JV
151
.A5713
1989

D1220717

27-1659 JV151 88-23966 CIP
Ansprenger, Franz. **The dissolution of the colonial empires**. Routledge,
1989. 337p bibl index **ISBN 0-415-00838-7, $49.95**
      Ansprenger takes a chronological and national approach in analyzing the re-
lationships within the French, British, Dutch, Belgian, Spanish, and Portuguese
colonial empires after WW I and the subsequent dissolutions after 1945. This
method tends to produce a fragmented text, yet surveys on decolonization are
scarce. Ansprenger suggests that a positive result of imperialism was its creation
of a global society. However, he views negatively the legacy of inequality and cells
of poverty created by imperialism. These are perpetuated through international
economic programs that still project a Western model upon Africa and Asia, fos-
tering a two-class society of "haves" and "have nots." Conjectures in the final chapter on prospects in 1988 in South Africa, Afghanistan, and Cambodia (in view of
recent events) illustrate the difficulties of treating the continuing and changing process of decolonization. The bibliography is incomplete, ignoring important works;
the index is limited to proper names only. College and university libraries.—*M.
S. Miller, University of Illinois at Chicago*

JACKSON LIBRARY
LANDER COLLEGE
GREENWOOD, S. C. 29649

OCLC

THE DISSOLUTION OF
THE COLONIAL EMPIRES

THE DISSOLUTION OF THE COLONIAL EMPIRES

FRANZ ANSPRENGER

ROUTLEDGE

London and New York

JACKSON LIBRARY
LANDER COLLEGE
GREENWOOD, S. C. 29649

First published in 1989 by Routledge
11 New Fetter Lane, London EC4P 4EE
29 West 35th Street, New York, NY 10001

© 1981 Deutscher Taschenbuch Verlag GmbH & Co. KG, Munich

Printed in Great Britain by T. J. Press (Padstow) Ltd
Padstow, Cornwall

All rights reserved. No part of this book may be reprinted
or reproduced or utilized in any form or by any electronic,
mechanical, or other means, now known or hereafter
invented, including photocopying and recording, or in any
information storage or retrieval system, without permission
in writing from the publishers.

British Library Cataloguing in Publication Data
Ansprenger, Franz
The dissolution of the colonial empires.
1. Decolonisation – 1900–
I. Title   II. Auflösung der Kolonialreiche.
909.82

ISBN 0-415-00838-7
0-415-03143-5 (pb)

OCLC

CONTENTS

CONTENTS

INTRODUCTION

THE BACKGROUND TO MODERN COLONIZATION

Whites have not always felt themselves to be the master race. It would be difficult to trace this outstanding element of the global history of the nineteenth and twentieth centuries back to the European Middle Ages, or into antiquity. To this day the king of the Moors in Christmas cribs bears witness to a culture oblivious to race. King Etzel of the *Nibelungenlied* is no representative of the yellow peril, the coloured knight of Wolfram von Eschenbach's *Parzival* no 'black shame' ('*Schwarze Schande*': slogan of German nationalists against black French soldiers of the occupation forces on the Rhine, 1919–30) for the kingdom of the Grail. The crusaders did indeed fight against the infidel, but they were far from calling Sultan Saladin a 'bicot' – this virtually untranslatable term was used by Algerian Europeans for their Muslim compatriots.

The Europeans of the Middle Ages had no reason to regard themselves as superior to the people of other continents. The Arab-Islamic culture was clearly superior to theirs. They charily dismissed Marco Polo's reports of China as bragging. Of course, the Europeans did have the true religion, a cause for pride, but on the edge of their own part of the world – in Scandinavia and in the east – for a long time heathens continued to live, whilst on the other hand Europeans shared Christendom with non-Europeans in Africa and Asia. At first these relations shifted only gradually: the last heathens were either killed or converted, and Islamic culture in Spain was wiped out, isolated schismatic churches in Asia became submerged under the ocean of Turkish hegemony. Gradually the concepts 'Christian' and 'white' became fused in common usage.

1

Then came the explosive extension of this world-view as a result of voyages of discovery – people of different race and colour on the islands and coasts of America, on the African trail, in India, Indonesia, China, and Japan. These people were not Christian (with the exception of Ethiopian Copts and a few Indians).

Were now the Christian, white Europeans superior to the heathen, coloured foreigners? Not always in terms of culture, and hardly in terms of state organization and land power, if we consider Japan, the China of the Ming dynasty and the early Manchu, or the Moguls and maharajas of India. They were superior, however, in terms of naval power and in similar branches of technology which were to be decisive for the future of the world: military technology, in a nutshell. At first it had not been possible for any European company to conquer a coherent colonial empire on the Asian mainland. Only in 1757 did Clive defeat the nabob of Bengal near Plassey and thus launch British hegemony over India. On the open seas, however, the whites were unassailable.

Something irrevocable occurred in America: gigantic states crumbled like dust at the hands of the scant *conquistador* troops. The people on the islands of the Caribbean died out as they had to perform slave labour. The Europeans, with their white skin, their horses and muskets, seemed like gods. So they began to feel like supermen themselves.

The Catholic Church had to ask itself whether what the Spanish and Portuguese were doing in newly discovered America was permissible. It is known that one pope drew a line across the globe: Spaniards to the left, Portuguese to the right! We know the name of the first bishop of Chiapa in Mexico, Bartholomé de Las Casas (1474–1566), who wanted to protect the Indians and thus unwittingly opened the way for the trade in Negroes across the Atlantic. Much less known is that in their debates theologians were already intoning almost all the theories and prejudices that are still a headache to us today when the colonial system is being discussed.

When Benito Mussolini sent his legions against Ethiopia – which was (up to now) the last colonial conquest carried out by a Christian European nation in good conscience, and consequently without dissimulation – the *Osservatore Romano*, official mouthpiece of the Vatican, wrote: 'In colonialization we see a miracle of patience, heroism and brotherly love. No nation and no race has the right to live in isolation.' This was on 24 February 1935.

2

In 1538 the theologian and lawyer Francisco de Vitoria gave a lecture at the university of Salamanca entitled 'De Indis recenter inventis' and 'De iure belli Hispanorum in Barbaros relectiones' on the contemporary history of the continent which was on the point of becoming Latin America. Vitoria himself started from the assumption that the Indians were barbarians. But was one therefore permitted to kill them and pillage their goods? No, he judged. On the arrival of the Europeans they were 'without doubt both in their private and political spheres *veri domini*, as much as Christians'.[1] This means that they were the true owners of that which was in their possession: in modern terms they had sovereignty and were masters of their own lands, and therefore entitled both to the right to self-determination and to equality. But . . . of course there was a 'but': Vitoria justified Spanish colonial rule using a range of arguments which are still topical today.

The first and most important of these is precisely the same as that put forward by the *Osservatore Romano* in 1935: the '*titulus naturalis societatis et communicationis*'. The earth is there for everyone, and if Indians oppose Spanish immigration or trade, this is reason enough for a 'justified war' against them. One can hear in this echoes of the British in the Opium War, beating on China's closed doors. One thinks also of Lord Lugard's thesis of 1922 on the mandate of the colonial powers: 'The tropics are the heritage of mankind, and neither, on the one hand, has the suzerain Power a right to their exclusive exploitation, nor, on the other hand, have the races which inhabit them a right to deny their bounties to those who need them.'[2]

Vitoria's second argument ran: the Spaniards were permitted to intervene in order to forestall atrocities, to protect Indians converted to Christianity from the revenge of the heathen. Here we recall the jump of Belgian parachutists over Stanleyville in the autumn of 1964: this was allegedly to protect white hostages from black monsters.

Thirdly, the Indians could themselves submit 'consciously and in true and free choice to wise and humane Spanish administration'. In this case 'a majority decision would be valid, even if others were opposed, since it is difficult to attain unanimous agreement'. As an example of this argument, in Algeria from 1945 to 1954 was witnessed a whole series of elections, which on repeated occasions 'magnificently' justified French rule. It was for a long time heard from South Africa that the majority of blacks were completely satisfied with apartheid, although they have never been allowed near a ballot box.

Vitoria puts forward for discussion a final legal title in favour of

Spanish colonial rule, one which interestingly, however, he himself does not accept: the barbarians are certainly not entirely irrational, but are so close to being irrational beings that one has to consider them incapable of either founding or running a legitimate state according to the norms of human dignity and civilization. Vitoria expressly refers here to the experts: 'Those men who have lived among the Indians report a mental underdevelopment [*hebetudo*] which is allegedly worse than that among the children and adolescents of other peoples.' If this were the case, argues the theologian, the Indians could be placed in guardianship, as is the case with orphaned minors among their own people. He does not trust the experts, however; such a guardianship should only be organized in the interests of the Indians, and not according to the wishes of the Spanish. This seems to him impossible, since the Spanish would immediately go one step further and maintain what Vitoria so firmly rejected initially, namely that all Indians were slaves by nature. 'Here', he argues by way of rejection, 'lies a serious danger for souls and their well-being.'

Do we not also recognize this argument today? They are children! They are quite incapable of governing themselves – the Africans and Asians and Latin Americans, the lot of them. . . . We the whites are their educators, ordained by God or nature. 'I am your brother, but your elder brother' was a saying Albert Schweitzer constantly used to remonstrate with his Africans. There is no doubt about it: the myth that non-European peoples have no reason, or at most only that of children, was a cornerstone of the European colonial system in recent times. On this conviction and the presumed natural right to trade and commerce, the *titulus societatis et communicationis* of Vitoria, rested the good conscience with which Europe from 1500 onwards extended itself across the globe and ruled over it.

Or is this trading right not a presumption? Much can be said in favour. Only in our own times is it becoming a fully topical issue. We can feel the economic, political, and moral consequences of it every time we meet immigrants or *Gastarbeiter* with darker skins on our streets and squares in London, Cologne, or Paris. President Kennedy essentially based his argument on the 'right to trade' when he initiated a new start for the western world by taking the free trade ideals of GATT seriously. It is here that the difference from the colonial age, and intellectual progress since the time of Vitoria and Lugard, become apparent. Not only the Europeans are now entitled to the right to buy spices, mine copper, or market ballpoint pens in the 'tropics'. Basing

4

themselves on precisely the same right to trade, the developing countries are making very precise demands on the industrial nations. Since UNCTAD I in Geneva in 1964 the word has got around. The *titulus societatis et communicationis* is only a presumption so long as only one society or race claims it as a privilege. The justification for this privilege of the white races, maintained and believed for centuries, was the assertion that coloured people are children. Psychologists and ethnologists have enlightened us on this long ago; the assertion is false.

Coloured people are human. This simple thesis embraces all criticism of the colonial system. It is not new. Colonial criticism, anti-colonial policy, or decolonization have not existed only since 1945. These movements ran through the centuries parallel with European colonial expansion.

A small brotherhood of Christian politicians took upon itself around 1780 in England the task of putting an end to Negro slavery. It took these 'Abolitionists', rallied around Wilberforce, however, more than fifty years to achieve their goal. Opponents constantly reiterated the argument that Africans were 'an inferior link in the chain of nature, created for slavery'. We can read how Thomas Clarkson, the leading theoretician of the anti-slavery movement, replies to this in his first essay in 1785:

> Had the Africans been made for slavery . . . it is clear . . . that
> they must have been created devoid of reason: but this is
> contrary to fact. . . . It is clear also, that there must have been
> many and evident signs of the inferiority of their nature . . . but
> this is equally false. . . . Nor is it less evident that they would
> have wanted many of those qualities which they have, and which
> brutes have not: they would have wanted that spirit of liberty,
> that sense of ignomiy and shame, which so frequently drives
> them to the horrid extremity of finishing their own
> existence. . . . We cannot suppose therefore that God has made
> an order of beings, with such mental qualities and powers, for
> the sole purpose of being used as beasts, or instruments of
> labour.[3]

Economic and political calculations were undoubtedly also involved when Europeans in the eighteenth and nineteenth centuries made a stand against the slave trade and slavery and against the acquisition of new colonies. Whoever believed Adam Smith and expected a prosperous future from free trade was obliged even in his own interests to be an anti-colonialist. In addition to 'anti-colonialism from the left', based on universal human rights, there was always – often in one and the same person – an egocentric 'anti-colonialism from the right'. It was in this spirit that Disraeli in 1852 called the colonies 'millstones around the neck of England', demanding in 1866: 'Leave the Canadians to defend themselves; recall the African squadron; give up the settlements on the west coast of Africa; and we shall make a saving which will, at the same time, enable us to build ships and have a good Budget.'[4] Cold calculation and moral disarmament were mingled with anti-colonialism just as indissolubly as were trading rights and racial arrogance in the justification for overseas expansion.

Around the middle of the nineteenth century colonial policy seemed to be receding increasingly into the past and to have less and less of a future. The mercantilism of the old colonial system seemed conceptually and politically dead, while the empires themselves were shrinking. This of course did not apply to those countries in the temperate zones in which white settlers had freed themselves from colonial strings (as in the USA) or were striving towards such a status (as in Canada). Where it was physically possible for the whites either to wipe out the native population, or shoot them down in such a way that all the necessary land lay 'unclaimed' and waiting for them, it was just seized without too many questions being asked. This undertaking was not entirely successful everywhere, however. The French in Algeria carried out destructive campaigns, systematically expropriating all the most fertile areas for settlement as soon as revolts presented them with an excuse to do so. They created their own encapsulated society within Muslim Algeria. France nevertheless continued to shrink throughout from imitating North American Indian policy, not seeking a 'final solution' for the 'problem' of millions of Arabs and Kabyles. South Africa evolved in a similar manner. The Cape and later the Boer republics in the interior came into the possession of the white Afrikaners, but the black Africans did not decline into the role of an ethnographical rarity as did the black Australians. Similarly, they did not allow themselves to be pushed into reservations, but began to form a new proletariat in the 'white' towns, bitterly opposed competition for the 'poor whites'.

In the tropics, on the other hand, a colonial lull prevailed. Wherever the Europeans had set up residence and were able to conduct at least some kind of business, they remained – although more out of lassitude than entrepreneurial spirit: the Dutch in Indonesia, the

French in Senegal, the British in India. A strategic imperative for seeking new footholds was lacking, since there was no longer any competition on the world's oceans as there had been at the onset of the voyages of discovery. Since Trafalgar, all the salt water of the world was effectively British territory.

THE AGE OF IMPERIALISM

Who or what was it that moved Europeans in the last quarter of the nineteenth century suddenly to throw themselves with enormous expenditure of energy once again into the competition for colonial possessions? This question is still waiting for a definitive answer. Lenin knew full well in 1916:

> Colonial possession alone offers full guarantee for the success of monopoly in the face of all contingencies in the struggle against competitors . . . the more highly developed is capitalism, the more keenly felt the shortage of raw materials, and the more sharply delineated is competition and the search for raw materials throughout the whole world, so the more bitter is the struggle to acquire colonies.[5]

It is thought today that he was thereby uttering a truth, but not the whole truth, about the age of imperialism.

History does not work with handy definitions, and certainly not with this or that 'alone'. We do nevertheless concede that in the decades prior to the First World War the white race did indeed take over the globe in a competition between old and new colonial nations, creating an expansion, indeed an explosion, of hitherto unknown force. '*Ce sont des continents que l'on annexe, c'est l'immensité que l'on partage*', as Jules Ferry wrote in 1890.[6]

The year 1914 suggests itself as the end of the age in which Europe filled the earth and which we have become accustomed to referring to as the age of imperialism. With it began the period of great European civil wars which we refer to as world wars. They destroyed the European state system and unleashed the collapse of the colonial system of the old type. At which point, however, should the historian mark the beginning of the age of imperialism? Various events present themselves which we should like to look at, since they disclose pointers towards the driving forces which contributed to this explosive expansion.

In 1874 the 70-year-old Benjamin Disraeli finally became prime minister after a Conservative victory. He, who more than twenty years earlier had uttered the watchword of 'anti-colonialism from the right', now launched his foreign policy by purchasing the Suez Canal shares from the khedive of Egypt: England laid its hands on the sea route to India. Strategic interests – but behind them we can discern the domestic political programme of the conservatives: pacifying the working class by means of social reform. A little later Joseph Chamberlain and Cecil Rhodes consciously perceived imperialism as a safety valve for social pressure, and the profits from the colonies as a lever with which to solve the welfare question.

In the same year, 1874, the British journalist John Rowlands, better known as Henry Morton Stanley, set out from the Indian Ocean to cross central Africa. He solved the riddle of the Congo river. This was on the face of it a purely scientific expedition, financed by American newspapers. 'By chance' it attracted the attention of the king of the Belgians, after other fruitless colonial speculations, to the Congo Basin. A few years later Stanley, now in the service of the King, Leopold II, laid the foundations for the Congo State. If Britain's seizure of Egypt was perhaps the chief cause, then Leopold's Congo policy was undoubtedly the immediate starting-point in the scramble for Africa, procedures being laid down at the Berlin Conference of 1884–5. We can note the chief actors in this scenario: the petty bourgeois loner who succeeds in accomplishing an apparently totally apolitical piece of research; and his connection with the rambling speculative interests of a business magnate.

On 1 January 1877 Queen Victoria was proclaimed empress of India. Still another scenario: a major matter of state: not an insignificant breakthrough into fresh territory, but a true crowning conclusion of past developments. It was preceded by the great uprising of the Indians. Old European accounts inform us that in 1857 a 'mutiny' broke out, as a result of bungling officers: Muslim and Hindu soldiers, issued with cartridges smeared with animal fat, feared an attempt to break their religious taboos. 'The civilian population was rather a spectator than a participant in the event,' wrote G. M. Trevelyan in 1937.[7] For Indians the uprising represented according to Jawaharlal Nehru a 'last despairing effort' of India's old regime to drive out the new foreign rulers.[8] Only now did they realize that the British were doing something fundamentally different in India from all former successful conquerors, who had ruled India but never changed it decisively. The British did not set themselves at the pinnacle of the old Indian social structure, they shattered it. They brought not only foreign rule, but also revolution: what was for India a totally new rhythm of life, the 'modern' way.

The uprising in fact took, as Nehru states, 'the character of a people's uprising and a war for Indian independence', which are like-wise modern, revolutionary concepts. But the British were victorious. In the age of imperialism it was the colonizers who determined the course of the first phase of this revolution, which dragged Asia and Africa into the One World of technological development.

We shall have to deal on several more occasions with the tension which existed between the resistance of the former, i.e. pre-colonial, regime on the one hand, and the struggle of the new, i.e. post-colonial, nationalist movements on the other. Here and there shrewd represen-tatives of the old order managed to switch themselves over to a promi-nent role in this new dynamic, for example King Mohammed V of Morocco, Emperor Haile Selassie of Ethiopia – at least for a time – or the monarchy of Thailand. Very often, however, aristocrats weighed down by pre-colonial tradition played the unhappy role of a Farouk or a Bao Dai.

Again a major act of state, this time on the international stage, was the Berlin Congress of 1878. It may truly be regarded as the prelude to the age of imperialism, since the major powers here secured the most important source of conflict on European soil – the powder keg of the Balkans – so effectively that serious detonation was deferred until 1914. In this way the 'excess' energy of European states was freed for extra-European policy. This was certainly the case for the two great antagonists of world policy around the turn of the century, Britain and Russia. Bismarck's role as 'honest broker' at the Berlin Congress furthermore points to the rapid growth of the German Reich to the stature of a more than merely European power. It is also true that Britain, with Bismarck's consent, gave the green light in Berlin to the new colonial expansion of France: the seizure of Tunisia, which again provoked Italy to demand compensation. Tunis itself was indeed com-pensation for the British occupation of Cyprus.

The machinery which kept international relations running in the age of imperialism thus manifested itself in the foreground of Europe. It was a highly complicated machinery of real and potential, territorial, economic and military compensation demands which could be set in motion at will from the most varied quarters. How cleverly constructed this machinery was! The slightest push of energy on the part of a government, or even a private person, was enough to set it going. Such a piece of machinery needed to be kept well oiled and could not afford to show much frictional resistance. Indeed all the major powers, including the clumsy Germany of Wilhelm II, spent the following decades in constant and expert servicing of this apparatus. Colonial rivalries continued to rumble in the background, but diplomats on the whole kept the level of friction so slight, the temperature so low, that the machinery did not seize up. The mutual slaughter of the major capitalist powers did not arise in 1914, as Lenin assumed, from the colonial competition which was pushing to the very ends of the earth: the First World War broke out as the insulation which had been installed around the *European* powder keg of the Balkans perished with age and burned through. In the long run, it was Lenin's arch-enemy, Karl Kautsky, who was proved right in having prophesied the non-violent formation of cartels: 'ultra-imperialism'. (The World Bank? The European Community?)

Seven powers shaped the age of imperialism with their advance into Asia and Africa. Britain, Russia, and France were the traditional colonial powers among these, Germany, the United States, and Belgium the newcomers. In addition to these was the non-white out-sider, Japan. Italy sailed alongside them, but only cautiously, after burning its fingers in Ethiopia in 1896: the victory of Emperor Menelik II at Adua was to stand for a long time alone in the annals of history as a successful repulsion of European colonial expansion.

The advance of the imperialist powers proceeded of course in the first instance at the expense of the 'native' peoples in Asia and Africa, having the secondary effect, however, of undermining the age-weakened colonial empires of Spain and Portugal. Spain lost its over-seas posts, apart from fragments, to the USA; Portugal only escaped the same fate when the two self-appointed inheritors, Britain and Germany, became bogged down in the First World War as they were just on the point (in 1914) of agreeing on the division of the spoils. The Netherlands shrewdly kept itself on the leeward side, its colonial empire thereby remaining safe from hostility.

A particularly interesting aspect of this imperial interplay is the role of Russia. It has since become clear that Russian expansion in Asia was built on firmer foundations than the colonial excursions of all other powers. The Russian empire is in fact the only one which still stands unshaken today, trimmed solely of its furthest outposts, set up in 1898 and recaptured for a short time in 1945, in Manchuria and Sinkiang, which were Russian spheres of influence from 1900 to 1950. A manifest difference between the Russian and all other expansion movements is the fact that only the Russian one essentially followed the land route in territorial unity with Europe. This puts into a questionable light the thesis of the earth-shattering importance of naval power, put forward in 1890 by the American Admiral Mahan, and uncritically adopted by Wilhelm II and others. The Soviet government doggedly maintains that its version of Marxism has allowed it to resolve the 'national question' and to transform the Tsarist people's prison into a voluntary people's community. As late as 1987 one might be permitted doubts as to whether the Estonians and Lithuanians, Georgians and former Crimean Tatars, Uzbeks and other Muslim peoples of central Asia really see it like this. Are they truly satisfied with the cultural autonomy offered by the Soviet system? Still, no one can deny that this Russian or Soviet empire does form an integral land mass.

Russia offered competitive imperialism fewer points of friction than any other colonial empire – this also as a natural consequence of its territorial unity and its lack of dependence on sea or (later) air routes across alien territory. Nevertheless, around 1900 German diplomats regarded the confrontation between Russia and Britain in central and east Asia, including Afghanistan, as one of the constants in world politics. It marked an embarrassing surprise for Berlin, indeed the true bankruptcy of its diplomacy, when the 'Bear and the Whale' were reconciled.

The path for this reconciliation was smoothed by the victory of Japan in 1904–5, which temporarily removed Russia from the centre stage of imperial rivalry. At the turn of the century this was the Far East, since it was here that the richest of the hitherto undivided spoils – China – beckoned to the imperial powers. Between the Sino-Japanese war of 1894–5 and the so-called Boxer Uprising of 1900, Russia, Germany, Britain, and France made ready to pounce on China: Russia and France from their neighbouring land bases in Siberia and Vietnam, Germany and Britain directly across the ocean. Why was it then that no division of China occurred, along the lines of the scramble for Africa? Why was it that Britain felt too weak to set up a 'second India' on the Yangtze Kiang (both the wish to do so and its renunciation were admitted by Joseph Chamberlain in November 1899 in talks with Bülow)? Only a few years earlier Curzon had been able to write with confidence: 'The Power which has been longest in the field, which enjoys the best geographical position for the distribution of its commerce, or the dissemination of its influence, and which can command the largest resources, must infallibly triumph in any such competition.'[9] It would seem that it was not primarily American Open Door trading policy, or even China's internal regeneration, which made the powers forgo dividing it up, but Britain's fear of too heavy a military engagement in view of the neighbouring Russian land mass. After 1905 Japan played the same deterrent role. Precisely because the powers were seeking overseas to bring in high returns in a more distant future, but were not prepared to stake particularly high investments for it, the 'Sick Men' of Asia – China, Persia, and in a sense also the Ottoman Empire – were spared euthanasia in so far as they lay within the sphere of Anglo-Russian tension. In the age of imperialism, the imperative of overseas diplomacy of the great powers really seems to have been to keep the machinery in motion, to treat it with due care, and to prevent havoc resulting from installing instruments which were too crude. The feeling prevailed that there was plenty of time. Europe's extension across the globe and the establishment of its economic and political universal hegemony seemed to conform to a pre-ordained law of history, fondly drawn from the 'survival of the fittest' concept of a vulgarized Darwinism.

In Indochina friction between Anglo and French imperialism was reduced by maintaining Thailand as a buffer state. Africa between 1890 and 1914 presents the image of a skilful mutual adjustment of colonial interests. No one relinquished the major aims with which the race had been entered or which had since emerged, although of course these aims conflicted with one another. Britain strove after the Cape-Cairo axis, largely it seems to protect the flank of its newest 'inland sea', the Indian Ocean. France wanted to round off its land possessions between the Mediterranean and the Congo; Germany toyed with the pipe dream of a new India, a powerful German Central Africa between Cameroon, Zanzibar, and the Orange River. In spite of this, however, all the African crises of imperialist competition before 1914 were defused without great effort, being converted into compensation deals. This formula still worked during the Morocco crises, which were potentially the most explosive on account of Morocco's closeness to Europe and the relatively late hour at which they erupted.

If we search with the eye of a contemporary for disturbing factors in the carefully worked-out balance between the interlocking European colonial empires just before the outbreak of the First World War, then we see Japan and Japan alone. Japan seems above all sinister to the Europeans, because it does not belong to the family. The Yellow Peril: this slogan was born in the very moment at which Japan first made its voice heard as an imperialist power in the circle of the imperialists, by beating Manchu China over the head in 1894. Britain was supposed to tame these clever students of power politics and industrialization by means of alliance and supervision: Japan's strength up to 1914 was much too limited to make demands on western Europe or the United States. But Japan the imperialist appeared as a dark cloud on the brilliant horizon of European imperialism. It represented a tangible contradiction to Darwinist racial arrogance, a hypothetical starting-point for an uprising of the coloured underworld against those who were after all only doing their duty in the face of history by carrying the 'white man's burden'.

THE COLONIAL EMPIRES AT THE OUTBREAK OF WAR IN 1914

In July 1914 more than 72,000 square kilometres and more than 560 million people were under colonial rule – more than half the land surface of the earth and a good third of the global population. Of course one should bear in mind that the majority of possessions settled by whites were by then already on the way to integration (Siberia) or to full self-government. The latter was the case for the 'Dominions' of the British Empire – Canada, Newfoundland, Australia, New Zealand, and the Union of South Africa, with some 11.5 million whites. On the other hand, enormous areas and states in Asia, especially China, Persia, and Turkey, were effectively 'semi-colonies' of the major powers, i.e. economically dependent entities with only formal sovereignty.

The guidelines of colonial policy differed from one nation to another and also altered in the course of time, but these differences may in practice have been more limited than appeared to be the case when seen from the committee rooms of European chancelleries, or from the perspective of research into colonial theory. The complicated differences in status between individual territories similarly merit only moderate interest from the political historian. In the British Empire, for example, distinction was made, according to the formalities of acquisition, between crown colonies and protectorates, to which were added the Sudan as an Anglo-Egyptian condominium, the leased territories on the Chinese coast, and of course the Dominions. France regarded Algeria as part of the republic, albeit with special status; it distinguished between the old colonies (the West Indies and Senegalese coastal areas), the inhabitants of which were French citizens, on the one hand, and the great bulk of the new colonies, where the natives were mere subjects, on the other.

This historically evolved diversity rapidly lost significance. The desire to rationalize colonization in order to make it more attractive to the critical taxpayers of the homeland (the gradual democratization of Europe affected colonial policy), made the revamping and unification of their overseas administration seem to all the colonial powers to be worth aiming for. Admittedly the British were not successful with 'Imperial Federation', as Joseph Chamberlain had called it. However, progress can be discerned if one compares the central administrations of 1914 with those of early imperialism! At first it was still believed in France that a sub-department of the naval ministry alone would be able to administer the colonies: a colonial ministry was not set up until 1894. In Britain and Germany (the Reichskolonialamt was only set up in 1907) it was hoped to dispense with direct state administration of colonial territories by farming them out to private companies. The example for this was set in 1885 by the internationally recognized Congo state of Leopold II. In 1885 the German Reich issued charters to the German East Africa Company (DOAG) and the New Guinea Company; the first collapsed within five years, the second gave up in 1900. Britain granted charters in 1886 to the Royal Niger Company, in 1888 to the Imperial British East Africa Company, and in 1889 to the Imperial British South Africa Company; the first handed Nigeria over to the Crown in 1900, the second being forced to give up in 1895 in the face of difficulties in exploiting Uganda and Kenya. Only the third, thanks to the energy of its founder Cecil Rhodes, held out beyond the First World War in the Rhodesia it had secured. Finally in 1908 the Congo region also passed into Belgian state administration, after hefty international criticism of the brutal exploitative economy of Leopold had made itself heard.

> The Congo state is by no means a colonizing state, it is not a state at all; it is a financial enterprise. . . . The colony was run neither in the interests of the natives, nor in the economic interest of Belgium. It was intended to bring the royal sovereign the maximum in income – this constituted the content of the work of government.[10]

When Stanley had acquired this land for Leopold in the 1880s, he estimated its population (albeit on the basis of only crude and limited clues) at 29 million. Estimates from around the First World War ranged between 8.5 and 11 million. . . . This decrease is attributable, not entirely, but nevertheless to a large degree, to the legendary Leopoldian 'Congo atrocities'.

Some colonizers continued to hope until 1914 to be able to open up vast new areas for mass white settlement: where climate and economic opportunity permitted, 'the white population would sooner or later push back, absorb or destroy the native one' wrote a German colonial expert in 1905.[11] The experiences of North America and Australia, however, did not repeat themselves. In southern Africa, Algeria, and Tunisia the whites remained a minority. Indeed the non-European population began to grow at a considerably faster rate – a development which was to prove more important for the future of colonization than most others, since it was in the backwater settlement colonies, to which Angola, Morocco, and Libya were later added, that the most dangerous anti-colonial ammunition was mounting up.

Elsewhere, reform of native policy set things on the right path even before 1914. If, above all in Africa, the local people had initially been regarded as a sort of burdensome addition to the natural wealth which was being sought after, people now began to realize that only the colonized would run the colonies successfully. '*Il faut faire du Nègre*', as some French people drastically put it. Bernhard Dernburg, first head of the German colonial office, expressed the same idea somewhat more delicately in 1907:

> Now, however, the native is the most important object of
> colonization, most especially in all our plantation colonies. Since
> slavery – thank God – has been abolished, and suitable workers
> can only come either under contract from other colonies or be
> drawn from the colony's own resources, the manual productivity
> of the natives representing the most important asset, so here lies
> a problem of eminent importance.[12]

If the native is needed as a labourer, one must also take him seriously as a person and offer him a humane livelihood. Initially this idea may have been concealed behind the disguise of guardianship, trusteeship, or paternalism, or may have entered the scene in a roundabout way in the form of the 'indirect rule' of the British or the 'association' of the French. Sooner or later, however, it was bound to end in the demand for the right to political self-determination. This development was to be interrupted, however, or even forestalled, where a voluble group of white settlers insisted on retaining its privileges – the obverse of a coin whose reverse meant the underprivilege, i.e. the oppression, of the non-whites.

THE ECONOMIC SIGNIFICANCE OF THE COLONIES

In the first decade of the twentieth century, public opinion in Europe understood that the acquisition of vast colonial empires did not necessarily bring with it immediate economic gain, and above all did not bring it for everyone. Aside from the bankruptcy of many private colonial businesses in all European countries, even the hope of many politicians (beginning with Bismarck and raised to the level of official doctrine in London) that the colonies would be able to raise their own state expenditure funds, was only rarely realized. France, for example, was obliged to raise the budget of its colonial ministry from just 43 million gold fr. in 1885 to 166 million in 1902 (it then declined somewhat, being 105 million in 1913). The contributions of the Reich in German East Africa rose from 5.3 million gold marks in 1901 to 41.8 million in 1908. Of all the German colonies only Togo managed without subsidies at that time. A famous saying was uttered in 1899 in the French National Assembly: '*Il y a deux choses dans la politique coloniale: d'abord la joie des conquêtes et ensuite la carte à payer!*'[13] The lack of viability of the colonies in the imperialist period, however, did not prevent hordes of interested parties, in anticipation, as it were, of the total economic effect, from making their fortunes. In addition to business people and shipowners one should not overlook the administrative officials and officers who were often able to forge careers far more quickly overseas than in their peaceful European homelands.

From 1874 onwards the newly acquired colonies were of no significance as a destination for European emigrants, the steady stream of emigration from central Europe generally drying up with rapid industrialization. In Germany, for example, emigration figures declined steadily from 1881 onwards. Nevertheless there was until 1914 a noticeable wave of white emigration – but this was moving from Europe to North America. In the mean time in South Africa the white population grew between 1880 and 1911 from 375,000 to 1.3 million, and in Algeria in the same period from 400,000 to 750,000. In addition to French people, many settlers from Spain, Italy, and Malta were also involved in this, blending in with a neo-French stratum of '*colons*', whilst in South Africa the British-Boer contradiction was not resolved with the founding of the union. Germany, on the other hand, in South-West Africa, its only settler colony, was able to install a mere 15,000 Europeans by the time war broke out.

The classical features of the colonial economy were the export of agricultural and mineral raw materials from the colonies to the 'motherland', which in turn sold industrially manufactured goods in its colonial possessions (predominantly consumer goods, since the development of industrial manufacturing plants in the colony itself would alter the structure of this '*pacte colonial*', as the French called it). This meant that the motherland gained considerably more from this trade arrangement than the colony. This is regarded as the reason for the perpetual, and indeed with time deteriorating, underdevelopment of the colony in relation to the 'metropolis', if not even the progressive impoverishment of the colony in relation to its own past: a view dominating academic debate chiefly between the late 1960s and early 1980s. There were and are many variations on this theory of *dependencia* or underdevelopment.

This theory, however, was never able to answer all the questions to which it gave rise and which were bound to strike even non-specialists. The Spanish term *dependencia* itself indicates that the theory originally evolved in Latin America as an argument against the 'dollar imperialism' of the Big Brother in the north – the USA. The countries of Latin America, however, allegedly still being kept in a state of dependence and underdevelopment, have nevertheless been independent states for almost two centuries. They are no longer colonies, and indeed never were colonies of the USA. The political system of colonial rule cannot therefore be put forward as a substantial element in the phenomenon of poverty in certain regions of the world.

Secondly, there is often some confusion as to what exactly is meant by the accusation that the industrial countries of the 'north' exploit the Third World or persistently impose disadvantages on it in mutual trade. Do we want to deduce this argument solely from the long-term development of the terms of trade, which, simply put, are based on the fact that a country such as Ghana, for example, must sell increasing numbers of sacks of cocoa on the world market in order to import a tractor? At the beginning of the *dependencia* debates we find precisely this approach on the part of the Argentinian Raúl Prebisch (1901–86) both to demonstrate and explain the long-term lapse in the terms of trade for developing countries. In 1964 Prebisch was appointed the first secretary-general of UNCTAD.[14] Or should one alternatively investigate the development of the profits for capital which were invested in the colonies or in other developing countries, and discover where they have gone? Such a question ought to suggest itself, in view of the tendency of classical theoreticians of imperialism to regard capital export as a prime characteristic of the system. There are no data on such 'terms of capital mobility',[15] however. Of no great help is the occasional random observation of higher sums of money flowing out of a developing country to the 'north' in some years than the sum of new development capital coming in.

In fact before these questions can be answered, some clarity first needs to be achieved as regards production conditions in the colonies and other countries of the Third World, since goods must be produced before they can be exchanged. In this respect some progress could perhaps be made, moving from the mere complaint that these relations are bad and unjust, towards some understanding of the reasons why they are so. Neo-Marxist theoreticians have framed this question within the concept of 'échange inégal/unequal exchange', attempting to apply the classic doctrines of Adam Smith, Ricardo, and Marx, according to which the value of a product is determined by the human work it 'crystallizes'. Can economic reality still be analysed in this way today, however? At all events the debate as to whether this or that author has really succeeded in determining the appropriate value of Third World products for the purposes of an 'equal exchange' does not seem to be nearing a conclusion.[16]

The actual political measures whereby the conditions of exchange for former colonies are supposed to be altered or improved in any case pay no heed to this theoretical debate – neither OPEC cartel politicians after 1973, nor the IMF strategists of the 1980s, who 'recommend' that Third World governments radically devalue their currencies in order to boost their exports.

For the moment, we are stuck with the simple historical fact that the independent states of Latin America, as well as those countries in Asia and Africa which were European colonies until the middle of the twentieth century, have also remained poor and backward, while the prosperity of society as a whole in western Europe and North America has increased.

The first, and for decades the only, state in Asia to compete with the white nations – Japan – was also the first to rebel politically and militarily against European world domination, defeating Russia, one of the white Big Powers, in a war in 1905. Since the 1960s, that is, since the dissolution of the colonial empires, on the other hand, a group of states known as 'newly industrializing countries' is forming in Asia and Latin America, and would seem to be on the threshold of the club of prosperous nations. South Korea, Taiwan, Malaysia, Brazil, and some other countries have at times shown substantially faster economic growth rates than the capitalist industrialized nations, even in per capita terms, despite rapid population growth. Whether this means, however, that the great leap forward of Japan is repeatable today or in the future, or whether the efforts of these countries are merely leading them into the dead end of underdevelopment at another level, remains to be seen.

In the few places on earth where colonial influence was never appreciable in its effects, further observations may be gathered which likewise put the alleged causal relationship between dependence and poverty into a questionable light. Have the peoples of Afghanistan or Ethiopia remained or become rich, for example, as a result of always having been left to themselves; are they industrial giants? Saudi Arabia's billions of dollars have certainly made more or less all the inhabitants of that country rich, but is the new economic structure that has been bought with these dollars at all self-reliant?

What would rather seem to be the case is that it is not the poverty of the colonies and former colonies which represents the extraordinary phenomenon of world history in the nineteenth and twentieth centuries, but on the contrary the explosive growth of the phenomenon we call wealth in western Europe, North America, and Japan. It cannot even be proven that the existence and 'exploitation' of the colonies was a substantial cause of the accumulation of wealth, or that the conquest of India was a crucial factor in the outbreak of the industrial revolution in Britain. Although efforts are constantly made to demonstrate this in the context of *dependencia* debates, they are equally regularly rejected by academics with different orientations.[17] There is no doubt that Britain by systematic competition drove India's textile manufactories into the ground at the beginning of the nineteenth century; whereas British cotton cloth had to pay customs duty of only 3.5 per cent when imported into India, Indian cotton had to pay 10 per cent when exported to Britain. This was the era of 'free trade', but for India it was free trade on a one-way street. Nevertheless, clear proof that several such simultaneously occurring events were causally linked, one being a cause of the other, is still lacking.

The scales were, however, to tip again soon after 1850. The British were building railways, both for strategic reasons and for the benefit of the steel industry, but in so doing they were exploding the boundaries of local markets. Indian entrepreneurs were able to set up new textile factories, in which they could now install modern machines (which of course in turn came from Britain). During the First World War Indian capitalists built the first steelworks on the subcontinent. It needed, even in 1923, a drastic protective tariff, and the British colonial government was moreover in agreement, since British and Indian industrialists were now jointly up against Japanese competition on the Indian market, economic rivalry between the colonizers and the colonized thereby losing importance.

By and large Great Britain adhered to the concept of free trade until the first global economic crisis – and thus also to the free movement of goods within the empire, since the industrial hegemony of Britain over its colonies had long been out of the question. The idea was to wait until the other colonial powers of Europe followed the same example. At all events one could expect the protection of one's own colonial empire from the trade competition of other motherlands.

France introduced just such a policy by changing over to protectionism in 1892. France's business people and industrialists regarded the colonial empire as a 'chasse gardée'. Germany, on the other hand, in spite of a protective tariff policy, kept the door to competition open in the colonies. The result of this was that German East Africa, for example, transacted half of its foreign trade with the Reich in 1912. The French colonies, however, exchanged in 1913 only 55 per cent of their goods with the motherland.[18]

For the economies of France and Germany the colonies were of practically no significance, so that even after the First World War nothing changed for France, in spite of a few pipedreams of the money-spinning 'mise en valeur' of Africa. If Britain paid somewhat more attention to its empire in the inter-war years, this was almost exclusively to the white settlement colonies, at all events India. The other tropical colonies were left economically to themselves, that is, to the resourcefulness of their British governors, who somehow had to achieve a balanced budget. For the mother country, Nigeria, Rhodesia, even Malaya, were and remained marginal – important as producers of certain products, as customers for certain firms, but not for the economy as a whole.

To this fact may be added the distribution of capital exports. Around

1914 an estimated total of $44,000 million was invested abroad – of which 57 per cent was invested in the white nations. South America, where by now a system of direct colonial rule no longer existed, led with $8.5,000 million the list of backward continents, followed by Asia with $6,000 million and Africa with $4.7,000 million. The picture becomes even more blatant if we look once again at France and Germany: of France's international capital in 1914 (45,000 million fr.) almost one quarter was invested in Russia, a bare 9 per cent finding its way into French colonies. Germany at the beginning of the war had some 25,000 million marks invested abroad, of which only 2 per cent were invested in its colonies. For Britain alone was there a substantially different picture: the empire absorbed 46 per cent of British capital export – the lion's share, however, being poured at an increasing rate into the 'white Dominions'.

The global economic crisis of the 1930s hit the backward colonies of Europe particularly hard and enduringly. The prices of tropical raw materials fell 'through the floor' and stayed there, while each of the industrial nations sought its own way out of the crisis, be it through Roosevelt's New Deal, Hitler's rearmament, or also (in this case completely independently of the capitalist world market) Stalin's five-year plans. The colonies were not able suddenly to run their economies autonomously, as the states of Latin America tried to do within certain limits. They remained chained to the world market.

The colonial economy in Asia and Africa in 1939 was still only a small enclave within conquered colonial territory – equally so whether its members earned income by extracting minerals (as in South Africa, Katanga, or later in Northern Rhodesia and in the oil-producing countries), by cultivating exportable agrarian produce on indigenous plantations (cocoa on the Gold Coast) or on those in European possession (Dutch East Indies), or whether there was already, as in India, incipient import-substituting industry. Those groups of colonized people who worked as entrepreneurs or wage-earners in these colonial economic enclaves, or who profited from trade with them, rapidly emerged as a specific and privileged social stratum among the colonized peoples. There were too few of them, however, and their interests were too strongly tied to colonial relations with Europe, for the 'modern' elements of the enclave economy to prevail in the country as a whole.

The real tragedy of the colonies, however, lay in the fact that the enclaves in spite of this did have sufficient links with the 'hinterland' to

21

instigate certain social changes there; these did not set any development in motion, however, but rather pushed the 'traditional' economy towards stagnation. Age-old craftsmanship collapsed in the face of competition from imported manufactured goods from Europe and later Japan – first of all in India. The cultivation of foodstuffs was neglected in favour of potential profits from the cultivation of agricultural export goods – particularly noticeable in Egypt, which degenerated into a cotton plantation. With the effects of western medicine the population began to grow at an increasing pace, even in the villages, but industrialization (even in India) was much too weak to 'liberate' an appreciable proportion of this excess peasant labour for wage-earning. The poverty of the masses became 'marginality' (Marx had a cruder German word for it: *Lumperei*), and the traditional social structures were overstretched. From a distance even the *lumpenproletariat* and *lumpen*-peasants could see the shimmer of the dynamic colonial economic enclaves with their regular wages, cinemas and cars for the whites, bicycles for the coloureds. They saw them clearly enough to hope for positive social change for themselves, but this hope was never fulfilled.

In many countries the colonial economy brought with it the first entrance of monoculture, by means of which dependence on the world market and its price swings exerted an even more extreme effect. Egyptian cotton and Gold Coast cocoa have already been mentioned; rice was to play the same role for Burma and Indochina, rubber and tin for Malaya, peanuts for Senegal, to name just a few examples. Even today some new states are still under hard pressure from these monocultures. Europe must fundamentally have known what effect this policy would have, Britain and France having introduced the sugar culture hundreds of years earlier in the West Indian colonies. 'In the West Indies you have a government of sugar for sugar by sugar,' exclaimed George Padmore in 1945 before the fifth Pan-African Congress in Manchester.

Some colonies did gradually achieve a favourable balance of trade – that is, they supplied more goods to the industrial nations than they received from them: India from as early as the 1880s; Malaya, South Africa, Nigeria, and the Gold Coast from immediately after the First World War, and likewise the Belgian Congo, the Philippines, and Indochina. The Dutch East Indies achieved a record in 1920 with 2.2,000 million guilders in exports to only 793 million imports. We should not forget, however, that the significance of a favourable balance of trade was quite different for a colony from what it was for an industrial country, where even today it is still regarded as a desirable thing. It showed (like other success statistics of the colonial economy) not progress in absolute terms, but merely progress in opening up the colonial enclaves.

The European colonial economy rapidly overcame the first phase of the brutal and ruthless exploitation of Asian and African resources. The shipment of Negro slaves to America, the simple squeezing of tribute out of India, the plundering of only ivory and rubber in the Congo, all proved at various times – in the latter case around the turn of the twentieth century – to be irrational. The colonizers learned to have the carrot to hand as well as the stick for their plantation workers, since it proved to be in their interests to treat so many natives with care, and even to have them learn a little of how they would be needed for the functioning of the colonial economy. It cannot be asserted that economic colonization – say around 1930 – was inhumane in principle (that would mean that all rule by people over people and all economic exploitation was inhumane): it was simply *colonization* in principle. This means that even rationalized, reformed, and humanized colonization, complete with clinics and schools, remained an economic system that compelled narrow sectors of the colonized societies in Asia and Africa to obey impulses from Europe which gave priority to serving the interests of Europe's ruling classes. For this reason Europe must admit the accusation from Asia and Africa, not only of not having developed these continents, but at the other extreme of having actively 'underdeveloped' them. *How Europe Underdeveloped Africa* – this is how colonial history[19] was written in the enthusiasm of liberation.

Part One

EUROPE AS MASTER OF THE WORLD, 1918–39

Chapter One

THE FIRST WORLD WAR

Germany did not reckon with a colonial war, when after the third Morocco crisis it stepped up the arms race on land and sea. Only colonial troops, consisting predominantly of natives, were stationed in the colonies: 2,500 men under 152 German officers in East Africa, 1,500 men in Cameroon, while in South-West Africa only whites served after the heavy Herero and Nama wars. No colony possessed a usable naval base.

The whole of German East Africa and parts of Cameroon lay within the conventional Congo Basin, for which it was specified in the General Act of the Berlin Conference of 1885 in article 11 that:

In the event of a power, which exercises rights of sovereignty or protection in the . . . territories placed under the regime of free trade, being involved in a war, the Parties undertake . . . to offer their good services, in order that the territories . . . should be placed under the regime of neutrality for the duration of the war. Then the belligerent parties would have to forgo extending hostilities on to the thus neutralized territories and to forgo using them as bases for military operations.

Germany made efforts to keep even Togo neutral; it lay outside the Congo Basin but was practically unarmed. A powerful radio station had been constructed there in Kamina for the transmission of bulletins to other African colonies.

Belgium and at first even France were not disinclined to respond positively to their opponent on this question. But then French and British troops invaded Togo on 5 August 1914. Three weeks later, on 26 August, the colony was obliged to surrender. In East Africa, where the British bombarded Dar es Salaam on 8 August, Lieutenant-Colonel von Lettow marched immediately towards the northern border with Kenya in order to threaten the Uganda railway, driving an Anglo-Indian division, which had landed near Tanga, into the sea, with heavy losses. German troops in East Africa during the war reached a peak total of 3,500 white troops and 12,000 black askari. Even with these, however, the borders of the colony could not be defended as soon as the enemy had mustered a strong and well-armed fighting force. At the beginning of 1916 the South African general Jan Smuts took command on the British side, occupying German East Africa with a concentric attack. In November 1917 von Lettow and the remnants of his troops were encircled on the Makonda plateau in the south of the colony. There he broke through on 18 November across the border river towards Mozambique, patrolling across the Portuguese colony for almost a whole year and bringing new war material from enemy stocks. In September 1918 he reappeared on German territory, then, however, taking evasive action towards Northern Rhodesia. Only when the armistice was declared on 13 November 1918 did the 20 officers, 10 doctors and officials, 125 other Europeans, 1,168 askari and 1,520 porters whom von Lettow still had at his disposal allow themselves to be interned.

The colonial troops of Cameroon did not last so long. At the end of September 1914 the British captured the important port of Douala, Garoua and Ngaoundéré in the north falling in June 1915. After a last-ditch defence in the district of Jaunde the Germans fled across to Spanish territory in February 1916.

The German authorities in South-West Africa at first hoped to join forces with rebellious Boers in the Union of South Africa. The majority of Afrikaners, however, remained loyal to the British Empire. The South African parliament voted on 14 September 1914 by ninety-two votes to twelve to enter the war on the side of Britain. Although some nostalgics did in fact subsequently again take up arms against the British – this time also against their own South African government – Prime Minister Botha was able to crush the rebellion by January 1915, immediately going on to invade German South-West Africa. The capital Windhoek fell on 13 May 1915, the Germans, wedged between Otavi and Tsumeb, surrendering on 9 July.

The scattered German possessions in the South Seas were occupied by New Zealander and Australian divisions in the first weeks of the war. Only the fate of the leased territory of Kiaochou on the Shandong coast proved more dramatic. This port had been occupied by the Germans in 1898 for strategic reasons. It now became clear that Tsingtau (Qingdao) was becoming a clean little model German town, but that it was useless from the military viewpoint. In August 1914 Count Spee, commander of the cruise fleet in the Pacific, ordered his ships to sail away from the South Sea islands towards the Chilean coast. On 23 August Japan declared war on Germany, in September 40,000 men landed in Shandong and on 10 November Tsingtau had to surrender.

The futile defence of the German colonies on land and the feeble attempts of the fleet, which had been built with so much pomp to disturb enemy sea traffic by means of cruise warfare, do not by a long way embrace all the disruptions set in motion by the First World War within the European overseas empires. Not only was the prestige of the white man weakened by the conflict of European or European-led colonial troops with one another: more than this the German government deliberately attempted to set off a wave of uprisings in the colonies of the enemy, above all in the British Empire. It was not by virtue of German sobriety, but through the weakness and romantic illusions which in Berlin evidently took the place of reliable information, that the Holy War of the Muslims against Britain was brought to a halt. Sought-after Persia, which in 1915 was promised Afghanistan and Russian Central Asia in return for entering the war on the side of Germany, remained neutral. The Egyptian officers and the Ottoman Turkish governor were careful not to provoke the British, in view of the fact that the Central Powers were conducting the planned campaign against the Suez Canal only symbolically in the form of a few raids. Leo Frobenius achieved as little on his visit to Ethiopia (it was intended to attack the Anglo-Egyptian Sudan) as did those emissaries who wanted to bring into play old contacts with undefeated Moroccan princes. Only the Senussi conducted a guerrilla war against Italy and France in the Sahara. Of greater military importance was the British counter-attack: the rebellion of certain Arab warriors against the Ottoman sultan. The German strategy of instigating an insurgence of the Islamic world turned out to be a boomerang.

This did not prevent Germany, however, from continuing to elaborate the fantasies of massive colonial expansion it had already been playing with before the war, and in which Africa formed the focal point. The 'German empire of Central Africa as the basis of a new German world policy'[1] was not only the subject of confidential memoranda, but extolled on the open market. The gaze of the German public alighted at first only on Belgian and French territories: the whole of the Congo (today Zaire) and French Equatorial Africa, as well as Dahomé (today Benin), Upper Volta (today Burkina Faso), and parts of what is today Mali; to these of course were also to be added the Portuguese territories, which had already been conceded to the Germans by London in 1898 and 1914.[2] The longer the war went on, however, the greater grew the appetite of German colonial strategists. The German Colonial League demanded in 1918 (in addition to the above-mentioned territories) the whole of West Africa south of the Sahara (including Dakar, Nigeria, and the Gold Coast), Uganda, Kenya, Northern Rhodesia, and Madagascar. There was virtually nothing left for other interested parties between the desert and the Zambesi! Kiaochou, however, was to be given to the Japanese.

On the side of the Allies the basis was lacking for such far-reaching expansion plans. Britain and France simply decided to retain the conquered German colonies in some form. It seemed that only Italy emulated Germany's example and expressed desires for a massive extension of its possessions. Ethiopia was at that time already – or once again – at the centre of Roman acquisitiveness: in addition the colonial minister Gaspare Colosimo called on the Allies in 1916 kindly to bestow on his country British and French Somaliland, two provinces of the Anglo-Egyptian Sudan (Kassala and Takai) and 2.5 million square kilometres of 'hinterland' from Libya down to Lake Chad.[3] This is the very same territory into which the Libyan revolutionary leader, Gaddhafi, tried to launch an armed attack after 1980.

Disappointment was great when Italy achieved with the peace settlement only a slight enlargement of its Somali colony at the expense of Kenya and came away empty-handed from the sharing-out of German possessions.

In 1919 Germany relinquished (by article 119 of the treaty of Versailles) 'to the benefit of the Allied and Associated chief powers, all its rights and demands with regard to its overseas possessions'. This condition embittered the German public all the more since President Wilson had agreed in the fifth of his Fourteen Points to 'a free, open-minded, and absolutely impartial adjustment of all colonial claims'. The quotation should not be cut short here, however: Wilson spoke of a settlement 'based upon a strict observance of the principle that in determining all such questions of sovereignty the interests of the populations concerned must have equal weight with the equitable claims of the government whose title is to be determined'.

With this formula the American president unquestionably approached his ideal of the right of peoples to self-determination, although 'interests' is a much more colourless and less clear concept than that of the national will, which demands self-determination. Did Wilson want to extend the right to self-determination to the colonial peoples? We cannot answer no to this at the outset, since in the last years of his presidency he attempted to obtain independence for the Filipinos, although he himself had earlier denied them the right to freedom, before their American mentors had provided them with the necessary 'maturity'. At the Paris peace conference Wilson was only peripherally interested in colonial issues. Even the first Pan-African Congress, which met in 1919 in Paris with Clemenceau's approval, only demanded in its Resolution that 'the natives of Africa must have the right to participate in the Government as fast as their development permits' so 'that, in time, Africa is ruled by consent of the Africans'[4] – which was likewise open to many interpretations; admittedly it was mainly Afro-Americans who met at this congress.

When the French diplomat Pierre de Margerie was asked in 1918 by the Italian ambassador what he thought of these 'ideas of Wilson and the Labour people' about colonial self-determination, he replied briefly and tersely: 'C'est simplement absurde.'[5] A year later Dr Solf, last head of the German imperial colonial office, wrote: 'Are we to deal seriously with the people's right to self-determination even in Africa? . . . This would mean cruelly throwing the natives back into the chaotic circumstances in which they were wiping one another out before the intervention of modern civilization.'[6] We can see that unanimity was restored, on this issue, over the trenches of the First World War. The national demands of oriental peoples, especially the Arabs, could clearly not be fully ignored. After all, Britain had promised the Arabs independence in 1916 – albeit to separate Arabs separately: in January 1916 to the Hashemites (Sherif Hussein of Mecca) in the form of hegemony over a united Arabia; and in July 1916 to the emir of the Wahabis, Ibn Saud, concerning all territory facing the Arabian/Persian Gulf! These two pledges were already contradictory enough. Then in May 1916 was added the Sykes-Picot Agreement with France concerning the demarcation of zones of influence in the Syrian-Mesopotamian region, and in November 1917 the Balfour Declaration, which promised Zionists a Jewish 'National Home' in Palestine. By the end of the war the Arabs represented an insignificant, but nevertheless really existing power, particularly the

35-year-old Emir Feisal, son of Sherif Hussein, who had fought against the Turks with Colonel Lawrence.

In order to save face with the Arabs, in so far as that was still possible, and in order not to violate Wilson's principles too brutally in the process of dividing out the German colonies, the mandate system was invented. Nominally, the newly created League of Nations was accorded ultimate authority over colonial war spoils, bestowing trustee administration on individual nations. The idea was not entirely new: the concept of international trusteeship had already cropped up at the beginning of the century during international criticism of conditions in the 'independent Congo state' of Leopold II. This time it was Jan Smuts, since 1919 prime minister of the Union of South Africa, who seized on it again. Originally he was thinking of the 'peoples and territories formerly belonging to Russia, Austro-Hungary and Turkey' when he proposed that 'the resort to the League of Nations should replace the plan for national annexation'.[7] Soon he extended his plan to Africa. Smuts's memorandum of 30 January 1919 was included almost verbatim in the statutes of the League of Nations.

Article 22 of the covenant of the League of Nations defines the mandate as 'the tutelage . . . entrusted to advanced nations' and as 'a sacred duty of civilization'. The text speaks of 'peoples not yet able to stand by themselves under the strenuous conditions of the modern world'. It thus concedes that one day the time of independence may come for all mandate regions. The prospect of such a definite possibility, however, is offered only to the so-called 'A' mandates, i.e. the Arabs: 'certain communities formerly belonging to the Turkish Empire have reached a stage of development where their existence as independent nations can be provisionally recognized subject to the rendering of administrative advice and assistance by a Mandatory until such time as they are able to stand alone.'

The German colonies in tropical Africa became 'B' mandates, their mandators undertaking only the obligation to remedy certain abuses ('such as the slave trade, the arms traffic and the liquor traffic'), not to build any fortifications, and to pursue an Open Door trade policy. With regard to the 'C' mandates, among which South-West Africa belonged, it was even expressly stated that they 'can be best administered under the laws of the Mandatory as integral portions of its territory'. The sole real competence of the League of Nations consisted of accepting an annual report by the mandatory for every mandated territory.

South-West Africa was taken over by the Union of South Africa. Great Britain, France, and Belgium shared out among themselves the remaining mandate territories in Africa, 'New Cameroon', which had been acquired by Germany in 1911, being reintegrated into French Equatorial Africa. In Arabia, Britain and France occupied the countries of the 'fertile crescent': Lebanon, Syria, Palestine, and Iraq. In the Pacific Ocean Australia, New Zealand, and Japan took over German island possessions as C mandates. Kiaochou was given back to China by Japan in December 1922.

Resistance to the new masters rose up above all in Arabia: on 8 March 1920 Feisal had himself proclaimed king in Damascus, while Britain and France were meeting in San Remo to discuss the demarcation of their mandate zones. Here Britain was able to improve its position in relation to the Sykes-Picot Agreement by taking over the crude oil region of Mosul, lying in the former French zone, for Iraq. In Syria France immediately exceeded the already occupied Lebanese coastal region: on 14 July (!) it presented Feisal with an ultimatum, on 22 July Arab troops were defeated, and Aleppo and Damascus were occupied three days later. The British were meanwhile kept busy until the spring of 1921 subduing Iraq, where the exiled Feisal acquired a new throne on 23 August 1921, whilst his brother Abdullah found himself transplanted to Transjordan as emir. In South-West Africa the mandate power put down a revolt of the Bondelswart-Nama in 1922 with the deployment of bomber aircraft.

The Turkish nation adapted itself to the loss of its Arab possessions. The leader of the national resistance – Kemal Atatürk – indeed regarded the amputation of the Ottoman Empire and the concentration of Turkish energy on the Anatolian heartland as a precondition for the political and military rebirth of his people. In Germany, on the other hand, there was vociferous complaint about the loss of the colonies – the same colonies which a broad sector of the public had only a few years before the First World War regarded as uneconomical, indeed as a political burden, since they formed a fertile soil for the master-and-servant mentality of so many officials. Now – in March 1919 – the Weimar National Assembly was demanding with 414 votes out of 421 the 'restitution of Germany's colonial rights'.[8]

Chapter Two

THE
BRITISH COMMONWEALTH

For the British Empire and for the British position as a world power, the victory in 1918 signified in the first instance the disappearance of the German war fleet from the oceans. This did not, indeed, restore former British naval supremacy; the USA had caught up with Britain in terms of maritime importance. In spite of certain frictions, however, chiefly concerning the distribution of crude oil sources, the Anglo-American alliance was so firm that the increase in US power since 1918 did not seem even remotely as dangerous as that of the Germans prior to 1914. Matters took a different turn when Japan began threatening to take its place with rapid steps among the prime maritime powers. Whereas, however, before the war all attempts to achieve an Anglo-German maritime arms control treaty had collapsed in the face of the more far-reaching diplomatic speculations of both sides, the powers now rapidly reached a preliminary agreement. The Washington Agreement of 6 February 1922 limited both the size and armament of battleships, heavy cruise ships, and aircraft carriers, and stipulated a total tonnage for the battleships of the five main naval powers. According to this, Great Britain and the USA were each permitted to build 525,000, Japan 315,000, and France and Italy each 175,000 tons.

In the event of future Japanese expansion in the Pacific (it was feared that Japan would fortify the former German mandate islands to the north of the equator), Britain and the United States, as the two powers interested in the status quo, remained far superior in maritime terms – even leaving the French fleet out of consideration. Britain nevertheless still set about covering the outposts of its Indian empire against attack. The fortifications of Hong Kong and Singapore in particular were established according to this concept. In other respects also India, the heart and almost indeed the *raison d'être* of the empire, was as well defended on all sides as it could possibly be. The Indian Ocean seemed more than ever to be a British inland sea: Germany had been pushed out of East Africa – the breach in the Cape-Cairo line thereby being closed – and its emergence in the Persian Gulf (the Baghdad railway) forestalled. Britain had its hand stretched across the whole of Arabia. Even when the protégé of Colonel Lawrence, Sherif Hussein, was driven out of Mecca in October 1924, the victor was another protégé of the British – if this time of the consul in Kuwait, Captain Shakespear, as well as of the emissary of the Indian government, H. St J. Philby: Ibn Saud. In 1922 Egypt was nominally granted independence, although British troops remained in the country. Not only the Suez Canal, therefore, and the oilfields of Mosul lay securely within the British sphere of power, but also the air routes to India, the significance of which was bound to increase in the near future. The Soviet revolution had thrown Russia back on itself, so that its pressure on Persia and the north-western frontier of India had momentarily disappeared.

INDIA

Even internally, British hegemony over India appeared perfectly secured. Some 60,000 whites and 150,000 Indian soldiers were sufficient to hold in check a subcontinent with by now almost 400 million inhabitants. In the 1920s a total of only 164,000 Britons were living permanently in India, of whom 45,000 were women. Never before in history had so small a group of foreigners ruled over so enormous a colonial empire. An unwritten but firmly rooted colour bar in social life separated the Britons from the Indians, even from those princely families, rich industrialists, and members of the new educational elite who had been educated at Oxford and Cambridge. European settlement had not been planned for any part of British India and did not in fact take place. The postings of British soldiers and officials were changed frequently, and as far as possible families had their children educated in Britain.

The political constitution of India was an amalgam of both direct and indirect types of hegemony and administration which had apparently grown up without planning, and which even in retrospect can be deciphered only by an expert. Internal shifts both during and after collapse of the Mogul Empire, Portuguese and French ad above all the transformation of British power from the private East India Company into a Victorian empire, and finally diverse border wars, had all left traces on India, being almost lovingly preserved by the colonial power. 'Divide and Rule'? One cannot help thinking of this old adage and holding on to the thought whenever one considers the history of British India. A question mark must nevertheless remain, since to omit it is to assert that the British consciously operated an extremely ingenious piece of planning, and this cannot be proved from the sources.

The most important distinction was that which lay between actual colonial possessions (British India in the strict sense) and the principalities which were only 'protected' by Britain. In India 40 per cent of the land surface and 23 per cent of the population fell within a total of 562 'states', ranging from the powerful Hyderabad (larger than the British motherland, with 12.5 million people) down to tiny entities resembling estates more than political units. A veritable maze of obligations and rights, tributes and subsidies, protocol honours and financial interests bound the princes both to one another and to the British rulers. British India likewise constituted until 1919 a patchwork of various forms of administration. After the First World War, it became imperative to make some concessions to the demands of the Indian national movement, whose strength sprang from quite different sources; first, the deteriorating poverty of the masses, which was becoming daily more apparent; second, the demand of European-educated Congress leaders for freedom and equality; third – a unique phenomenon among the many anti-colonial movements of Asia and Africa – from the contradictory personality of a single man, a source of fascination both to his contemporaries and to posterity, to friend and foe alike: Gandhi.

The often described and photographed poverty of the Indian population can be explained by the coincidence of two historic events: rapid population growth and a colonial regime which for too long pursued the economic interests of the motherland alone. All efforts on the part of the British administration to alleviate the distress of famine, to improve agriculture, to introduce irrigation measures, and to establish co-operatives, even the battle against profiteering, did not change the fact that the industrialization of India began too late because it ran counter to the interests of British industry as they were then understood. Only in the 1930s did Indian iron and steel production figures begin to rise by leaps and bounds. In the decades prior to that time the

36

economy stagnated (the previous fate of pre-colonial Indian manufactories has already been mentioned on p. 19). Economic growth did
not keep pace with the growth in population. Around 1890, out of
some 280 million Indians 65 per cent lived as peasants, while in 1930
the proportion was 75 per cent out of 350 million. These few figures
encapsulate the poverty of British India, which was in such dispropor-
tion to the natural wealth of the country and to the courtly splendour of
the viceroy and the princes.

Clearly organization and leadership were needed to transform this
social need into political anti-colonial action. In the 1920s India found
a leader of genius, whose spiritual power enabled him not only to
understand the masses, but also to mobilize them, and whose ethic
pointed the way for the nationalist movement even beyond his death.
Precisely this accident of history, however, led to the anti-colonial
movement remaining organizationally under-developed; it did not
need a strictly disciplined party, because it had Gandhi, and it was
unable to develop into such a party because on the one hand Gandhi
rejected the idea of being bound to a party apparatus as its permanent
helmsman, and on the other no one disputed his spiritual leadership
of the movement. Apart from Subhas Chandra Bose in 1939, no one
either wanted leadership or sought it.

The All-India National Congress is much older than Gandhi's public activity. It was founded in 1885, incidentally by a retired British
official, already rallying itself to political activity after the turn of the
century. At that time (1905–11) an attempt by the viceroy, Lord
Curzon, to divide the province of Bengal and create a new administrative region with a Muslim majority out of East Bengal-Assam was
incensing the Indian masses. It was during this time (1906) that the
Muslim League was founded which was to bring about the separation
of Pakistan after the Second World War. The hard wing of Congress –
temporarily banned from the party – was at that time under the leadership of a Brahman from the warrior Maratha people, Bal Gangadhar
Tilak (1857–1920), who was imprisoned, however, from 1908 to 1916.
Subsequently, in the middle of the First World War, it was he who
made an agreement in Lucknow with the Muslim leader Mohammed
Ali Jinnah (1876–1948) and who was the first to demand '*swaraj*' for
India: literally 'self-rule' (also 'self-control'). 'Home rule', as it was
first translated on the basis of the Canadian and Irish model,
'Dominion status' or 'independence in the framework of the
commonwealth': that is how we would put it today. The Indian people

were not yet fully aware of this agitation. The British Indian government did evidently perceive the situation after the end of the war as a threat; on 18 March 1919 they promulgated the Rowlatt Act, which permitted the detention of 'agitators' without trial. We know that this summary procedure today forms in many countries – even commonwealth members – a tried and tested resource in the art of government. At that time, however, it created a sensation, being clearly contrary to British legal principles. Exactly one month later the bloodbath of Amritsar took place. Compared with this, arbitrary measures on paper (and paper protests) pale into insignificance. Not even this massacre, however, had supra-regional causes, nor did it lead to direct consequences beyond the strictly closed-off Punjab boundary. Since Amritsar was later regarded as a beacon for Indian nationalism and since the event is indeed symbolic of the lack of leadership of the masses at that time, an account should be quoted here; this is how Sir Valentine Chirol, *Times* corespondent in India in 1919, remembered the event decades later:

> Order had been restored before General Dyer reached Amritzar, but on an ill-omened day he thought himself justified in opening fire without warning upon a great crowd assembled in the Jalianwala *Bagh* in defiance of his orders prohibiting all public meetings. . . . The *Bagh* – once a garden – has long been, save for one clump of old trees, an open space covering perhaps the area of Trafalgar Square, enclosed on every side by mud walls with tall houses rising in many places close up against and above them. The approaches are few and extremely narrow. By one of them, leading on to the highest ground in the *Bagh*, General Dyer with a party of fifty Ghurka entered the *Bagh* and saw, at a distance of perhaps a hundred yards, a dense crowd, variously estimated at from 6,000 to 10,000, most of them engaged in listening to speeches. General Dyer assumed, rightly enough, that this was a public meeting in contravention of his orders and a seditious one. Without a word of warning he opened and kept up upon them a fusilade that did not stop until, as he himself said, his party's ammunition was almost exhausted, though the panic-stricken multitude broke at once, struggling to escape through the narrow exits or attempting vainly to climb the walls, or in despair throwing themselves flat on the ground. General Dyer, according to his own statement, personally

directed the firing to the points where the crowd was thickest. The 'targets', he declared, were 'good' and by the time he and his men went off by the same way they had come, they had killed 379, according to the official figures given some months later by Government, and they left about 1,200 wounded on the ground for whom he did not consider it his 'job' to provide any help whatever.[1]

Although the House of Commons condemned (not by a very large majority) General Dyer's act, there was no mention of appropriate disciplinary action.

It was in this climate that London policy pressed forward on 23 December 1919 with the proclamation of a new constitution for India (Government of India Act), which was intended to mark a new epoch as the Montagu-Chelmsford Reform.[2] The heart of the Act consisted of the unification of directly administered British India, which was ordered into eight provinces of identical structure, the governors of which were now all to be of equal rank under the viceroy. The constitution accommodated Congress only at province level and even here not extensively; England was granting a small degree of self-administration, but was keeping the door closed to self-government, to *swaraj*. The legislative councils of the provinces, at least 70 per cent of the members of which (ranging between 53 for Assam and 140 for Bengal) were to be elected, were given jurisdiction over local administration, health and education services, public works, agriculture, and industry – known as the 'transferred subjects'. All the remaining, 'reserved subjects', continued to be the privilege of the governors and their executive councils, in so far as they did not fall within the competence of the central government, i.e. that of the viceroy and his cabinet in New Delhi, and of the India Office in London. Elected representatives of the Indian population obtained virtually no share in central government. The new constitution did, it is true, create a central two-chamber parliament, consisting of a council of state, the upper house, and a legislative assembly, the lower house, both with a majority of directly elected members. A census franchise was at that time in effect which even after extension in 1932 allowed only 6.8 million men and 300,000 women to the ballot box. This parliament was in any case powerless: the viceroy could still promulgate bills which it had rejected, and reinsert deleted budget items on his own authority. The central government was responsible solely to the parliament in London, while the Indian ministers in the provinces (not the executive councils and of course not the governors) theoretically required the confidence of the legislative councils. The whole system came to be known as dyarchy, meaning a division of rule into two columns: the British colonial regime and Indian representation. But within the central government 'dyarchy' was deprived of all meaning, since there continued to be only one, British, authority. In the provinces the 'transferred subjects' were politically harmless, if still extremely important for the daily life of the population. In 1921, 139 out of 1,000 boys and men aged 5 years and above, and 21 out of 1,000 girls and women, were 'literate', that is, capable of writing a few words in one of the country's languages. This statistic included Burma, where Buddhist monasteries maintained a relatively high level of education even in the villages. The reform of 1919 gave the green light to the battle against illiteracy. By 1927 the expenditure of the provinces for primary education had risen from just £3 million to £7 million. May we say that Britain knew how to shift the growing pressure of poverty on to Indian shoulders, so that the Indian ministers would be the scapegoats for the shortcomings of the previous administration? This would be an exaggeration, since London did not intend the new constitution to be a bone of contention thrown among the Indians, but genuine reform, a step towards a kind of federal dominion status to be reached by India at some distant later date.

The Montagu-Chelmsford Constitution, contrasted with the bloodbath of Amritsar, highlights under the magnifying glass of a single year the oscillation of British India policy between rule by force and step-by-step emancipation. Depending on temperament and conviction, we may speak of ingenious juggling with several balls, or of the stick and carrot, a struggle among various interest groups, or simply of confident pragmatism. Whatever it was, this policy characterized Indian history until the end of the Second World War and beyond. As a result of (or in spite of?) this seesaw policy, India achieved its independence without the bloody sacrifices of an anti-colonial war such as those which devastated Indochina and Algeria. In the moment of freedom, however, India paid with a separation. And the blood price for this internal event, even at its first stage, was high.

When the shots of Amritsar were ringing out and 6 million Indians were being called to the provincial elections which two-thirds of them boycotted, Mohandas Karamchand Gandhi (1869-1948) had already been back in his homeland for five years. He had first left India as a

19-year-old to study law in England, and had then emigrated to South Africa in 1893, living there until the beginning of the First World War. Gandhi entered politics in 1916, but it was only in 1920 with his first *satyagraha* campaign that he stepped into the vanguard of the nationalist movement. Even so early he could see the danger of an estrangement between active Hindu forces and the Muslims. He campaigned in the interests of the so-called Khilafat agitation, which began as a protest by Muslims against the humiliation of the caliph, the Ottoman sultan, by the entente powers.

'*Satyagraha*' – non-violence, or literally 'holding fast to the truth' – is the great instrument in the arsenal of world politics that Gandhi has bequeathed to us all. He used it for the anti-colonial struggle which had at one and the same time to be a mobilization of his own people and a conflict with the foreign power if it was to promise success, thus exactly marking the seam between internal and foreign politics. This conscious and precisely calculated dovetailing of national and international politics is something just as innovative as non-violence. It has been understood and adopted by countless politicians of the present day, in both poor and rich countries, while the persistent refusal of Gandhi to use violence still affects us today like an inexplicable, mysterious alien thought. It is wondered at by all, while by no means professed on the same basis by all. Only a few (Albert Luthuli, Martin Luther King) remained true to it when hard-pressed. It has been said that Gandhi was only able to practise *satyagraha* because his opponent was democratic Britain; if he had been dealing with one such as Stalin, Hitler, Mao Tse-tung, or Verwoerd. . . . There is much truth in this, although we know that democratic and reformist Britain in India was at the same time also the Britain of the Rowlatt Act and the bloodbath of Amritsar. Gandhi's success, however, which even more than the taming of the British lion was marked by his precarious victories among his own people, victories over special interests, narrow-mindedness, and fanaticism, cannot be extinguished from the outside. How does Jawaharlal Nehru explain it? The fact that this man, from a totally different way of life, of a totally different world-view, and furthermore of opposing socio-political conviction, could remain loyal to Gandhi is in itself mysterious.

And then Gandhi came. He was like a powerful current of fresh air that made us stretch ourselves and take deep breaths; like a beam of light that pierced the darkness. . . . He seemed to emerge from the millions of India, speaking their language and incessantly drawing attention to them and their appalling condition. Get off the back of these peasants and workers, he told us, all you who live by their exploitation. . . .

Congress was dominated by Gandhi and yet it was a peculiar domination, for the Congress was an active, rebellious, many-sided organization, full of variety of opinion, and not easily led this way or that. Often Gandhi toned down his position to meet the wishes of others, sometimes he accepted even an adverse decision. On some vital matters for him, he was adamant.[3]

Gandhi immediately cut short his first *satyagraha* campaign when it broke into sudden violent rebellion in some places; on 4 February 1922 peasants burned down the police station of Chauri-Chaura: twenty-two officers lost their lives. The British administration nevertheless took action, Gandhi being arrested in March and sentenced to six years' imprisonment. He remained in prison only until February 1924, Congress electing him as its president in the same year. Gradually the influence of more radical politicians began to increase again. In 1927 they won a majority in the All-India Trades Union Congress, which since its foundation in 1920 had initially steered a liberal course. In Congress the moderates prevailed again in 1928; their speaker Motilal Nehru (1861–1934), Jawaharlal's father, was elected president. His son, however, led the extreme wing to victory a year later. '*Purna Swaraj*' – complete independence – was now the watchword.

Jawaharlal Nehru (1889–1964), from an aristocratic Kashmiri family, throughout his life in terms of sentiment and bearing more gentleman than populist leader, nevertheless intellectually understood the Indian freedom struggle as simultaneously a nationalist and a social liberation movement. He wanted to be a socialist:

A study of Marx and Lenin produced a powerful effect on my mind and helped me to see history and current affairs in a new light. . . . Much in the Marxist philosophical outlook I could accept without difficulty; its monism and non-duality of mind and matter, the dynamics of matter and the dialectic of continuous change by evolution as well as leaps.[4]

He wanted not only to awaken the collective anti-colonial consciousness of all Indians, but also immediately to show Indian peasants that, in addition to the British, Indians were also exploiting them – princes, capitalists, profiteers. Gandhi's actions, on the other hand, often amounted to a strengthening of emerging Indian capitalism; when, for example, he called for a boycott of British textile imports, wearing '*khadi*', homespun coarse cotton, this political fashion in fact worked to the benefit of Indian textile industrialists. Gandhi's aversion to modern machines and his preference for '*swadeshi*', primitive domestic working methods, were also intended to strengthen Indian self-awareness; many people today are enthusiastic about the use of 'appropriate technology' for developing countries, but this legacy of Gandhi can also be done to death. Anti-machine sentiment still has an anti-progressive aspect even today.

Nehru showed little enthusiasm for these aspects of Gandhi's activity. The European category of 'left-wing revolutionary' fits him better than the Mahatma, although not entirely. In 1926–7 Nehru travelled in Europe, after having spent some time in prison (1921 to 1923) and before entering the vanguard of the Congress opposition against his father in 1928. He took part in the founding congress of the League against Imperialism and for National Independence, in Brussels in February 1927, saying there:

> What is the situation of India today? We are speaking here of exploitation! It is amply felt. Not a simple exploitation, but often double and treble. We have a part of India, the so-called Indian states, in which the feudal system operates under the protection of the English. The English often point to this and say: look at these parts of India where a form of self-government exists. Other parts of India are much more advanced. I will admit that this accusation is not entirely false. . . . Unfortunately those who live there submit themselves not only to oppression and exploitation resulting from British rule, but one must also admit that they are not able to develop because of their own incapable rulers. . . . Besides the policies of the British government in India we must also take into account the Indian princes and landlords as their compatriots, who feel that they are not able to greet a free India, because a free India would lead to the liberation of the peasants from exploitation. Again, we often see a dependent relationship between British capitalists and Indian capitalists.[5]

In reality, however, Nehru also held firm to the unity of the Congress Party which embraced all social classes. That constituted its strength. He knew as well as Gandhi did that Indian politicians had now of all times to present as united a front as possible to Britain, because in London a new constitutional reform was being worked out; a further step towards internal autonomy, new responsibilities for Indians in regional administration, but still refusal to grant independence. Indian politicians were now confronted with the same dilemma as before 1919; were they to compromise by co-operating with British rule, so as to keep the bird in the hand, or were they for the sake of the bird in the bush to boycott the reform, adhere to their policy of non-cooperation, and pursue the 'civil disobedience' on which Gandhi had resolved in 1921? In 1928 a British royal commission headed by Sir John Simon visited India to observe the effects of the Montagu-Chelmsford Reform. In view of the fact that there was not a single Indian on the commission, Congress boycotted it. In March 1930, while a round table conference was being prepared in London to evaluate the committee report, Gandhi began his second great *satyagraha* campaign with the symbolic violation of the government's salt monopoly on the beach of the Gulf of Khambhat (Cambay). Once again non-violence broke out into bloody unrest, Gandhi again applied the brakes, and again he was arrested (on 5 May) with tens of thousands of his supporters. The constitutional conference thus began in November 1930 without representatives from the Congress Party, that is, without any authentic Indian representatives. This time, however, London no longer wanted to dictate reforms, but really to negotiate. The viceroy Lord Irwin brought Gandhi out of prison to see him and made an agreement with him on 4 March 1931. In return for the release of political prisoners (obviously excluding 'terrorists') and the legalization of his '*khadi*' campaign, Gandhi relinquished non-cooperation: this led him in the autumn to England, to the second round of the constitutional conference.

Had Gandhi capitulated? The subsequent course of events proved the opposite. He remained master of his own decisions and allowed the conference to break down when the British side insisted on reserving for the 50 million 'untouchables' of India a fixed number of seats in the parliamentary assemblies and to group them into a separate voters' roll, that is, to isolate them from the mass of Indian voters. Whilst the British saw themselves as the protectors of an oppressed caste, Gandhi protested against further political splintering of the people whom through his teaching and work he was in the process of forming into a nation.

The problem of the various 'communities' within the Indian people justifiably dominated both political debate and struggle in the period before the Second World War. This was the cardinal question, not only for the political, but also for the social, future of India. The transition into 'modernity' demanded from Indians as much as from all other peoples a new consciousness of the scale and framework in which this new way of life was to grow, and a revolution in the relationships among innumerable fixed groups.

The British thus made themselves the advocates of the small communities in India. This 'communalism' was intended to safeguard minority groups from all forms of dictatorship. In this way the British government became the protector of the particular interests of the Muslims and Sikhs, Indian Christians and European business people, the so-called Anglo-Indians (Eurasians), untouchables and in the last resort also of the princes, although they were not generally considered one of the communities. Undoubtedly there were tensions among these groups. In 1926 alone 140 people died in Calcutta during disturbances caused by Hindu music being played in front of mosques (1,300 people were injured). Narrow majority ratios increased nervous tension, the more clout the representative bodies gained. The British electoral system of single-member constituencies and simple majority vote had been transferred to India as a matter of course (as to nearly all other British dependencies). The hazard element of this system made things worse. In the province of Bengal (in which Calcutta is situated) 55 per cent Muslims were counted, in Punjab province 56 per cent.

British concern seemed dubious, however, when the groups who were allegedly in need of protection were split off from Congress in the first place, as the government succeeded in doing in the case of Dr Ambedkar, the best-known spokesman of the untouchables; other minorities even struggled against the parliamentary privileges intended for them – e.g. Christians. The Muslim League, on the other hand, was already in the 1930s probably more highly representative of those professing Islam than congressional leaders were prepared to admit. There is no doubt that the political backwardness of India – contributed to of course by British cultivation of certain 'nature reserves' such as the principalities – resulted in the fact that large sections of the population still did not know how to organize themselves politically.

Various models suggest themselves for this. A 'community' can attempt to preserve its special identity within the larger modern nation by forming a lobby, or even its own political party; the classic method of socio-economic groups such as the workers and peasants of Europe in particular, but also of, for example, the Catholics in the German Reich after 1871 where they found themselves in the minority.

Where the 'communities' are geographically separate to a certain degree, a federal solution may be considered, such as was in fact later chosen by independent India. Where this fails, however, there is often an attempt at secession, that is, the founding of a separate smaller nation based on the community. The Catholic majority in southern Ireland accomplished such a solution after 1919, although this does not help the Catholic minority of Northern Ireland. This path is likewise proving to be a dead end for the Sikhs in India.

The British were definitely disposed towards discovering as many communities as possible and playing them off against one another. Gandhi, by contrast, defended the ideal of an All-Indian nation, an ideal which he himself embodied to the utmost degree humanly possible. When the untouchable question was played up, he responded with a fast 'to the death' (20–5 September 1932), since the political amputation of this caste would politically and socially disable the Indian nation, leaving it definitively to fossilize in an historical museum. On the other hand precisely the European parallels which have been mentioned above indicate the dangerous and explosive character of 'community' problems, even in industrialized, well-informed, and rich continents.

With his fast Gandhi achieved the British government's modification of its 'Communal Award' (arbitration) of 4 August 1932 by the so-called Poona Treaty: the untouchables did retain reserved seats – in fact double the number originally envisaged, but the separate voting roll was scrapped, so that there was no more splitting of the electorate into Hindu castes and oppressed classes (scheduled castes and depressed classes being the official terms).

In the mean time, however, conflict with the British administration had once again reached a serious watershed. As soon as the Mahatma set foot on Indian soil after the failed second constitutional conference – on 4 January 1932 – the new viceroy had him and all notable politicians arrested. The era of the Irwin-Gandhi agreement was over. Congress was banned for two years. This failure of his attempt at compromise moved Gandhi in October 1934 to withdraw from active politics. He nevertheless remained the spiritual leader and adviser of Congress, and when he feared wrong turnings he still knew how to intervene in everyday politics with skill and firmness of purpose.

London – the 'national coalition government' under the former Labour leader Ramsay MacDonald, effectively, however, dominated by the Conservatives – would not be deterred from passing the new constitution for India through parliament in August 1935, enacting it on 1 January 1937. A fresh exchange of the stick for the carrot – or fresh proof of the patience and ingenuity of British pragmatists? The constitution removed Burma and Aden from the Indian imperial federation. Again it did not apply to the princely states, but only to British India, now organized in eleven provinces. The plan for a federation between the provinces and the states remained a dead letter; one could not 'force' the 'independent' states to incorporate themselves into one state federation with the semi-democratically administered provinces! The idea of 'dyarchy' in British India was given up. Each province obtained true autonomy under a government of Indian ministers to be formed on parliamentary principles and to be responsible to a legislative assembly; Madras, Bombay, Bengal, the United Provinces, Bihar, and Assam obtained two-chamber parliaments. All members of the Legislative Assembly – from 50 to 250 in the various provinces – were directly elected, many seats being reserved for specific population groups on the principle of communalism. Approximately every tenth adult Indian now had the right to vote. The British governors retained a limited right of ruling by decree within limited spheres – and a practically unlimited right to declare a state of emergency and then to exercise all functions which they deemed important. In this event the governors were subordinate only to the control of the viceroy and the British parliament.

Congress decided to keep the bird in the hand, thus making the constitution a success for Britain, but at the same time also bearing out the success of Gandhi and his disciples. It had simply become clear that Congress decided the fate of the experiment with a yes or a no. From now on the aim of the British could only be to win over Congress, not to eliminate it.

In the elections of 1937 the Congress Party carried 715 seats out of 1,585 in the provincial assemblies; in Madras, Bombay, the United Provinces, Bihar, the Central Provinces, and Orissa they obtained an absolute majority. In these places, as well as in Assam and the North-Western Frontier Province, Congress formed the governments. Only in Punjab (18 seats out of 175) and Sind (7 seats out of 60) was the party really defeated, while in Bengal the majority was taken away from them by the disproportionately large representation of Calcutta Europeans; they constituted only a few thousand voters, but had 25 seats as a result of the communalist principle, while 17 million non-Muslim Indians had to make do with 50 seats.

The Congress ministries remained in office until the outbreak of the Second World War. A co-operation which was drastically curtailed by external circumstances, but which was nevertheless genuine, and a constitutional framework demarcated by London came into being. The fact that Gandhi was willing to accept and practise loyal co-operation and to defend it against extremist criticism within Congress is shown by the fate of Subhas Chandra Bose (1897–1945). This administrative official, educated at Cambridge, was among the leaders of Congress from 1921, but was forced into lengthy exile in Europe, from which he returned only in 1936. He launched a severe attack on Gandhi, accusing him of inconsistency and escape into non-political charitable works, played ideologically with a synthesis of communism and fascism ('*samyavada*' – translated by him as the 'doctrine of synthesis of equality'), and was elected as Nehru's successor to the Congress presidency in February 1938. In order to take advantage of the threat to Britain by Hitler in Europe, he proposed a six-month ultimatum for granting freedom to India, and a fresh campaign of non-violent passive resistance when this period expired. In 1939 Bose was re-elected, but Gandhi exercised an effective veto: at the end of April he forced Bose's replacement by his loyal follower Radshendra Prasad, later a president of the Indian Republic. In this way the Mahatma may have prevented the flaring up of a revolutionary war in India at the same time as the outbreak of the Second World War in Europe, or two years later in the Pacific. This would certainly not have been a bloodbath for England, but it would have been for India. Gandhi had not foreseen the Second World War. Was the constitution of 1937 that he wanted to save in 1939 worth Bose's expulsion?

Perhaps the question is wrongly formulated. Today the British-Indian government and the nationalist movement inspired by Gandhi no longer look like opponents entering into compromises, but more like allies taming the inclination of a gigantic nation towards chaos and extremism. In the light of the subsequent India-Pakistan conflict we cannot simply dismiss communalism as hypocrisy and camouflage for British divide-and-rule calculation. Gandhi certainly did personally overcome the inner contradictions of the Indians more strongly than official Britain admitted at the time, but these contradictions

were nevertheless still threatening enough, so that governmental communalism now seems to us a sort of safety valve which complemented, if
not even actually permitted, the merger of a national consciousness by
Gandhi. The struggle for a united Indian nation, waged in this way on
opposing fronts, ended with a semi-victory for reason: with the principalities, castes, and regions the merging was partially successful, but it
failed with the Muslims. In the case of the various language communities (there was astonishingly infrequent mention of these in the 1930s),
it is still on probation. The struggle against extremism, however, waged
by Gandhi and the British in a united front, supporting and comple-
menting each other, brought unequivocal victory. Independent India
has so far been spared fascist experiments of the kind that appealed to
Bose, and it has been spared communist ones. We have failed to mention
the Indian Communist Party, founded in 1933 by M. N. Roy,[6] as it was
banned between 1934 and 1943 and therefore unable to influence pre-
war politics. In the elections of 1951–2 it all the same gained 6 million
votes against the 48 million of the Congress Party and the 12 million
votes of the socialists. We do not know how the party would have developed if a definitive break between Gandhi and the British had brought
the leaders of Congress under lock and key. It was in this way that
France and the Netherlands either destroyed or permanently weakened
the non-communist nationalist movements in Vietnam and Indonesia.

In the event of an all-or-nothing test of strength between Congress
and Great Britain before 1939, the victor would undoubtedly have been
Great Britain. It was thus in the very nature of things that the colonial
power remained in charge even during peaceful reform, and that it
compelled Gandhi to make compromises which went more than halfway to correspond with British expectations.

Gandhi, ostensibly a dreamer, had enough realism not to challenge
these real power relations to no purpose. He thereby preserved the valuable potential of a colonized people, its modern educated strata, from
too severe losses, keeping the door open for an opportunity in future,
with a change in these power relations, to make decisive steps forwards
towards independence.

THE DOMINIONS

What did this dominion status mean, that the British so stubbornly
denied India in the inter-war period? The concept was first introduced
as a definite datum into the political language of the empire in 1907. In

that year New Zealand obtained full internal autonomy; a Dominion, according to the original conception, is simply a colony whose white inhabitants control their own affairs: an 'internally self-governing colony', as distinct from other colonies ruled by a governor – advised by a legislative council representing the inhabitants only in part – under the supervision of the secretary of state for the colonies, in London.

It would be too simple to depict the history of the Dominions between the wars as a progression from internal autonomy to full independence, i.e. above all to international sovereignty. The development of the commonwealth would then appear as a process of progressive disintegration. In the Westminster Statute of 1931, evidently the peak of this development, the *centrifugal* elements come to the fore when looked at in this way. We read of the 'free association' of the Dominions and interpret it as a 'right to secession', as was in fact demanded by South Africa's Afrikaner Nationalist prime minister, James M. B. Hertzog (1866–1942).

This way of looking at things, however, is one-sided. The history of the transformation of the British Empire into a Commonwealth of Nations is not analogous to any physical process. The progress of the Dominions to independence rather became possible precisely because it no longer jeopardized the integrity of the whole. This was because parallel to the 'secessionist' development new common solutions were being worked out to a range of questions (especially of an economic nature) which could not be answered by simple retention of the empire as it had come into being in the nineteenth century. These new solutions may well be regarded as a consolidation of the commonwealth, that is, as a *centripetal* force.

Even before 1914 there had been an economic dilemma in the commonwealth. The Dominions wanted to protect their young industries against competition from external, above all British, imports, whilst at the same time seeking secure outlets for their traditional agricultural produce on the British market. The first desire led to a loosening, the second to a tightening, of the imperial clamp. British industrial producers likewise had dual demands: preference in the Dominions and the free importing of foodstuffs, in order to be able to keep wages down. They also therefore sought both a consolidation and a loosening of the empire. There were at the same time a foreign policy dilemma and a military dilemma. The Dominions could either seek their own competence in these spheres, or they could demand a right of consultation with the British government in decision-making. The former thus led again to independence of the members of the empire, the latter to the formation of an imperial federal state with authorities superior to those of the British government. Britain rejected both of these developments before 1914, not being prepared to grant the Dominions more than internal self-government, and certainly not even entertaining the idea of restricting its own freedom in foreign policy decisions. Prime Minister Asquith rejected in 1911 a New Zealand plan for turning the empire into a political 'federation'.

The First World War put an end to this state of suspension, when the British prime minister, David Lloyd George, called the prime ministers of the Dominions to an 'Imperial War Cabinet'. It is indicative that the overseas politicians all saw their independence confirmed by joining this common War Cabinet. The prime minister of Canada (1911–21), Sir Robert Borden, said in his speech of 21 June 1918 to the Empire Parliamentary Association:

> We meet there on terms of perfect equality. We meet as prime ministers of self-governing nations. We meet there under the leadership and the presidency of the prime minister of the United Kingdom. . . . Every prime minister who sits around that board is responsible to his own parliament and to his own people; the conclusions of the War Cabinet can only be carried out by the parliaments of the different nations of our Imperial Commonwealth. Thus, each Dominion, each nation, retains its perfect autonomy. I venture to believe . . . that in this may be found the genesis of a development in the constitutional relations of the empire, which will form the basis of its unity in the years to come.[7]

Autonomy of the members and unity of the whole, seen a priori not as a contradiction, but as two sides of the same coin: this approach was to overcome all difficulties in practice. There were certainly enough of them: Joseph Chamberlain had wanted to resolve the economic dilemma by relinquishing in 1903 the traditional British policy of free trade, but this trend had come to a standstill halfway. Lloyd George was equally unsuccessful in resolving the foreign policy dilemma by calling the imperial war cabinet. It was unable to function after 1918, precisely because the parliaments of the Dominions refused in peacetime to sanction decisions which served predominantly British interests. In 1922 Turkish nationalists under Kemal burst through the

British stronghold on the Dardanelles, a crisis came and London appealed to the Dominions. The governments of South Africa and Canada, however, wanted to consult their parliaments before entering into agreements, and the crisis meanwhile passed. The 'Chanak Incident' revealed the internal weakness of inconsistent imperial federalism. The next swing of the pendulum therefore constituted a further loosening of the structure. In the nineteenth century Canada had set the pace; now for a few years turbulent Ireland took over the role.

Britain's Ireland policy was under an unlucky star during the First World War. Although King George V signed the Home Rule Bill, the actual granting of autonomy was postponed until after the war. At this point an armed uprising of the Sinn Fein movement broke out, which Britain suppressed. On 23 December 1920 its neighbouring island was divided in two by the Government of Ireland Act. One year later the Dominion status of southern Ireland was complete, and a year after that, on 6 December 1922, the Irish Free State was proclaimed in Dublin. In Irish domestic politics the Republicans under Eamon de Valera stood against the moderate wing of the former Sinn Fein Party. The latter group, which until 1932 formed the government, was prepared to continue giving formal allegiance to the British king, which at that time was an indispensable precondition for membership of the commonwealth. However, all the Irish demanded their own international representation – which was conceded to them. As late as 1920 London had still stressed the 'principle of the diplomatic unity of the British Empire', when a Canadian envoy became active in the context of the British embassy in Washington. In 1924 the Irish Free State sent its own accredited envoy to the USA. A precedent had thus been set which had to be seized on by other Dominions so as not to leave their status in any doubt. The decision came at the Empire Conference of 1926 (19 October to 18 November), after Britain had already declared in article 9 of the Locarno Treaty (October 1925) that its signature did not bind the Dominions until they themselves had declared their consent. In 1927 the Inter-Imperial Relations Committee chaired by the earl of Balfour (at that time the most prestigious elder statesman of Britain) coined the famous formula for the future of the commonwealth:

> The Committee are of opinion that nothing would be gained by attempting to lay down a Constitution for the British Empire. Its widely scattered parts have very different characteristics, very

different histories, and are at very different stages of evolution; while, considered as a whole, it defies classification and bears no real resemblance to any other political organization which now exists or has ever yet been tried.

There is, however, one most important element in it which, from a strictly constitutional point of view, has now, as regards all vital matters, reached its full development – we refer to the group of self-governing communities composed of Great Britain and the Dominions. Their position and mutual relation may be readily defined. *They are autonomous Communities within the British Empire, equal in status, in no way subordinate one to another in any aspect of their domestic or external affairs, though united by a common allegiance to the Crown, and freely associated as members of the British Commonwealth of Nations.*

The Balfour formula is often quoted thus far, but it continues as follows:

A foreigner endeavouring to understand the true character of the British Empire by the aid of this formula alone would be tempted to think that it was devised rather to make mutual interference impossible than to make mutual co-operation easy.

Such a criticism, however, completely ignores the historic situation. . . . No account, however accurate, of the negative relations in which Great Britain and the Dominions stand to each other can do more than express a portion of the truth. The British Empire is not founded upon negations. It depends essentially, if not formally, on positive ideals. Free institutions are its life-blood. Free co-operation is its instrument. Peace, security, and progress are among its objects.[8]

In less than five years this Committee Report took shape in the form of law; not a 'Constitution for the British Empire' or for the commonwealth, but a normal Act of Parliament passed at Westminster: *An Act to give effect to certain resolutions passed by Imperial Conferences held in the years 1926 and 1930, 11 December 1931.* This is the 'Statute of Westminster'.[9]

Its preamble states that it stands 'in accord with the established constitutional position that no law hereafter made by the Parliament of the United Kingdom shall extend to any of the said Dominions as part of the law of that Dominion otherwise than at the request and with the consent of that Dominion'. Article 2 states that the parliaments of the Dominions may in future also pass such statutes as 'are repugnant to the law of England', and that they are further free to change valid former laws in their countries. Article 3 grants the Dominions the right to conclude international treaties. One would nevertheless look for one word in vain in the Statute of Westminster – the word 'independence'. Instead of this, articles 7 and 8 guarantee the constitutions of Canada, Australia, and New Zealand; in other words: prevent the parliaments of these Dominions adopting constitutional changes. Since this is an Act of the United Kingdom, this clause ultimately means that London reserves for itself constitutional competence for Canada, Australia, and New Zealand. But does this not again drastically limit the independence of those countries? Could a future British parliament not change or waive the whole statute like any other law it chooses? This question is in practice so absurd that it is hardly ever raised, even in theoretical discussion. The reservations of articles 7 and 8 can be quite simply explained in a practical light: they were intended to pacify the provincial governments within the federations of Canada and Australia, who in fact felt their rights more severely threatened by their own central governments than by London.

In terms of practical application, the Statute of Westminster has proved itself superbly well. The international independence of Canada, Australia, and New Zealand has developed beyond all doubt, whilst their friendly relations – vice versa and with the United Kingdom – have not suffered from it, either during the hard test of the Second World War, or in the stresses and strains of world policy since 1945. Until 1961 the same also applied to South Africa, and even in this case the expulsion of the apartheid state from the commonwealth was a lesson in smooth and effective co-operation among the remaining members.

In 1932 at the Empire Conference in Ottawa, a successful preliminary solution of the economic dilemma was also reached. Only in 1930 had the customs federation plans, revamped once again by Lord Beaverbrook and Lord Rothermere, finally been laid to rest. The sole form of economic co-operation which offered a promise of success and which could be reconciled with the new conditions was an elastic system of mutual benefits, this being drafted in Ottawa in the form of the 'Imperial Preferences'. Of course, these benefits were not of equal importance for all the Dominions in the ensuing period. They were certainly a thorn in the side of the USA, impeding as they did the possibilities for direct trading with Canada, its immediate neighbour.

Subsequently, during the Second World War, therefore, the USA took advantage of Great Britain's economic plight to force a waiving of the Imperial Preferences, achieving this on paper with the conclusion of the GATT agreement in 1947. The Imperial Preference concept was nevertheless a tenacious one, and continued to preoccupy experts even in the 1960s and early 1970s during London's negotiations on entry into the European Community (EC). At that time, Australia and New Zealand would have been faced with crisis if the economic fabric of the commonwealth were to collapse entirely. A comparison of the foreign trade figures of the 1920s with those of 1965 and the mid-1980s gives the following picture:

Table 2.1 Commonwealth trade figures 1928–85

| | Commonwealth share (in %) | | | | | |
| | exports | | | imports | | |
	1928-9	1965	1985	1928-9	1965	1985
Great Britain	40*	28	9	32**	29	11
Canada	36	18	5***	18	11	5***
Australia	44**	38	20	54**	39	21
New Zealand	85	58	36***	69	66	33***
South Africa	60	50	16	48	34	16

Notes:
* 1927
** 1923-4
*** 1984

In addition to the shared 'positive ideals' referred to in the Balfour formula, the Imperial Preferences and the Sterling Zone, now only of historical importance, and other less conspicuous linchpins which hold the commonwealth together should be mentioned. Until the Second World War the common citizenship of all citizens of all Dominions (and of the inhabitants of the crown colonies) as 'British subjects' was undisputed. Only in 1947 did a commonwealth conference resolve that each member country should introduce its own citizenship and establish regulations for obtaining it and losing it, although all members pledged to continue to recognize citizens of all the commonwealth partners as 'British subjects' or 'Commonwealth citizens'. In practical terms this meant that these persons would receive preferential treatment over other foreigners, and in particular that they would enjoy greater mobility and easier naturalization. The Irish incidentally also enjoy these advantages, in spite of Eire's withdrawal from the commonwealth. Only when Great Britain began to discriminate against coloured immigrants from Pakistan and the West Indies in the 1960s was this pillar of unity of the commonwealth dealt a blow.

One of the judicial links was represented by the function of the Judicial Committee of the British Privy Council. This council, originating from the Middle Ages, constitutes the historical background from which the more compact cabinet later emerged. Since then the term 'Privy Councillor' (PC) is a purely honorary title which in the 1930s decorated some 350 respected persons from Great Britain and the Dominions. Only the Judicial Committee was at that time of any political significance. This included judicial members of the House of Lords and, from the end of the nineteenth century, specialists from the Dominions and India, and was at one time the supreme court of appeal for the whole empire. From 1875 onwards, however, Canada, followed by Australia and later South Africa, endeavoured to pave the way for the replacement of the Privy Council, and the establishment of their own courts as the highest judicial authority. The question nevertheless remained in the balance for decades, being discussed once again at the Empire Conference in 1926 – and again postponed. In 1933 South Africa and the Irish Free State banned appeals to the Privy Council. Canada (on civil matters) and India followed this example in 1949, and Australia in 1968. Those commonwealth states which were decolonized after 1960 all chose this judicial path either immediately or a short while after achieving independence. The Privy Council today is only responsible for appeals lodged from the non-sovereign territories of the commonwealth.

Whoever wishes to make an historical assessment of the changes in the British Empire between the wars must recognize the fact that success, given the exceptionally complicated nature of the material to hand, was as complete as world policy successes can be in view of the weaknesses of human nature. The statesmen of Britain and the Dominions achieved a near-optimal combination of freedom and unity, self-sufficiency and co-operation. Although the last thing they wanted was to pave the way for the elimination of European dominance of the world (as British tactics towards the Indian nationalist movement until the Second World War show), they were nevertheless preparing a model whose usefulness was to prove invaluable to smooth decolonization after 1945. This truly earth-shattering revolutionary movement, which nevertheless managed to an astonishing degree to be bloodless, would very probably have come together far more clumsily and lost itself in many more culs-de-sac, had it not constantly had the 'spider's web' of the commonwealth at its disposal as a means of orientation. It is a remarkable thought that the worthy white gentlemen who met every couple of years without much fuss in London (or even in Ottawa), were still able decades later effectively to bridle, or even direct, the impetuousness of the people's tribunes of India and Africa who were leading the distressed millions - the truly 'damned of the earth' - in uprising against the white overlords. This is nevertheless how it was. These same tribunes later sat happily and gratefully in the only club on earth (and where would its domicile be if not in London?), which is so distinguished that it accepts only the prime ministers of independent nations as its members. Who knows a better paraphrase of the commonwealth? 'Considered as a whole, it defies classification.' The Balfour formula of 1926 is still valid today, whereas so many of the brilliant achievements of the diplomacy of that time - the Polish Corridor and Locarno, the Young Plan and the Cordon Sanitaire, not to mention Munich - are now of no more significance than historical fossils.

THE SPECIAL CASE OF SOUTH AFRICA

Since today we can recognize the emancipation of the white Dominions as a prelude to the liberation of the coloured peoples and to the setting-up of a multiracial commonwealth, the ease with which the Union of South Africa was despatched into full independence is a source of wonderment. Could one not have included a clause on the protection of 'non-white' South Africa in the Statute of Westminster in addition to the provisos for the benefit of individual states within Australia and Canada? Of course the 'free institutions' on which the Balfour formula so proudly bases itself were in all the Dominions political institutions for the white man, preferably for white men of the British kith and kin. White supremacy in the Dominions, however, responded in 1930 to an overwhelming white population majority everywhere - with the sole exception of South Africa. Almost 9 million people were living in Canada, of whom only 110,000 were Indians and 40,000 Chinese; in Australia some 6 million, of whom 100,000 were Aborigines and 30,000 Asians; in New Zealand 1.5 million, of whom 50,000 were Maoris and 4,000 Chinese. In South Africa, on the other hand, there were 7 million, of whom almost 5 million were black Africans (or 'Bantu' as they were later officially known), 555,000 people of mixed race ('coloureds') and 200,000 Indians.

Since prior to the Second World War only the white countries in the British Empire obtained Dominion status, we can assume that no one seriously entertained the notion of transforming white supremacy in South Africa into 'free institutions' for non-whites. Furthermore, since 1924 the National Party of the white Afrikaners[10] had been ruling in Pretoria! This in itself probably explains the forbearance towards South Africa in the Statute of Westminster. In order not to drive Hertzog towards secession along de Valera's road, London sufficed itself with older, weaker provisos.

When in 1909 Britain had merged the self-governing colonies of the Cape and Natal with the 'Boer' republics, defeated ten years earlier, into the Union of South Africa (not a federal state such as Canada or Australia, but in fact a unitary state), British politicians were fully aware of the racial problem and had a clear answer to it, which corresponded largely to the *'Baaskap'* (supremacy) concepts of the white Afrikaners. On 18 May 1903 Lord Milner, British high commissioner responsible for reconstruction policy, said in Johannesburg:

> What is the good . . . of perpetually going on shouting that this
> is a white man's country? Does it mean that it is a country only
> inhabited by white men? That, of course, is an obvious
> absurdity, as the blacks outnumber us at five to one. Does it
> mean a country which ought only to be inhabited by white men?
> Well, as an ideal that would possibly be all very well, but as a
> practical statement it surely is perfectly useless. If it means
> anything, it means that we ought to try and expel the black
> population, thereby instantly ruining all the industries of the
> country. What it does mean, I suppose, if any sane meaning can
> be applied to it, is that the white man should rule. Well, if that is
> its meaning, there is nobody more absolutely agreed with it than
> I; but then let us say that plainly, and do not let us only say it,
> but let us justify it. There is only one ground on which we can
> justify it, and that is the ground of superior civilization.
>
> The white man must rule, because he is elevated by many,
> many steps above the black man; steps which it will take the
> latter centuries to climb, and which it is quite possible that the
> vast bulk of the black population may never be able to climb
> at all.

Later in the same speech Milner did tell the whites 'that the general standard of native civilization should be immensely raised'. With political vagueness, although with emotional impressiveness, he continued: 'Mind you, it will take years and years to raise them even so far as to the level of your waist, although it stands to reason that a certain number of them will rise to the level of your shoulder. Are you going to put back the whole progress of civilization by banging them on the head the moment that they do so?' Referring specifically to people of mixed race, he went so far (how carefully!) as to take a step further, using politically unequivocal concepts: 'Speaking again my personal opinions, opinions perhaps not shared by the majority of those here, perhaps not shared by any of them, I shall think it an unhappy day when any large British community in South Africa completely and finally repudiates the doctrine of one of the greatest of South African statesmen [Cecil Rhodes] – 'Equal Rights for Every Civilized Man'.[11]

The South African constitution of 1909 consequently did not force the white Afrikaners to make any political concessions to the black Africans, but did make it somewhat difficult for them to restrict further the already existing rights of non-whites. Once again one can discern here the British principle of not bringing matters to a head, but rather postponing them and hoping for future reconciliation between those of goodwill. In South Africa this recipe failed. When the Union became a Dominion, and thus autonomous in its internal affairs (1910), there was still no female suffrage. In the Cape Colony every man could vote who was 21 years of age, could read and write, and had either a yearly income of at least £50 or possessed land to the value of £25. Numerous black Africans and people of mixed race fulfilled these requirements. In the 1880s the proportion of black voters had even risen to as much as 47 per cent. This did not suit the Cape government, which since 1872 had been a 'Responsible Government', with an indigenous white prime minister. Under Prime Minister Sprigg in 1887, a law was enacted depriving all black Africans who cultivated tribal land (that is, those who did not earn individual income from the land) of the vote. In this way, the danger of the Cape whites being outnumbered was eliminated, as some 30,000 black voters were then struck from the roll. Several thousand nevertheless remained. The Cape electoral law, which was 'colour blind' at least in principle (there was still only one electoral roll for everyone), remained a thorn in the side of politicians from the Transvaal and the Orange Free State. In their provinces, only the white man had ever enjoyed civil rights. In predominantly British Natal, non-whites were theoretically free to be registered on the electoral roll, but needed for this a special paper, a 'Letter of Exemption', which was as good as unobtainable.

The Union's constitution stipulated that only both houses of parliament together and with a two-thirds majority could curb the right of non-whites to vote. When the Balfour formula was being discussed in South Africa at the end of the 1920s, Prime Minister Hertzog declared himself expressly in favour of the continued validity of this clause. As early as 1930, however, he granted women the right to vote – only white women! In this way the meagre political weight of the non-whites was indirectly nullified. In 1936 the government, formed in 1933 by a Great Coalition of the National Party (Hertzog) and the South Africa Party (Smuts), proceeded to their next attack. The African voters of the Cape province were put on a separate roll, and were in future to be represented by three special (of course white) representatives in the Lower House of Parliament. All remaining Africans of the Union were to send four (white) senators to the Upper House.

Voter statistics in the Cape Colony altered during the critical years as follows:[12]

Table 2.2 Racial representation in Cape electorate 1929, 1931, and 1936

Year	white voters	%	coloured voters	%	African voters	%	total voters
1929	167,184	= 80.1	25,618	= 12.3	15,780	= 7.6	208,582
1931	352,658	= 90.2	26,378	= 6.7	12,271	= 3.1	391,307
1936	382,103	= 91.5	24,793	= 5.9	10,628	= 2.6	417,524

In the Transvaal there were some 349,000 voters in 1936, in the Orange Free State 101,000 – exclusively white, as has already been mentioned. Among 92,116 voters in Natal there were only 353 people of mixed race and one (!) black African.

It cannot be said, therefore, that this legislation of 1936 signified a break with previous developments for the Cape Colony. It simply set the seal on the policy of repressing non-white influence which had been pursued by all governments since 1887.

The cementing of white minority rule in South Africa proceeded legally and without any discernible attempts, either on the part of London and other commonwealth governments, or the public at large, to exert any effort to check it. As yet, only very few realized that this regime was bound to become a foreign body, indeed a seat of disease, within the commonwealth.

THE WOULD-BE WHITE DOMINIONS: RHODESIA AND KENYA

If the commonwealth and Britain accepted white minority rule in the Union of South Africa as normal and legitimate between the wars, why was the same 'emancipation' then denied to the white settlers of Rhodesia and Kenya? This question can be answered only with reference to population statistics and chronology, not in terms of principle. Europeans in Central and East Africa, where they formed significant settler communities, naturally based their claims on the precedent set by South Africa. They set the same development in motion – but did not bring it to its conclusion.

Before the First World War, Southern Rhodesia was administered by the British South African Company, a creation of Cecil Rhodes, which was still the most successful operator of all the European 'chartered companies' established at the end of the nineteenth century. The white settlers obtained a majority in the Legislative Council in 1907. In 1922 they were called to vote – having in the mean time increased to some 50,000 – in a referendum on whether Rhodesia should be annexed to the Union of South Africa, or whether it should become a self-governing colony under the British Crown. At that time the majority of the settlers were almost exclusively British, and, with an eye to the gulf between themselves and the 'Boers', they chose the second alternative. They counted on soon being raised to dominion status, and on forcing the black majority population – at that time numbering a million – into reserves, as South Africa was at that time just trying half-heartedly to do. Thirty-seven per cent of the land of Southern Rhodesia was declared black land – for a million Africans. In 1936 the settlers called for union with Northern Rhodesia, where only a few thousand whites were living. At this point, however, London was already listening with one ear to the concern of the black population, expressed both by chiefs and colonial administrators. North of the Zambesi the idea of falling under the rule of self-governing settlers was strongly disliked. The two colonies thus remained divided, and even white political progress in the south was stopped. Southern Rhodesia did not obtain the status of a Dominion, although its prime minister had been taking part in the empire conferences since 1931. In particular, a constitutional clause of 1923 remained in effect which required the consent of the secretary of state for the colonies in London for legislation concerning the affairs of the African population.

In Kenya there were only 12,500 Europeans living at the end of the 1920s, mostly as farmers in the 'White Highlands' which had been occupied by them since 1902. In 1920 London declared the whole region of the former East African Protectorate a crown colony, with the exception of the Arab Zanzibar coastal strip. Elected representatives of the settlers occupied eleven of the twenty-two seats in the Legislative Council. The other races were at first left with nothing. One year later the 50,000 Indians were offered two, and in 1923 five seats, which led to boycotting and lengthy disagreements. In 1927 an Arab entered the council. The interests of the Africans, of whom at that time there were over 3 million, were represented by a European appointed by the governor. The settlers successfully blocked every plan to introduce racially mixed electoral rolls. London, however, regarded this policy with suspicion. It handed over even fewer keys for future development than it had done in Rhodesia. The governor of Kenya continued to hold a majority of seats in the Legislative Council with 'Official Members', who were obliged according to the traditions of the British colonial government to vote along the lines set by him, that is, along the lines of London policy. The number of these official members was simply increased accordingly with each extension of elected representation.

'INDIRECT RULE' AND REPRESENTATIVE GOVERNMENT

In those African possessions which attracted no white settlers, as well as in relatively quiet Asiatic colonies (Ceylon, Malaya, Burma) and in those parts of Central America which had long been British, the political order consolidated itself during the 1920s and 1930s under the persistent effect of an administration which was preoccupied with two ideas: the exploitation of the natural wealth of these almost exclusively tropical countries, and the fiduciary care of the indigenous population. The fact that these two principles went together, that the ruthless exploitation of nature also destroyed the basic living conditions of the 'primitive' natives, while on the other hand the neglect or even decimation of the population also devastated the land, had been recognized by all European colonial powers long before 1914. In this the British had been aided by the legacy of the anti-slavery movement of the time around 1800 and the tradition of their philanthropists and missionaries. It should be recognized that they had become thoroughly rooted and confident in their role of paternal protectors, guardians, and trustees of colonized Africans and Asians – everywhere, as we have seen, where they themselves did not want direct settlement. There was also at that time concern that raw material resources would soon be exhausted (especially oil). This concern has since proved to be unfounded, but before the Second World War it intensified interest in economic revaluation of the colonies.

Although united in their basic attitudes, British colonizers nevertheless recommended until the Second World War various ways of anchoring their benevolent trusteeship among the colonized peoples. They needed the loyalty of the indigenous populations, and African and Asian assistants. Should they seek their co-operators predominantly among the culturally westernized educational elite, who were fascinated by Europe? This young, still very thin social stratum appeared to most colonizers as a dangerous ferment, politically volatile, morally dubious, and socially uprooted. Much more reliable seemed to them the bearers of authority which was firmly rooted in religion and history, the rulers or aristocratic leading circles of the pre-colonial state world, which had indeed often apparently remained intact, having only secured for themselves British 'protection'. Of course there were differences between the nizam of Hyderabad, a Malaysian sultan, and a minor sheikh somewhere on the Arabian 'pirate coast'. There were indeed substantial differences between a Fulbe emir, a Yoruba town king, and an apparently chiefless Ibo village community in one and the same dependency of Nigeria. The pragmatic British would have been the last to overlook this.

Only a few pre-colonial state and social systems proved resilient and elastic enough as political units capable of effective action, to survive the collision with the modern world economy, with annexation into vast territories, and with inclusion in the British Empire. The new educational elites were essentially more homogeneous, and the exchange of ideas and techniques with and among them took place more easily, even across continents and oceans. This was ensured not only by the English language they had in common and in which they learned to read and think, but also by their common orientation towards a closed, intact, self-aware, almost arrogant culture – that of the British Isles. Whether the first generation of the new Afro-Asian educational elite immediately penetrated the strongholds of British life, such as Oxford and Cambridge, as did certain privileged Indians, or whether they had to make do with the reflected glory passed on by some teachers' seminar in West Africa, its British flavour was basically the same and, as any visitor to a commonwealth country can see for himself in conversation with that now elderly generation, it was no less strong than the effect of French assimilation policy.

Until the First World War the colonizers did nevertheless prefer the traditional elites as middlemen and associates in their rule, especially in Africa. This doctrine became known as 'Indirect Rule'. Lord Lugard (1858–1948) is correctly regarded as the man who had coined it (characteristic for its pragmatism) even before 1914 and elaborated it theoretically after 1918. He understood Indirect Rule not only as a practical and economical method of government, but also as an excellent, timely tool of the mission of civilization and trusteeship bestowed on the colonial powers by humanity. His main work, first published only in 1922, is entitled *The Dual Mandate in British Tropical Africa*.

Part of this mandate, of this colonial 'responsibility', is in Lord Lugard's own words the 'training of native rulers; the delegation to them of such responsibility as they are fit to exercise; the constitution of courts of justice free from corruption and accessible to all; the adoption of a system of education which will assist progress without creating false ideals; the institution of free labour and of a just system of taxation; the protection of the peasantry from oppression, and the preservation of their rights in land, etc.'.[13]

Indirect Rule was thus not synonymous with neglect, with a mere supervision of indigenous despots so that they would not become a danger to the colonial power. The 'Native Authorities' created in West Africa were not conservative, but reformist authorities, be it of an Islamic emirate or a heathen principality. British administrators also worked there, if only as 'advisers' to the African rulers. The more stable the pre-colonial order, however, the more powerful the rulers, and the clearer their political doctrine, the less the British were able to change and indeed the less they wished to change.

Uganda, which had been occupied in 1890 by the young Captain Lugard after the Anglo-German Heligoland Treaty, and Northern Nigeria, administered by Lugard as high commissioner between 1900 and 1906, were particularly stamped with the mark of Indirect Rule. Kabaka (King) Mutesa II of Buganda, from 1963 to 1966 president of the united state of Uganda, and the sardauna of Sokoto, Alhadji Ahmadu Bello, who ruled Northern Nigeria until his murder in January 1966, set up no more blameless political systems than the modern leaders of national liberation movements. They were decried as conservatives, indeed as reactionaries, even before their demise in Africa. They did nevertheless embody a synthesis of tradition and willingness for reform, and tried to safeguard their peoples from extremism and from stagnation. We should be careful not to dismiss the Indirect Rule brought about through the kabakas and sardaunas as a mere blind alley of colonial policy. It was certainly abandoned as a doctrine after 1945, and had certainly also failed in many other colonies before in which there had been a desire to follow the model of Northern Nigeria. In Tanganyika, for example, the Arab slave hunts of the nineteenth century and wars of rebellion during the German period had simply not left enough of the indigenous authorities intact. Even the French, however, who liked to pour scorn on Lugard and Indirect Rule, today concede him at least partial success.

> Indirect Rule was a convenient formula for subjugation. It created as little unrest as possible, and was intended to keep Africa on the ancestral African track. . . . This was the golden age of ethnographers and colonial administrators bent on picturesque exoticism. These traditional societies, completely conserved, with their centuries-old structures and decorative celebrations, their noble deportment, their sedans and crowns, their holy stools, perfect accommodation with nature, their order and satisfaction, offered our romantics an idealized picture of the distant past. . . . I can imagine that my British colleagues, as true subjects of the Crown and of the venerable institutions surrounding it, felt more comfortable in this anachronistic world than I did myself.

In this way the Paris professor of history and former colonial governor-general, Hubert Deschamps, fenced ironically with Indirect Rule as late as 1963 in a Lugard memorial lecture. He did this, however, only to state seriously at the end:

> Your system was based on the conviction that peoples are different, and on respect for their own ways. You believed in the possibility of allowing Africa to develop in the forms of the past and with the people of the past. This separate existence was

bound to lead to separation later. Even if you did not see it consciously, centrifugal movement was the logical consequence of your premises. The belief of the eighteenth century and the French Revolution . . . postulated by contrast the fundamental similarity of all human beings and their ability to develop according to one and the same concept. Africa should thus have obtained its place in the modern world by means of a swift revolution replacing old structures with new forms. Then there would no longer be any obstacle to assimilation in one and the same political structure. And now let us count up the score: you lost in developing in traditional forms, but you gained in African autonomy. I won in terms of the victory of modern man and institutions. I lost in terms of political assimilation. *Un but à un*, Lord Lugard. *Match nul.* In reality we were both deceived by absolute values. People are at the same time both similar and different. The Africans reacted in a healthy way: they both demanded the same political forms as those of the Europeans, and defended the uniqueness of their culture. In the words of Senghor, they wanted 'to assimilate, but not be assimilated'.[14]

If Deschamps were not only to debate with the spirit of Lugard, but also to examine Britain's policy of colonial trusteeship as a whole, he would look not only to Africa, but also to Asia, thereby perhaps conceding his counterpart additional points after all; because while Britain was confirming the emirs of Northern Nigeria in their offices, having the exiled king of the Ashanti return to his homeland (1924), and leaving the Indian principalities out of all constitutional reforms, it was resolutely adopting quite a different path in Ceylon. The island at the heart of the British inland sea that the Indian Ocean had become was developing into a model for the democratic participation of the colonized in the political regime. There, the representatives of the modern education elite were the first to be given free rein to prove themselves as colleagues, critics, and very soon as designated heirs of British power.

In 1920 the Legislative Council of Ceylon obtained a majority of 'non-official members', that is, partially appointed, partially elected representatives of the population who were able to vote at their own discretion. There were twenty-three of them to fourteen official members with the imperative mandate of the governor; in 1924 their preponderance was further strengthened to a ratio of thirty-seven to twelve. Admittedly only some 4 per cent of the population had the right to vote, and the colonial administrators continued to rule in the Executive Council. Three years later a commission of enquiry visited the island. Their report (the Donoughmore Report) came to the conclusion that it was pointless to give indigenous politicians parliamentary power but deny them governmental responsibility; such a state of affairs was bound to arouse heated criticism. As a consequence, Britain in 1931 not only proceeded to introduce a new franchise giving the vote to 50 per cent of the population, but also reformed the Ceylon executive. Until the outbreak of the Second World War, this then consisted of three colonial officials, who remained responsible for external affairs, finance, and justice, and seven indigenous ministers, who were responsible to the Legislative Assembly. The system which had only half succeeded in India in 1935 because it was restricted to provincial level, was thus at first successfully implemented in Ceylon.

The African inhabitants of Freetown (Sierra Leone), descendants of slaves bought up along the full length of the west coast who had been freed from the slave vessels after 1807 by English warships and settled in this colony, call themselves 'Creoles'; they recognize no traditional ties with a specific African nation or tribe and speak no African language. Indirect Rule was pointless here. *Mutatis mutandis*, the same applied to the coastal towns of what were later to become Ghana and Nigeria, where the upper trading class in particular had often cut itself off from 'tribal ties' for generations.

In West Africa it was also a question of finding formulas for combining modern representation and Indirect Rule: intermediate solutions, since anything else was out of the question, while safeguarding in the first instance free decision-making authority for the British trustee power. It was also by no means clear whether the scales would tip in favour of one principle or the other in the long term. In this way, in addition to the 'Native Authorities' of the hinterland, more and more obviously competing institutions came into existence. In the legislative councils, the modern elite of British West Africa found its first, if still very modest, foothold in politics. In 1922 Nigeria obtained a legislative council, significantly responsible only for the southern regions, not for the territory of the Fulbe emirs in the north; the council also still did not have a non-official majority; in addition to twenty-seven official members sat only fifteen non-officials appointed by the governor, and three elected representatives of the cities of Lagos and Calabar. In 1925 the Gold Coast and Sierra Leone followed suit. In the Legislative Council in Accra, which was similarly only responsible for the coastal area (Gold Coast Colony), not for Ashanti or the northern region, there were nine elected representatives in addition to five appointed non-officials and fifteen officials. In Sierra Leone the ratio was eleven officials to ten non-officials, of whom three were elected; nevertheless in this latter dependency Britain completed in 1925 the union of the crown colony (around Freetown) with the hinterland, which had been a protectorate.

Lugard himself writes:

> When the Europeanized African has qualified in the school of municipal training, and proved his ability to control his own community and improve its conditions, he can claim, and rightly be accorded, increased representation on the legislative and other councils, and selection by elective vote. . . . But it would be unjust to place under their control the interior tribes, who themselves have a right to a measure of self-rule.[15]

Elections bring political parties into being. The first organizations of this kind, which emerged in West Africa after the First World War, would have been glad to see themselves as sole, or even only as main, partners of the colonial power, but they were not stable enough and in fact not an expression of the people, but of only the small 'educated' stratum restricted to the towns. In March 1920 Joseph Casely Hayford (1866–1930), an African lawyer from the Gold Coast, founded the National Congress of British West Africa. From 1922 to 1925 he set in motion through his petitions the reforms of the legislative councils which have just been described. His more far-reaching demands, however, fell on deaf ears:

> 1. Self-government be implemented so that peoples of African descent should participate in the government of their own country. – 2. Elective franchise be granted. – 3. The system of nomination to the Legislative Council be abrogated because it is not democratic. . . . – 9. Chiefs be appointed and deposed by their own people, without interference by the Governor. – 10. Racial discrimination be abolished in the civil service. . . . – 16. A university be established for West Africa.[16]

Men such as Casely Hayford were too weak, their voices too quiet for them to be able even to initiate such revolutionary changes.

Only in East and South Africa had political contact between the modern intelligentsia and the peasant masses already been established in the 1930s. The reasons for this may be sought above all in the severe land shortage of some peoples, which as a rule was a consequence of the influx of European settlers. Settler policy, however, as we have seen, in its turn blocked reconciliation between the African protest movements and the ruling regime. The politicians, although probably better legitimized and representative of much broader social strata than their West African colleagues, did not have a chance in the settler colonies. The African National Congress (ANC) of South Africa is the oldest modern anti-colonial movement of black Africans. It was founded in 1912 and grew out of even older roots, which had established as early as 1884 in the eastern Cape a 'Native Electoral Association'. The ANC was not consulted, however, when South African policy was being debated. Its explicitly moderate stance, its support of the war efforts of 1914 and 1939, its co-operation in the Native Representative Council created in 1936 by the Union government, were all to no avail. Nonwhites were considered politically non-existent in South Africa.

Matters were hardly any different in Kenya. Whereas, however, the ANC extended beyond tribal boundaries from the outset, thus demonstrating greater political maturity of Africans in the Union, the early anti-colonial movement of Kenya restricted itself to the Kikuyu people. This made it easier for the administration to take a negative view of it. Harry Thuku, leader of the Young Kikuyu Association, was imprisoned from 1922 until 1931. Jomo Kenyatta (c. 1893–1978), from 1927 general secretary of its daughter organization, the Kikuyu Central Association (KCA), was allowed to present the grievances of his people without hindrance in London, but in Kenya itself the KCA was suppressed, and its president, Joseph Kangethe, sentenced to two years' imprisonment for having held a public meeting against the orders of a chief installed by the authorities. There was no mention of introducing African representation. No wonder, therefore, that the KCA became bogged down in internal discord, and that its influence only began to radiate outwards beyond the Kikuyu nation in 1938. Force of circumstance threw it back in its organization, and therefore also in its demands and interests, into the old Africa of secret societies and magical customs. In the 1930s the KCA fought not least against the demand of missionaries to give up the traditional clitoridectomy of Kikuyu girls; the majority of teachers of mission schools went along with the KCA and were thereby driven into the arms of indigenous African churches. They organized Kikuyu schools into an independent association. As later with the Mau Mau movement, we can already see here a mingling of energies directed both forwards and backwards in African nationalism, which did damage to its potential recognition as a modern political force capable of responsibility.

THE CONTAINMENT OF ARAB NATIONALISM

The force of nationalism, which could still almost be overlooked in East and South Africa, was by contrast in the Arab countries of the British sphere of influence so strong, that only an orderly retreat from political rule could be considered. Extending the Protectorate of Egypt, legalized in 1914, or the mandates in Palestine, Transjordan, and Iraq, into lasting colonial rule appeared Utopian, and was moreover not in accordance with the League of Nations statute.

In **Egypt**, the 'Father of Independence', Sa'ad Saghlul Pasha (1860-1927), led the famous deputation (*Wafd* in Arabic) on 13 November 1918 to the British high commissioner, Sir Reginald Wingate. The Wafd Party was to develop in the inter-war years into the great National Party. Saghlul wished to represent the Egyptian right to independence at the Paris peace conference. Instead he repeatedly found himself a prisoner, on Malta, in the Seychelles, and in Gibraltar. The people, however, knew him well as education and justice minister in pre-war cabinets. Unrest broke out and London gave in and granted independence. In March 1922 Fuad I of Egypt acceded to the throne. The Wafd Party was to stay excluded from government, the British high commissioner retained substantial influence, the British army was still in the country, and the Sudan remained in any case an Anglo-Egyptian condominium. The floodgates had nevertheless now been opened. Saghlul, released in March 1923, achieved the first electoral victory for his party in September: 190 out of 214 seats. In the ensuing years the Wafd Party won again and again as long as the electoral law gave them a chance to do so. The Egyptian people remained loyal to the party, although the latter's leaders were often in dispute among themselves and although the governments of the country were dissolved and alternated with colourful regularity. Saghlul became prime minister for only ten months in 1924. He had to avoid British pressure and royal mistrust as much as Mustafa Nahas Pasha (1876-1965), his erstwhile secretary, would later have to do when he took over leadership of the Wafd Party after Saghlul's death. Prime Minister Nahas fell in 1928, 1930, and 1937, on each occasion after only a short time in office, but he and his party could not be ignored for long. Britain was basically fighting a rearguard action. On 26 August 1936, when Faruk I had just acceded to the throne, Nahas safely accomplished an alliance treaty with Great Britain. He was now able to secure the 14-year-old independence at least to the extent of having British troops, 10,000 strong, withdraw to the Suez Canal zone. Even the Capitulations of the nineteenth century, which had bestowed extra-territorial rights on Europeans in Egypt, were now revoked.

In 1926 London pledged independence to **Iraq** and at the same time ensured the oil-rich Mosul area for its protectorate, which Turkey did not want to relinquish for nothing. In 1932 Iraq was received into the League of Nations.

Only in **Palestine** did mandate policy run aground. The hopes of Zionists for a 'national home' and the national claims of the Arabs were in all too obvious conflict. Great Britain did not want to arbitrate between them. Perhaps the British even added fuel to the fire, in order to make themselves indispensable on the land bridge between Africa, Asia, and Europe, which had been in dispute since time immemorial. The Jews of Palestine, who until 1948 originated predominantly from eastern and central Europe, managed, in spite of cultural diversity and internal contradictions between religious and secular Jews and disputes as to the political goal of their movement, somehow to achieve a national unity capable of effective action. They recognized the authority of democratically elected leaders, who after 1930 came mainly from the Labour camp. The Palestinian Arabs, on the other hand, although rapidly overcoming after 1919 the contradiction between their Muslim and Christian elites, nevertheless became caught up in the labyrinth of parochial politics and extended family loyalties on their way to acquiring national consciousness. From this an Arab Palestine policy of All or Nothing emerged. Up to 1948 London was not willing to give All to the Arabs (which would mean the elimination of the Jewish national home and a ban on future Jewish immigration). In the end Nothing remained for them, whilst the Jews gained more land step by step and consolidated their polity within Mandatory Palestine.

In 1922 the British initiated indirect elections to a legislative council: the Arabs boycotted it and the council did not come into being. In 1928 an Arab congress called for the introduction of 'representative government' and London agreed, but in August 1929 an anti-Jewish uprising destroyed the project. It broke out as a result of a dispute as to what Jews were and were not permitted to do while praying at their shrine, the Western Wall of the Temple Mount in Jerusalem. This dispute cost the lives (official figures) of 133 Jews and 116 Arabs.

At that time the Jews would still have been hopelessly outnumbered in a democratically convened representation, or any kind of body elected by the people: in 1931 the British authorities in Palestine counted 784,557 Arabs and 174,610 Jews. Jewish immigration was at that time just going through a dramatic decline, from 34,386 (the record figure of 1925) to 4,075 (1931). At that point Hitler's seizure of power in Germany abruptly drove tens of thousands of Jews to Palestine; in 1935 immigration reached a new peak with 66,472 Jews. If Arab landowners continued to sell to the Jewish National Fund 'infertile land', on which a proportion of the immigrants were later to work the well-known miracle of reclamation, Arab national leaders nevertheless now had to take seriously the emergence of the nation of Israel in their country. Indeed, by imposing an economic boycott on the Jews they played into the hands of the Zionist ideal of creating a closed body of Jewish people in their own economic sphere.

At the beginning of the 1930s, Hadj Amin el-Husseini (1890–1974), mufti of Jerusalem, emerged as the most powerful force of Arab nationalism in Palestine. At first a protégé of the British, who in 1921 secured him his influential key position in the Muslim establishment, he became head of the Arab Higher Committee in April 1936. At the same time an Arab uprising inspired by him broke out – this time not only against the Jews (who now knew how to defend themselves), but also against the British Mandate. Only now did Jewish efforts towards compromise begin to wane, those feelers of leftist and bourgeois Zionists which had been stretched out after 1929 in order to find out whether an Arab-Jewish agreement would be possible; Palestine as the jointly ruled fatherland of both peoples? A few stubborn men, who continued with (German?) thoroughness to discuss among themselves the idea of a *bi-national* state (the Brit Shalom group, the Association for Peace), now found themselves isolated, whilst the political father of the emerging Israel, David Ben-Gurion (1886–1973), after 1939 no longer returned to his earlier proposal of Jewish-Arab 'parity' in an independent Palestine.[17] On the Arab side, the mufti in his armed struggle succeeded *de facto* mainly in making war on the partisans of rival Arab leaders; of 2,176 Arab dead during the time of the uprising from 1936 to 1939, 1,369 lost their lives at the hands of the army or police, only 243 as a result of Jewish violence, and 494 were killed by other Arabs (British figures). Who would still have dared to mention among Arabs the possibility of an agreement with the Zionists?

The British government added to the statute book of history the closing item on its programme for a joint Palestinian legislative council: in December 1935 it had proposed once again that twenty-three people's representatives be chosen, either elected (twelve) or appointed (eleven); that is, eleven Muslims, three Christians, seven Jews and two 'business men', the latter as a *community* apparently constituting an auxiliary structure. The outbreak of violence made this plan pointless.

London seized on another tried and tested method in its overseas policy; a royal commission of enquiry. The report of the Peel Commission in July 1937 recommended the foundation of a Jewish state. Therefore, before there occurred in India the idea that 'communal' difficulties could be solved, not by loosening the knots but by severing them, dividing the disputed country, it occurred here in Palestine. A British presence was to remain in Palestine as mandate power for the holy cities of Jerusalem, Nazareth, and Bethlehem. The report remained only literature, however. The struggles went on, the British arrested the Arab Higher Committee, the mufti fled to Syria (and in 1941 to Berlin). The majority of Jews, however, did not want division, and the fronts gradually reversed. The Chamberlain cabinet appeared impressed by Arab arguments, introducing an appeasement policy there also. After a fruitless tripartite conference, it promised the Arabs officially on 18 May 1939 to restrict Jewish immigration until 1944 to a total of 75,000 people and thereafter to set it at the discretion of the Arabs. This effectively meant not a single Jew more to Palestine. In 1949 the Mandate was to be concluded and the country to become independent. This meant an Arab Palestine with a Jewish minority.

However well the protection of minorities propagated since 1918 had been functioning at times, in 1939 it was possible everywhere in Europe to grab failure with both hands. The Jewish population of Palestine was determined not to be enclosed in a ghetto by the Arabs. The outbreak of the Second World War spared them, for the moment, an open conflict with the mandatory power.

It would be presumptuous to pause at this point and attempt some kind of conclusive statement about the British Empire. It is likewise impossible to summarize the contents of the countless volumes which have been written on this, the greatest colonial empire of modern times. It would perhaps assist the reader, however, for me to say a few brief words about this historical phenomenon, as an outside observer without direct experience (neither as a Briton nor as a citizen of any country which was at some time a British colony, although I was admittedly for some years after 1945 an inhabitant of the British Sector of Berlin – it is difficult in this world to keep absolute distance from the British Empire).

There are two questions that need to be asked. The first is, what kind of an impact did the empire make on the 'motherland', Great Britain; the second is, what have the Asians and Africans colonized by the British made out of this fate?

In both cases one can draw a comparison with France, the second largest of the West European colonial powers, and for this reason one can look for the answer to the second question predominantly to Africa, where British rule and French rule were practised among peoples of the same or similar types. France was never able to conquer anything equivalent to India, much to the chagrin of its colonialists.

At first glance, today in 1988 Great Britain is having a harder time than France. 'What until a few years ago constituted the heart of a mighty empire, will rapidly transform itself into an over-populated island lying somewhere off the Danish coast,' wrote the Dutch-American popular academic Hendrik W. van Loon around 1930. Seldom has a carelessly made prophecy hit the nail on the head with such accuracy. The reason behind this of course is the advanced age of British industry, whereas France, which was industrialized much later and which has retained to this day a much more pronouncedly agricultural character, was able to carve itself out a key economic and political niche within the (West) European Community at just the right time. To this must be added the fact that Britain was obliged to fight out the Second World War against Hitler's German Reich, whereas France could allow itself to be liberated.

To move on to the second question, however, what have the Asians and Africans made out of the British imperial impact? Here the balance is a good deal more positive, in that the two great aims of the empire in the inter-war years, which have just been discussed above, have been achieved: the securing of India and the maintenance of the ties among the Dominions. But why secure India? British viceroyship is a thing of the past. India and Pakistan (and Sri Lanka, although not Burma), however, continue to seek their way into the world of modern life according to the European model imparted by Great Britain. India has even largely preserved the political forms of British democracy. In other words the Indians have taken up and continued with substantial elements of that to which the British conquerors initially coerced them.

Only one member of the family of Dominions settled by Britons and other Europeans has so far broken away: South Africa, where the white citizens have been following a different political tradition and style since 1948. In Canada, on the other hand, the quality of life originating from the British is holding its own not only against US economic power, but also against separatism in Quebec. The elasticity and pragmatism which characterized colonial policy in the British Empire are thus preserved under new conditions.

These qualities also ensure that Canada, Australia, and New Zealand today form a solid bridge between western Europe (including Great Britain) and the Third World. This can be observed above all in their diplomatic confrontation of the white government in South Africa. In South Africa itself as late as 1986, the mission of a 'group of eminent persons' from the commonwealth made more impression on whites and blacks alike than any other démarche from the outside world.

In the internal politics of the majority of African states which were formerly British colonies, on the other hand, there is less evidence of elasticity and pragmatism, and indeed their systems are (on the surface) scarcely distinguishable from those of their francophone neighbours. The latter countries can at least be given credit for having been visibly marked by the centralist character of the *République une et indivisible*, including its penchant for judicially fixed abstracta. A rigid adherence to state sovereignty, which is perfect only on paper, nevertheless characterizes both British and French-influenced post-colonial African states. Other, more powerful nations shrug their shoulders at it, and the transnational corporations do not even bother about it, whilst the ordinary Africans are obliged to fall back on 'tribalist' loyalties in the face of the socio-political failure of 'their' state apparatuses, thus leaving the way open in 'national' politics to virtually any lieutenant who can shoot his way to the presidential palace. In spite of this, however, there are states in former British Africa where the call for impartial justice, a free press, a multi-party system, and free elections is still stubbornly making itself heard despite decades of coups and dictatorship. This could have something to do with memories of the foreign rulers of yesterday.

Chapter Three

THE GREATER FRANCE OF
THE THIRD REPUBLIC

Between the wars, the focus of French policy lay in Europe. Whereas for London the victory over the German Reich meant in the first instance the disappearance of the threatening fleet of Wilhelm II, for Paris it meant the promise of military and political hegemony on the old continent. The colonial acquisitions raked in by France in 1919 served chiefly to bridge the gaps in its compact African mainland empire. Togo (two-thirds of the German protectorate) was annexed to the Federation of West Africa (Afrique Occidentale Française = AOF), Cameroon (four-fifths of the German colony) to French Equatorial Africa (Afrique Equatoriale Française = AEF). The formal supremacy of the League of Nations over mandated territories did nothing to change this: France regarded this war booty as a permanent possession. Overseas expansion underlined the claim of France to be a world power, serving prestige more than any greater strategic concept, whereas for Britain it served the purpose of securing all conceivable routes to India. Actual French colonial policy, the administration and exploitation of overseas possessions, was left to a small cluster of experts and interested parties for as long as the Third Republic continued to exist. Colonial policy was in general not an object of political controversy, or if so then only an incidental one. Prior to 1945, the majority of peoples colonized by France had no organization or representation with which to make themselves heard in the chorus of the Paris state leadership. Investment in their own colonial empire was in any case regarded by the French bourgeoisie as bad business.

The administration of the colonies was based on antiquated juristic principles. Apart from the West Indies, Réunion, Algeria, and the protectorates of Tunisia and Morocco, the basic constitutional document of the French Empire consisted of a decree of Emperor Napoleon

III (3 May 1854), which ruled: 'The colonies, with the exception of Martinique, Guadeloupe and Réunion, will be ruled by the Emperor by means of decrees.' They were thereby removed from the competence of parliament, which otherwise in the Third Republic, as later in the Fourth, assumed full political power, setting up a 'Régime d'Assemblée'. The frequently changing cabinets in fact functioned as a kind of executive committee for the Chamber of Deputies (and the Senate), consequently emitting only weak impulses for colonial policy. In the constitutional texts of 1875 the overseas territories are hardly mentioned; the majority of them were in any case acquired later. The result was a surfeit of high colonial bureaucracy, of 'proconsuls' in Saigon, Dakar, or even Algiers, in all matters of colonial government.

From 1889 there was an Ecole Coloniale in Paris, a special college for the education of overseas officials. Its graduates had a uniform, clearly and precisely defined course before them, as was also the case for other great bodies of civil servants within French administration. A considerable, often remarkable *esprit de corps* was deliberately inculcated into the '*administrateurs*'. Under certain circumstances it was possible to make a rapid career in the French colonial service. This also applied, incidentally, to the military service overseas, which explains something of the attraction of the colonial empire for certain officers and officials.

Joost van Vollenhoven, from 1917 to 1918 governor-general of AOF, drafted a text which not only applied to AOF but also expressed a general principle of French colonial government. He formulated it precisely, perhaps even too punctiliously. Having dealt with the theses of Lord Lugard on Indirect Rule, however, we can justify this extract from a circular issued by the governor-general of AOF on 15 August 1917, which heads a chapter on French colonial policy:

I consider it neither possible nor desirable to create an administrative corps of native chiefs with classes and promotion schedules. . . . Because the characteristic feature – and I would add, the value – of the order we should give the native chiefs lies in its heterogeneity, the opposite of that among our own administrative cadres. Individual chiefs must not be interchangeable. . . . The following rule must determine the competences of native chiefs: they have no authority of their own of any kind, since in the *cercle* [intermediate administrative unit

of the colonies] there are not two authorities – the French and
the native authority – but only one!

The [French] Commandant commands alone. He alone is
responsible. The native chief is only a tool, an assistant. It is true
that this assistant is not merely an intermediary: he puts not only
his work and his loyalty into the service of the Commandant, but
also his knowledge of the country and the real influence he may
perhaps exert over the natives of that country. The native chief,
however, never speaks or acts in his own name, but always in
the name of the Commandant, both on his formal and on his
tacit orders. I hope I have formulated this absolute principle
clearly enough to leave no room for doubt. . . . I have stated the
reasons which allow us to resort to support from chiefs. These
reasons do not arise out of the interests of the chiefs. They are
not former sovereigns whose thrones we wish to protect; either
there was no such throne or they have been deposed by us and
will not rise to power again. The reasons for our action arise
exclusively out of the interests of the population which is
subordinate to our authority. There must be a hinge between us
and this population, and that hinge is the chief, not because he
has imposed himself on us, but because we have chosen him.
And we have chosen him because he is the best.[1]

French colonial regimes were in the main rigid, authoritarian, and
hence often bureaucratic and occasionally cruel. They nevertheless
always contained a spark of desire for egalitarian reform and a
humanitarian concern emanating from the spirit of 1789. This
'*humanisme*' assumed more or less the same position occupied in the
British system by respect for established powers and the impulse
towards sooner or later granting self-government to every human
community (once having recognized it as human!).

French '*humanisme*' cannot simply be taken as synonymous with the
willingness to assimilate. It was by no means in all periods the official
goal of colonial policy to educate Africans and Asians to become
'coloured Frenchmen' and to accept them at the successful conclusion
of this experiment as equal citizens of the one and indivisible republic
of the French nation. France has on the contrary only asserted
assimilation doctrine during particularly revolutionary flights of fancy
in its own national consciousness: 1792, 1848, 1945–6. It may be said
that France always relied on its strength to absorb people from all over

the world in its own nation when it was in any case convinced of its ability to win the battles of the whole of mankind and attain its goals ('*Humanité*') within its own country, pinning global victories on the French tricolour.

In quiet times, when reason returns, France too sees the dangers and absurdities of uncompromising assimilation policy. The colonial expansion of the young Third Republic between 1880 and 1919 led to there being as many yellow, brown, and black 'Frenchmen' as white. The only possible solution, which was recognized increasingly clearly from 1910 onwards and adopted in practical policy up to 1939, consisted of not treating coloured French people as *citoyens*, but as subjects of the republic. This is what happened, and it was named the policy of association, as opposed to assimilation.

This policy follows recognizably – at least in theory – the British pattern: the colonized were to remain excluded from the political life of France. This did not mean, however, that the French wanted to keep them in a state of servitude without rights. Or did they? Was it not that now, after Woodrow Wilson or Lenin had proclaimed the right of peoples to self-determination, it was no longer possible to do so? We are bound to fail in deciphering the conscious or unconscious motives of the colonial politicians of that era. One of the most prominent among them, Albert Sarraut (1872–1962), in 1931 entitled a book which had mass circulation *Grandeur et Servitudes coloniales*. Sarraut, who was counted as a left-of-centre politician in parliamentary life, had governed Indochina during the First World War and later served on more than one occasion as colonial minister (ending his career in the Fourth Republic as president of the semi-parliamentary Assembly of the French Union); he wrote in 1931:

> The natives are people like ourselves. They must be treated as such, which means securing for them the basic guarantees of such individual and personal rights as we claim for ourselves. This is a categorical demand of association policy: it has moral and practical consequences. Secondly, the colonized races must be protected from the diseases which strike and decimate them and which reduce the yield of this mighty workforce. This is the task of medical aid. They should be protected against acts of violence and fraud which may threaten their person, work or possessions. From this arises, with the concern for general security in the country, the effort towards a guarantee for

personal security through the work of a non-partisan, regular judiciary. . . . The native worker must be protected appropriately by means of humane work regulations. The moral and spiritual value of this mass of human beings must be raised. This means the development of education.[2]

All this, it should be noted, was to be either bestowed or forced on the 'natives', or at any rate offered by the colonial government. They were not to achieve it by themselves. In 1931, however, one could not persist in such a stance alone; Sarraut therefore continues:

Finally our protégés must be rendered capable of taking part to a legitimate and appropriate extent in the administration of their own countries. It must therefore be made possible for them to hold public office, and the setting-up of representative bodies must enable them to express their wishes. In a word, they should be associates, and not serfs, of the power that has taken the fate of their fatherland into its hands.[3]

This was at that time the reform programme – repeat – of a left-wing bourgeois politician. Clearly the '*organismes représentatifs*' were to express wishes, but not to make decisions – over the budget, for example. By '*emplois publics*' there was no thought of the higher ranks of the bureaucracy. Sarraut quite certainly wanted the legitimacy of the planned self-administration (the colonized were to participate in the 'administration' of their country, not in its government) to be delineated from above and from overseas, that is, from Paris. In a word, albeit a word in retrospect from the distance of decolonization: the tutelage of the colonized and the 'paternal' supremacy of the colonizers who always know better and thus always have the last word, were all fully retained in the policy of association, and indeed lay at its very core.

Practice, however, that is, everyday colonization somewhere in the African bush or in the Vietnamese jungle, had its own special face and a policy of its own. At this level the difference between association and assimilation became blurred. Whilst the dispute over doctrine was of interest in Paris, perhaps even in Dakar or Saigon, the *commandant de cercle* in his residence or on the march had other worries. The typical French colonial official did see himself as a kind of chief, definitely the commander of his 'population', but also as a kind of teacher or guardian. He liked to hear devoted natives pleading to him as 'father and mother in one'. He had to do more than keep the peace, and was certainly not there in the first instance to 'advise' native princes. He had to teach the colonized something, and what else could it be but '*la civilisation*'? It did not suit him to observe a strange 'primitive culture' from a distance, which created the mentality of the colour bar, to protect them as far as possible from contact with his own European world – even if only so that people could write books about these 'primitives' and perhaps deduce from them how their own forefathers had lived in the Old Stone Age. That was (to render the positions crudely) the interest of the ethnologist. Books have been written on the permanent friction (still continuing today) between French social anthropologists and French colonial officials. The friction was always sparked off by the fact that the administrators in fact wanted to be guardians, that is, to educate and change. In the final analysis the whole policy of association resulted once again in assimilation, at first (until the Second World War) in the strictly individualistic sense: the assimilation of individual black, brown, or yellow people into the French nation, with cultural integration counting as a sort of diploma for political integration. In this way not only did the France of the bourgeois, Catholic-socialist intelligentsia recruit its Léopold Sedar Senghor, but also the France of the Communist Party its Ho Chi Minh.

The dilemma which had led at the turn of the century to the official demise of assimilation had clearly not yet been resolved. It was not possible to integrate the millions without turning France, according to the famous formula of Edouard Herriot in 1946, into a 'colony of its colonies'. It was similarly not possible, however, in the France of the Third Republic, especially in the France of the People's Front, to persist in pursuing a colonial policy which saw these millions simply as passive human material, as a '*vaste main-d'oeuvre*' or '*masse de vivants*', to quote Sarraut once again, and nothing more. Cynics could object here that the late Third Republic, in the face of this dilemma, decided to pursue no colonial policy at all. It nevertheless remains true that practical everyday work in the colonies continued and produced results – individual people, careers, printed papers, as well as institutions – which were usable as mosaic pieces for decolonization.

INDOCHINA

As has already been mentioned, the experiences of Albert Sarraut, which we have quoted as chief evidence for the policy of association, stem from the years in which he was in charge of Indochina as governor-general: 1911 to 1914, and 1916 to 1919. He was the first to be able to make use of the far-reaching powers granted to the governor-general in a decree of 20 October 1911: as '*Dépositaire des pouvoirs de la République*', he dealt solely with the colonial minister, over the heads of the governor of Cochin-China and the *résidents* of Annam, Tongking, Cambodia, and Laos. He was able, almost like a head of state, to deal directly with French diplomatic representatives in the Far East, and had all the authorities of Indochina at his disposal. Sarraut must have succeeded in amassing a certain basis of trust among the intellectual elite of the country, because after the end of the First World War one can see that this elite made efforts to construct a modern political life, in the first instance urging legality and opportunities for safeguards within the context of colonization. In 1922 a publication appeared under the title *Essais franco-annamites*. In 1923 one Bui Quang Chieu returned from his studies in Paris and founded a Constitutionalist Party in South Vietnam (Cochin-China, which had been French for the longest time, and where indigenous representatives sat beside French ones in the Conseil Colonial[4]). The politico-religious movement of Caodaism began in 1924 to merge Buddhist, Christian, and rationalist elements into a new teaching; Victor Hugo was among those it revered! In 1927, however, a new, illegal party was founded, which drew its impetus not from the preserves of French civilization and colonization, but from the traditional teacher and cultural guardian of Indochina – China.

The National Party (Vietnam Quoc Dan Dang, abbreviated to VNQDD) of the teacher Nguyen Thai Hoc imitated both in its ideas and organization, although without lasting success, the National People's Party (Kuomintang) of Sun Yat-sen. At first, however, it gained support rapidly: by 1929 the VNQDD in Tongking already had 120 cells, with some 1,500 members.

A reform decree issued by France on 4 November 1928 granted Indochina a 'representative body'. The Grand Assembly of Economic and Financial Interests, as it was called, comprised thirty-eight Frenchmen (twenty-eight delegates from regional bodies and chambers of commerce, ten members appointed by the governor-general) and twenty-eight Indochinese. Among the latter a majority (twenty-three) were considered 'elected', that is, they were delegated by the Conseil Colonial of Cochin-China and by the Assemblées Consultatives Indigènes, which had been in existence since 1913. Only five indigenous members of the Grand Assembly were directly appointed by the governor-general. Leaving aside the top-heavy representation of French interests, the Grand Assembly was empowered to advise the governor-general in devising the budget and the allocation of public works. It could pass decisions (with the agreement of the governor-general) only on certain forms of taxation, having no other authority. This may perhaps even have been a certain protection for the indigenous population, precisely because French interests were so strongly represented in the assembly! At all events the whole structure offered up-and-coming indigenous politicians no platform for legal and responsible work. It revealed the policy of association for the dead end that it was. Since the colonial government left no alternative, Indochinese politics were forced on to the road to illegality. Out of the theoretical relations of guardianship between colonizers and colonized emerged a *de facto* relation of enmity – at first for the elite, but soon also for the masses. Colonial policy in Indochina became colonial war. The sweeping 'victories' of the French in the first phases of this war wiped out the first wave of national pioneers. The leadership of the people of Vietnam thereby fell to the men of the second wave, who began to cause a stir only in the 1930s: the communists.

Nguyen Van Cung, later to be known as Nguyen Ai Quoc, and from 1941 as Ho Chi Minh ('The Enlightener'), was born on 19 May 1890 in the province of Nghe An, in what is today North Vietnam (he died on 3 September 1969). His father had been Chinese-educated, but he himself attended for only a short time a French higher education establishment in Hué, the former capital of Annam, being at sea from 1911, becoming acquainted with America and Europe, and settling as a photographer in Paris during the war. As is stated in the introduction to the first volume of his *Collected Works* (Hanoi, 1960), he wrote mostly in French until 1926. He joined the Socialist Party of France (SFIO) and was one of the delegates at the famous Congress of Tours, which in 1921 declared allegiance to the third International of Lenin and Trotsky.

In 1923 Ho Chi Minh left France to study at the Workers' University of the East in Moscow. In June–July 1924 he spoke for Vietnam at the fifth Comintern Congress. In 1925, when his first larger work appeared under the title *Le Procès de la Colonisation Française*, we find him in Canton as secretary of the Comintern adviser to the Kuomintang government, Mikhail Borodin. He organized an 'Association of Revolutionary Vietnamese Youth' among Vietnamese emigrants, continuing this work in Hong Kong in 1929. In the mean time in 1927 Chiang Kai-shek had shifted the Chinese revolution to an anti-communist course, and Borodin and his associates were deported. The association put feelers out towards Vietnam and gained some 1,000 supporters, chiefly in the north. The Communist Party of Vietnam emerged out of an internal split in 1931, now to present serious opposition to the VNQDD, which had recruited 1,500 members.

The VNQDD attempted to launch an armed uprising on 10 February 1930 by organizing a mutiny of Vietnamese soldiers in Yen Bay. The Chinese revolution of Sun and Chiang, however, was not so easy to imitate. The party leader Nguyen Thai Hoc lost his life in the sup-pression of the revolt. From May 1930 until September 1931 the French also put down communist peasant uprisings in Annam. Once again the parallel with China is clear, this time with the unsuccessful struggles of Mao Tse-tung for his 'Soviet territories' in Kiangsi in 1934. In both cases, the communist leaders saved themselves, but whereas Mao led the core of his army through the long march to Yenan in person, Ho did not take part in the battles and was isolated from the movement by forces beyond his control. On 5 June 1931 the British put him behind bars for two years in Hong Kong. Although he was free again at the beginning of 1932, he returned to Moscow via Vladivostok a year later. The Comintern took him out of the front ranks when Stalin began in 1934-5 to court the West European democracies and dropped his anti-imperialist campaign. Ho studied at the Moscow Research Institute for National and Colonial Ques-tions and at the Lenin Academy for top Comintern functionaries. The end of 1938 found him in Yenan with the eighth army of Chinese communists, and a little later in the entourage of a Chinese general loyal to Chiang Kai-shek (the Kuomintang and communists were at that time fighting together against the Japanese). It was only now that Ho Chi Minh could think of making direct contact with the communist cadres in northern Vietnam.

France made one more attempt in 1932 – in the wake of a shift to the left in the Chamber elections which brought Sarraut once again into the colonial ministry – at reform policy based on the theories of association, this time explicitly under the influence of the reasoning of Lugard on Indirect Rule. In September 1932 the 19-year-old Bao Dai was permitted to return to Vietnam, having been educated for ten years in France; since 1925 he had been nominally the emperor of

Annam. He announced his decision – in reality of course an experiment on the part of the colonial government – to set up a constitutional monarchy.

In May 1933 the emperor reshuffled and revamped his ministry, which up to that time had led only a shadow existence. The French *résident* continued to chair cabinet meetings, obtaining indeed even more room for manoeuvre, since Bao Dai abolished the office of prime minister in order 'to be able to conduct the business of state himself'. The most important new man, however, envisaged as minister for the interior and chairman of the 'Reform Commission', took office only when he had been expressly assured that he would have genuine freedom of action. This man was a 32-year-old mandarin of the Catholic faith, of rather a conservative turn of mind, but clearly not corrupt and moreover intelligent: Ngo Dinh Diem.

The reform failed. The subordinate French departments refused to play ball, and the old guard of Annamite mandarins also held back. In September 1933 Ngo Dinh Diem resigned, at which point the experiment ceases to be of interest to us.

Instead the communists began to make their presence felt again, when in 1936 the French People's Front government permitted, at least in Cochin-China, political activity, a free press, legal political parties, and trade unions. In 1937 they won the local elections in Saigon. Then, however, they were afflicted by the contemporary ills of the international communist movement: the Trotskyites and Stalinists fell out, the party split, and when in April 1939 there were elections for the native seats on the Conseil Colonial, the Trotskyites had the advantage, obtaining 80 per cent of the votes.

Further to the north, political parties remained illegal. The VNQDD obviously lost ground rapidly, because their leaders fled to China, where they were subjected to the not exactly wholesome influence of the Kuomintang. The communists, on the other hand, camouflaged themselves as the Democratic Front, found young and excellent leaders in Pham Van Dong, born in 1906, the son of a mandarin, who was able to leave prison in 1936 after a six-year sentence, and in Vo Nguyen Giap, born in 1910, who had passed his school-leaving examination in the humanities only in 1934, receiving a law diploma in October 1938, and who after a short period of imprisonment earned his living as a history teacher at a Catholic school. This relative freedom for political activity in Tongking was short-lived, however. After the outbreak of war in 1939 the police smashed all communist organizations; understandably, since this was the time of the Hitler-Stalin pact and the desertion from the French army of Maurice Thorez! Madame Giap, daughter of the dean of the Arts Faculty at Hanoi, was put in the penitentiary and died there. Her husband was kept out of the clutches of the authorities: Pham Van Dong had sent him on a military course to China.

SYRIA AND LEBANON

The history of the French mandate in Syria is likewise chiefly a history of the collapse of political experiments and of related attempts to bring the benefits of civilized guardianship to the people by force. After 1920, when the newly declared Arab King Feisal had been ejected from Damascus, France proceeded with measures in which no attempt at all was made to conceal the old doctrine of 'divide and rule'. General Gouraud set about the foundation of a Greater Lebanon 'half the population of which consists of Christians and is well disposed to us' as it was curtly expressed in a colonial history as late as 1950.[5] Once this was in progress, separate districts were also created for the Druse south of Damascus and for the Alawis on both sides of the port of Latakia; these two religious communities are outside both Sunni and Shi'ite Islam. Alexandrette, the northernmost part of the coast, obtained a special statute because Turkey claimed it (and obtained it in July 1939). There remained a Syria which did not even happen to possess an outlet to the Mediterranean. The whole entity was an A mandate, therefore qualifying for independence according to the covenant of the League of Nations. France, however, only formed a semi-autonomous government in Lebanon. The French high commissioner alone governed the 'Syrian states'. General Sarrail was able to prove himself in this office as early as 1925-6 by putting down a Druse uprising. Unrest did not even respect the boundary between the allegedly mutually hostile denominations, affecting Damascus in October 1925. The rebels were brought to heel with the aid of bombers. A new, more liberal-minded high commissioner, Henri Ponsot, finally permitted the Syrians to elect a parliament in 1926 and 1930. The formal independence which Britain had granted to Egypt and in 1930 to Iraq, the dissolving of the Syrian parliament in 1934 by a new French high commissioner, Damien de Martel, the Italian invasion of Ethiopia in 1935, and finally a wave of arrests of Syrian nationalists in January 1936, constantly refuelled the fires of anti-French resistance.

A general strike and an impressive campaign of passive resistance, perhaps also the growing strength of the People's Front in the motherland, caused the Paris government – Albert Sarraut was at that time prime minister – to grant the Syrians a cabinet at the end of February 1936 and to pledge independence on the Iraqi model. Negotiations were led by the People's Front government of Léon Blum, in which Pierre Viénot showed remarkable steadfastness when it came to implementing reforms against the onslaughts of the colonial conservatives. On 9 September 1936 France, Syria, and Lebanon signed agreements extending the mandate for a further three years. Fresh elections in November 1936 confirmed that the Syrian people were behind the nationalists. Although the agreements secured for France for twenty-five years two air force bases with garrisons of unlimited strength on Syrian soil, the Syrian parliament (likewise the Lebanese) ratified the treaties unanimously. The year of independence – 1939 – moved nearer. But then Georges Bonnet, foreign minister of the Daladier government, announced on 14 December 1938 that he would not present the set of agreements to the chamber for ratification. The spirit of the People's Front had evaporated. Once again it was believed possible to box the ears of the 'natives' without repercussions. At the outbreak of war in 1939, Syria was just as much under direct French rule as it had been in 1920, and a strong army, soon to be missed on the European battlefield, ensured peace and order.

MOROCCO AND TUNISIA

In Morocco, a protectorate acquired just before the outbreak of the First World War, international law prescribed a policy of association to the French government. Moreover, indigenous Moroccan authorities continued to exist, which had been recognized for centuries by the whole of Europe as sovereign partners in international relations. This opportunity was heightened by the personality of the first French 'proconsul' in Morocco, General Lyautey (1854–1934), who was appointed when the Protectorate was established in 1912. He was an aristocrat of the old school and a convinced royalist who had no time for the Republican ideals and the theses of freedom and equality of 1789. Instead of this he respected the Moroccan aristocracy, admiring the solidity of Islam and its power to imprint itself on society. Lyautey was determined to brook no interference from Paris, and to pursue a genuine protectorate policy in Morocco.

He left untouched the Moroccan government apparatus, the Maghzen, allowing it to exist side by side with the new French authorities which underpinned his own office as *résident*. He gave the state a secure position economically by exploiting its mineral resources; in August 1922 he set up the Office Chérifien des Phosphates (OCP) as a public monopoly for working what was then (and is still) Morocco's most important export commodity. Only four representatives of private French economic interests sat on the supervisory committee of the OCP, beside eight state representatives, of whom four were Moroccan ministers. By June 1916 some headway had been made in establishing an Office de la Propriété Industrielle, which developed into another branch of the bureaucracy. Lyautey did not think much of the immigration of French settlers either. Inasmuch as they did come to Morocco (attracted by economic exploitation) they were denied the political rights which Algerian Europeans were successful in procuring for themselves. Lyautey wanted, if he was not going to be allowed to save France from itself (towards the end of his life he dreamed that he could have become a French Mussolini), at least to preserve Morocco as an island bastion of the old virtues. There was clearly no place in this concept for the rising young Moroccan intelligentsia, freshly filled with progressive ideas from Europe. But without newcomers, the Maghzen could not be modernized. In other words, the Moroccan central authorities remained old-fashioned, and consequently weak. By relying on tribal princes, Lyautey doubly damaged the Maghzen, the conflicts between these two forces having in fact been the cause of the anarchy of the late nineteenth century. Lyautey's policy therefore carried within itself the seeds of its own destruction, in spite of the fact that among French colonial politicians and proconsuls he was the most sincere champion of association.

During the First World War, Lyautey managed to secure the protectorate from the military point of view, excluding the still unoccupied, high mountainous regions and the desert behind them. After the war, the revolution of the Rif Kabyls under Abd el-Krim (1880–1963), at first directed against Spain, did spread to the French zone. This cost Lyautey his office, from which he resigned in 1925. Abd el-Krim declared a 'Republic of the United Tribes of the Rif', but was unable to defend it, in spite of support from European officers and the third International, when a military campaign was launched on the French side by Marshal Pétain and on the Spanish side by General Primo de Rivera. On 26 May 1926 Abd el-Krim surrendered to

Lyautey's successor, being deported to Réunion and released only in 1947; he spent the rest of his life in Cairo.

The French took warning from the Rif war that a complete 'pacification' of its north-west African protectorate would be necessary. Up to 1934 military operations in the Atlas and the Sahara were carried out successfully. Politically, there was no thought of abolishing the protectorate and replacing it by open annexation, but Lyautey's fears of 1920 – namely that there would be an increasing tendency towards direct administration,[6] were confirmed. Increasing numbers of colonists now flowed into the country – 100,000 Europeans were counted at the beginning of the Second World War. About a million hectares passed out of state, collective, or private Moroccan possession into the hands of Europeans (40 per cent to large landowners, who acquired more than 500 hectares). Europeans were appointed to the Conseil de Gouvernement and gained political power; when pressed, they acted over the heads of the protectorate administration through direct relations with Paris. The notorious '*Dahir Berbère*' (Berber decree) of 16 May 1930 seemed to compel the sultan to continue Lyautey's course: it strengthened the authority of certain feudal lords in the mountains by conserving political arrangements which deviated from the Islamic-Arab norm in the Berber-speaking areas. But had France really found worthy partners for a policy of indirect rule in the aristocrats of the Moroccan mountains? A figure such as that of the pasha of Marrakesh, el-Glaoui, who embodied this group after 1945 and who was played off by the French against the sultan in Rabat, gives occasion for doubt. The Berber decree certainly outraged young educated people, who sensed here a particularly odious mixture of reaction with 'divide and rule'. The political instruments of the protectorate were as inadequate to contain this new force as to accommodate the settler minority, which despised everything non-European.

The Sultan, who had to seal the Berber decree in 1930, was Mohammed ben Yusuf, later King Mohammed V. He was born in 1910, educated at home by tutors, and succeeded to the throne in 1927 on the death of his father, being put under a regency for three years. With this background, he seemed destined for the course of a Bao Dai. Mohammed, however, made contact, albeit at first only loosely, with that stream of the young intelligentsia which called itself, in imitation of the former Turkish revolutionaries, the 'Young Moroccans'. In May 1933 at a great rally in Fez they hailed him not only as sultan or sherif, but as 'malik' (king). On the other hand, the Young

Moroccans had no exceptional leaders within their own ranks, so that Mohammed ben Yusuf suited them as a symbol. In the ensuing period, the traditional monarch and the modern nationalist movement in Morocco grew not apart but closer together as a result of a chain of partly coincidental events; they could not be played off against each other by the colonial power, as France had done with Bao Dai in 1932 and 1950, and as Britain tried to do with the sultan of Zanzibar as late as 1963. Instead the monarch and the nationalist movement in Morocco achieved independence together, subsequently managing to retain a kind of equilibrium, although its stability is becoming increasingly doubtful.

In 1934 the Young Moroccans organized themselves into the Comité d'Action Marocaine, but this broke up two years later. A more rural and comparatively more peaceful wing under Mohammed Hassan el-Ouezzani formed the Mouvement Populaire, the more go-ahead ones forming the National Party under Allal el-Fassi (1910–74), who came from a respected, originally Andalusian family and who had obtained in 1930 the diploma in Islamic law at the traditional Karaouyine University in Fez. He was thus the product of a classical Arab education, and learned French properly only when he was exiled by the protectorate power in 1937 to nine years in Gabun after feverish activity and a two-month prison sentence in the People's Front year of 1936.

With his elimination, the path of the Moroccan nationalist movement was at first blocked. The sultan waited until the Second World War provided him with fresh avenues.

The second French protectorate in North Africa, Tunisia, can boast no Lyautey in its history. The indigenous authorities there had never been respected as a self-sufficient establishment, even if only formally. The colonial administration there was rather of a mixed French-Tunisian character, with the French of course predominating. European settlement was promoted by competition between French and Italians, who accounted for some 90,000 colonists around 1930. Intellectual contact between the Islamic population and Europe was much closer in Tunisia than in Morocco: the land of old Carthage opened itself up to foreign influence much more readily than the kingdom of the sherifs. Thus occurred in this protectorate a particularly strong assimilation of Frenchness. The monarchy of the Husseini beys paled into insignificance. The tone was set by the Tunisian bourgeois intelligentsia, followed directly by a powerful, self-assured trade union movement.

In Tunisia too the nationalist movement made its first appearance on the Turkish model – before the First World War – with the name 'Young Tunisians'. In 1919 intellectuals put Wilson's ideas to good use, demanding civil liberties, ministerial responsibility to a genuine parliament, and above all a constitution, the latter demand providing the party with its name, Destur (which means constitution in Arabic). The local notables were agitating far too cautiously, however, for the taste of one young man who had returned home in 1927 with diplomas in law and political science, and with a French wife, and who in true French tradition combined a flourishing law practice with political journalism. Habib Bourguiba was born in 1903 in the coastal town of Monastir, the son of a Tunisian officer. In 1934 he began his political campaign among the people and in the villages, founding at one stroke a new newspaper and a new party: the Neo-Destur. This immediately made the French administration uneasy, and the leaders were exiled to the southern desert, from whence they returned heroes in 1936, as the People's Front was loosening the reins in Tunisia as well. From this time onwards no more was heard of the old Destur. Bourguiba now embodied Tunisian nationalism. For the moment, however, he met a similar fate to that of Allal el-Fassi. He was arrested in April 1938 and kept prisoner without trial until after war broke out – not in some distant colony, however, but in France.

ALGERIA

The heartland of the Maghreb had a much more difficult time than its neighbours in finding its way to an effective, unified nationalist movement. It was French from 1830; the last great resistance struggle, the uprising of the Kabyles under El Mokrani, was crushed in 1871. Although here, as in Tunisia, some intellectuals founded in 1921 a 'Young Algeria' party, it did not take root. No autonomous statehood continued to exist, such as Algeria's eastern neighbours could make use of to demand their own constitution. There was no monarchy here, unlike Morocco, to which a nationalist movement could have clung. Instead, French colonial doctrine denied that Algeria had ever been a nation, disputing that before 1830 the deis of Algiers had exerted authority over the hinterland. It could not be ignored that Islam united the Algerian population, and yet some of the French attempted to assert that the Kabyles had only really been converted to Islam by means of certain egalitarian decrees of the French administration. Whatever the truth of this may be, there is no doubt that a genuine assimilation policy on the part of France in Algeria would have had good prospects for success. Some 100,000 Jews resident in Algeria since antiquity obtained through the Décret Crémieux on 24 October 1870 full French citizenship rights, and rapidly became integrated. Among Muslims too there developed a group whose members, of indeterminate number, for decades desired nothing more earnestly than to become French. The majority of them belonged to the petty bourgeoisie. From the mouth of an expert witness, however, that of Gastu, a member of parliament for the Algerian Europeans, we can hear the following episode:

> In the first days of September 1871, the population of Bougie
> observed to its surprise numerous groups of natives, from
> various tribes, coming into the town and repairing to the Justice
> of the Peace in order to see to the necessary formalities for their
> naturalization. What did the military authorities do who were
> responsible for these natives? They put the most influential of
> them into prison, in order to shut the others up. They then sent
> the horsemen of the Arab Bureau in all directions to order the
> Kabyles to stay at home.[7]

If the spontaneous impulse on the part of these Kabyles was perhaps not typical, then the reaction of the authorities certainly was. They did not want masses of Algerians becoming French citizens. But had not Napoleon III just declared in 1865 that all Algerians were French? He had, but neither then nor now under the Third Republic did this make them citizens. If they retained their 'Islamic Personal Statute', they were French subjects (subjects as opposed to citizens). They were then permitted, for example, to have several wives, according to Islamic law. They were not permitted to vote. Theoretically they could obtain full rights of citizenship by relinquishing the Personal Statute; this procedure was known as 'naturalization', similar to the naturalization of foreigners. The above quotation, however, suffices to illustrate actual practice. Cultural assimilation, however, in particular the daily use of the French language, soon spilled over to the 'subject' majority of the Algerian population. Ferhat Abbas, as a typical representative of the petty bourgeoisie, never made any bones about his ignorance of the Arabic language, even after becoming one of the leaders of the anti-colonial movement. In the days of French rule, many Algerian town dwellers adhered no more seriously to Islam than their French counterparts did to Catholicism. Some 172,800 'native' Algerians were allowed to fight in the trenches of the First World War, almost 20,000 to lose their lives; still they were obviously not in the same league as French citizens.

In the years between 1881 and 1896 the young Third Republic had at least made a start in integrating Algeria both administratively and technically into the motherland. Had this succeeded, progressive governments in Paris might have been able to pave the way for a gradual assimilation of Muslims. The full powers of the governor-general (who was a civilian from 1871 onwards) were reduced, and as many authorities as possible directly linked with the respective administrative branches of France. This policy failed, however, the so-called 'rattachements' having to be revoked even before the turn of the century. This was the first great success of the European settlers, the 'colons' or 'pieds-noirs'.

The colons naturally claimed the same rights and liberties as the French in France, and a right of consultation in French politics. They elected MPs to the Paris Chamber – after 1871 at first six, then eleven, finally nine. They favoured the speedy naturalization of the Spaniards, Italians, Maltese, and all other Europeans who had set up in Algeria, since their 'assimilation' of those immigrants reinforced their political weight vis-à-vis the 'natives'.

But there was clearly no question of catching up with the Muslim majority. Algeria's population statistics[8] show the following picture:

Table 3.1 Ethnic ratios in Algerian population 1856–1954

Year	'Natives'	Europeans	Others	Total population
1856	2,307,349	180,330	8,388	2,496,067
1872	2,125,052	279,691	11,482	2,416,225
1882	2,842,497	412,435	55,480	3,310,412
1891	3,577,063	530,924	16,745	4,124,732
1901	4,089,150	633,850	16,331	4,739,331
1911	4,740,526	752,043	71,259	5,563,828
1921	4,923,186	791,370	89,719	5,804,275
1931	5,588,314	881,586	83,553	6,553,453
1948	7,679,078	922,272	80,435	8,681,785
1954	8,449,332	984,031	96,363	9,529,726

The colons knit their brows, however, whenever the 'Frankawi' (as they called the French of France in a kind of pidgin Arabic) were about to make pronouncements on Algerian matters – 'about which they understood nothing', or make any rulings on native policy from the committee room in Paris. It was for this reason that the *rattachements* disappeared in 1896. The ultimate power of the governor-general, who himself worked in the country and was therefore under the constant influence of the settlers, was reinstated. In 1900 Algeria received its own budget and in the 'Délégations Financières' a representative body to administer it.

The Délégations Financières consisted of three sections which as a rule consulted separately. The gulf between colonizers and colonized, and the prevailing power of the former, were institutionalized: in the first section sat twenty-four directly elected representatives of European landowners; in the second section sat twenty-four representatives of those Europeans who possessed no land (all Europeans over the age of 25 were eligible to vote for this section, only being required to have been French citizens for twelve years and domiciled in Algeria for three years); and the third section comprised seventeen Arabs and seven Kabyles. Some of these were elected indirectly until 1919; the electorate consisted of the indigenous committees in the so-called '*communes mixtes*'[9] and of the *chefs de familles* of Kabyle extended families. Representatives of those areas which were still under military rule (that is, 43 per cent of Algeria, not including the southern territories, i.e. the Sahara, which had been made administratively separate in 1902) were appointed by the governor-general. In the main, all of them were recruited from the 'Beni-Oui-Oui' tribe, well known too in the English colonies as 'yes-men': the docile tools of the colonizers. . . .

Algerian politics were unable to function within this representative body - even along the lines of the *colons*, who considered themselves to be the true Algerians. When France promulgated a reform law on 4 February 1919 in gratitude for the loyalty of Muslims during the war, this did little to change things. It was hardly worth the trouble: from then on the third section of the Délégations Financières was directly elected in the 'regular communal districts'. Only 420,000 Algerians, however, fulfilled the legal conditions for inclusion on the electoral roll; they were either landowners or business people, former soldiers, administrative employees, holders of certain honorary titles, or were able to read and write in French. In addition the Muslims in these regular communal districts received slightly greater local representation and were able to participate in the election of the - of course European - mayor. In the *communes mixtes* everything remained as it had been: authoritarian administration by administrators appointed by the general government, and the indirect election of the 'finance delegates' by those notables admitted to the 'indigenous committees'.

Naturalization was also formally made easier in 1919, although until 1936 only some 8,000 Algerians availed themselves of this 'privilege'. Administrative posts were opened to Muslims – with the exception of 'functions, in which authority is exercised'. For heaven's sake no Muslim could be the superior of a European! In 1923 the military territories disappeared from the map of North Algeria; military administration remained in the Sahara. All in all these changes were mere drops in the ocean.

Under the People's Front, Paris set out for another large-scale reform project: Prime Minister Léon Blum and his state minister for Algeria, Maurice Violette, wanted to grant citizenship to certain categories of Muslims without compelling them to undergo the procedure for naturalization. Between 20,000 and 30,000 Algerians would have been allowed to the ballot box in the following year. At least Violette knew what he was letting himself in for: he had been governor-general in Algeria from 1925 to 1927. 'Because he had made the great mistake of relying on the natives as opposed to the Europeans',[10] the Délégations Financières had had him removed from office. He had urged the Europeans: 'Take heed! The natives of Algeria still have no fatherland – undoubtedly through your fault. They seek a fatherland. They demand of us the French fatherland. Give it to them soon! If you don't, they will create another one for themselves.'[11]

As late as June 1936 a 'Congress of Algerian Muslims', in which at least one politically influential Algerian body took part (the *ulema*, of whom we shall be hearing shortly), still swore allegiance to France, although demanding the right to vote. The Blum-Violette project did not get as far as this: it was only a first step towards that end. The colonists, however, were still as stubborn as they had been nine years before. The project was killed off in the Paris chamber, when an assembly of Algerian mayors overthrew it by 298 votes to two.

Is it to be wondered at then that the settlers strenuously boycotted even the setting-up of schools for the 'natives'? In this case the republican swing in the motherland proved strong enough to uphold the principle that public primary schools for Muslims were a good thing; France began setting them up in 1883. Their main aim was the dissemination of the French language (in March 1938 Minister Chautemps was even to declare Arabic a foreign language for

Algeria). The colonists, however, protested vigorously. In March 1908 a congress to which they sent representatives adopted a resolution, according to which 'the education of natives signifies a real danger, both from the economic point of view and for the French community. The congress thus expresses the wish that the primary schools for natives be closed.'[12] It marked a defeat for the *pieds-noirs*, therefore, that the number of schools and pupils grew slowly, but at least steadily. Even in 1938, when the total number of Muslim pupils had reached as many as 108,000, there were by contrast 124,000 European pupils in Algeria. One hundred years after the occupation, an official brochure boasted:

> The great test of 1914 to 1918 has demonstrated that the
> Algerian school also knows how to train good Frenchmen . . . it
> has the legitimate ambition of taking the entire youth of the
> colony into its constantly growing classes in the near future. . . .
> Here France . . . has accomplished a moral victory which was
> not achieved even in Rome to the same degree.[13]

The Algerian people were later to show that this self-praise was a little premature. Before the Second World War, however, one could in fact find only the feeble beginnings of an anti-colonial movement on Algerian soil. Emir Khaled, a grandson of Abd el-Kader, was the sole intervener in favour of the independence of Algeria at the Paris peace conference in 1919. In a catalogue of demands published by him in 1922 we can find on the other hand that of 'representation in the [French] parliament to the same degree as that of the Algerian Europeans' – that is, not even proportional to the population ratios! – and 'access possibilities for Algerian natives to all civil and military ranks'.[14] Was Emir Khaled a forerunner of Messali and the FLN, or was he demanding genuine assimilation? This question can be left open, since he did not bring about any political organization.

In 1931 Abdelhamid Ben Badis (who died in 1940) founded the Association des Oulemas d'Algérie, an association of educated men of Arab culture who were concerned about the decadence of Islam and who followed the ideas of the great Mohammed Abdu (1849–1905) on religio-cultural renewal. Ben Badis declared: 'Islam is my religion, Algeria my fatherland, and Arabic my language.' The *ulemas* called on the people to donate money for the foundation of Arabic schools which would not be controlled by the colonial administration: traditionally the government administered the Habu assets, religious endowments, from the proceeds of which, according to Islamic law, education was to be financed. This expropriation of an important pillar of Muslim society had been largely responsible for the collapse of the traditional Arab education system after 1830. In the Constantine *département* the *ulemas* scored initial successes. At first the French administration sufficed itself with close surveillance and a disposition that only imams (priests) and *muftis* (magistrates) paid by them out of the Habu assets were allowed to preach in the mosques, whereas according to Muslim tradition every educated person has the right to do so.

The *ulemas* did not create a political mass movement. Indeed as late as 1936 they showed sufficient readiness to make concessions by taking part in the Congress of Algerian Muslims, mentioned above, which pledged its loyalty to France. At that time a revolutionary spirit stirred only those Algerians whom material need forced to emigrate to France. Soon after the end of the First World War they formed a relatively numerous, particularly ruthlessly exploited sub-proletariat in Paris and some other industrial centres. At the beginning of the 1920s an Algerian militant of the Communist Party (CP) of France, Ali abd el-Kader, founded the North African Star organization (Etoile Nord-Africaine, ENA). In 1927 Messali Hadj (1898–1974), a worker from Tlemcen in West Algeria, became head of the ENA. He had fought in the First World War, and spoke as Algerian representative in February 1927 at the founding congress of the League against Imperialism in Brussels:

> Our struggle for independence will be hard. . . . Thanks to the uniting of all oppressed peoples and with the support of the world proletariat we hope to accomplish the destruction of imperialism and create a truly humane society. I greet the representatives of the fraternal peoples present at this congress. I heartily greet the French proletariat, which has supported us and continues to do so . . . I conclude this speech with the call: Long live the socialism of the oppressed peoples! Long live the Soviet Republic, which liberates the world! Long live the Chinese revolution! Long live the Congress![15]

These sincere friendly terms between Messali and the French CP did not last long, since it became clear both then and later that French communists for tactical reasons were at best cultivating a peripheral alliance with Algerian nationalism. Basically they regarded Algeria as a French country just as much as all other political groups in France.

Among the European settlers in North Africa there were a number of communists who thoroughly despised all 'natives', and whose stance had to be acknowledged by the party leadership. Messali therefore soon distanced himself from the communists, although retaining communist organization tactics in the ENA. In 1929 the ENA was banned, and in 1933 Messali went to prison for having continued his association underground. He was released in May 1935, but a new warrant for his arrest was issued only four months later. Messali fled to Switzerland, where he was influenced in the direction of anti-communist pan-Islamism by the Lebanese Druse Chekib Arslane, a former member of the Turkish Grand National Assembly and publisher of the *Arab Nation* journal. Some people at that time took Arslane to be an agent of Hitler, as they did the mufti of Jerusalem. The People's Front victory of 1936 allowed Messali to return to France; now the ENA could at last also make a start in Algeria, where by dint of intensive propaganda thirty sections were formed immediately. At the end of January 1937 the Léon Blum government banned the ENA once again. Messali countered this move immediately from Paris with the foundation of the Algerian People's Party (*Parti du Peuple Algérien*, PPA), which slightly camouflaged its independence programme. This time Messali wanted to remain legal. In June 1937 he travelled to Algeria to stand as a candidate in local elections. On 27 August, however, he was once again behind bars and sentenced to two years' imprisonment and loss of civil rights for 'incitement to unrest against the sovereignty of the state'. His sentence came to an end as the Second World War broke out, Messali was immediately interned, the PPA dissolved, and its active members subjected to severe police persecution. The popularity of the party and its leader did not suffer from this, however – quite the reverse. It was Messali's tragedy never to be given a chance to live and work for any length of time in his country.

Ferhat Abbas, on the other hand, a year younger than Messali and from 1944 to 1954 his great opponent in Algerian politics, never saw the inside of a prison before the Second World War. His career is symbolic of the lack of orientation within broad sections of the Algerian petty bourgeoisie, and for the honesty with which this group built on the pledge of French assimilation. Ferhat Abbas came from the Constantine *département*. His father was a rich man, a dignitary favoured by the French administration and a commander of the Légion d'honneur. He himself studied pharmacy. While at university he founded in 1924 a union of Muslim students and led it for five years. In Sétif, where he opened a chemist's shop, he was elected to the town and *département* councils, being delegated from there to the Délégations Financières. The motto heading a collection of his press articles, which Abbas published in book form in 1931 under the title *Le Jeune Algérien*, reads '*De la colonie vers la province*'. Abbas was prepared to become French, speaking in quite a different tone from Messali: no mention of independence. Abbas warned of communism at a time when Messali was still in favour of it. Despite all this, Abbas's language sounded no less rebellious to the ears of the *colons*, because his recognition of France was not intended as homage, but as a demand. Even in 1931 his criticism of policy was sharp and open. It would be a fundamental error to see the young Ferhat Abbas as a 'Beni-Oui-Oui'.

> Only one policy can preserve the interests of France and of civilization: our loyal emancipation and improvement of our status. Do you want to make a sister country for France out of Algeria? Then educate the Algerian, link him economically and administratively with the French motherland, make him interested in the work of French construction! Do you want to civilize this country? Civilize its inhabitants! There is no other way. If instead of this you artificially create a European people and treat the true owners of the country as underlings, then you expose yourselves to the danger that nature will one day demand its day of retribution and destroy this work in an instinctive movement – a work which has remained alien to it, which has caused it suffering. . . . A century of occupation has unfortunately not bestowed any sense on this work, apart from the fact that 600,000 Europeans have settled here while the Nineteenth Army corps keeps the mass of Arabs and Berbers in check.[16]

These lines of Ferhat Abbas should be quoted more often, and not only his article of 1936, where we read that 'neither history, the living nor the dead, not even the graveyards spoke to me of a fatherland Algeria'.[17] Certainly Abbas wants France to become his fatherland, but his pride at being an Algerian and a Muslim is unaffected and unbroken by this wish. An attempt to show double loyalty – to his Muslim homeland and to a political nation called France – was the hallmark of his ideas of Utopia, which were also the ideas of some other Africans. France could not accept double loyalty, which was a slap in the face of the 'one, indivisible nation'. It was precisely those

French people who felt allegiance to these values who most persisted in confusing the distinction between universal and national French 'human rights'. How could people who lived under the tricolour seek progress and civilization (or *Liberté, Egalité, Fraternité*) outside the French nation? It was no problem for this 'leftist' France to integrate individuals – such as Jews – into the French nation, but it tolerated the self-awareness and independence of groups within the state only to the extent that these restricted their specific character to the level of folklore. Even collective adherence to non-French cultural values, much less specific nationalisms, was regarded politically as mortal sin. Apart from some extremists, the Bretons, Corsicans, Alsatians, and Basques have adapted themselves to this expectation, which also prevailed on Martinique and Guadeloupe. One French colonial historian wrote optimistically in 1949 – and in terms of the example he chose he was in fact right:

> One can give French civilization to those who have no other.
> This was the only way in which the slaves of the Antilles could
> escape their spiritual and moral servitude.[18]

In the case of the Algerians, however, there was no *tabula rasa*, which ultimately proved the undoing of their assimilation. The incompatibility between French (albeit 'leftist') assimilation doctrine and the self-awareness of those very Algerians who were prepared to assimilate was not apparent to either side until the Second World War, because the narrow-mindedness of the colonists came between them, preventing any genuine sounding-out. When in 1957–8 the army of the French homeland and a socialist minister for Algeria wanted to make a serious attempt at assimilation, it was precisely this which led to the most horrific excesses of the war of liberation.

BLACK AFRICA AND MADAGASCAR

What was happening at that time in the vast African colonial possessions of France south of the Sahara? A sideward glance will suffice for the period before 1939, for there still prevailed in this area a practically undisturbed calm and order. '*La paix française*' extended now even to the Tuareg of the desert. On the Ivory Coast the last revolts of the old style were put down. '*Soumission parfaite de l'indigène*', perfect submission of the native, was confirmed by the governor-general of AOF, J. Carde, in November 1923:

The political situation . . . is in the main extremely satisfactory to us. Complete calm prevails in the whole country. Everywhere the native devotes himself to his work, with no other concern than for the growth of his flock, the yield of his harvest, the fruits of his labours or of his trade. Generally speaking he is impervious to external provocation . . . some provocateurs, who belong to certain extremist circles of the homeland, have attempted to disseminate their extremist doctrines among the most highly advanced natives of the coast and to find supporters there; they have had no success.[19]

As was the case in the neighbouring British colonies with Lugard's theses, so in AOF and AEF the doctrine of association led the field undisputed. The special status of Togo and Cameroon as League of Nations mandates was of no importance: France was acting in accordance with League of Nations stipulations in treating these countries in exactly the same way as the neighbouring colonies.

Only the four municipalities of the Senegal coast, the nucleus for the extension of French power, amounted to a hangover from the old days before imperialism, when assimilation of the colonized had been the ideal aim of France: Gorée, an island off Cape Verde which with brief interruptions had been French since the end of the sixteenth century; Saint Louis, the capital of Senegal, founded in 1641; Dakar, across from Gorée, founded in 1857, which grew in leaps and bounds by virtue of its good harbour to become the capital of AOF; and finally Rufisque, a neighbour of Dakar. For the natives of these towns a law of 24 April 1833 applied, without distinction as to race or religion, granting 'every free-born or person who had attained freedom legally in the French colonies 1. civil rights, 2. political rights'. Until 1890 the administrative authorities in Senegal made no fuss about acknowledging the civil rights of the natives in the four cities. At that point, however, they began to limit them. A decree of 5 January 1910 withdrew those Senegalese who were not naturalized (that is, those who were subject to the Islamic jurisdiction set up in 1857) from the list of those eligible to vote, grouping them into a 'second voters' roll' (*deuxième collège électoral*). In practice, there remained only Europeans and people of mixed race on the first roll. A further decree of 16 August 1912 deprived Africans in the four cities of regular French jurisdiction as soon as they left those municipal districts; if then they went as colonial officials or on their own business to the newly conquered countries of French Africa, they were to be treated there as mere subjects, like all other 'natives', for whom there was no separation of executive and judiciary authority.

The First World War presented the Africans of the four cities with a good opportunity for making a stand against discrimination without throwing doubt on their patriotism. They demanded the right to be called up to the same troops in which their white or mixed race fellow-citizens were serving: to the colonial infantry or artillery, not to the 'tireilleur' units formed of colonial subjects. A new law of 19 October 1915 gave them a dispensation, and in September 1916 they achieved still more: it was no longer the place of birth but the place of origin which was to decide who counted as 'Senegalese from the four municipalities'. The privilege had become hereditary. Since the chamber elections of 1914 a black man, Blaise Diagne (1872-1934), had been a member of parliament for Senegal; it was largely due to him that France now unequivocally recognized the citizenship of Africans from the four cities. Clearly, however, he paid for this privilege with the blood of his African compatriots. Diagne the African proved himself in 1917 as West African recruiting commissioner for the Clemenceau cabinet. The white governor-general, van Vollenhoven, protested in vain against the blood-letting demanded of his charges.

In 1920 the colony as a whole obtained representation. In the Conseil Colonial there sat twenty directly elected spokesmen for the citizens (that is, all inhabitants of the four municipalities, as well as the Europeans of other parts of Senegal) and twenty spokesmen for the subjects delegated by the 'chiefs'. In 1925 this ratio was modified in favour of citizens to 24:16, but in 1939 a gesture was made for the benefit of former soldiers: although they were to remain subjects, they were to be able to elect eighteen additional members in the Conseil Colonial.

A modern form of political life nevertheless developed in the inter-war years only in the four cities, and even here it remained at the level of French local or *département* politics: a dispute over elected offices among local notables, whose followers provided themselves with political party labels. Diagne defended the mandate in the chamber of deputies until his death, but was obliged in 1925 to resign his office as mayor in Saint Louis to Amadou Lamine-Guèye (born 1891), who entered office under the socialist SFIO banner. After 1934, Lamine-Guèye continued to fight against a protégé of the administration, Galandou Diouf, who went to Paris as Diagne's successor. For the overwhelming majority of inhabitants of French Africa these disputes were irrelevant, and possibly even entirely unknown. In 1932 only 71,121 French African citizens were counted in the whole of AOF compared with 14,365,150 subjects.

Astonishingly, the much more sparsely populated and less developed French Equatorial Africa (AEF) produced a movement in the 1920s which manifested at least partially a modern political character: Matswanism, which as a religious community belongs to the messianic revivalist movements which have abounded in Africa – particularly the Congo – since the beginnings of the Christian mission. André Matswa Grenard (1899–1942), however, did not at all want to found a religious community. He came from Brazzaville and at first studied his catechism at a Catholic mission. He then moved on to the customs service, went over to France at the beginning of the 1920s and volunteered for military service against the Rif Kabyles. In 1926 in Paris he founded a club for his compatriots, the Amicale des Originaires de l'AEF.

At first, Matswa organized only mutual assistance and welfare. In 1928, however, he was making political demands in letters to the minister for the colonies, demanding exactly what Ferhat Abbas was demanding at the same time in Algeria: civil rights.

Two delegates sent home to the Congo by Matswa in 1930 in order to collect money for the association encountered spontaneous enthusiasm among the Bakongo people; in only a few weeks 100,000 fr. had been collected, donated out of the paltry possessions of the Africans of Brazzaville and its environs. It seems the Bakongo believed they could buy their land free from the French, in accordance with their indigenous law. The governor-general of AEF sensed danger. Although he had given a friendly reception to Matswa's envoys and even promised them a yearly subscription of 1,000 fr., he now had them arrested, as well as their founder in Paris, who was brought back to Brazzaville. He had them up for fraud before the native courts. Matswa was sentenced to three years' imprisonment. Violent protests on the part of the Bakongo – a genuine mass action, above all in Brazzaville – came to nothing. The Amicale lived on in semi-legality, but while waiting for Matswa's return from prison it gradually transformed itself into a religious community, while the political internee took on the qualities of Christ, the suffering saviour. The Matswanists withdrew into a strict hostility towards foreigners and for decades repudiated all participation in public life.

What political life there was in Madagascar until 1939 drew on a student conspiracy of the First World War era, known as the VVS secret society (Vy Vato Sakelika = Iron, Rock, Branches), which doubtless alarmed the French more than was warranted. At all events stiff sentences abounded. Only when an amnesty was declared in 1921 did some young men return to freedom: political martyrs, among them the medical student Joseph Ravoahangy (born 1893). After 1945 he was to become one of the foremost spokesmen and leaders of Malagasy nationalism, but in the inter-war years he himself still oscillated aimlessly between pro-communist, socialist (in 1936 he joined the SFIO) and loyal-assimilationist political activism. As with Ferhat Abbas and Matswa, the call for civil rights was also heard on Madagascar. A 'French league for the admission of the natives of Madagascar to French civil rights', founded after 1918 by a war veteran, had some limited impact in the 1920s. Its leaders were placed under arrest in May 1929 after turbulent political rallies, the name of Ravoahangy also being mentioned among them. Incidentally Madasgascar had only achieved 8,000 naturalized French citizens of indigenous origin by 1939.

To recap: the failure of the Bao Dai experiment in Vietnam and of mandate policy in Syria, and the dilution of the Lyautey protectorate regime in Morocco, highlight the weak points of the association policy which formed the professed colonial doctrine of France before the Second World War. The blind spot in the treatment of Algerian Muslims, and the intransigence in black Africa and on Madagascar, made plain by the absurdly small number of naturalizations, show equally that the traditional assimilation tendencies which were still active under the surface were not destined for success. In general there emerges an impression of half-heartedness in colonial matters which was scarcely if at all affected by changes in political majorities in Paris. The colonies were a subject of equal indifference to all sections of public opinion and for all French political parties and their leaders. In France during these years even committed colonialists must have sounded like voices in the wilderness, much more so anti-colonialists. Can this be attributed to the fact that the colonies were so uninteresting to France economically? Prior to the First World War (1912) the colonies contributed a mere 10.8 per cent to the imports of the homeland and 13.5 per cent to its exports. In 1928 these ratios had risen to 13 per cent imports and 16.8 per cent exports. After the world economic crisis (1932) these did leap to 27.6 and 31.5 per cent, but only the decline in trade with other countries was reflected in these figures. Private investment by the French in their own overseas territories was as meagre before 1945 as the development expenditure of the state, although French policy had now grasped, in contrast with the pre-war period, how to diminish foreign competition by means of protectionist measures.

No Frenchman of course wanted to dispose of the colonial possessions: people were used to them. The vast territory which appeared under the colours of the fatherland in the atlases, and the loyal regiments from Algeria, Morocco, and West Africa, were all part and parcel of the fixed assets of France's position as a great power. Was it seen as a kind of second, imaginary Maginot line, to which nothing more was to be added and behind which one could rest in peace? Let us do justice to Léon Blum: his People's Front cabinet did try to reform, or at least co-ordinate, overseas policy. He showed goodwill, gave an ear to critics, and even took responsibility for them. Not only the half-successful Pierre Viénot and the unfortunate Maurice Violette should be mentioned here, but also men such as Charles-André Julien and Robert Delavignette, who were working their way up the public service at that time. Both of them, one in academic life, the other as a colonial administrator and writer, later contributed a great deal during the Fourth Republic towards smoothing the path towards decolonization.

In 1936, however, nothing was achieved by just putting a socialist – Marius Moutet – in the colonial ministry. Syria, Morocco, and Tunisia, theoretically also Cameroon and Togo, were under the ministry of foreign affairs, and the ministry of internal affairs maintained its key position on all Algerian matters. Here reform plans of the Popular Front met with resistance, or at least with lack of interest. Was it more a question of sabotage or of obstruction? At all events the shock of 1940, the destruction of the real Maginot line, was needed to jolt France out of its colonial lethargy.

Chapter Four

THE NETHERLANDS, BELGIUM, AND PORTUGAL

In the inter-war years, the lesser European colonial powers were noticeably under the influence of the two major ones, Britain and France. Even where they did try to go their own way, avoiding pedantic imitation, it is still not difficult to discern British or French models in individual elements of their overseas policy. The Dutch colonial empire lay in Asia; as an economically valuable and relatively well-developed region, the main island of Java was severely exposed to the pressures of the great economic crisis, while the proximity of China, Japan, and India (as well as the Philippines) gave rise quite early on to a modern nationalist movement, thus causing problems for the Dutch. Belgium and Portugal, on the other hand, whose colonies were predominantly in Africa, had no serious protests of an anti-colonial nature to face before 1939.

It may nevertheless have something to do with the similar ethnic character of the Dutch and the Flemish that the policies of the Netherlands in Indonesia and of the Belgians in the Congo were guided by similar impulses, which are popularly summed up under the heading of 'paternalism'. The colonizers wanted to bring their possessions economically into bloom, and expected the increasing prosperity of the colonies to alleviate social deprivation among the natives. A reasonable living standard, at least for that section of the population working directly in the modern economic sector and for the colonial administration, would – it was anticipated – keep this 'elite' happy, so that one would be spared the necessity for political reforms. Otherwise it was advised not to proceed 'with too much haste' in disseminating western education: Asians or Africans were only to learn as much as they needed to know in order to fulfil the role allotted to them, that is, in the lower ranks of colonial society.

Out of this approach arose an economic orientation which made the British model look more interesting than the French one. **The Dutch** liked to speak of 'ethical policy'.

In some respects this may be seen as the forerunner of modern development policy: there was a genuine attempt to provide the colony in **Indonesia** with a modern infrastructure. We should not forget, however, that the Dutch were taking up ideas which in England had already been expressed by Joseph Chamberlain in 1894 ('What is wanted for Uganda is what Birmingham has got – an improvement scheme')! In terms of putting these ideas into effect, however, the major powers took their time until 1945. Independence, of course, was not in evidence as a future aim of 'ethical policy'; instead, the majority of Dutch people who went out to Indonesia wanted to make the colony a new, permanent homeland. Unlike the British in India or West Africa, they often did not even send their children to school in Europe. They sought a kind of peaceful symbiosis between western bourgeois and colonial elements in the 'East Indies society' of the future, whereby they themselves would be able to make a comfortable living as the securely established upper class. To make room for bourgeois capitalist economic incentive, the colonial government dismantled from 1870 onwards the mercantile monopolies which they had inherited from the former Dutch East India Company; the coffee monopoly went in 1915. The peasant population of Java saw themselves freed from compulsory labour; but did not wage labour for European planters or the hopeless competition against Chinese small traders amount to a move from the frying pan into the fire? In addition to rubber, sugar, and tobacco cultivation, oil revenues soon began to interest European capital. The Netherlands could not of course alone, or even predominantly, keep up with the rapidly expanding foreign trade of the colony, which was heading towards the world economic crisis: the Netherlands' share in Indonesian imports dropped from 33.3 per cent in 1913 to 17.7 per cent in 1929, its exports dropping in the same period from 28.1 per cent to 16 per cent. The profits nevertheless did predominantly find their way to the Netherlands. A total investment of 5,000 million guilders was planned for Indonesia in 1929, four-fifths of this Dutch capital; every hour, the historian Jan Romein asserted,[1] some 50,000 guilders in profits flowed from Indonesia back to Holland.

Only after 1900 did the Dutch secure their effective military hegemony over the whole enormous archipelago. Analogously with

British policy in India, they considered it a good idea to allow numerous native principalities (a total of 269, of which only two were on Java) to continue to exist on about half their territory outside Java, while 93 per cent of the surface area of Java was administered directly. On directly administered territory there lived around the year 1930 about 36 million people, 12 million in the principalities. The preservation of the indigenous aristocracy as a prop of the colonial regime, however, misfired for the Dutch in the long term more seriously than it did for the British on the Indian peninsula. The princes sank into total insignificance, the importance of the Dutch bureaucracy increasing proportionately.

One cannot deny that the blessings of 'ethical policy' – irrigation plants, school buildings, sanitary provision – were chiefly to the benefit of the towns and those zones in which there were European plantations. The 240,000 whites in the Dutch East Indies also set the tone in the representative body – here one can discern French models – which was granted to the colony in 1916. In this 'Volksraad' in the first period (1918–21) sat twenty-three Europeans (nine elected, fourteen appointed by the governor-general) and only fifteen Indonesians (ten elected, five appointed). After the competences of the Volksraad had been somewhat extended in 1925 – it now gave advice on the budget and legislation, although the governor-general was not obliged to follow its suggestions – the representation of the indigenous population improved. In the last period (1931–42), the European section consisted of fifteen elected and ten appointed members, the Indonesians numbering twenty elected and ten appointed members. There were an additional three elected and two appointed representatives of foreigners, which means chiefly Chinese. The Indonesians in the Volksraad – in 1939 there were 2,228 voters – were elected not directly by the people, but indirectly through local councils. They were nevertheless able to formulate certain moderate demands, and above all to develop a sense of community which united the population of the various islands.

The living standard of the lowest and medium peasant strata did not improve, since they were subject to the increasing pressure of the tax burden, which in 1940 was two and a half times as great as it had been in 1920. They saw little of the public facilities created with this tax money. Their produce was systematically discriminated against in favour of the products of European plantations, particularly when the crisis forced a cutback in production. A European planter thus received for the same amount of rubber six to twelve times what an Indonesian was given. In 1925, there were 61,425 Indonesian children attending modern primary schools, in 1940 only 88,223 – an increase of 44 per cent in twenty-five years, which in view of the marked growth in the population indicated not stagnation but retrogression. Even Algerian indigenous schools recorded in the same period a 102 per cent increase in attendance. But why educate intellectuals, when after all the governor-general, Jonkheer D. C. de Jonge (1931–6), had frankly declared: 'We have been ruling here with the stick for 300 years and that won't change in the next 300 years.'[2]

The slender stratum of Indonesians with a modern education nevertheless proved sufficient to call active political parties into being, which were to develop considerably beyond the official spheres of the Volksraad. A handful of Eurasians (the majority of people of mixed race were more colonialist than the colonizers) and a few Dutch people assisted in their birth, such as Hendrik F. J. M. Sneevliet, who founded the Indian Social Democratic Association in May 1914, thus introducing the ideas of Marxism into Indonesia. The second main root of Indonesian politics consisted of the Partai Sarekat Islam Indonesia, which grew out of a tradesmen's association during the First World War (usually Indonesian tradespeople, who had to combat Chinese competition in order to survive, had Arabic rather than Dutch education). Sarekat Islam and social democracy became interwoven, although a rift occurred in 1920–1 between the right and left wings of the new movement. On the left the Partai Kommunis Indonesia (PKI) was formed, which ignored Comintern instructions to make an alliance with bourgeois revolutionaries on the Chinese model. Even before the expunging of Chinese communists from the Kuomintang, the PKI was making a lone bid for revolution. The storming of the prison and the telephone exchange of Batavia on the night of 12–13 November 1926, accompanied by similar actions in other parts of Java and in January 1927 in Sumatra, ended in total defeat after only a few days. The deportation of 813 communist leaders was enough to extinguish the PKI (which was of course immediately banned) into the 1940s era, even as a serious underground movement.

While the right wing of the nationalist movement was seeking the beginnings of reform policy in the Volksraad, the chance presented itself to graft a non-communist leadership on to the now fallow leftist forces. Under the slogan 'New Dynamism', a fresh graduate of the

Bandung Technical College, Sukarno (1901–70), founded on 4 July 1927 the Partai Nasional Indonesia (PNI), which grew rapidly and in December of the same year pulled a number of smaller groups into its wake: Sukarno created the Permufakatan Partai-Partai Politik Kebengsaan Indonesia, the National Union of Political Parties, (PPKI), as an umbrella association.

Conflict with the colonial government was only a matter of months away, however. Fear of a repetition of revolutionary unrest had rooted itself deeply among the Dutch. On 29 December 1929 there was a series of raids on the PNI; Sukarno was arrested and sentenced to four years' imprisonment a year later. He was released in December 1931, but found his political legacy divided. Mohammad Hatta, who had already become acquainted with a prison cell as a student in the Netherlands in 1927–8, and Sutan Schahrir grouped the socialist-orientated PNI cadres into the PNI-baru, numbering only 1,000, the others having established themselves as the Partai Indonesia (Partindo), numbering approximately 20,000. Sukarno's efforts towards reunification (1932) were in vain. His freedom was to be shortlived; at the beginning of February 1933 Indonesian sailors mutinied on the armoured vessel *De zeven Provinzien* (with twenty-three dead), and once again the fuses blew in the government: there came a political party membership ban for government employees – which meant the majority of the 'elite'! The leaders were once again arrested, and Sukarno was deported to Flores island in 1934, where he remained until the Japanese freed him in 1942. The left continued to vegetate under various names, the personal prestige of Sukarno being retained, but a counterpart of the Indian Congress movement was denied to Indonesia on account of Dutch nervousness. As if defini-tively to alienate their last remaining friends in the intelligentsia, the government roundly rejected the tentative petitions of right-wingers in the Volksraad. A petition of 1936 that urged granting Indonesia an autonomy statute within ten years on the Philippine model (without relinquishing Dutch sovereignty) was put on ice until 1938 and then rejected. Even more timid sounded a new proposal in February 1940: now there was talk only of the responsibility of the colonial govern-ment to the Volksraad and of limiting the powers of the governor-general. Not even this request to the Netherlands government, which had in the mean time fled to London, found sympathy. No wonder that the gaze of educated Indonesians began to turn towards Tokyo!

In the **Belgian Congo**, the stability of the paternalist order was not subjected to any comparable testing, which may perhaps explain the pompous good conscience of the Belgian public; until as late as around 1958, they were convinced that they had discovered the philosopher's stone for the treatment of 'natives'. Belgian welfare and development policy in Central Africa arose, as has already been suggested, out of similar motives to those of the Dutch in Indonesia. There was a laudable desire to be distinguished from the *ancien régime* – although in the case of the Congo not from the mercantile colonialism of the seventeenth and eighteenth centuries, but from the ruthless exploitation of the resources of the subcontinent which had been pursued by Leopold II in the 'Independent Congo State' from 1880 to 1907.

The instability of Belgian domestic policy between the wars largely gave the colonial authorities a free hand: between 1918 and 1939 there were sixteen changes of colonial minister in Brussels, and only four changes of governor-general in Léopoldville. The foremost of these 'proconsuls', Pierre Ryckmans, was in office from 1934 to 1946. It was he who coined the phrase '*Dominer pour servir*', which most aptly expresses the colonial ethos of the Belgians:

> To dominate in order to serve. This is the sole excuse for
> colonial conquest; it is its full justification. To serve Africa
> means to civilize it. Not only to awaken new needs and provide
> the means for meeting them; not only to exploit and grow rich:
> but to make men better, happier, more humane . . .
> ethnographic research and contact with the black soul offer white
> men who come to Africa astonishing surprises. . . . When he
> sees that in the apparent chaos of primitive society a profound
> order prevails, the colonizer is seized by a wholesome shudder.
> He will then refrain from destroying the order while thinking
> that he is ordering chaos. Not that the experience has taught him
> to doubt himself and his mission. . . . But he will take a less
> lordly hand to the old building.[3]

Thus wrote Ryckmans in 1931 in the foreword to his collection of essays.

The Congo colony rested securely on the three pillars of authoritarian administration, mission schools, and big capitalism, which after the collapse of rubber prices before 1914 resorted increasingly to the exploitation of mineral resources. The administration was guided by the British doctrine of Indirect Rule, desiring to leave the Africans as undisturbed as possible in their traditional chiefdoms. In the Belgian

Congo there were, apart from a Lunda monarchy in Katanga, now quite powerless, no more large African states, at least nothing comparable with the Fulbe emirates in northern Nigeria, or even the Buganda kingdom in neighbouring Uganda. The situation was somewhat different, however, in the mandate territories acquired after 1813, the Hima monarchies of Rwanda and Burundi (former German East Africa). Nevertheless, with the painstaking care of the ethnologist, Belgian colonial officials discovered over 6,000 chiefdoms, which they recognized and gathered together into '*circonscriptions*': the more the better, since no political danger could possibly issue from such fragmentation. Unruly tribes were carefully watched by the 17,000-strong, well-trained paramilitary force, the '*force publique*'.

This system of indirect administration was not tailored to the masses of workers who poured into the mining areas and administrative centres, chiefly into the capital, Léopoldville, and who in 1940 already numbered 50,000. At the beginning of the Second World War, more than a million Congolese, 10 per cent of the total population, were living in the '*milieu extra-coutumier*', that is, outside the traditional tribal communities. Admittedly the administration did try to remain true to its principles, setting up chiefs in the towns; but these remained artificial institutions without authority. The few Congolese who had been able to acquire a modern European education, the '*évolués*', rejected the regiment of chiefs, thus being regarded by conservative colonial politicians as an unforeseen, indeed disruptive element.

It was not made easy for them to obtain a modern education. Catholic and Protestant missions did set up a superb network of primary schools in the inter-war era which was without parallel in Africa at that time: in 1935, 254,000 children were attending Protestant schools and 213,000 attending Catholic schools, that is, altogether 35 per cent of the school age population.[4] Instruction, however, was largely limited to African local or colloquial languages, such as Swahili in the east and Lingala in the west. Few Congolese learned proper French. Secondary schools, apart from seminaries, were virtually entirely absent.

For good or ill, the economy was obliged to make provision for the training of a reliable workforce since, as has already been mentioned, mining was acquiring increasing importance in the economy. While the trade balance in the 1920s was still passive (1925: 629 million fr. in exports, as against 876 million fr. in imports), this trend was reversed in the 1930s: in 1935 the Belgian Congo had 1,203 million fr. worth of exports for only 525 million fr. With 23 per cent, gold now topped the list of export goods, followed by copper (20 per cent), cotton (12 per cent), diamonds and palm oil (9 per cent each).

Mining works such as those established by the Union Minière in Katanga were unthinkable without qualified workers and, unlike in South Africa and Rhodesia, only a few tasks were available for white labour. The mining companies thus moved away from the short-term employment of migrant workers, and set about providing roots and social security for their staffs over several generations. This policy was in the main so successful that the Congolese industrial workforce emerged in the turbulent days of independence not as instigators of a proletarian revolution, but as a markedly conservative element. The Belgians made sure that this section of the population had more to lose in 1960 than just its 'chains'.

Obviously, industrial workers and similarly privileged administrative employees formed only a small minority of the people: some 400,000 in 1935, 500,000 at the outbreak of the Second World War. Something had to be done for the peasants. The organization of '*paysannats*' set up in 1933 along Dutch-Indonesian lines, however, never got off the ground. Some 300,000 Congolese peasants were urged to modernize their working methods and to produce coffee, maize, and cotton for the market. There were too few funds available, however, to make these enterprises viable, while bureaucratic paternalism was not capable of inspiring lively co-operation among the people.

Before the Second World War, **Portugal** was only able to pursue a feeble colonial policy, being crippled by inner confusion until the military *putsch* of 1927 which brought General Carmona to power. Antonio de Oliveira Salazar (who became minister for financial affairs in March 1928, and took over the office of prime minister in July 1932) did from the outset establish firm goals for the 'new state' he wanted to build, in terms of overseas policy. He was obliged, however, to direct his attention chiefly to the neighbouring country of Spain. Initially, therefore, colonial policy in Lisbon was limited to published manifestos, often in statutory form, and to intensive propaganda designed to make the Portuguese people 'colonially aware'.

Despite a centuries-old tradition of Portuguese activity overseas, this was desperately needed. A poor country, Portugal was obliged year after year to lose tens of thousands of people as emigrants, who by no means settled in 'their' own colonies. In 1920, 33,621 Portuguese emigrated to Brazil, only 1,153 to Angola and Mozambique; in 1928 the ratio was 27,705:189. In Angola around 1930 there lived only about 40,000 Europeans, in Mozambique barely 18,000.

The first great proclamation of Salazar's colonial policy was a bill of 1930, which was later incorporated into the constitution; in order to draft it, the dictator himself took over the colonial ministry for a short time. The chief aim of the bill was to unify and centralize the administration. It was urgently necessary once and for all to create order overseas and effectively to exert Portuguese authority. All too often up to that time they had made do with keeping Africans under superficial control in the hinterland, trading with them and forcing them to provide labour. This sloppiness was now gradually to be replaced by purposeful development. Put crudely, Portugal in 1930 was still where the great colonial powers had been in 1905.

This was particularly apparent in 'native policy'. As a Latin nation, whose cultural background gives little ground to racial and colour barriers, Portugal under Salazar was predominantly guided by the French model. Whereas France in the 1930s, however, was already discussing approaches to equipping Africans with improved civil rights, Portugal had only just established its *regime do indigenato* in 1930. It was not Salazar's intention in this to hold back progress, however, but to encourage it: he banned the recruiting of forced labour for private entrepreneurs, impressing upon Europeans that they should make a habit of paying for African labour. These were problems that the British, French, and Germans had resolved before the First World War.

The attempt to improve the quality of European officialdom in the colonies by means of better education and supervision is also only to be found in Portugal for the first time under Salazar. Even his critics conceded that he was successful in this. The governors-general of Angola and Mozambique were now made true proconsuls with far-reaching legislative powers by a bill of 1928.

It was of great economic significance for Angola when in 1931 the Lobito railway was built with British funds, linking the harbour with the copper mines in Katanga. The Portuguese province, however, profited mainly from the through traffic, which meant that it remained dependent to a large extent on foreign economic activity. The same phenomenon may be observed in Mozambique: its ports of Beira and Lourenço Marques flourished while serving as emporia for the Union of South Africa and for Rhodesia. Economic impulses arising out of this transit business did of course radiate out as far as the land itself: those regions, for example, through which the Lobito railway passed, were more easily developed than others. The Salazar government likewise made efforts – again lagging decades behind Britain and France – to deprive the private concessionary companies of their power, these having up to then set the tone of the Mozambican economy, and to reinforce the leading role of the state. With every large-scale project, however, the poor Portuguese state was obliged to resort to foreign private capital. Diamond production in Angola, for example, which in the 1930s began to have a substantial effect on the balance of trade, was built up by the South African Oppenheimer Trust.

Chapter Five

FASCIST ITALY IN CLOSE PURSUIT

As a rebellious 'have-not' among the saturated powers of Europe, and as an embittered ally which felt cheated of its rightful share of the colonial booty of the First World War (the British having thrown it only the barren Jubaland between Somalia and Kenya like a spare crust), Italy was pressing forwards with calculated ruthlessness in the circle of colonial powers. Admittedly, its European competitors, especially Britain, concerned with its naval power in the Mediterranean, felt the force of fascist brutality only in words. To work off their fury in deeds, the Italians had to turn against the 'natives'. Fortunately for Libyan Arabs and for Ethiopia, Italy remained incapable, even under Mussolini, of pursuing a truly totalitarian colonial policy. The memory of Italian rule in North and East Africa does not seem fundamentally to deviate towards the worse compared with that of British or French colonization.

Between the two world wars, Italy obtained no real opportunity for peacefully administering or developing its colonies. It became entangled in military actions – initially to reconquer recognized Italian territory, later to heap new laurels on the Roman eagle. It trod international law underfoot in attacking and conquering the sovereign empire of Ethiopia. For Italy, however, the march into Ethiopia seemed a logical continuation of its newly completed war of conquest in North Africa. All its colonization was now under a military star. There was no other choice for poor Italy but to use elbow power. The Italians responded with all the more outrage, therefore, to the sanction threats of League of Nations members, which did much to drive Mussolini into Hitler's arms.

Italy had to conquer Libya for a second time, since with the exception of a few coastal places the Senussi and local aristocrats, egged on and advised by Turkish, and allegedly also by German, officers, had in the course of the First World War 'liberated' the colony annexed in 1911. At first Rome tried this by means of an appeasement policy, aimed at recognition of a partnership relationship with the indigenous rulers, and offered autonomy of Tripolitania and Cyrenaica within an Italian federation of states. In April 1919 Italy signed the truce of Kallet-es-Seituna with the leaders of the Tripolitanian Arabs, granting them a 'statute' in September. A parliament was to be set up, all inhabitants were to become Italian citizens, but not to do military service and initially not to pay any taxes. Italy pledged to convert the still circulating Turkish paper money into the lira. For Cyrenaica there followed on 25 October 1920 the Treaty of Regima with the Senussi brotherhood; their head, Mohammed Idris (1890–1983), who had just taken over leadership from his cousin Ahmed es-Sherif, was recognized as emir, that is, as a legitimate political authority.[1] From 1950 until 1969 he was Idris I, king of Libya.

Successful co-operation did not arise from these treaties of 1919 and 1920, however. Perhaps this was impossible as long as the military humiliation of the Italians was not overcome; perhaps also in Rome they did not have a reasonable concept of the extent of the task. Did they perhaps just want to 'muddle along' until Italy regained its strength? The question remains open as to why they did not seek the support of the League of Nations, although the treaties of 1919 and 1920 pointed in just the direction indicated by the mandate system (A-mandate). At all events, local Italian military commanders began, even before the victory of fascism at the end of October 1922, to launch offensive actions off their own bat in the Tripoli region. At the beginning of February 1922, the coastal area of Misurata Marina was taken after several weeks of fighting. By the end of the year, however, only a few places had been secured, none of them more than 100 km from Tripoli. In April 1923 an attack was launched on the Senussi to the east; Italian soldiers occupied Ajdabiya without prior warning. Emir Mohammed Idris fled to Egypt, leaving the conduct of the struggle in Cyrenaica chiefly to a tried and tested Senussi brother, Omar el-Mukhtar (1862–1931).

In 1923 and 1924 the Italians concentrated on putting down uprisings in already conquered territory and on the cautious extension of their rule, which they managed about as far as the Ghadamis-Sirte line. Only in 1928 did they once again go on the offensive in the grand style, conquering the Jufrah oases, then at the beginning of 1930 also bringing the Fessan under control after raids on Ghat and Murzuq. They had to fight rather more doggedly for Cyrenaica. The Jarabub oasis, from the middle until the end of the nineteeth century the political centre of the Senussi and as the burial place of the founder an important religious shrine, was occupied in February 1926, so that Omar el-Mukhtar felt obliged formally to submit in June 1928 (at Barke). On 8 November of the same year, however, war broke out again. By contrast with the Tripolitanians, the Senussi were already employing important elements of modern guerrilla strategy. Even in areas where there were Italian military, they put the population under the authority of disguised administrative bodies (or 'threatened them by means of an underground organization' – the description one uses depending on one's point of view). Exactly as in Algeria after 1954 or in Vietnam, people said that the Italians were the 'daytime government', the Senussi the 'night-time government' of Cyrenaica. Of course the Italians, now under the command of General Rodolfo Graziani, responded with the same methods which were later to be used against guerrilla fighters by the French, the Americans, and the British (in Kenya or Malaya): first by gathering the population together in camps which could be placed under military surveillance, and which at that time in Libya were still honestly described as 'concentration camps'. Second, by means of the most massive possible deployment of the air force, with hardly any distinction being made even in those days between fighters and civilians. Graziani publicly praised the ruthlessness of Cato, rewording the latter's famous formula into '*Senussia delenda*'. In May 1930 the brotherhood was banned throughout the whole of Italian territory. On 19 January 1931 an Italian column reached the Al Khufrah oasis, which had hitherto served the Senussi as a refuge. When on 11 September 1931 Omar el-Mukhtar fell into Italian hands, Graziani put him up before a drumhead court martial and had him executed on 16 September in Benghazi. By 1932 these military operations in Libya could be regarded as successfully crowned in victory.

All these battles took place, as has been mentioned, within a territory which had been recognized as Italian by the powers. On 7 January 1935 Mussolini even achieved French withdrawal from 114,000 square km of the great desert region between Libya and the Chad colony, from Pierre Laval, who had just entered office as French foreign minister in the Flandin cabinet. With this, the Italian frontier was shifted to the Tibesti massif. At the Red Sea also Italy extended its colony of Eritrea, somewhat at the expense of French Somaliland. The rock island of Doumeira, which it thereby acquired from the British possession of Perim in the Bab al Mandab strait, was regarded as a potential eastern Gibraltar. Italy never found the time to fortify it.

Mussolini set about expunging the 'disgrace of Adua', where the Ethiopian emperor, Menelik II, had wiped out an Italian army of 17,500 men in 1896. This time Italy was not going to allow itself to go into a campaign against Ethiopia with such a puny force! A pretext for creating a crisis between Rome and Addis Ababa was to hand, despite the friendship treaty which had been signed as late as 2 August 1928: on 5 December 1934 the British-Ethiopian border commission, accompanied by Ethiopian troops, had come up against an Italian position at Walwal in Ogaden. There was as little of a mutually recognized border between (Italian) Somalia and Ethiopia then as there is now. Emperor Menelik had agreed with Major Nerazzani on a line in 1897, but neither the map nor the text of that agreement was ever published. There is still disagreement today as to whether the 'Menelik line' runs parallel with the Indian Ocean coast at a distance of 180 km, or of 100 to 130 km. A treaty of May 1908 clarified nothing, since it referred to the (unpublished) agreement of 1897, adding, to make confusion complete, that 'all territory belonging to tribes living as far as the coast was to be Italian; the whole region of Ogaden and the whole region of tribes living behind Ogaden, was to be dependent on Abyssinia'.[2] Walwal lies further than 180 km from the coast and in the Ogaden region. Italy, however, could point to the fact that the Miyyertein Somali, who live close to the coast, tend their cattle in this area at certain seasons of the year. At all events the Italians had stood unchallenged for five years in Walwal when the Ethiopians appeared, and were victorious in the skirmish which followed: 200 Ethiopians fell. The crisis came before the League of Nations, but in view of the irreparably contradictory texts, arbitration was hopeless; even today the Ethiopian-Somali border conflict is a hot potato, and preferably given wide berth by everyone, including the Organization for African Unity (OAU)!

In 1935 Ethiopia had an estimated 12 million inhabitants, the capital Addis Ababa 100,000. Emperor Haile Selassie I (1892–1975), a great-nephew of Menelik II, reigned from September 1916 as regent for the Empress Zauditu (Menelik's daughter), and de jure from the time of Zauditu's death in April 1930. He made efforts towards reform, and in particular towards combating slavery. As recognition for his endeavours, the League of Nations accepted Ethiopia as a full member in 1923. The authority of the emperor over the Amharic lords, however, was until 1935 by no means complete, whilst economic and military modernization was still in its infancy, in spite of European aid. Between 1925 and 1935 Ethiopian imports consisted of 40 per cent salt, 21 per cent cotton, and only 2 per cent metal goods. As for military forces, only the emperor's guard (a troop of some 20,000 men), which was at least semi-modern, equipped and trained, was really at his disposal. He had no artillery – above all no anti-aircraft guns – practically no aeroplanes and only twenty-five tanks. His feudal vassals could call up around 350,000 warriors, whose medieval training and weapons, however, could not be made competitive even with enthusiasm . . .

The Italians, on the other hand, had in the course of 1935 mustered some 125,000 European soldiers, 72,000 fascist militia men ('blackshirts') and 44,000 African askaris deployed under General de Bono. An additional 35,000 men were recruited as police troops, and 30,000 Italians and 45,000 Africans as work troops. It is estimated that the Italians concentrated 1,400 heavy guns, 500 planes and as many tanks in Eritrea and (as a substantially smaller southern army) in Somalia. Rome, publicly and unabashed, prepared for a war of aggression, leaving the world in no doubt as to its motives. The newspaper *Popolo d'Italia* wrote on 31 July 1935:

> There is slavery in Abyssinia . . . but it is not for this reason that
> Italy is preparing herself to act. . . . The racial question is not
> a significant reason. . . . Not even civilization is Italy's
> argument. . . . There are two essential and indisputable
> arguments: the vital necessities of the Italian people and its
> security in East Africa. . . . Of the two the second is the decisive
> one. . . . There can only be a total solution of the question. All
> expansion and every protectorate must be accompanied by
> military measures. . . . The question only admits of one
> solution, with Geneva, without Geneva or against Geneva.

Haile Selassie hoped to be able to put up resistance for years in his impassable country. The fact that he completely failed in this was not only the result of the technical superiority of the Italians and their brutal use of poison gas, in defiance of international law. The emperor either understood nothing of the guerrilla strategy which had just been put into effect by Omar el-Mukhtar in Cyrenaica, or he did not want to use it. Instead, his generals went into open battle at the northern front, at which initially the Ethiopians would even go on the offensive against Italian machine-guns. Although there was not a complete lack of modern means of communication, there was no co-operation between individual army groups. At least one Amharic aristocrat, the Deyazmach[3] Haile Selassie Guksa, reprimanded by the emperor in 1932, went over to the enemy. Since de Bono's tactics were over-cautious, he was replaced in the middle of the first skirmish (18 October 1935) by General Badoglio. Badoglio demanded a further 90,000-man reinforcement, as well as additional guns, aeroplanes, and gas. In February and March 1936 he defeated the Ethiopian northern armies under the war minister Ras Malugeta, Ras Kassa, and Ras Imru. On 31 March Haile Selassie positioned himself with his core troop at Ashangi lake, about halfway between the northern border and Addis Ababa. Once again he was the first to attack, and the Italian counter-attack on 4 April destroyed the Ethiopian army. The Oromo deserted and the emperor returned as a refugee to his capital, escaping on the train to Djibouti. On 5 May Badoglio moved into Addis Ababa, where there was no longer a central government.

Graziani, in command of the southern army, had a harder time, particularly in the two-week battle of Sassabauch in April 1936; the Ethiopian leader Deyazmach Nasibu was being advised by a Turkish general – Wehib Pasha – and therefore made fewer tactical errors. On 10 May, however, Graziani was able to take Harer, and with that the campaign was essentially at an end. Compared with other African mountainous countries such as Morocco, Algeria, or, in Libya, Cyrenaica, Ethiopia was quick to lay down its arms before the colonial conquerors. Italian losses were stated as 2,313 dead Europeans and 1,593 African soldiers, as well as 453 dead workers. Of the European soldiers, 1,273 fell to enemy weapons, 1,000 died of disease, and twenty Italian aeroplanes were lost to the gun defence fire of the Ethiopians. No one even counted the Ethiopian dead; estimates speak of 50,000 fallen.

The swift end to the campaign contributed to sanctions by the League of Nations being allowed to fizzle out, as well as the propaganda and material support actions introduced in the coloured world for Ethiopia, chiefly among Afro-Americans and in South Africa. All the same, these did lead to a reappraisal in the Pan-African movement, especially among intellectuals from America and Africa gathered in London. However grandiloquent and naive these support programmes may have been, they nevertheless strike the later observer more positively than the hypocritical sanctions policy of those governments represented in the League of Nations. Despite the fact that the league apparatus worked relatively quickly, so that sanctions came into effect on 18 November 1935, just six weeks after the outbreak of the war not even Britain was prepared for real intervention. If it had been, it could, referring to article 20 of the League of Nations Covenant, have closed the Suez Canal to Italian military transport.[4] The only really dangerous sanction was the oil embargo. Italy successfully circumvented it by purchasing oil from Romania and from the recently admitted League of Nations member, Soviet Russia.

The constitutional order of the Italian colonial empire remained heterogeneous until 1939. On 25 October 1938 the fascist Grand Assembly declared northern Libya to be an 'inseparable part of the homeland', thus copying the Algerian model. Four provinces were set up: Tripoli, Misurata, Benghazi and Derna. As in Algeria, the south remained under a military administration.

Italy proclaimed the annexation of Ethiopia as early as 9 May 1936. King Victor Emanuel III assumed the title 'Emperor of Ethiopia', thus following the example of Britain's Queen Victoria for India in 1877. Marshal Badoglio, soon replaced by Marshal Graziani, became as viceroy the highest official in the whole of Italian East Africa. He had a state council consisting of Italian officials and a 'consulta', to which eleven natives were appointed, at his side; both institutions together corresponded roughly to the legislative council of a British colony in its earliest phase. Italy made efforts to pay heed to ethnic tensions in East Africa, that is, to play off other groups against the Amhara, the former rulers of Ethiopia.

The Amharic aristocracy lost its special status, their land and property, including imperial assets, being expropriated. There was no mention of bestowing political rights on the population, although the Arabs and Berbers of Libya in 1938 at least had the possibility of acquiring a 'minor Libyan citizenship', which put them roughly on a par with the 'subjects' of French colonies. Nevertheless Italy made no provision for introducing a policy of racial segregation. People of mixed race were recognized as full citizens as long as they descended from an Italian father, even if out of wedlock.

Mussolini regarded the colonies primarily as settlement territory for the Italian population surplus. Settlement was to proceed under strict state control in accordance with fascist principles, although permitting the acquisition of private property and securing wealthy settlers a privileged position as large landowners overseas as well. In 1932 the state organization Ente per la colonizzazione della Libia was founded; by the beginning of the Second World War it had acquired 757,840 hectares of land in Tripolitania; a reservation of a total of 3 out of the 35 million hectares comprising Tripolitania was planned for Italian colonization. In fact by 1938 just 9,000 Italians were settled in Tripolitania in 623 agricultural enterprises on 127,000 hectares. Of this, 88 per cent was allotted as large estates. In Cyrenaica at the same time there were 3,500 settlers on 1,600 farms on 45,000 hectares. In October 1938, 15,000 new settlers then arrived in Libya, and further transports were planned. By the outbreak of the war some 120,000 Italians were living in the North African colony.

The settlers were to receive progressively reduced salaries from the 'Ente' for five years; their houses and equipment were at their disposal from the first day. After this they were expected to manage themselves and to pay the value of their new property back to the state in twenty to thirty years. As was the case with the French in Algeria, Italy also placed the main emphasis of its agrarian colonization on wine-growing, although the employment of indigenous labour was not envisaged. Grain cultivation was not viable in Libya, while the forest-ation programme introduced in Cyrenaica could not expect to bring profits for a long time. Italy initially allotted 12,000 million lire for East Africa, divided up on the basis of a six-year plan which came into effect in 1937 – exactly the sum which the military campaign had absorbed within six months. Road building was top priority: an immediate programme of 2,800 km was begun. Colonization by Europeans was also envisaged for the future. It was hoped to make the East African highlands a home for 5 million Italians. Before the out-break of the Second World War the Italians had succeeded in achieving a sharp rise in coffee production; they exported 22,000 tons in 1937, as much as 27,000 tons in 1938 (the 1954 harvest was 37,600 tons). The search for minerals, however, was unsuccessful.

One question suggests itself at the end of this chapter, whether, in the inter-war years, as the political dividing line in Europe between democracies and dictatorships was deepening, a similar difference could be discerned in colonial policy: whether the policies pursued by the Italians and the Portuguese in Africa differed fundamentally from the conduct of the British, French, and Belgians, or indeed from that of the Dutch in Indonesia.

The preliminary answer to this question must be no – without wishing to pre-empt future historical research, of which there still remains much to be done on all colonial empires. In terms of colonial policy, the fascists and semi-fascists of Europe in the 1930s seem to have continued to regard their competitors, France and Great Britain, with which they were in other respects in a state of enmity, rather as models to emulate. By the same token, until 1939 the democrats of Europe did not question the right of the fascists and semi-fascists to rule over colonies.

One may ask whether the reason for this mutual 'tolerance' did not perhaps lie in the fact that colonial rule, even in those places where it was practised by democrats, gave vent to the instincts of white racism, thus allowing people to live them out in a way which would already have been unlawful at home in Europe. Conversely, it is quite clear that racism was fundamental to many fascist and semi-fascist ideologies and movements, although of less importance in Italy and Portugal than in Hitler's national socialism: the German Reich in the Second World War set about establishing a new colonial kingdom in Poland and Russia, complete with apartheid, and implementing the genocidal trend of the Herero war (1905) in most cruel ways. Africans and Asians were spared the experience of this system of colonial domination.

Chapter Six

SUPRA-REGIONAL COLONIAL AND ANTI-COLONIAL MOVEMENTS

There has been no mention in the previous pages of planned co-operation among the various European colonial offices. We have noted a certain osmosis of colonial theories between Britain and France, and a radiation of ideas outwards from the two main powers to the minor ones. In terms of practical policy, however, it was a case of each nation for itself. Each power saw to the securing and development of its own empire and endeavoured, if necessary, to contain anti-colonial movements.

It may be that this picture is an incomplete one. Most accounts so far of overseas history have been written from the point of view of European national statehood: the history of British, French, or some other colonization, or individual studies within the national framework. If the sources were to be read and interpreted again in the light of international co-operation, it is possible that this picture could be complemented. It might, on the other hand, offer rather more insights into mutual mistrust on the part of the colonial powers and into envy between European rivals, against the USA or Japan, than into co-operation in colonial policy.

Prior to the Second World War, Europe had no need of a defence alliance of colonizers against the colonized because the superior power of the colonizers was immense. Every colonial power, even a relatively weak one such as Portugal, could afford to go it alone. Only in Germany, which had lost its colonies in 1919, were voices to be heard discussing an international arrangement. By means of this back door, the Weimar Republic intended to regain its place in the circle of colonial powers. The first plans for a 'Eurafrica' arose out of these colonial revision concepts. At Locarno in 1925, Streseman sought to link the entry of Germany into the League of Nations with obtaining a

125

mandate. The president of the Reichsbank, Hjalmar Schacht, proposed on 24 March 1926 in a speech to the German Colonial League:

> The capitalist business leaders of the world have enormous interest in a solution to the colonial question. With their help it will be possible to bring into being a great colonial chartered company to which an appropriate colonial territory could be assigned, with the express intention of giving the highly developed German industry and technology an opportunity for colonial-economic activity and to settle sections of the German population without damaging anyone's political prestige or any hitherto sacrosanct political interest. . . . Of course certain sovereignty rights cannot be entirely disregarded. . . . It would be quite possible to place the required legal apparatus either under the existing government, or under a former regime which is to be reinstated, or even to place it under the auspices of an international committee, which admittedly I should not like to propose to the League of Nations in its present form, but for which international guarantees could doubtless be found in an international court of law.[1]

The shrewd way in which Schacht covers his rear against potential criticism from traditional nationalists does not alter the fact that this plan bears hallmarks which are clearly (perhaps even embarrassingly) reminiscent of the standard way in which capital is invested today in overseas countries, where sovereignty has become a secondary issue and 'legal protection' or 'investment guarantees' have come to the fore. When Hitler came to power in Germany, this discussion of international 'neo-colonialism' naturally died down – Schacht himself had given his speech the title 'The new colonial policy' – on the spur of the moment.

Consequently, the internationalization of overseas policy did not proceed from the 'have-nots' within the colonizer camp, but from the colonized themselves. It was realized that Asians and Africans would have to strive towards supra-national and supra-regional associations, in order to strengthen their hopelessly inferior forces, at least by forming alliances. Admittedly success was pitiful at first. Europe's colonizers did here and there take note of diverse 'Pan' movements, but did not take them *hic et nunc* seriously as a threat to their power positions.

Where a rebellion of non-European peoples against European rule was either partially or wholly successful in the 1920s and 1930s, it was a matter of a strictly national movement, and indeed of the successful or attempted rebirth of a nation. Peoples who had previously been embedded in non-European imperial structures of a universal or at least a supra-regional character, and who were consequently handicapped, or who had dissipated their political forces by nursing old conflicts, withdrew into narrower spheres, where they remained among themselves and thus gained new strength. This was the case of the new China of the Kuomintang; the best example of it, however, is offered by the Turkey of Kemal Atatürk. Here during the 1920s was accomplished the truly successful emancipation of an oriental people which had previously declined from the status of a great power to that of a semi-colony. Kemalism should be ranked among decolonization movements not only because of its military resistance to Greek expansion, but also because of its self-assertion against Britain and France. The fact that Kemal systematically and indeed forcibly 'westernized' the Turkish people, is only an apparent contradiction. Anti-colonial movements bent on modernization (as they generally are) differ from conservative resistance to colonial conquest precisely in the fact that in addition to military hardware, they also borrow political, ideological, and organizational ammunition from their opponents. By struggling against colonial rule, they deepen the influence of the modern world on the colonized people – generally in the particular stamp of the former colonizing power.

Calling on the ideals of self-government against British rule, on the words of 1789 against a French governor, is only paradoxical at first sight. National rebirth or 'nation-building', the mustering of political, economic, and military power, is only possible in colonized or semi-colonized countries through the modernization of the society. Modernization, however discredited a concept this may be among some European theoreticians of political economy, does mean 'westernization', and from among the various models of western society, that of the country's own colonial rulers is always the most accessible.

It is because of this that decolonization so often takes the form of a dialogue between the erstwhile rulers and subjects, a dialogue little understood by outsiders, who may even disrupt the process, despite having intervened with the best of intentions. For the same reason, the various decolonization movements rarely extend beyond the former imperial, or even regional, context.

We should nevertheless not overlook the fact that certain concepts between the two world wars were already moving towards assuming tangible form as supra-regional, anti-colonial movements. These 'Pan' movements did not arise out of the specific national experience of the Turks, the Chinese, the Kabyles, or the Indians (not even of the Arabs!), but partly out of old and partly out of brand new universal concepts. Pan-Islamism was rooted in the fundamental values and concepts of Islam, and continued to be guided by these even when it was in fact developing much more into narrower Pan-Arabism. Early Pan-Africanism was based on more or less reinforced racial concepts, such as can also be seen at work in German national socialism and (mostly much milder) other contemporary versions of fascism. The anti-imperialism of the Comintern ultimately made use of the theses of Marx, Engels, and Lenin, who both prophesied and wanted to lead a world-wide revolution.

All these anti-colonial 'Pan' movements paid for their universal orientation with a preliminary lack of strength and success. On the other hand they did not as a rule become the tool of some Asian or African government. An exception to this were Pan-Asiatic or Pan-Mongolian tendencies, which were taken over by the Japanese state leadership and turned to propaganda use.

PAN-ISLAMISM AND PAN-ARABISM

Pan-Islamism is not an Arab product. Its founding father is considered to be Afghane Jemal ud-Din (1838–97), who was brought up in Buchara and took up teaching at the El-Azhar University only in 1871. In his person we can find the essential characteristics of every modern decolonization movement. He strove after the defence and renewal of Islamic society, which is at one and the same time a political and a religious entity, by means of the adoption of western methods, that is, the methods of the challenger and the opponent: economic education, industrialization, nationalism. In the case of his pupil, Mohammed Abdu (1849–1905), an Egyptian, the movement shifted predominantly towards the cultural aspect; the defeat of Arabi Pasha in 1882 by the British strengthened Abdu (who had predicted it) in his apolitical tendency. The Pan-Islamic Society, founded in London in 1903, had an Indian secretary. Incidentally, it became a tool of the Ottoman sultan, Abdul Hamid. The First World War repoliticized Pan-Islamism, which was now something distinct from Pan-Arab nationalism.

The first Arab National Congress had met in Paris in 1913. Christian Arabs, chiefly from Lebanon and Palestine, played an important role in the movement. For this reason alone, Pan-Arabism was never able to find a steady home with the government of any Arab state, since all governments ruled over Muslim majorities. This did not prevent them, however, from attempting to justify expansionist desires at the expense of their neighbours in Pan-Arab terms, as Nasser did after 1945, and Gaddhafi and others continue to do today.

It is worth noting that at that time Pan-Islamism likewise had no firm 'base' in any of the young Arab regimes. The Hashemite dynasty failed directly after 1918 with its plans for a united Arab kingdom, which for a brief while even laid claim to the caliphate. The Hashemite monarchs in Transjordan and Iraq none the less managed to hold their own, even after having been formally released from the British mandate in 1930; in 1946 political potency and the will to expand bestirred themselves more energetically, however, in the Wahabi prince Abd el-Aziz ibn Abd ar-Rahman, known in Europe as Ibn Saud (1880–1953); in 1921 he annexed the Rashid state to the north of his Nejd homeland; he threw the Hashemites out of the Hijaz; in 1932 he proclaimed himself king of Saudi Arabia and on 19 May 1934 forced the defeated Imam Yahya of Yemen to a treaty expressly referring to 'Islamic friendship and Arab fraternity'. Despite the fact that Pan-Arab nationalists pinned their hopes on Ibn Saud, he paid them as little heed as the Hashemites. Was this only because conservative monarchs were in no hurry to modernize their countries? Or was it because Pan-Arabism was so obviously pulling no punches with London and Paris, whereas the kings were too weak to challenge the great powers? Chekib Arslane (a Druse, and thus likewise a member of an ethno-religious minority), from 1930 the driving force behind Pan-Arabism, set up his headquarters in Geneva, where he published the newspaper *Arab Nation*, and where he made contact with politicians from Morocco and Algeria. In the orient, only the mufti of Jerusalem, Amin el-Husseini, sought a Pan-Arab resonance, but one can also find Pan-Islamism in his actions. He was not responsible for the fate of a sovereign country, but as the self-proclaimed spokesman for Palestinian Arabs, the enemy of Britain and of the Jewish immigrants was in fact more comparable with someone like Arslane than with Ibn Saud. In December 1931 el-Husseini organized a World Islamic Congress in Jerusalem. Government representatives from Turkey, Egypt, Iraq, and Saudi Arabia, however, would have been sought there in vain.

In the 27 August 1932 issue of the Jerusalem newspaper *Al Arab*, we can read an article by Abd er-Rahman Azzam Pasha which, with its sweeping non-committal manner, as well as its claim to universalism, may be quoted as a typical example of Pan-Arabism. It reads:

> Arab unity is a reality of today and a reality of history. . . . The splintering of the Arab nation into peoples and tribes is not a sign of its disintegration or loss of life force; it is simply one of the marks of ignorance and one of the forms in which the oppression of the European races manifests itself in the Orient. This state of division, however, will not prevent the Arab nation from attaining its appropriate power. . . . When the Arab race has reached its superior power, its perfected qualities will predominate. There is no doubt that the Arabs need unity; there is also no doubt that the world needs the Arabs. Shift your gaze to the nation of the future, to the Arabs.[2]

Azzam Pasha, a doctor born near Cairo (1893–1976), was at that time a member of the Egyptian parliament for the Wafd Party, although he did not yet have any executive responsibility. Only in 1939 did King Farouk promote him to foreign minister. In 1945 he became general secretary of the newly founded League of Arab States. Azzam Pasha remained a 'Pan-Arab'. Is it not, however, typical of the remarkable unworldliness of early Pan-Arabism that, of all times, in 1952 after the victory of the Young Officers, he resigned from office? The new government was for his taste too concerned with Egyptian questions and was neglecting the Pan-Arab ideal! This false estimation he made of Nasser indicates the extent to which early Pan-Arabism allowed itself to be seduced into Utopianism. Universalist exuberance and racial arrogance did not prove sound advisers in the real world.

PAN-AFRICANISM

Early Pan-Africanism, which in fact carries this name unjustly, since it was a 'Pan' movement of people with black skin, was similarly isolated from the only two states at that time ruled by blacks: Haiti and Liberia. More than this, the radical wing of Pan-Africanism, the Garvey movement, was destroyed by the resistance of Liberia to every practical attempt to realize the 'Home to Africa' slogan. Ethiopia's emperor may have regarded the Pan-African support campaign, launched for him in 1935, as hardly welcome, since the Amhara by no means considered themselves part of the 'black race'. Only in the late 1950s when Pan-Africanism began to free itself of racial concepts and to define itself geographically, was Haile Selassie willing to take over a senior, arbitrating role within it. Early Pan-Africanism was a cause which appealed to the intellectuals of the American black diaspora, the cause of men with political passion and sometimes also a talent for political leadership, but without state political responsibility.

Its kinship with fascist racist doctrine is particularly clear in the case of Marcus Aurelius Garvey (1887–1940), originally from Jamaica, who inspired the masses in New York (Harlem) from 1917. The slogan of his Universal Negro Improvement Association (UNIA) was 'Home to Africa!', but in 1924 it failed, among other things, because of the refusal of Liberia to provide land and aid for a Garvey colony. The opposition of the Liberian president, Charles D. B. King, is understandable: after all, Garvey had in 1920 been proclaimed 'provisional president of Africa' by the UNIA. The history of the Garvey movement, which remained restricted to America, particularly the USA, is of less interest here than its ideology. It can be found in concentrated form in a letter from Garvey of 1 August 1921 to the League of Nations, protesting against the Pan-African Congress organized by DuBois:

DuBois and his associates who call the Congress are making an issue of social equality with the white race for their own selfish purposes. . . . We believe the motives of the Congress are to undermine the true feeling and sentiment of the Negro race for complete freedom in their own spheres, and for a higher social order among themselves, as against a desire among a certain class of Negroes for social contact, comradeship and companionship with the white race.

We further repudiate the Congress because we sincerely feel that the white race, like the black and yellow races, should maintain the purity of self. . . .

We appeal to the sense of race pride among the white people of Europe not to encourage those Congresses in misrepresenting the attitude of the Negro. The Negro feels socially satisfied with himself and means to maintain the dignity and purity of his race, and therefore renounces any attempt . . . to foster a campaign of miscegenation to the destruction of the race's purity.[3]

No wonder that Garvey could honestly say that he was the inventor of fascism, and that Mussolini (Hitler was at that time unknown) had learned from him. No wonder that the Ku Klux Klan seems to have been interested in an alliance with the Garvey movement, which after all promised to make America 'Negro free'. Nevertheless, Garvey influenced African liberation policy of the future indirectly, if we are to believe Kwame Nkrumah: while a student in America he read the writings of Garvey and later said that they had had the strongest influence on him of all the works he had read. By that time, Garvey had already been pulled under by a whirlpool of lawsuits (he was deported from the USA in 1927). It was probably a blessing for African decolonization that Garvey was not able to exert a direct influence on it.

It is far more difficult to think oneself into the conceptual universe of his rival W. E. B. DuBois (1868–1963) and the Pan-African Congress movement set up by him. His level of operation is higher, so that it eludes the primitive echoes of contemporary European barbarism. DuBois saw the 'black race' oppressed throughout the world by white hegemony and wanted to launch a world-wide action to change this situation. On his initiative, the second Pan-African Congress resolved in 1921:

> The absolute equality of races, physical, political and social, is the founding stone of world and human advancement. . . . The doctrine of racial equality does not interfere with individual liberty: rather it fulfils it. And of all the various criteria of which masses of men have in the past been prejudged and classified, that of the color of the skin and texture of the hair, is surely the most adventitious and idiotic. . . .
>
> The beginning of wisdom in interracial contact is the establishment of political institutions among suppressed peoples. The habit of democracy must be made to encircle the earth. . . .
>
> The Negro race through their thinking intelligentsia demand:
>
> I. The recognition of civilized men as civilized despite their race or color.
> II. Local self-government for backward groups, deliberately rising as experience and knowledge grow to complete self-government under the limitation of a self-governed world. . . .
> V. Co-operation with the rest of the world in government,

industry, and art on the bases of Justice, Freedom, and Peace.
VI. The return to Negroes of their land and its natural fruits
and defense against the unrestrained greed of invested
capital.[4]

As one can see, no bridge to fascism is to be found from the
emancipation concepts of this former student of the universities of
Harvard and Berlin – rather a bridge to the democratic socialism of
Europe, or to the degenerate form of it which was to dominate Soviet
Russia after 1917 under Lenin and Stalin. At the peak of his career, in
the 1920s, DuBois maintained a critical position in relation to the
Comintern and to American communists; only as a 90-year-old –
living as an honoured guest in Nkrumah's Ghana – did he join the
Communist Party of the USA.

Only in the USA did an organized group stand behind the Pan-
African Congress movement: the National Association for the
Advancement of Colored People (NAACP), in whose founding in
1909 DuBois was involved. It had at best only a sentimental interest in
African colonial problems. The NAACP, as Garvey had quite correctly grasped, was struggling for the integration, with equal rights,
of Afro-Americans in American society, not for their collective
isolation. They and the Pan-African congresses had no theoretical
basis for dealing with Africa. With their general turns of phrase, the
congress resolutions raised claims which could be met by an enlightened, rational colonial administration.

The third congress (London, 1923), however, did adopt a more
militant posture by claiming 'as long as white folk bear arms against
black folk, the right of blacks to bear arms in their own defense'; in
practical political terms the very same resolution restricted itself to
such demands as 'a voice in their own government . . . trial by juries
of their peers . . . free elementary education for all' and the like.[5]

It was precisely this blurring of far-reaching theoretical goals and of
the experience of internal US colour compromises, however, which
allowed DuBois at the second Pan-African Congress in August–
September 1921 to make precise proposals for a specific policy. The
only platform which could be considered for this was the League of
Nations: Garvey had after all also written to Geneva. He, however,
had baldly demanded the granting of former German East Africa 'to
us', that is, to him personally, and thereby remained in his Cloud-
cuckoo-land. DuBois, on the other hand, was concerned to be taken

seriously by the league. With the second Pan-African Congress, which met consecutively in London, Brussels, and Paris, he had brought about an impressive representation of the black race: 110 delegates, of whom 41 were from various African countries (reported to be Nigeria, the Gold Coast and Sierra Leone, Sudan, Tanganyika, Senegal, the French Congo and Madagascar, the Belgian Congo, Sao Tomé, Angola and Mozambique, Liberia and Ethiopia), 7 from the West Indies and 35 from the USA. The petition presented at Geneva proposed:

> 1 The setting-up of a section at the International Labour Organization, the special task of which is to be the detailed study of the living conditions and needs of native workers in Africa and elsewhere. . . . The Congress believes that a serious investigation of native work would mean the first step towards the emancipation of work in the world. 2 . . . The mandated territories which are populated mainly by blacks have a right to decide that a man of African origin, well-prepared in character and education, should be appointed as member of the mandate commission as soon as a seat becomes available.[6]

At the League of Nations, however, no thought was entertained of recognizing Mr DuBois in this way as spokesman for African mandated territories which he had never seen in his life. Seen from the European point of view, his Pan-African ambition was as high-handed as the self-styling of Garvey. None the less, objectively one can distinguish two differences: first, DuBois would in fact have been capable of familiarizing himself with the practical matters of mandate government, certainly no worse than any European governor or minister; and second, he strove for co-operation within the existing international organization, whereas Garvey was taking money out of the pockets of Afro New Yorkers at mass rallies and parades or through press propaganda, in order to colonize off his own bat.

The League of Nations did no more in 1921 than to acknowledge the petition of the second Pan-African Congress and to have it delivered to all delegations: on the matter itself it did not lift a finger. At this point the DuBois movement, as far as Africa was concerned, had reached the end of its tether. It is significant that the failure of this attempt at practical co-operation was followed by a collapse of the entire movement. Even the third congress (London, 1923) was a mere shadow of the second, and the fourth congress (New York, 1927) was almost exclusively a meeting of Afro-Americans only.

Political circles of African and West Indian blacks survived in Europe, especially in London. Although in quantitative terms they represented mere fragments of what had in fact never been an over-strong Pan-African movement, they did not withdraw into a dreamworld, but began to exert more and more pressure on colonial realities: certain efforts at reform on the part of the up-and-coming black bourgeoisie of the Gold Coast, whose envoys could be useful in contact with British politics; Kenya's uncertain future – whether it was to be based on the South African or West African model; and above all in 1935 the invasion of Ethiopia. Among the organizers of the International African Friends of Abyssinia (IAFA), which met in London, one finds Dr J. B. Danquah of the Gold Coast (1895–1965), who from 1949 was Nkrumah's opponent and dogged by misfortune, Jomo Kenyatta (1893–1978) (he passed his examinations at the London School of Economics with the famous anthropologist Malinowski), and George Padmore (1903–59), who from 1953 until his death was Nkrumah's foreign policy adviser. These men of a younger generation – compared with DuBois, who was born in 1868 – and some others stood by one another when the lobbying for Ethiopia was taken out of their hands by a largely British committee. During the Second World War they prepared for a renaissance as the 'Pan-African Federation' and for closer African unity, more in accordance with the realities.

Padmore originated from the communist camp, having broken with the Comintern when their seventh congress in July 1935 had gone along with Stalin's swing to the 'People's Front'. In order to make way for an alliance with the social democrats of the West European colonial powers, the communists had had to relinquish the anti-colonial policy which they had been building up for years – and did this without batting an eyelid. Men such as Padmore, for whom anti-colonialism was top priority and protection of the USSR a secondary issue, were dropped. This discredited communism in the Third World to a degree which is still being felt today. The practical policy of the Comintern in the colonies and semi-colonies had in any case already fallen into disarray in 1927 in its most important field of operations, China.

COMMUNISM

It was towards not African but Asian models that the communists, after having seized power in Russia in 1917, looked in developing theoretical and practical guidelines for an anti-colonial revolution, which they considered useful for the victory of their own 'socialist' revolution. Observers are aware of a fundamental sense of wonder at the breadth of vision of Soviet leaders – whether Lenin, Trotsky, or Stalin. They took anti-colonial tendencies more seriously than any other European government of that time. Lenin correctly foresaw that nationalist movements in the European colonies would soon be playing an important role in world politics. Soviet interest intensified and took shape with the efforts they themselves were making to retain Russian colonial possessions in Asia. On these fringes of the former Tsarist empire, nationalists, including some thoroughly revolutionary Marxists, such as the Tatar Sultan Galiyev (who was expelled from the Soviet Communist Party in 1923 and arrested), were pressing for self-determination.

Lenin used the right of the peoples to self-determination as a tactical weapon in 1917:

> Muslims of Russia, Tatars of the Volga and the Crimea, Kirgiz and Sarts of Siberia and Turkestan, Turks and Tatars of Transcaucasia, Chechens and mountain Cossacks! . . . Build your national life freely and without hindrance. It is your right. Know that your rights, like those of all the people of Russia, will be protected by the might of the revolution![7]

In 1913, however, Joseph Stalin had seen the question somewhat differently. His work *Marxism and the National Question* raised him to the status of a Marxist theoretician, moving Lenin to entrust Stalin from 1921 to 1923 with the People's Commissariat for Nationalities.

In 1913, Stalin did not mince his words:

> The Transcaucasian Tatars as a nation could, let us say, meet at their national assembly, and under the influence of their Begs and Mullahs restore the former situation and pass a resolution to separate from the empire. Would that be in the interests of the working classes of the Tatar nation? Can then social democracy stand idly by while the Begs and Mullahs are gathering the masses behind themselves in the solution of the national

question? Should not social democracy intervene here and up to a point influence the will of the nation? . . . Since when do social democrats carry fuel to the fires of reactionaries? . . . No, that is no solution to the national question. The national question in the Caucasus can only be solved in the context of a drawing of the late-arrived nations and peoples into the general stream of the higher culture.[8]

Soviet policy thus put its own colonial political house in order in terms of the interests of the Russian Communist Party, not in terms of the pledges of 1917. The Islamic government in Kokand was swept aside in January 1918 by the Russian military, as was the independence of Christian Georgia in February 1921. Uprisings, such as the Turkestan Bamashi revolts in the early 1920s, were crushed. All that remained of the promised right of peoples to self-determination in Soviet Asia was the formal independence of certain Soviet republics, which were prudently divided up according to 'tribalist' principles (e.g. Uzbekistan/Tadjikistan), with a pinch of cultural autonomy added, to make the political and social domination of the centre in Moscow more palatable.

This systematically 'integrative' colonial policy in the former Tsarist empire has never prevented the Soviet Communist Party from encouraging anti-colonial movements in the western sphere of influence, or from forcing local communist cadres into more or less happy coalitions with non-communist nationalists. Nikolai Bucharin's formulation of the resolution of the first Comintern Congress of March 1919 states:

> In contrast to the yellow social-patriotic international,
> international proletarian communism will support the exploited
> colonial peoples in their struggles against imperialism, in order
> to promote the final downfall of the imperialist world system.[9]

The same Bucharin commented on the same proclamation in the same month at the eighth congress of the Russian Communist Party with the frank words:

> If we propound the solution of the right of self-determination for
> the colonies . . . we lose nothing by it. On the contrary, we
> gain. . . . The most outright nationalist movement . . . is only
> grist for our mill, since it contributes to the destruction of
> English imperialism.[10]

It was now a question of finding the theoretical formula, the 'line' for co-operation between the Soviet government, local communists, and non-communist, anti-colonial movements. The Communist International had as little success with this until their seventh congress as the Soviet and Chinese communists had after 1945. At the second Comintern Congress in July–August 1920 Lenin and the Indian delegate Manabendra Nath Roy presented opposing theses. Lenin counted on weak communist parties in Asia (there was hardly any mention of Africa at this stage); since the imperialists were holding back with the industrialization of the colonies and semi-colonies, there was consequently no powerful proletariat. In order to score rapid successes, therefore, Lenin was prepared in the first revolutionary phase to subordinate the communists to the leadership of non-communist, anti-colonial movements, which he – analogously with the historical development of Europe as seen by Marx – defined as 'bourgeois-democratic'. Roy on the other hand feared non-communist nationalists; they could secure their power after victory over colonialism, keep the communists down, and lead the new states on to a capitalist road. Although ready, like Lenin, to guide the first phase of the anti-colonial revolution according to 'petit-bourgeois, reformist demands' ('such as division of the land, etc.'), the organizational leadership was nevertheless to rest from the beginning with the 'communist avant-garde'.[11]

The congress did not want to choose between Roy and Lenin, and Lenin himself made efforts towards a compromise. He conceded that 'we as communists are only obliged to support bourgeois liberation movements in the colonial countries when their representatives do not prevent us from educating and organizing the peasants and the broad masses of the exploited in the revolutionary spirit'.[12] The organizational independence of the communist parties was thus the precondition and price to be paid for communist support of stronger, non-communist, anti-colonial movements! Theoretically this was a shrewd solution, although Roy himself remained dissatisfied: he gave another urgent warning at the fourth Comintern Congress in November 1922 against alliances with the 'bourgeoisie', and he himself experienced the failure of this Comintern policy in China in 1927. Later, however, Roy was to accuse the Comintern of underestimating the revolutionary tendency of the bourgeoisie of India, his homeland; this was at a time (between 1928 and 1934) when Stalin was exerting himself for the international struggle of the communists with the slogan 'class against class', thus breaking off all co-operation with non-communists. Roy fell into increasingly sharper conflict with Moscow, until the twelfth plenary of the Comintern Executive in September 1932 summarily condemned him as a 'leftist, nationalist-reformist Menshevik renegade'. In spite of all subsequent de-Stalinization and *glasnost,* this condemnation does not seem to have been lifted, and in communist literature one will search in vain for an appreciation of this Indian pioneer of a communist anti-colonial revolution.

Roy's theses of 1920 did not have to be tested in practice, however. Before the Second World War, no communist-led revolutionary movement was successful in any Asian or African colony. After 1945 Mao Tse-tung did take over the leadership of China, and Ho Chi Minh the leadership of Vietnam – both heading movements which formally embraced non-communist elements.

Nasser, Boumedienne, Sekou Touré, and others like them, on the other hand, made no bones about repressing their internal communists as soon and inasmuch as they deemed it correct to do so. The willingness of Moscow, and likewise of Peking, in spite of this to seek out the friend-ship of anti-colonialist dictators, must have been demoralizing for com-munist cadres in the prisons and underground movements of Asia and Africa. This is an old experience; in 1922 a Turkish communist at the Comintern Congress was given a rebuff when he described the suffering of comrades persecuted by Kemal. Would they be kind enough to sup-port the 'national liberation', i.e. Kemal, retorted Radek.

Chiang Kai-shek's strikes at Chinese communists in 1927 hit at a time when Stalin was making his way to his lone peak of power in the communist world movement. Precisely because the opposition in the Soviet Communist Party tried to gain ammunition against Stalin out of this fearful, partially self-inflicted defeat, Stalin silenced all theoretical discussion on the colonial question. He allowed Lenin's doctrines to petrify into something which could serve as a treasury of quotations, but which no longer had hardly anything in common with the realities of the colonized world. Lenin's head start in having correctly evaluated the significance of the anti-colonial movements before any other European government, was now lost. Communists were now increasingly active as dividers of anti-colonial forces, and were even proud of the fact, since co-operation with non-communist nationalists had become as good as impossible, now that Stalin in 1928 had prescribed the 'class against class' strategy.

In the process he also allowed the collapse of a front organization which, at the beginning of 1927, just before the China débâcle, had emerged with a great deal of skill and aplomb and undeniable chances of success: the League against Imperialism and for National Independence. The brilliant German communist Willi Münzenberg (1889–1940) organized a founding congress in Brussels in February 1927. He knew how to bring representative delegates of the colonial peoples to his conference hall: Jawaharlal Nehru, Mohammed Hatta from Indonesia, Messali Hadj from Algeria, Haya della Torre from Peru. Telegrams were received from Gandhi and Wang Ching-wai, as well as from the Tunisian Destur Party, the Cocoa-Growers Union of the Gold Coast, and of course intellectuals such as Romain Rolland, Ernst Toller, and Albert Einstein.

Münzenberg said at Brussels:

> Our opponents . . . rule the greater part of the globe. Even today, however, one can recognize that our opponents have passed the peak of their power. . . . The nations, classes, races, and organizations represented by us will in later days be the creators of a true League of Nations spanning the whole globe. The future belongs to us! The coming decades of development of the peoples and nations will not be determined by the old capitalist motherlands in Europe, but by the development of the struggles in China, India, and in the Pacific. . . . The centre of world history has shifted.[13]

He was right. What role would this little-educated, but instinctively sure-footed and shrewd, business-minded communist have been able to play in the decolonization of later years, if his party had not been curbed by Stalinism! Thirty years later Padmore openly voiced his admiration for Münzenberg, who broke with Stalin shortly after he did:

> For him, all his life's work had been destroyed. Münzenberg was left a broken and disappointed man, a little later to meet a violent death. He was strangled in a forest in the south of France while trying to escape before the advancing Nazi forces. Some say he was murdered by the Gestapo, others say GPU agents. I just don't know. One fact I do know: the colonial peoples lost a sympathetic friend in this likeable German.[14]

Had Stalin continued with the impetus given in 1927, communism might now have a better position in the Third World; it might also be a different, freer communism. As it was, the league atrophied. Nehru condemned it in 1931 for entering into a compromise with Britain; four years later Stalin himself joined the 'limited company of imperialism', as Münzenberg had described the League of Nations. Independent non-communists in the League against Imperialism's leadership were replaced either by Communist Party people or reliable yesmen – 'This is typical communist behaviour,' commented Padmore. In 1933 the league disappeared into oblivion.

Where in the inter-war years were communists at all able to found parties that are worthy of the name? In the Executive Committee of the Comintern, India (until 1928 represented by Roy), China, and Indonesia had been represented since 1925; in 1928 came Turkey and South Africa (with one candidate), while a further candidate represented Egypt, Palestine, and Syria. In those days these were the only countries in which there were the beginnings of communist organizations. In the 1930s, communist cadres were added in Vietnam, Algeria, and Morocco. The latter two, however, consisted almost exclusively of European settlers. Even in the Central Committee of the South African Communist Party, which accepted blacks as members with full equality from the very beginning (1921), whites still formed the majority.

EUROPE'S WITHDRAWAL FROM ASIA AND AFRICA

Chapter Seven

THE SECOND WORLD WAR
AND THE COLONIES

The second European civil war of the twentieth century and, above all, Japan's meteoric succession of victories of 1942, damaged the prestige of the white man among the colonial peoples far more seriously and lastingly than the First World War. Since 1945 Europe has no longer been master of the world. The dropping of two atom bombs on large cities with 'coloured' populations at the light-hearted command of a white president may seem to later generations the last outburst of the white hubris of world domination.

Among the outward reasons for this loss of prestige was the rapid collapse of two secondary colonial powers: Italy and the Netherlands. The Italians were defeated by another European power, the British – but by no means by superior armies. On the contrary, Italy, unlike the German Reich before 1914, had prepared for an African war. The Italians had more than 100,000 men in Libya, twice as many in East Africa. An advance by some 30,000 British into Cyrenaica at the end of 1940, however, swept the Italians aside. On 18 May 1941 the duke of Aosta capitulated in Ethiopia.

In **South-East Asia** it was 'coloured' Japan which drove the Dutch out of Indonesia, pushed the British and the Americans to the brink of defeat, and forced the French colonizers in Indochina into submission. The attack on Pearl Harbor on 7 December 1941 was followed by the surrender of 70,000 men at the Singapore stronghold on 15 February 1942. At the beginning of March the occupation of Java was ended; on 6 May the blockaded island of Corregidor near Manila fell. Japan could perhaps have transformed the glory of these victories into political energy, into a direct anti-colonial uprising of the peoples of South-East Asia, but it merely toyed with such ideas. The decolonization process did not draw to an abrupt conclusion in this agitated environment, but took some years, or even decades, until after the end of the Second World War, proceeding for the most part bloodlessly, or at least in a politically controlled way.

It would be shooting in the dark to try to convey the actual political programme of Japanese imperialism during the Second World War. How was the Great East Asian Sphere of Prosperity intended to look? What was the significance of propaganda actions such as the 'AAA', with which Japan extolled itself in Indochina as the 'Light of Asia, Protector of Asia, and Leader of Asia'? The history of earlier Japanese conquests, in particular the fate of Korea since 1905 or Taiwan since 1898, reveals a hard and authoritarian rule, in which 'native policy' served to keep peace and further the interests of the colonial power, in exactly the same way as in European possessions. During the Second World War Japan did not pursue the same course in South-East Asia, but on the other hand did not forge a completely different one either.

On 8 December 1941, Thailand managed to put up just five hours' resistance to the Japanese. On account of this its sovereignty remained untouched, and it indeed gained territory on its borders with Malaya and Kampuchea. Malaya, on the other hand, was administered as a Japanese colony. Burma obtained independence on 1 August 1943 at the hands of the Japanese, and likewise the Philippines on 14 October. In both cases the occupation power came to an arrangement with recognized national leaders. Ba Maw had already led a semi-autonomous Burmese goverment in the 1930s under British sovereignty, and had built up the National Revolutionary Party. His foreign minister in the Japanese era was the socialist U Nu (born 1907). The Philippine president tolerated under Japanese rule was José P. Laurel, who under the Americans had been a member of the Supreme Court. Manuel Quezon (1878–1944), however, who had been elected in November 1935 as first president of the autonomous Commonwealth of the Philippines (the USA had pledged in 1934 to grant their colony independence after ten years), withdrew with General MacArthur to the Bataan peninsula, and later flew to America.

In Indonesia, Japan permitted in March 1943 the setting-up of a political umbrella movement, the Pusat Tenaga Rakjat (PUTERA), under Sukarno and Hatta, who had decided to co-operate with the temporary conquerors. A 120,000-man militia was mobilized – even with indigenous officers, whereas in Ba Maw's Burmese army, commanding posts were occupied exclusively by Japanese. While Burma formally received independence, however, the Japanese stalled in

Indonesia and sought to build up opposition against Sukarno. Only in September 1944 did Tokyo pledge independence to Indonesia; and only in August 1945 was Sukarno invited to negotiations in Japan, over which the shadow of defeat already hung. He was just in time to fly home to proclaim the independence of the Republic of Indonesia on his own initiative, two days after the Japanese surrender, on 17 August 1945.

It is somewhat easier to understand the confusion of Japanese occupation policy if one knows that the Japanese had every reason to distrust the 'Great Asian' loyalty of the nationalists. They were all playing with marked cards. Everywhere there were close contacts, even secret co-operation, between pro-Japanese collaborators and other elements of the nationalist movements, who were holding back in order to present themselves to the Allies as an anti-Japanese resistance movement, should the fortunes of war change. There was a particularly dramatic about-face in Burma. While British-American-Chinese units were pressing forward to Mandalay, the Burmese army mutinied in March 1945 against its Japanese officers. When MacArthur returned to the Philippines in 1945, he ordered the lenient treatment of collaborators, and assisted his personal friend, Manuel Roxas, who had been a minister under Laurel, in making a new career; he was successful in the first post-war presidential elections. The Americans showed less generosity, however, with the Filipino guerrilla army, which had been fighting against Japan since March 1942. This 'anti-Japanese people's army' (Hukbalahap, short for Hukbong Bayan Laban sa Hapon), was outside the rules of the game: it had fallen under too strong a communist influence.

In the case of Vietnam we have seen the communists on the brink of taking over the leadership of the national movement before 1939. During the war years the juxtaposition of French and Japanese authority in Indochina, complicated by the internal feuds of the French, brought about a plethora of developments which are essential to this account.

For years Japan preserved the French colonial system, which remained loyal to Vichy under the governor-general, Admiral Decoux. Until the end of 1944, Japan never stationed more than 35,000 men in Indochina: internal security was entrusted to the French – who eagerly looked to their own interests. On 22 November 1940 communist cadres in South Vietnam initiated a peasant uprising, which was energetically crushed within a fortnight. French planes bombed the rebellious villages. The Communist Party proclaimed at the time an 'armed struggle against French imperialism and Japanese fascism', in other words making itself the enemy of both the powers present in the country. This hapless strategy arose out of the general confusion of Asian communists at a moment in which Stalin was making a pact with Hitler and Mao Tse-tung forming a united anti-Japanese front with the Kuomintang.

As soon as Ho Chi Minh took over the real leadership of the Vietnamese communists, heroic adventurousness gave way to planned, shrewd strategy. Ho had come to South China in the entourage of the Chinese general Yeh Chien-ying, there becoming at the end of 1940 head of the Communist Central Committee which had fled from North Vietnam. On 8 September 1941 he founded – still under his old pseudonym Nguyen Ai Quoc – a new organization, the Front for the Independence of Vietnam (Viet-Nam Doc Lap Dong Minh, abbreviated to 'Vietmin'). Hitler's invasion of the Soviet Union had clarified the positions. A good communist no longer needed to struggle against all imperialists at the same time, but could seek suitable allies among them. Tactics and politics once again became possible. On 25 October 1941 the first manifesto of the Vietmin was issued. It spoke of 'unity of all social strata, all revolutionary organizations, all ethnic minorities. Alliance with all other oppressed peoples of Indochina. Co-operation with all anti-fascist French elements. One goal: destruction of fascist colonialism and imperialism.'[1]

At this point the future president of the Democratic Republic of Vietnam still stood on extremely unsure ground. At the turn of 1942 he was arrested by the Chinese authorities and went to the Liuchow prison. Chang Fa-kwei, military governor of Chiang Kai-shek in Kwangsi, gathered 600 Vietnamese in his town to employ them as partisans in their homeland. Several non-communist emigrants were to form the political leadership and absorb the Vietmin, which was known to be a communist front organization. Even substantial injections of funds from Chungking did not help, however. There was only one single firm core in the whole house of cards, the only possible initiator of effective action, and that was the Vietmin, which was based on the cadres of the old Communist Party. Giap was already training the first guerrilla units. Chang Fa-kwei found himself exposed; in Chungking he was accused of secret alliance with the Japanese: in other words, he needed a success in Indochina, and for that he needed the Vietmin. Nguyen Ai Quoc, the imprisoned communist leader, was prepared to co-operate, and Chang Fa-kwei suddenly announced to his superiors that he had found an entirely new Vietnamese to head the liberation organization, a so far unknown but highly deserving fighter by the name of Ho Chi Minh. In February 1943 the coup was successful: Ho stood with the blessing of Chungking and of the Americans at the head of the recognized exiled resistance movement for Vietnam. Since that time the Vietnamese communists have never allowed themselves to be forced into the isolation which was to prove the undoing of the Filipino Huks and the Malaysian-Chinese communists.

On the other side of the border, tension mounted between the Japanese and the Vichy French. Admiral Decoux sought support among the Vietnamese educated elite against the military superiority of Japan. He forbade the French to address the Vietnamese – as usual – like small boys, and permitted the use of the Vietnamese language in school lessons. In the middle of the war the number of schoolchildren doubled to 700,000, although this still amounted to only 14 per cent of school-age youth. At the same time the shortage of supplies caused by the war compelled the setting-up of a modest consumer goods industry. Not only were holes being punched, therefore, in the cultural colonial doctrine of France, but also in its economic doctrine.

The Japanese for their part began in the summer of 1943 to carry over into Indochina what they were simultaneously trying out in Burma and the Philippines. They too were on the look-out for allies among the Vietnamese intelligentsia. The French police countered this, arresting pro-Japanese people, and a skirmish between the Sûreté and the Kempeitai by no means always ended with the victory of the stronger. In October 1943 the Japanese were obliged to remove their most important right-hand man, Tran Van An of the old Constitution Party, from Saigon to Taiwan. Some weeks later Ngo Dinh Diem, who had likewise staked his money on the Great East Asian card, fled to Hué under Japanese protection. Less prominent nationalists were given up to the French. In this way the Japanese and the French hoed the political field together until it presented the ideal ground for cultivating the seed being prepared by Ho Chi Minh in Chinese exile.

Far away in Paris, de Gaulle had meanwhile walked along the Champs Elysées; the Vichy regime went under and Admiral Decoux trimmed his course to the prevailing wind: he began to conspire with the Allies via Chungking, a fact which did not remain hidden from the Japanese. From November 1944 the admiral was in office merely as a front for an 'Indochina Council' which in fact received its directives from de Gaulle. The Japanese attacked on 9 March 1945, over-powered all but a handful of the French troops, and had Emperor Bao Dai declare the independence of Vietnam in Hué on 11 March. Unlike Sukarno, however, Bao Dai was not a truly representative national leader; only a few Vietnamese politicians were prepared to take passage in his ship, which was so obviously chained to Japan's sinking one. Ngo Dinh Diem in particular, generally regarded as the future prime minister, dismissed imperial invitations with contempt.

Some months previously, on 6 August 1944, Ho Chi Minh had analysed the political climate of his country with sharp vision and published the result in a Vietmin circular:

> Our maxim is the removal of our enemies one by one. It is a question of using others without being used ourselves. Internally we must make pacts with the Gaullists and the Chinese, because the Gaullists will fight against the French fascists, and the Chinese will turn against the Japanese and the French as soon as their armies set foot in Indochina. . . . We must step up the partisan war and transform it into a general uprising. We must keep the enemy out of breath with constant attacks. . . . Our aim is to set up zones under revolutionary government, and thus gradually form a unified state rule in the whole country. The armed uprising of our people should break out in the last phase of the world war: when England, America and China are trying to take possession of Indochina; when Gaullists are opposing French fascists in Indochina; when the French and Japanese are slaughtering each other and the Franco-Japanese fascists come into conflict with the Democrats. . . . All incapable and weak puppet regimes will then fall. Indochina will fall into anarchy. We will not need to seize power then, because there will no longer be any power.[2]

This is exactly how it happened. On 7 August 1945 – one day after the dropping of the atom bomb on Hiroshima – Ho Chi Minh formed a Liberation Committee for the Vietnamese people and declared his guerrilla fighters to be the liberation army. On 10 August he commanded the uprising. On 16 August – one day after the general armistice – the Japanese released all political prisoners in Hanoi. On 21 August the Vietmin was in charge of the city without encountering any resistance. On 25 August two Vietmin delegates made Emperor Bao Dai hand over the state seal in Hué and the red flag was hoisted over the palace. The monarchy of Annam disappeared without so much as a murmur. Even in Saigon, where there had been no more communist cadres since the failed uprising of 1940, Vietmin emissaries took over the leadership – and with it control of the Japanese arsenals. On 2 September Ho Chi Minh proclaimed the Democratic Republic of Vietnam in Hanoi. The proclamation opens with a quotation from the American Declaration of Independence (1776) and a reference to the Paris Declaration of the Rights of Man (1789).

In Indochina, French internal strife between Pétain and de Gaulle played only a secondary role beside that of Japanese expansion. In **Africa**, however, it was this discord in the ruling nation which caused colonial history to be transformed into the history of decolonization. The fact that Frenchmen took up arms there against other Frenchmen was not the decisive factor; this occurred only in Gabon at the beginning of 1940 (and later in Syria). The initiative did not proceed from the side of the colonized at all, but remained in French hands: in order to strengthen his questionable legitimacy by deeds, Charles de Gaulle introduced a reform policy in 'his' Africa about which he clearly nurtured illusions.

De Gaulle believed that he could bolster the renown of France among Africans by means of reform and thus reinforce the French position. This was certainly also the goal of the man who had declared himself a supporter of de Gaulle as the first administrative head of a French territory – the governor of the Chad colony – in August 1940, and who was rewarded by de Gaulle in November 1941 with the office of governor-general of the AEF: Félix Eboué (1885–1944).

Eboué came from Cayenne, and his skin was black. Nevertheless he was by no means an African nationalist, but a French patriot. A career colonial official, he was already a man of 51 when he became governor of Guadeloupe; white Frenchmen made quicker progress in the overseas service. Under the People's Front government, in 1936, he had organized in Guadeloupe the first elections which were not manipulated, in which the population and not the administration determined the result. In 1939 the Third Republic's last minister of the colonies, Georges Mandel, posted him to Chad.

Eboué was an assimilationist on principle, but not a dogmatist.

The colour of his own skin may have taught him that it is not enough to do honour to the abstract human worth of the African by bestowing on him French civilization and, in the last resort, French civil rights. In his programme for a 'new native policy for AEF' in November 1941, Eboué wrote:

> If we [i.e. the French] want to set up or remodel a society [in Africa] – perhaps not according to our model, but at least according to our thinking habits – we are bound to fail. The native has mores, laws, and a fatherland [*patrie*] which are not ours. We cannot bring him happiness according to the principles of the French Revolution, which is our revolution, nor by introducing the Napoleonic Code, which is our book of statutes, nor by placing our officials in place of his chiefs. Because our officials will indeed think for him, but not with his head. On the contrary: we can only ensure his equilibrium if we proceed from his own self in our treatment of him.[3]

In practice Eboué wanted in the first instance to create local self-administration, the proponents of which were to be men of a new type, the 'notable *évolué*': Eboué wanted to open up the world of modern civilization to a number of Africans without at the same time uprooting them culturally. They were to remain anchored in their own *patrie*, but nevertheless to exercise those civil rights which Eboué, like de Gaulle and every other Frenchman, tended to imagine were the prerogative of the French Republic. We can see today that there was an error of judgement concealed in this aim, that the path being trodden would one day lead to the demand for autonomy, and then to independence. The fact remained hidden during the war years, since the reforms themselves were in any case impeded by a range of practical difficulties. This political decision nevertheless pointed the way for the post-war period: France was putting into operation in tropical Africa, of its own volition, without pressure from an anti-colonial party, its hitherto lethargic native policy, an operation characterized by an intentional synthesis between cultural-political modernization and respect for African autonomy. Eboué deserves the credit for having conceived this policy; de Gaulle merely had the honour of giving him the green light.

The carrying-over of this new policy to French West Africa, which came under Gaullist administration in 1943, presented no great difficulties. In North Africa, on the other hand, de Gaulle was not able to call the shots as he liked. There he had to take into consideration indigenous national parties which were already in the middle of a maturing process and which thought themselves able to make use of this hour of French weakness to suit their own ends. The Allies – the British and the Americans – were also pursuing their own policies in this part of the world, which did not necessarily suit France's interests. France was politically on the defensive in Morocco, Algeria, and Tunisia in the final phase of the Second World War, although by no means as hopelessly as in Vietnam. During the Casablanca Conference, on 22 January 1943, President Roosevelt met Sultan Mohammed ben Yusuf, by now 33 years old, and in the same year Moroccan nationalism formed itself, with the monarch's blessing, into a new party, which took the name Istiqlal – 'independence'. When on 10 February 1943, in Algiers, Ferhat Abbas and twenty-eight other representatives of the Muslim population signed a 'manifesto of the Algerian people', they handed this document not only to the French governor-general, Peyrouton (the right-hand man of the Americans, not de Gaulle), but also to the US diplomat R. D. Murphy, and to the Soviet representative in North Africa, Alexander Bogomolow, as well as to a British official. With express reference to Roosevelt and the Atlantic Charter, the manifesto demanded the 'condemnation and lifting of colonial rule, that is the annexation and exploitation of one people by another . . . the application of the right to self-determination of peoples to all small and large countries, the granting of its own constitution to Algeria and the guaranteeing of absolute equality of all its inhabitants without regard to race or religion'.[4]

The Algerian manifesto did not demand independence. Ferhat Abbas was apparently prepared even now to remain loyal to the French republic, if France was only prepared to recognize honestly the separate existence and human equality of the Muslim Algerian people. Basically, therefore, the ideas of Ferhat Abbas and Félix Eboué were by no means worlds apart. De Gaulle, however, who was generous enough to give a free reforming hand to a French governor-general with a black skin, was not willing to consider backing down before North African nationalists, who were furthermore trying to seek support from America.

At the end of May de Gaulle set off for Algiers, glossed over the former Vichy administration and friends of America among the French with an elegance which still merits admiration today, and had the new governor-general of Algeria, the Gaullist General Catroux, announce forthwith: 'Algeria is an integral part of France.' The manifesto was disregarded, and Ferhat Abbas was placed under house arrest for a couple of weeks in September 1943. In January 1944 in Morocco the Istiqlal leaders found themselves under lock and key. In Tunis, the French General Juin removed from office the Bey Moncef, because he had collaborated with the Axis powers during the months of German-Italian occupation. Habib Bourguiba did allow himself to be liberated by the Italians when the French Vichy zone was occupied in November 1942, and even spoke via Bari radio to the Tunisians, being transferred back to his homeland at the beginning of April 1943, a few weeks before the German capitulation. Bourguiba was far too shrewd, however, to have any truck with the Axis powers. He clearly foresaw their military defeat. Instead, towards the end of the German occupation, he sought the sympathy of the US consul. Neither this protection, however, nor the call 'Form a bloc with France now, outside France there is no well-being!', could keep the people's tribune from fresh arrest by the French protectorate authorities.

After the elimination of North African nationalist leaders, de Gaulle was also prepared to reform in this part of the colonial empire. On 7 March 1944, he granted French citizenship to about 60,000 Algerian Muslims, increased the number of Muslim subjects who were eligible to vote (for the third chamber of the Délégations Financières) from 200,000 to 1.6 million, and indeed also addressed these 'Français Musulmans' as 'potential citizens'. To put it crudely, he warmed up the Blum-Violette assimilation plan of 1936. These measures came exactly eight years too late, however. The 'manifesto of the Algerian people' was no longer going to be silenced.

At the end of January 1944 de Gaulle gathered the governors of West and Equatorial Africa at a conference in Brazzaville, the direct importance of which is often overestimated in France. Brazzaville in 1944 did as little to herald decolonization as the Berlin Congo Conference had done in 1885 to parcel out Africa among the great powers. The reforms introduced at Brazzaville petered out in the technical sphere. High-ranking colonial officials, who kept to themselves in Brazzaville (Africans gaining the floor only indirectly through memoranda, according to an account by Félix Eboué), did not want to decolonize, but to colonize better, and probably also more humanely. The political resolution of the conference states categorically at the very beginning:

The purposes of the civilizing work being carried out by France in its colonies exclude any idea of autonomy and any possibility for development outside the French imperial bloc; the possible future establishment of self-government in the colonies is – even in the remote future – excluded.[5]

Among the Allies, de Gaulle could count on sympathy from Winston Churchill for his wartime colonial policy, which combined a willingness for reform with principled steadfastness against anti-colonial demands. Through the mouth of Stafford Cripps (1889–1952), the British government promised in 1942 to grant **India** dominion status – after the war. It did not back down, however, when Congress rejected the formation of an all-Indian war cabinet in order to exert pressure on London. On 8 August 1942 the Congress Committee went so far as to adopt its famous 'Quit India' resolution asking for an immediate ending of British rule

both for the sake of India and for the success of the cause of the United Nations [meaning at that time the anti-Axis war coalition]. The continuance of that rule is degrading and enfeebling India and making her progressively less capable of defending herself and of contributing to the cause of world freedom.[6]

Britain once again showed an iron hand. The unrest unleashed by Congress with its appeal for non-violent mass struggle cost, according to official reports, the lives of 100 members of the security forces and 1,028 rebels. Nehru later considered a figure of 10,000 dead more probable.

In spite of its enormous military and economic strength, the United States was powerless against this tough policy of the British and French colonial administrations. Even in conjunction with the hard-pressed Soviet Allies, Roosevelt had not been able to force the more minor partners into the policy of international trusteeship he had in mind. He nevertheless continued to try to persuade them, since this dream was one of Roosevelt's favourite concepts. The words of Wendell Willkie, his unsuccessful rival in the 1940 presidential election, written at the end of 1942 in his report of a world tour, could have been taken out of the president's mouth: 'In Africa, in the Middle East, throughout the Arab world, as well as in China and the whole Far East, freedom means the orderly but scheduled abolition of the colonial system. Whether we like it or not, this is true.'[7]

In 1944, Stalin showed a cautious interest in Roosevelt's ideas, since if the future International Organization was to inherit from the colonial empires, the Soviet Union might obtain a right to consultation in South Asia and Africa. Stalin was a realist, however, and was not willing to anger the British for the sake of such vague speculations. As the Yalta conference was being prepared, Roosevelt himself felt obliged to keep a low profile and to present a watered-down proposal for international trusteeship: only in the former mandated territories of the League of Nations and in those regions to be taken away from enemy states was the world organization to set up trustee administrations under its own power. For the other colonies the ruling powers were to make a general pledge to lead them to independence and to give the United Nations Organization progress reports within certain limits.

Even to this project, Winston Churchill reacted at Yalta with some well-directed footwork; the conference protocol states:

> The Prime Minister interrupted with great vigour to say that he did not agree with one single word of this report on trusteeships. He said that he had not been consulted. . . . Under no circumstances would he ever consent to forty or fifty nations thrusting interfering fingers into the life's existence of the British Empire. As long as he was Prime Minister, he would never yield one scrap of their heritage. . . . He asked how Marshal Stalin would feel if the suggestion was made that the Crimea should be internationalized for use as a summer resort. Marshal Stalin said he would be glad to give the Crimea as a place to be used for meetings of the three powers.[8]

The meeting was interrupted, and Stalin left the Anglo-Saxons to it. Roosevelt and Churchill agreed on the arrangement which was subsequently included in the UN Charter: trusteeship, not under direct UN administration, but as with the former mandate system exercised by individual, colonially experienced nations. This marked the definitive burial of Roosevelt's plans. Only in 1967 did the United Nations (so far unsuccessfully) attempt directly to take over the administration of a dependent territory – Namibia, former South-West Africa.

All things considered, the interference by foreign powers – even the mighty United States – in colonial affairs during the Second World War did not carry a lot of weight. Decolonization, furthered by the shattered prestige of the white man, was preparing itself within the old imperial frameworks: in the bilateral relationship between colonizers and colonized. For the immediate future the most important thing was how the individual colonial empires stood at the end of this great struggle. Apart from Italy and Japan, they were all theoretically in the victors' camp. But what did that really mean?

Who were the victors of the Second World War? Anyone who wants to answer this question without facing too much derision must proceed from the allocation of the five permanent seats in the Security Council of the United Nations. The USA, the Soviet Union, China, Great Britain, and France, according to the wish of the UN founders, were to set the tone of the post-war world, as a kind of 'Holy Alliance'.

The weakest of these 'great powers' in 1945 was undoubtedly the China of Chiang Kai-shek – a former semi-colony. Perhaps China was *in abstracto* called to be the crystallization core of the anti-colonial movements of Asia and Africa, but on account of its exhaustion from decades of war and civil war, the Republic of China was unable to play such a role. The strongest, and indeed the only truly victorious power, was the United States – the most important white industrial nation, trapped in a world of anti-colonial feeling flavoured by memories of its own historical origins. Roosevelt had tried to pursue a policy on this basis, but Roosevelt was dead; none the less the repercussions of his emotional anti-colonialism continued to have an effect. Between the two extremes of the United States and China stood the three other major powers, who themselves had colonial interests to protect: the Soviet Union, Britain, and France. Moscow denied being a colonial ruler; it was strong enough to prevent anti-colonial outbreaks in its empire (or to conceal them), and was above all too strong for other powers to dare to interfere in its 'internal affairs'. France had been so enfeebled by the war that it had had to conquer an important part of its empire – Indochina – all over again; it was in such a state of inner turbulence and so filled with the critical reforming zeal of the resistance movement, that many representatives of colonized peoples placed their confidence in it. Great Britain was in a comparably secure middle position. Exhausted by the war effort, it had after all been humiliatingly defeated in one part of its empire – Malaya. Between 1939 and 1945, not only had the colonized peoples in the main kept quiet – with the exception of India – but also the independent white members of the commonwealth had respected their moral ties with the old motherland – even if, as in the case of South Africa, not without a certain hesitation. Only Eire understood its neutrality, maintained until 1945, as a demonstration of its resolve to separate from the British Commonwealth; the formal secession was proclaimed on 18 April 1949.

The commonwealth policy of the inter-war period, culminating in the Statute of Westminster and the contemporary British colonial policy of 1945, had thus successfully weathered the storm of the Second World War. From the psychological viewpoint, the British nation could have defended its empire as it had defended India after 1918. Instead, however, it entered upon a course of withdrawal from Asia and Africa. The weaker European colonial powers – France, the Netherlands, and Belgium – had no other choice but to follow suit. What in fact was British and European colonialism retreating from, however? From indigenous anti-colonial movements of a non-violent character – that is, from Gandhi, Nkrumah, and Nyerere? From the few national leaders, such as Ho Chi Minh, Ben Bella, or Sukarno, who were prepared to shoot? From US pressure or communist infiltration? None of these questions can be answered with a straight yes, especially not in the case of Britain.

The picture becomes clearer only when the perspective is shifted away from the concept of a retreat bordering on a defeat. Admittedly the Netherlands did experience its relinquishing of Indonesia as a defeat, as later Belgium did its loss of the Congo, and France the end of the first Indochinese war. Great Britain, however, preserved throughout all decolonization operations an awareness, not of retreating, but on the contrary of moving forwards in the direction of a better and healthier world order, or (to put the same thing in different words) of amicably and conscientiously cultivating and furthering a natural process of international growth. For lengthy periods the France of the Fourth and Fifth Republics had similar feelings. The paradox of the 'victorious retreat', so thoroughly ridiculed by Hitler's propagandists after Dunkirk, and which was nevertheless at that time justified, can claim even greater applicability in the case of the history of decolonization. Seen in this light, Britain after the Second World War was not dismantling an empire, but building a commonwealth.

Chapter Eight

THE MULTIRACIAL COMMONWEALTH

The nature of the structure previously known as the 'British family of nations' altered very rapidly after 1945. Now, it was being transformed into the 'multiracial commonwealth'. This term can be traced to the title of the fifth unofficial conference on commonwealth relations, which took place in March 1954 in Lahore (Pakistan). Even the fourth conference in the same series – in September 1949 in Ontario, Canada – had spoken vaguely of a 'changing commonwealth'.[1]

The racial emphasis touches the heart of the historical process marked by the independence dates of India and Pakistan, Ceylon, Ghana, Nigeria, Tanganyika, Zambia, Jamaica, Malaya, and the other commonwealth states. It is not the done thing nowadays – and for good reason – to work with the racial concept. 'Race' here, however, does not mean a biological term, but the 'spontaneous' arrogance of 'whites' in relation to black, brown, and yellow people. In the 'commonwealth club', so exclusive that it accepts only prime ministers, dark faces suddenly appeared, and in fact even formed the majority. This did not signify a catastrophe, however, since in this exclusive club no voting of course ever takes place. It is nevertheless an interesting fact, in general appreciatively noted, that no newcomer disputed his title with the club's aged chairman, Great Britain. It was not until 1965–6 that this reverent manner, the foundation of club life, began to falter when some members broke off relations with London during the Rhodesia crisis. Earlier, a senior member – South Africa – had departed, but there had been no real shedding of tears over this: South Africa was regarded as a crank. The new members, on the other hand, showed their best side, as gentlemen, as soon as they appeared in the club. So it was possible to look discreetly away from certain rumours which showed their morals at home in a bad light. The club was content with itself for many years.

It was not even necessary to change the rules of the club in order to accept the new members: there were no rules on admission. One had only to reinterpret traditions. Exceptions became the rule: such as, for example, the membership of republics. They did not pay homage to the Crown in the usual way, but only to the 'head of the commonwealth'. Above all the procedure for acceptance was speeded up. Who saw to it that it was? No single member can take the credit for it alone.

The election victory of the British Labour Party in July 1945, in the middle of the Potsdam Conference, was of great significance for the future of the commonwealth. The colonial policy theses of the Labour Party and the Conservatives had never been in stark opposition to each other, either before or after 1945, if one views the parties as a whole. Since Winston Churchill, however, had risen in the war years from an 'outsider' to undisputed leader of the Conservatives, his own tough colonial doctrine must be taken into consideration. After victory, this doctrine would perhaps have come to the fore in a purely Conservative government even more colourfully (and perhaps disastrously) than it did within the war coalition. Clement Attlee did not have such strong control of his party. The still lively criticism of British colonialism, which since the time of Wilberforce had appealed both to the Christian-humanitarian and the socialist conscience which had persistently been demanding human rights for the oppressed, and to which the 'unscrambling' of the empire did not sound nearly so terrible as it did to Churchill, was relatively easy for Labour policy to assert. The conscience of the Labour Party had been particularly quickened by the colonial debates of the 1920s and 1930s, not least in the second International; in the Fabian Colonial Bureau and in the Imperial Advisory Committee, the intellectual energy the government needed after 1945 for a generous overseas policy had been accumulating during the war. Arthur Creech Jones (1891–1964), chairman of both institutions, was Attlee's secretary of state for the colonies from 1946 to 1950. Clement Attlee knew how to harness this energy. It is futile to ask how Churchill would have handled individual issues, but the collision between the prime minister and the leader of the opposition on 20 December 1946 shows that we can by no means be certain that Churchill would have opened the doors to the independence of India and the other colonies as Attlee did, or done it so quickly. It is true that Churchill's Conservative colonial secretary, Oliver Stanley (1942–5), had introduced reforms; he had prepared the Colonial Development and Welfare Act of 1945 which laid down the principle of British development aid for the dependencies – at first with the modest allocation of £120 million for the ten years after 1946. This very measure, however, was more proper to an enlightened colonial policy than to politically planned decolonization.

On 20 December 1946, Prime Minister Attlee said in the House of Commons debate:

> I would repeat, so far as Burma is concerned, what I have already said with regard to India. We do not desire to retain within the commonwealth and empire any unwilling peoples. It is for the people of Burma to decide their own future. . . . It is the desire and intention of His Majesty's Government to hasten forward the time when Burma shall realize her independence, either within or without the Commonwealth, but for the sake of the Burmese people it is of the utmost importance that this should be an orderly – though rapid – progress.

To this, the leader of the opposition, Churchill, replied:

> It was said, in the days of the great Administration of Lord Chatham, that one had to get up very early in the morning in order not to miss some of the gains and accessions of territory which were then characteristic of our fortune. The no less memorable Administration of the right hon. gentleman opposite is distinguished for the opposite set of experiences. The British Empire seems to be running off as fast as the American Loan. The steady and remorseless process of divesting ourselves of what has been gained by so many generations of toil, administration and sacrifice continues. In the case of Burma it is hardly a year since . . . the Japanese were forced to surrender, destroyed, or driven out, and the country was liberated. And yet . . . there is this extraordinary haste that we should take the necessary measures to get out of Burma finally and for ever.[2]

This romantic enthusiasm for the old and the recent past, this refusal to look in any other direction than backwards, are too much in accordance with Churchill's resistance to Roosevelt's trusteeship plans during the war to be explained away merely by the tension of a parliamentary debate. The fact that the same Churchill, on his return to power in August 1951, refrained from stopping the process of decolonization does nothing to alter his potential policy of 1946 or 1947.

Labour policy was summarized in 1947 in the formula: 'to guide the colonial territories to responsible self-government within the commonwealth in conditions that ensure to the people both a fair standard of living and freedom from oppression from any quarter'.[3] This formula goes beyond Attlee's words of December 1946 in two respects. On the one hand, Labour was trying to retain the new independent nations for the commonwealth; on the other it was seeking to impart to them on the way certain economic and political structures which seem wholesome in British eyes. 'Freedom from oppression' clearly meant not only the capacity of the new states to survive in the international arena (meaning their military potential), but also a certain guarantee of constitutional freedom. One can assume that the decolonization policy of the Labour government of 1945–51 took for granted that it would leave behind in Asia and Africa democracies on the Westminster model. Of India, Attlee said with pride on 15 March 1946 in the House of Commons: 'She has learned from us principles of democracy and justice. When Indians attack our rule, they base their attack not on Indian principles, but on the basis of standards derived from Britain.'[4] This is certainly not the whole truth. Attlee seems at that time to have known little of Gandhi's personal philosophy and Nehru's Marxist leanings. The sentence nevertheless throws light on the self-assured confidence with which the Labour government embarked on its policy of decolonization.

THE CEYLON MODEL

They did not need to coin new formulas and procedures. Away from the violent disagreements over India and far from the paternalistic stagnation of the African colonies, Britain had evolved a serviceable model for the emancipation of a 'coloured' crown colony: Ceylon. The transfer to a 'coloured' people of rules of evolution which had been applied since 1839 to white colonists, culminating in the Statute of Westminster, was already well under way in Ceylon. It is not possible to state who at what point decided to make such a transfer: no debate as to whether or not the principles which held good for Canada, Australia, and among the whites in South Africa were also good for the Sinhalese (and Tamils) seems to have taken place, either in Britain or in the colony itself.

The 'semi-responsible government' of Ceylon linked from 1931 extensive and unified franchise (without the encapsulation of ethnic-religious 'communities', without provisos concerning property or education, and without discrimination against women) with genuine powers of people's representation in the State Council and genuine responsibility in the hands of indigenous executive officials. Until the war, however, ministers remained more dependent on the British governor than on the elected people's representatives. The State Council was nevertheless representative enough to formulate in 1943 the desire of the population for complete self-rule, and to inform London of this. Exactly as Cripps had promised the Indians, so the war coalition now promised similar reform to the people of Ceylon – albeit after the victory. However, what had sounded in the ears of Congress politicians, who had so far been kept away from genuine state power, like cheap consolation, was judged in Ceylon to be a reliable prediction. In 1944–5 a commission under Lord Soulbury was working out British proposals, and the State Council voted in favour by fifty-one votes to three. In 1946 Ceylon received the insignia of 'responsible government': a prime minister with a cabinet, and instead of the State Council a two-chamber parliament. The democratically elected first prime minister, D. S. Senanayake (1884–1952), was able without dramatic gestures to negotiate the transfer of the last state functions remaining before Ceylon could achieve full independence: military jurisdiction, foreign policy, and full control over its civil servants.

Whereas in the Statute of Westminster the word 'independence' does not appear and no 'white' commonwealth member has ever been released from the motherland into independence by way of express legislation,[5] this path was adopted for Ceylon, as it had been a few months earlier for India and Pakistan; the same procedure also became the rule for the decolonization of British Africa. In December 1947, the British parliament passed the Ceylon Independence Act, which came into effect on 4 February 1948 complete with two 'Ceylon Independence Orders in Council'. Since that day the island has been a sovereign state, with loyalty to the Crown retained, as it has also been in Canada, Australia, and New Zealand. Until 1972, Queen Elizabeth was head of state in Ceylon with the title 'Elizabeth the Second, Queen of Ceylon and of Her other Realms and Territories, Head of the Commonwealth.'[6]

Ceylon, today Sri Lanka, was not exactly tailor-made for harmonious decolonization. Both before and after 1948 the building of a unified nation has been impeded by ethnic and religious diversity,

exactly as on the Indian subcontinent. In the mid-1950s, the population of Ceylon consisted of 61.4 per cent Sinhalese and 23.3 per cent
Tamils, or 64.4 per cent Buddhists and 19.9 per cent Hindus. A
census in 1981 showed 73.9 per cent Sinhalese and 18.2 per cent
Tamils. Nevertheless the democracy left behind by the colonial power
did function until 1981, allowing the people (a rarity among the new
states of the Third World) to change its government several times by
means of free elections. Only then did the tension between the
Sinhalese and Tamils break through the protective political barriers,
plunging Sri Lanka into civil war.

INDIA AND PAKISTAN

With a greater or lesser number of modifications, the Ceylon model
was implemented in numerous African regions. However, this process was not entirely successful on the Indian subcontinent. Had the
British colonial government adhered for too long to the defence of
'community' interests? Or was the gulf between Muslims and non-
Muslims really so much more difficult to bridge than that between
Sinhalese and Tamils – or, to pre-empt the African situation,
between northern Nigeria and the southern regions? Whatever the
case may be, the Muslim League did not back down from its demand
for Pakistan, put forward in 1940. In September 1944, negotiations
between Gandhi and Mohammed Ali Jinnah were broken off after
just three weeks. On 14 June 1945, one month before elections to the
House of Commons, the Conservative secretary of state for India,
Leopold Amery, announced to the House that the new Indian constitution would have to be devised by the Indians themselves, and that
Great Britain would not impose any constitution against the will of
India. He continued, however: 'His Majesty's Government does not
intend to make any alterations against the wishes of the important
Indian "communities".'[7] The 'will of India' was not, therefore,
equated with a majority decision. In practical terms London was now
finally planning the infusion of democratically legitimated Indian
ministers into the central executive. A constitutional conference was
to clarify the procedures.

This set another precedent to which London was to resort whenever
the decolonization of a region encountered a particular problem, especially inner discord: all the disputing parties met with the British
government at a round table, in order either to find a compromise –

or to let responsibility rest again on the British government.

On 19 February 1946, Attlee officially pledged full self-government. In the spring of 1946 a cabinet commission made a last-ditch attempt to preserve the unity of India. Although it did not succeed in assisting Congress and the Muslim League to unity, it did publish a constitutional plan on 16 May. According to this, a federation was to be created out of the whole of British India, including the principalities – in terms of European concepts more a confederation, since only foreign policy, the military, and long-distance traffic were to be federal matters, all remaining power to reside with the 'provinces'. Special arrangements were envisaged for Punjab, the North-Western Frontier Province, Sind, Baluchistan, Bengal, and Assam. These were the critical regions, in which the population, according to the census of 1942, was divided as follows:[8]

Table 8.1 Regional distribution of Muslims and non-Muslims in India, 1941

	Muslims	Non-Muslims
Punjab	16,217,242	12,201,577
North-Western Frontier Province	2,788,797	249,270
Sind	3,208,325	1,326,683
Baluchistan	438,930	62,701
Bengal	36,005,434	27,301,091
Assam	3,442,479	6,762,254

Every province was to have the right to separate from the Indian Union by means of a re-election of its parliament. The 296 members of the constitutional assembly were to be delegated by the provincial parliaments according to communalist principles.

This proposal gave the Muslims a chance to break their Pakistan away from the Indian Union soon – but only after independence. This was not enough for the league. They demanded that Great Britain take responsibility for the division, after having ruled India for centuries and made it what it was. The viceroy Lord Wavell now came down decisively on the side of the Congress Party, winning it over to co-operation in a provisional national government. On 2 September 1946 Nehru and other Congress politicians joined the Executive Council, which was thereby transformed into an All-India cabinet. Severe disturbances were the direct result, this time no longer directed against the withdrawing colonial power, but an attack by Muslims and non-Muslims against one another – in Calcutta, Dacca, and

Bihar. Who was responsible? The Muslim League had already called for 'direct action' before 2 September, and one must therefore admit that they were the first to call openly for violence. The reaction on the part of militant Hindus, however, was no less violent.

In October 1946 Muslim leaders were suddenly prepared to take part in the provisional central government; the hour of compromise had already passed, however, and co-operation of the disputing parties proved impossible. The Muslim League boycotted the formation of the constitutional assembly, and Britain capitulated in the face of the forces of 'communalism' which it had once so carefully nurtured.

At the end of February 1947 Attlee recalled the viceroy, appointing Lord Mountbatten of Burma as the last holder of this office: he was not only to lower the British flag over India honourably, but above all to observe the proprieties with regard to the division of the subcontinent. Mountbatten fulfilled this thankless task as well as could be expected, and it is indeed his accomplishment that the decolonization of India may for the most part be regarded as a success, in some respects even as exemplary. On 3 June he announced the plan for division over the radio. The Punjab and Bengal were to be divided; the Muslims in those provinces in which they formed a majority could now create their own dominion with a constitutional assembly. Britain was to grant independence simultaneously to the truncated India and to Pakistan – and indeed as soon as possible, without awaiting the outcome of the two constitutional assemblies.

Jinnah grieved over the 'mutilated and moth-eaten Pakistan' he had been presented with but, like Congress, came to terms with the last word of power of Great Britain. On 1 July 1947 the British parliament passed the India Independence Act and on 15 August India and Pakistan stepped on to the stage of world politics as independent states.

Successful decolonization? The division of British India meant the shedding of much blood and mass expulsions for the population. It is said that 8 million Muslims were expelled from India to Pakistan, and as many Hindus from Pakistan to India, and that there were at least 200,000 dead (excluding those who died of hunger or destitution caused by expulsion).[9] The assassination of Gandhi by a Hindu extremist on 30 January 1948 vividly highlighted the outbreak of uncontrolled passion. The new states did not even become homogeneous entities. In the middle of the 1950s almost 10 per cent of the population of India were Muslims; this did not disturb the political philosophy of the Congress government, who did not want to build a Hindu but a secular state. There were, however, almost 13 per cent Hindus in emphatically Islamic Pakistan. The conflict between West Pakistan and Islamic Bengal which led to the foundation of Bangladesh in 1972 was at that time still latent – the Indian-Pakistani conflict over Kashmir, on the other hand, all the more virulent.

The only indisputable success was in fact achieved by Britain itself, which had managed to relieve itself of India without the trouble and expense of a colonial war, and furthermore to the applause of world public opinion. Looking a little further one may add that at least India has up to now preserved the principles of the democratic form of government it inherited from Britain. India, in spite of its economic and social problems – indeed precisely because of the free and honest exposure and discussion of these problems – bears witness to the effective power of certain basic concepts of political conduct which managed to find their way into the baggage of colonizers going to Asia and Africa. It is not the transferability of western democracy, pack and parcel, which is at issue here, but much more modestly the capacity of a few great universal ideas to germinate in Asian and African soil: personal freedom, the right of consultation of the ruled in the political process, the governing of political action by human reason, and at all events the validity of majority decisions . . . the fact that these ideas are still showing signs of life in India, and that in Pakistan also the democratic alternative to authoritarian military domination continues to be stubbornly lodged in the political awareness of the people, must be attributed to the full range of British colonization and decolonization, and not solely to the latter.

BURMA

In the case of Burma, already mentioned briefly (pp. 146f.), it should be added that the London government really did – as Churchill stated in the House of Commons – press the country into independence with a certain amount of haste, without waiting to clear up the complicated political relations which Japan had left behind. At the end of 1946, Attlee recognized the Anti-Fascist People's Freedom League (AFPFL) as a negotiating partner, this having been formed in the latter phase of the Second World War. Its revered leader was the young Aung San (born 1915), previously minister of defence in the collaboration government of Ba Maw. Ba Maw's foreign minister, U Nu, also found a place for himself in the AFPFL. The communists originally played an important role: at the first AFPFL congress in January 1946 the communist Than Tun became general secretary, and thus second-in-command to Aung San, who had been elected president. In October 1946, however, both men were overthrown, and the Burmese Communist Party, known as the 'Communists of the White Flag', withdrew from the league; prior to this a second, left-wing, radical Communist Party of Burma, known as the 'Communists of the Red Flag', was already in opposition under U Soe.

Aung San took over the leadership of the interim government formed by the British governor, concluding on 27 January 1947 in London a transition agreement which was intended to lead Burma to independence. On 9 April a constitutional assembly was elected, in which as expected the AFPFL obtained a substantial majority: the communists took only seven seats. A former prime minister, U Saw (born 1901), however, whose career had been cut short by post-war politics, and who had been interned by the British in Uganda from 1942 until 1946, saw fit to have Aung San and six other ministers attacked and shot by an armed commando group in the assembly hall of the council. U Nu was also intended to die, but escaped his assassins. The governor immediately offered him the leadership of a new government; U Saw was seized, condemned, and hanged in May 1948.

In spite of this bloody incident, Attlee did not delay the decolonization of Burma. On 17 October U Nu concluded a definitive treaty with London, and on 4 January 1948 (astrologers determined the exact date) Burma became independent. It did not apply for membership of the commonwealth. Burdened with the immediate outbreak of a partisan war with the 'White Flag Communists', and with tribal disturbances and bands of Nationalist Chinese soldiers in the north of the country as well as unresolved economic problems to boot, Burma embarked on its journey into the future, which was to lead it into persistent isolation from the rest of the world.

PALESTINE AND THE SUEZ CANAL

Britain under the Labour government similarly made attempts to throw off both its heavy colonial 'millstones' and the responsibility of the colonizer, in its 'solution' to the Palestine question. In this case the

United Nations intervened since, as a former League of Nations mandate, Palestine was one of the few territories in which Roosevelt's trusteeship ideas could be put to the practical test. The result was not particularly encouraging: the United Nations abandoned its own ideas and resorted to the British plan for division, made in the pre-war period. A two-thirds majority of the General Assembly voted on 29 November 1947 for division: the west and its friends (apart from Great Britain and China, who abstained, as well as Greece and Cuba, who voted against) together with the USSR and its followers. Only Muslim UN members, including Pakistan and Turkey, seconded by India, came out against the setting-up of a Jewish state. As planned by the UN the Jewish state was of course considerably smaller than the Israel of 1949–67, western Galilee and access to Jerusalem in particular being absent; the holy city itself was to come under international administration.

In neighbouring Egypt, British troops did leave the country in 1946, but concentrated in the strategically important zone around the Suez Canal, which Britain did not intend to give up. In Palestine, British fighting forces did not seriously intervene when Jews and Arabs entered upon civil war in earnest at the end of 1947. They concentrated instead on unsuccessful attempts to suppress the anti-British terrorism of Jewish extremists, the Lehi or 'Stern band' (after their founder, Abraham Stern), and after the end of the Second World War the Irgun of Menachem Begin, who on 22 July 1946 blew up the British headquarters in Jerusalem's King David Hotel (ninety were killed).

On 14 May 1948 at midnight, as London's Palestine mandate expired, the proclamation of the state of Israel merely marked the beginning of another, even more bloody phase in the war. Through decades full of terror, passages of arms, and uncertain pauses, Palestine has remained a problem without a solution – one of the ugliest monuments to misfired decolonization.

THE GUERRILLA WAR IN MALAYA

Malaya is not typical, since here Britain squarely faced the forces that wanted to oust it, even allowing itself to be drawn into guerrilla warfare, and fighting its way through it tenaciously to victory – before implementing decisive constitutional transitional measures towards independence.

In July 1948 – after Stalin's victory in Prague, but long before the victorious offensive of Mao Tse-tung against the cities of North China – the Communist Party of Malaya struck out against the returned British power. The cadres of the former Malayan People's Anti-Japanese Army, whose modest deeds had been supported in 1942–5 by British material supplies, despite the fact that the Communist Party had previously been banned in Malaya, transformed themselves into the Malayan Races Liberation Army (MRLA), 90 per cent of which was Chinese. The Chinese-Malayan communists opposed a constitution imposed by London on 1 February 1948: out of the nine sultanates and the two British possessions of Penang and Malakka emerged the Federation of Malaya, but of the seventy-five members of its central Legislative Council not a single one was to be elected. The princes retained their rank, and the British high commissioner, i.e. the governor of the new federation, 'advised them on all matters concerning the government of their states'. The anti-monarchist elements among Malayans were disappointed, while the Chinese, who constituted 40 per cent of the population, must have felt particularly neglected. Moreover, Singapore, the island city with a Chinese majority at the southern tip of the peninsula, remained for strategic reasons, as well as in order to prevent a Chinese majority in the new state structure, excluded from the federation. A shorter way to independence could not at that time be discerned, either for Malaya or for Singapore.

Chin Peng, from 1948 until 1957 general secretary of the Malayan Communist Party (a Malay later took his place for cosmetic reasons), could probably never muster more than 5,500 fighters at any one time. Until 1952 their influence on the Chinese section of the population grew, and it almost began to look as if by means of strategic concepts laid down by Mao Tse-tung and Vo Nguyen Giap, they would be able (before the Vietmin) to bring a colonial power to its knees. They met their match, however, in Lieutenant-General Sir Harold Briggs, who from April 1950 was 'Director of Operations' with all appropriate powers. Briggs was able to deploy 40,000 soldiers (among them 10,500 Gurkhas) and 80,000 auxiliary troops. He cut the guerrilla fighters off completely from their supplies. It has been estimated in the press that one dead enemy cost the British an average £20,000; for the Vietnam war fought by the United States, the corresponding figure was only some 10 per cent higher.[10] Six thousand guerrilla fighters were killed, 1,200 were taken prisoner, and 1,700 went over to the other side. Civilian losses were likewise high, but essentially Briggs stifled the uprising by resettling half a million Chinese who lived on the edges of those jungle regions 'infested' with guerrillas. The communists were thus starved out; harvests which they attempted to produce on patches of cleared woodland were destroyed by the Royal Air Force by means of chemical weapons.

It was no cleaner a war than the one in Vietnam, and yet it was hardly noticed in Europe, chiefly because the British public reacted quite differently from the way the French or the Americans did later. By the end of 1951, when the Labour Party had to step down in London, the war in Malaya had already essentially been won. The communists never went beyond the first stage of guerrilla terrorism called for by Giap – terrorism in order to influence the peasant population; they did not succeed in creating 'liberated zones' anywhere on the peninsula.

What was the motive behind this tough British policy? Perhaps the fact that the enemy represented only a small political minority within a minority population; perhaps its communist creed. One must also remember the rubber, however, which in 1950 by a long way outstripped any synthetic substitute, unlike the products of today. Foremost – as in the case of the Suez Canal – was also the strategic interest, painfully heightened by the memory of the fall of Singapore in 1942. Evidently London still believed in the military importance of the commonwealth.

We may furthermore assume that the British government objected to shifting the burden of self-government in former colonies to unknown partners. How Nehru, Jinnah, the politicians of the western-educated upper class of Ceylon, or U Nu would conduct themselves could to some extent be predicted by British politicians. Even the Tunku Abdul Rahman, of whom mention will be made later, came from circles which British colonial politicians tended to take notice of. This was not the case with communist guerrilla leaders of Chinese origin.

LABOUR POLICY IN WEST AFRICA

A man such as Kwame Nkrumah was likewise unpopular with the British and, as we know, they would have preferred to place political responsibility on the Gold Coast in the hands of men from that bourgeois class which had already been represented – albeit sparsely – in the Legislative Council since the end of the First World War. There is no indication that Labour would have paid less heed to this preference for known, 'sensible' partners in decolonization than the Conservatives did. All the same, Attlee saw to it that Britain relinquished this tendency on the Gold Coast soon enough to spare both himself and the colony inconvenience.

Constitutional reform for the most extensively developed British colony in West Africa had been on the agenda since 1939: at that time Lord Hailey wrote a report for the Conservative government, which was not published on account of the outbreak of war. There was general agreement on the direction: the doctrine of Indirect Rule was to be superseded by a new evolution aiming at self-government. But on what kind of time-scale was this to be achieved, and which geographical entities were to prepare themselves for self-government?

When the Labour government put into effect the new Richards and Burns constitutions, named after the governors of Nigeria and the Gold Coast respectively in 1946, these now extended to the interior the partially representative system which had previously applied only to the coastal belts. In Nigeria, the Legislative Council acquired jurisdiction over the whole country; in what would become Ghana, over the Ashanti region; the especially backward north thus remained undisturbed. At first it seemed as if Nigeria was about to take over the leadership of a modern political liberation movement in West Africa. It was here that Nnamdi Azikiwe had founded the National Council of Nigeria and the Cameroons (NCNC) on 26 August 1944. 'Zik', as Azikiwe is known among his compatriots, was at that time 40 years old; he had studied in the USA, and after his return in 1934 had acquired in Accra and Lagos the reputation of a fiery anti-colonial newspaper founder, journalist, and writer. His book *Renascent Africa* (1936) especially pre-empted many of the theses of African post-war nationalism. In 1945, seventeen Nigerian trade unions with a total of some 30,000 members – two-thirds of all workers of the colony who were organized in trade unions – called a general strike. They demanded the raising of the basic daily wage to 2s 6d in order to catch up with the 200 per cent rise in prices of the war years. The strike lasted thirty-seven days and ended with a promise from the colonial government to set up an investigative committee. It wrecked the trade union organizations, which were not fit for such strain, but it nevertheless brought the impulses of modern political life to the whole country for the first time.

172

In Manchester – in October 1945 – the fifth Pan-African Congress met, following on from the meetings organized by W. E. B. DuBois in the 1920s. DuBois was now 77 years old: a younger generation was taking over the active leadership from him, a group of Africans from Africa who wanted to prove themselves in their homelands as practical politicians and not only as ideologists. These included above all Kwame Nkrumah, born on the Gold Coast in 1909, who held degrees from American universities and who had for a short time been a law student in London. The congress called uncompromisingly for 'complete and absolute independence for the peoples of West Africa'; it repudiated not only Indirect Rule as 'obnoxious and oppressive', but also the current constitutional reforms as 'spurious attempts on the part of alien imperialist powers to continue the political enslavement of the peoples'.[11] It was not the future president of Ghana alone who set the character of the congress; the list of participants also included Jomo Kenyatta, Hastings K. Banda, and three Nigerians who were to play an important role in political life later: Jaja Wachuku (NCNC) was minister of foreign affairs for many years; H. O. Davies wrote an authoritative book in 1961 about the chances for democracy in Africa, later also taking over a federal ministry; finally, Obafemi Awolowo (1909–87) struggled for key functions in Nigerian politics as long as he lived.

At home the NCNC preferred less explosive slogans than that of 'complete independence'. Its declarations spoke of 'political freedom' or 'democratic principles'. Of the two open questions concerning British West Africa which have been mentioned above, Azikiwe predominantly took up the second: he wanted the whole of Nigeria to be merged into a single nation, with the NCNC as its backbone. He left the first question, the pace of emancipation, in the background.

The Gold Coast was more backward in every respect. Only in 1947 was a modern political organization formed there, the United Gold Coast Convention (UGCC), which was influenced by a man ten years Azikiwe's senior who had made a name for himself as a lawyer and also as a historian of the medieval kingdom of Ghana: Joseph K. K. B. Danquah (1895–1965). The UGCC criticized the constitution of 1946, which was regarded by the governor, Sir Alan Burns, as a far-reaching plan and by means of which he believed he was already introducing democracy. Were there not two Africans (appointed by him) in the Executive Council? In contrast, the UGCC was demanding 'that by all legitimate and constitutional means the direction and control of government should pass into the hands of the people and their chiefs in the shortest possible time'.[12] The word 'independence' was avoided.

Nigeria's lead in terms of political self-awareness was lost when the leaders of the UGCC decided in 1947 to recall Kwame Nkrumah from London and make him general secretary of their association. At the beginning of 1948 in Accra – as had happened three years earlier in Nigeria – the anger of poorer people at the economic consequences of the war erupted in turbulent political action. There was no strike on the Gold Coast, but a boycott movement against European and Lebanese traders, the effecting of which (on 28 February 1948) led to a demonstration, orders for the police to shoot, and unrest in some cities; there were 29 dead and 237 injured. The UGCC had done as little to organize the boycott as it had to promote the excesses, but it sent a telegram to the colonial secretary in London asking 'in the name of the oppressed, inarticulate, misruled and misgoverned people and their chiefs, that special commissioner be sent out immediately to hand over government to interim government of chiefs and people and to witness immediate calling of Constituent Assembly'.[13] The London Labour government did not act so hastily, however. They sent out the usual royal commission, which after a few months reached the conclusion that the Burns Constitution of 1946 was already outdated. This in itself was no revolution in terms of British colonial thinking. The practical proposal of the commission did, however, cause a sensation: the working-out of a new constitution was to lie entirely in African hands. Britain was for the first time forgoing the prerogative of imposing reforms, or at least determining them in negotiations between Britons and 'natives' while the responsibility for the country remained for the time being in British hands. In India/Pakistan in 1947 the constitutional assemblies had been allowed to work freely, but at a time when the two new states had already obtained independence.

Justice Henley Coussey took over the chairmanship of a committee of forty Africans in December 1948 in order to provide the Gold Coast with a new political order. He had never been politically active, and chiefs and conservative men from the urban bourgeoisie predominated among his colleagues. Whilst the committee worked, Kwame Nkrumah split the UGCC, gathering the radical anti-colonialists, above all youth, from 12 June 1949 into a new party, the Convention People's Party (CPP). Using methods borrowed chiefly from American campaign management, he was able to popularize the CPP among the whole people. His specific anti-colonial fighting tactic was borrowed from Gandhi. In organizational terms the CPP likewise was and remained more similar to an American party or the Indian Congress than the parties built up in some of the French colonies.

Even if the foremost elder politicians in Accra, and especially the British officials, did like to turn their noses up at the CPP, saying of them that Nkrumah drew his support mainly from the 'verandah boys', unemployed young men who hung around in all African towns, a political force was none the less growing there which would soon cut loose from the leading strings of colonial willingness to reform, in order to take the fate of Ghana (as they called the Gold Coast, incidentally after a former suggestion by Danquah) into their own hands. It is to the credit both of Nkrumah and British government staff that in spite of this there was not a complete rift, and that decolonization was achieved with harmony between the rulers and the ruled. The initiative in Ghana, however, lay from 1949 onwards at least as strongly with the 'natives' as it had in India since Gandhi's second *satyagraha* campaign of 1930.

Justice Coussey presented his report on 17 August 1949 and on 14 October the colonial secretary, Creech Jones, agreed to it. The whole country (including the northern region) was to obtain a legislative assembly. By a tiny majority, the committee proposed a two-chamber parliament in order to be able to dispose of the chiefs in the Senate. On this point alone London went against the report, decreeing the formation of a single-chamber parliament: of the eighty-four members, five were to be directly elected in the larger cities (Accra, Cape Coast, Sekondi-Takoradi, and Kumasi), thirty-three from the country districts of the south and the Ashanti territory through electors, nineteen from the north through a special voting body; eighteen members were to represent the chiefs and were to be delegated by their assemblies. There were an additional three high colonial officials as *ex-officio* members and six representatives of the business world, of whom, however, only two had the right to vote. Elected people's representatives thus had a clear majority. Eight African ministers, members of the Legislative Assembly and carried by the confidence of their majority, were to form part of the executive (presided over by the governor), in addition to three colonial officials. One of them was to act as 'leader of the house', that is, leader of the majority and unofficial prime minister. Creech Jones remarked expressly in a message to the British governor of 14 October that this system could only function if a party system emerged on the Gold Coast. He can hardly have been thinking of the predominance of the CPP, although this is of secondary importance, more important being the conscious and intentional breakthrough to a modern, representative democracy on the Gold Coast, even if the former indirect rulers were to be infiltrated into it. In this way the Coussey Constitution stamped itself as a transition arrangement to be followed in the short or long term by full self-government, and thus also independence.

Nkrumah was not satisfied with this. He proclaimed the slogan 'self-government now', rejected the constitution and began in January 1950 a campaign of 'positive action'. By this he meant Gandhi-type 'non-violent non-cooperation' with the colonial government, in practice strikes, a boycott on trade and administration, and demonstrations. The new governor, Sir Charles Arden-Clarke (1898–1962), who had arrived in 1949, countered with a state of emergency and a wave of arrests, which brought Nkrumah himself to prison on 22 January. He was sentenced to three years.

The British could see clearly that Nkrumah was working on the Indian model, but they did not believe that he would succeed. 'You must think seriously before you take this step,' Nkrumah was told by Reginald H. Saloway, an ex-Indian civil servant and colonial secretary to the governor, in a private meeting at the end of December 1949. 'Take India, for instance. Now India was a very different matter. The Indian was used to suffering pains and deprivations, but the African has not that spirit of endurance. Mark my words, my good man: within three days the people here will let you down.'[14]

Saloway was proved right – in the end. But it took the people of Ghana fifteen years to let Nkrumah down, a bit longer than he had predicted. For the moment, Saloway himself and the governor made it easy in 1950–1 for the CPP to hold out. The state of emergency declared on 11 January was lifted again six weeks after Nkrumah's arrest – on 6 March – to make preparations easier for the district and legislative elections. Important CPP leaders, chiefly Komla A. Gbedemah (born 1912), were released after serving only short sentences. A readiness for compromise also prevailed on the other side. Although the CPP rejected the Coussey Constitution, it did not consider boycotting the elections which were to make that constitution a reality. Nkrumah was spared the long years of struggle for the principle of self-government in a central governing body, such as Gandhi had had to go through. 'Positive action' raised Nkrumah's prestige and that of the CPP, chasing other political elements, above all the conservatives and the chiefs, out of the field.

On 1 April 1950 the CPP gained all the seats on the city council of Accra, and in November all seats in the city council of Kumasi. This victory in the Ashanti capital, the stronghold of the chiefs, came as a surprise. The chiefs had still tried to secure the candidate nominations for parliament by pre-empting the one-party system with the intention of merging all parties into a Gold Coast National Congress controlled by themselves. The CPP was already too strong, however. Not only in the towns, but also in the rural districts of the south and of the Ashanti country, the elections of 8 February 1951 were marked by a party contest between the CPP and conservative groups. In the towns the CPP gained 58,858 votes against the 5,574 of all other candidates; of the rural electors they could put 1,936 against 788: thirty-four of the thirty-eight seats to be held by these two groups fell to the CPP. Even some chiefs (out of their eighteen representatives) and northern members (out of their nineteen representatives) soon went over to the side of the victors. Kwame Nkrumah was elected by 22,780 out of a possible 23,122 votes in his own constituency in Accra. On 12 February he left prison, was presented to the governor and entrusted with the selection of the African ministers for the Executive Council. With this he took the government of Ghana into his hands.

This result was thus achieved by both sides forgoing a rigid adherence to principle. The colonial government left off what had in any case not been a particularly energetic attempt to crush the CPP before the elections, and certainly after Nkrumah's victory. The 'promotion' of a prisoner to the status of prime minister was celebrated as a sporting achievement, and indeed later successfully repeated in several cases (Banda, Kenyatta, Makarios). Nkrumah contributed even more to the success of the compromise, by working loyally with the instrument of a bedevilled constitution, and consequently did not relinquish his goals, although still quietly omitting the 'now' part of his call for self-government. He thus brought about precisely what the UGCC had been calling for since 1947. Was this only so that he, Nkrumah, could stand at the head, and not Danquah or another? It would be unjust to attribute to him such personal ambition and nothing else. In truth Nkrumah had created an instrument of power in the CPP which no politician on the Gold Coast had possessed before him, and which permitted him alone to co-operate with the British power, which was so much stronger. Without the 'hotline' to the masses of the common people which the CPP represented, at least in the beginning, Nkrumah might well have become a tool of the British. He himself must have feared changing his prison cell in the end for a golden cage.

One week after being sworn into office, Nkrumah wrote to CPP members:

> There is a great risk in accepting office under this new Constitution which still makes us half slaves and half free. . . . Hence we call for vigilance and moral courage to withstand the evil manoeuvres in imperialism. Bribery and corruption, both moral and factual, have eaten into the whole fabric of our society and these must be stamped out if we are to achieve any progress. Our election to the Assembly shows that the public has confidence in the integrity of the Party, and that we will not stoop low to contaminate ourselves with bribery and corruption at the expense of the people. The trust which the people have placed in the CPP is the most precious thing we possess; and as long as that trust and confidence is maintained, there is victory for us. . . . What the people of this country want is real political power to manage their own affairs without leaving power in the hands of a single person appointed by an alien power, however paternalistic in kind.[15]

Macabre prophecy? We must not judge from the experience of later years. In 1951 Nkrumah stood alone in a wide arena as the African head of government of a British colony. On the strength of his own skill and obstinacy, he had to create a precedent and open the way to independence for the whole of British Africa. This was no self-aggrandizement, such as Nkrumah cultivated later in the Organization of African Unity (OAU), when he made enemies of important heads of state with his demand for the immediate setting-up of a union government for the whole continent. In 1951–7, his role as forerunner and pioneer, at least for the British colonies in Africa, was sober reality.

Nigeria in the mean time had not by a long way achieved anything comparable. Azikiwe had not swept to the position of a generally recognized national leader, and indeed could not do so in Nigeria, which was so much larger and structurally more complicated. Whereas the CPP, at least in the first phase and among the younger generation, managed to overcome tribal boundaries, the NCNC only became a firmly rooted party among Azikiwe's own people, the Ibo of the eastern Nigerian region. It was precisely the fact that Nkrumah did not stem from any great ethnic group which had initially favoured the 'national' claims of the CPP; only later did Nkrumah feel compelled to weave around himself the pseudo-sacred aura of the 'Osagyefo', seizing upon a princely title in order to triumph over the real princes of the more powerful communities, above all the Ashanti. Initially, Azikiwe was able to rely on a loyal following among a relatively important people. He did always seek 'national', that is, all-Nigerian effectiveness, but it was just this weight of the Ibo which frightened many other groups away from the NCNC. In 1951 Awolowo reorganized among his people, the Yoruba of the western region, a cultural association to the rival political party, the Action Group (AG). Almost at the same time the emirs of the northern region, the privileged and exemplary pillars of the *ancien régime*, also decided to don the cloak of modern party politics. They founded the Northern People's Congress (NPC) under the leadership of the sardauna of Sokoto, Alhaji Ahmadu Bello (1910–66).

Creech Jones brought a certain buoyancy and elasticity into the colonial government of Nigeria by appointing two conciliatory officials to key positions: Sir John Macpherson became governor and Hugh Foot (after 1964 Lord Caradon) his chief secretary. Before its resignation in 1951, however, the Labour government did not have to make any such momentous or dramatic decisions for this colony as it did for the Gold Coast. Political radicalism in Nigeria remained restricted to a splinter group, the Zikist Movement, founded in 1946, which adopted Azikiwe's name, but was never in fact directly led by him. The Zikists (among whom were many brilliant intellectuals, who later rapidly became more moderate) spoke gladly and often of 'positive action' and tried to organize a general strike and a tax boycott. The masses, however, did not co-operate, and when the British banned the Zikist Movement in April 1950 the excitement soon subsided. The fulcrum of political life in Nigeria lay with the counterpart of the Coussey Commission, that is, the various regional reform committees which reported from March until September 1949 and then finally co-ordinated their results at a 'General Conference'. This consisted of fifty-three people (of whom only three were non-Nigerians) and met in Ibadan in January 1950. From the multi-level discussion, in which the predominant concern was that the north should not be under the tutelage of the more highly developed south, emerged the new Macpherson Constitution of 1951.

Nigeria obtained a federal parliament (House of Representatives) with an elected majority and indigenous ministers in a central executive. The federation, however, remained as loose as possible. Three regions were chosen as constituent states: the north, the south-east, and the south-west; the substance of governmental power, placed in the hands of Africans, now lay with the regions. The south was thereby split and the north remained a giant conservative bloc, embracing not only the former Fulbe kingdom of Usman dan Fodio (including conquered territories in Yoruba country), but also peoples such as the Tiv (to the north of the eastern region), which had never been subdued by the emirs. The federal parliament consisted solely of delegates from the three regional parliaments. It may be said that this constitution represents a variation on the theme of the old Anglo-Indian 'communalism', although the 'communities' were geographically fixed from the outset. In this way Britain under Attlee saw to it that federalism could put down roots in Nigeria; this did not prevent the Biafra civil war (1967–70), but it did survive it.

This shrewd foresight did not impede the dynamic elements within Nigerian politics – Azikiwe in particular – or the creators of new Ghana, from thoroughly condemning the Macpherson Constitution. They saw African nationalism as the loser in this game, which had ended in the first instance in favour of continued British control, but above all in favour of the aristocrats of northern Nigeria.

CONSERVATIVE POLICY IN WEST AFRICA AND SUDAN

The colonial balance of the Labour years amounted to some new, independent commonwealth members in South Asia; withdrawal from Palestine and Egypt, albeit without relinquishing the Suez Canal military zone; a successful anti-guerrilla campaign in Malaya; and the beginnings of self-government in West Africa. But there was also recalcitrance in East and Central Africa. The Conservatives, victorious in the British elections of October 1951, were not taking over a unified, reformed empire, but a gigantic building site.

They continued to build. One can appreciate what this must have meant to the new prime minister, Winston Churchill, who nevertheless accommodated himself to the facts and made no attempt to restore a colonial empire. Even in an earlier Conservative election brochure of 1949, which still bears the proud title *Imperial Policy*, we read:

180

The Conservative Party reaffirms that self-government within the British Empire and Commonwealth is an aim to be achieved as soon as Colonial peoples are ready for it.

It is impossible to state in black and white the precise moment at which a country is ready to govern itself, but the Party considers that two conditions should be laid down which should be fulfilled before full self-government is achieved:

(1) That the country is economically sound and that social services have reached a reasonable standard of efficiency.
(2) That power can be transferred to the people as a whole and not to a small and unrepresentative political, racial or religious oligarchy.[16]

The years of Conservative administration until 1964 demonstrate that both decisive concessions of this programme were seriously intended: self-government for everyone, and the setting aside of the autocratic upper social strata who had exercised Indirect Rule, in favour of democratically legitimated majority representatives.

Nkrumah was able to implement his concept of a constitution for Ghana. He deprived the chiefs of power, permitted no regional autonomy, and secured for the CPP – not least by virtue of the British system of majority vote in single-member constituencies – an incontestable parliamentary majority. The opposition called in vain for a federal constitution or other insurances against a one-party dictatorship – such as an upper house of chiefs. Not only did Nkrumah shrug off all resistance, including the moderate decentralization plans of the British constitutional adviser, Sir Frederick Bourne, whom he invited himself in 1955; the London government likewise turned a deaf ear to warnings and federalist proposals, put forward largely by Ashanti politicians.

Nkrumah recognized only the new nation of Ghana. London (now the Eden Cabinet, in which Alan Lennox-Boyd was colonial secretary) demanded, before Ghana was to be given independence, only one more general election, in order to test the influence of the CPP. In the first general and equal parliamentary elections of the future Ghana on 15 June 1954, the CPP had obtained seventy-one seats (with 391,817 votes), five opposition parties and independent candidates together obtaining thirty-three seats. In July 1956 the CPP renewed its victory, winning all forty-four seats in the coastal zone, eight out of thirteen seats in British Togo, but in Ashanti country only eight out of twenty-one, and in the north eleven out of twenty-six. Since one Independent went over to the CPP, Nkrumah had seventy-two MPs at his disposal, the opposition (which later amalgamated to form the 'United Party') thirty-two. Until 1969 this was the last parliamentary election in Ghana. In July 1960 there remained thirteen of the opposition members, at the official introduction of the one-party system in January 1964 only seven, the others having joined the CPP.

Britain granted independence to Ghana on 6 March 1957. Three years later Nigeria attained the same goal, likewise without any dramatic incidents. Conferences in London and Lagos had prepared a new constitution in 1953, named the Lyttelton Constitution after the colonial secretary then in office (later Lord Chandos). The particularism of the regions was at its height: they obtained cabinets and prime ministers – Awolowo in the west, Azikiwe in the east, the sardauna of Sokoto in the north. The moderate party leaders had entrenched themselves in their strongholds.

The east and west regions immediately obtained internal autonomy, and the north would also have done so, had its leaders expressed a wish to have it. Since, however, they still feared their southern compatriots more than they did the British, they deliberately allowed the machinery of constitutional reform to run slowly. The federal clamp was thus put under renewed strain, in spite of the fact that the Lyttelton Constitution represented a great step forward for the Nigerian central government. Fears that Britain wanted to obstruct the independence of an all-Nigerian state proved unfounded. In 1954 Nigeria obtained a directly electable federal parliament with a fixed catalogue of legislative competence, and in 1957 (after the clarification of the internal political situation by means of regional elections) the candidate of the strongest party was called on to become federal prime minister; Alhaji Abubakar Tafawa Balewa (1912–66), a right-hand man of the sardauna, but a man of sufficiently impressive stature in his own right to be able to hold office with respect from all sides.

Prior to independence, which had been set for 1 October 1960, after the sardauna had received all conceivable guarantees for a permanent leading position of the northern aristocrats, elections to the federal parliament were held twice. In 1954, out of 184 seats 79 fell to the NPC, 61 to the NCNC, and 27 to the AG. In 1959 the NPC attained 134, the NCNC 89, and the AG 73 seats out of a total of 312.

The seats were allotted in 1954 in such a way that the northern region obtained exactly half, so that the possibility of an outnumbering by the north, even if all seats there were to fall to the NPC, was excluded. This limitation of northern power disappeared in 1959: the north now obtained a majority of eighteen seats. This did not help the NPC, however, to obtain a parliamentary majority in Lagos, because the Action Group, which had not even been fully successful in the west in 1954, was now in 1959 firmly installed there, and in addition proved to be a most dangerous eroder of the domestic power of the Fulbe aristocrats, in part of the northern region – the 'middle belt'. This compelled the sardauna and Prime Minister Abubakar to seek a coalition with the NCNC. They were successful, Azikiwe at first taking over the chairmanship of the Senate (a form of upper house in the federal parliament), and then with independence the office of governor-general, that is, head of state as representative of the queen. Awolowo emerged as leader of the opposition in the federal parliament. With this coalition, Nigeria became independent as a member of the commonwealth. Britain's political withdrawal from West Africa was now only a matter of time: in 1961 Sierra Leone was released from colonial rule, in 1965 Gambia.

The contradiction between the decolonization of Ghana and Nigeria – in one country the encouragement of a unified state, in the other of federalism – is easy to explain. London sought continuity and stability of power in the new states, and therefore worked pragmatically with the strongest political force in existence. In Accra this was Nkrumah, in Lagos it was the aristocrats of the northern region. It cannot be asserted either of one or the other that the guarantee of democratic rights and freedoms, or the transferral of Westminster parliamentarianism to Africa, was a matter close to their hearts. None the less Britain, as long as it held responsibility, insisted on the retention of certain democratic forms.

This was not the case in Sudan. There too London opened the way to self-government soon after 1945, and Conservative governments after 1952 had to decide in what form the country was to become independent. Here too one can discern an effort on the part of the departing colonial power to achieve stability – also with the wish that Egypt, neither the country of King Farouk, nor of Naguib, nor of Nasser, should rise to become master of the whole Nile valley. In internal political terms the stabilization of Sudan was a failure: on 1 January 1956 it became independent with a parliamentary constitution, but as early as November 1958 General Abboud set up a military dictatorship. Territorial integrity was nevertheless successfully retained. Revolts on the part of military units in which the anger and fear of the south Sudanese at the hegemony of the north Sudanese exploded had already broken out under British rule – on 18 August 1955. This was because there too, as in Ghana, Britain had encouraged the centralists and after the first elections in November 1953 had had the north Sudanese Ismail el-Azhari (1902–69) as prime minister safeguard internal autonomy. The special administration of the south, by means of which the British until as late as 1945 had prevented the Islamicization and Arabization of the black inhabitants, was hastily dismantled. The politicians of the south, and probably the great majority of the population, felt betrayed and reacted violently. In this late stage of decolonization, however, Britain did not lift a finger. The government in Khartoum began a bloody campaign of repression that was only to be punctuated in 1972 by a short-lived political compromise.

THE FATE OF WHITE SETTLERS IN EAST AND CENTRAL AFRICA

Conservative British cabinets experienced serious difficulties in Africa where the privileges of European settler minorities became caught up in the fabric of the anti-colonial movement. The defence of the most important strategic positions also led to crisis: withdrawal from the Suez Canal zone, promised by Churchill in October 1954, was carried out by his successor Eden in June 1956. But it is known that Eden then attempted, in conjunction with France, at that time conducting the war in Algeria, to turn back the historical clock – far back into the era of gunboat diplomacy. The story of the Suez crisis, however, belongs to the field of international relations between the Great Powers, not to this history of decolonization.

The way of life of white British settlers was mainly at stake in Southern Rhodesia, and in Kenya. British political skills were able to tackle these thorny problems – partially; credit for that is due to Harold Macmillan, prime minister from 1957 to 1963, and to Iain Macleod (1913–70), his secretary of state for the colonies from October 1959 until October 1961.

The big issue was the Central African Federation, a bold and promising experiment according to its planners. The idea of creating closer economic and administrative ties between the quasi-dominion of **Southern Rhodesia** on the one hand, and the two protectorates of

Northern Rhodesia and **Nyasaland** on the other, originates from the inter-war period. There was particularly extensive discussion after 1945, when the Northern Rhodesia 'copper belt' was experiencing a major industrial boom. The self-confidence of the Europeans settled in Central Africa, just 300,000 of them, increased to a point where they were firmly convinced that it was within their capabilities to build a model society, both for themselves and for the black Africans, between Katanga and the northern border with the Union of South Africa. By no means did they want to copy South Africa, which since the electoral victory of the National Party in 1948 was implementing the doctrine of 'apartheid' or 'separate development'. The old anti-Boer reflex, originating from the founding years of Rhodesia (created as a barrier against the extension of the Transvaal) which had already shown itself in 1923 in a referendum of the white settlers on their future, played its part in the setting-up of the Central African Federation. The British Rhodesians wanted to do it better than the South Africans. Whereas among the latter, besides all the pride in their achievements, an old defensive spirit against being swamped by blacks was still very much alive, so that they permanently saw themselves in a state of defence, in the Rhodesia of around 1950 white optimism prevailed unequivocally. 'Partnership' was the name given to the Rhodesian programme for a society to be formed of several races, and to offer a model of progress and economic success, above all to East Africa. There was no doubt that the white man claimed the senior role for himself for a considerable time to come, referring to the old doctrine of Cecil Rhodes: 'Equal rights for every civilized man'. Garfield Todd (born 1908), prime minister of Southern Rhodesia between 1953 and 1958 and later a man of the 'left', expressed the prevailing mood with the words: 'We're taking the African people by the scruff of the neck and saying "Come with us into the twentieth century." But they'll be glad they came.'[17]

The Africans tried to protest against the formation of the federation, but their voice did not carry far, as they were not significantly represented in any governmental bodies of the three territories. Their political organizations around 1950 were substantially weaker than their counterparts in West Africa. Only in Southern Rhodesia was there at least a tradition of African trade union work, influenced from South Africa. Since, however, only the white Rhodesians had to agree to the federal constitution by means of a referendum (25,570 votes to 14,729), the two remaining territories, through their legislative councils, the new 'Federation of Rhodesia and Nyasaland' came into existence on 3 September 1953.

Until 1955 the prime minister was G. M. Huggins (1883–1971; in 1955 made Lord Malvern of Rhodesia) and after him Sir Roy Welensky (born 1907), the thirteenth son of a Jewish immigrant from Lithuania, in his youth an amateur boxer and in the 1930s leader of the white railway union of Southern Rhodesia. The federal government obtained significant jurisdiction on matters of defence, immigration, European education, European agriculture and health policy. *De facto* they pursued their own foreign policy, British influence with the federation being minimal. None the less the white politicians of Central Africa did not succeed in pushing through full independence in London.

What made Eden and Macmillan shrink from this last and irrevocable step? Certainly no economic consideration, since in this respect the federation was proving even the boldest optimists right. Until 1959 almost £1,000 million were invested in the federation, 27 per cent of this foreign capital. As a symbol of the rise and at the same time the cohesion of Northern and Southern Rhodesia, the Kariba roller dam was built on the Zambesi, exactly on the border between the two territories. It cost some £80 million and in 1962 supplied 2.7 thousand million kilowatt hours of electricity (two-thirds of the requirements of the federation), predominantly to the Northern Rhodesian copper mines. The Europeans also boasted educational successes. In 1953, 634,008 African children were attending primary schools and (only) 1,962 higher schools; in 1962 African primary school children numbered over 1.2 million, higher school pupils 13,839. Steady immigration also seemed to be vindicating the founders of the federation; 137,735 whites went there between 1953 and 1957, of whom just half were from Great Britain and almost as many from South Africa.

One cannot assert that the development of 'European' politics must have alarmed Britain. As during the inter-war period in Southern Rhodesia, so in the years of the federation too the whites – at least until 1960 – did not permit the rise of any extremist groups. The Dominion Party, which called for a tougher racial policy, suffered a defeat as late as 1958 in elections to the Southern Rhodesian Assembly, albeit only as a consequence of a complicated majority electoral system with preferential possibilities; in this way the ruling party of the centre, Welensky's United Federal Party (URP), was able to gain seventeen seats with 17,516 votes, and the Dominion Party only thirteen with 18,314 votes. Liberal voters supporting Garfield Todd, who opted with their preferential votes for the UFP, went away empty-handed. Todd himself was toppled as prime minister of Southern Rhodesia at the beginning of 1958 for wanting to raise the minimum wage of African industrial workers by 30 per cent up to £6 10s per month.

In the federal elections of 1959, which resulted in another victory for the UFP, voters were divided into two rolls, in which race theoretically played no part. In fact, however, the lower or B roll (5,546 voters) consisted of 95 per cent Africans – mostly Northern Rhodesians. They could vote for eight African members of parliament, while forty-four seats were reserved for the upper or A roll, which numbered 91,495 voters, of whom 85,644 were whites. In fact the 64,622 white Southern Rhodesians of the A roll constituted two-thirds of the total electorate of all three territories. The result was not surprising; the UFP obtained a two-thirds majority.

It must have been mounting African objections to the tutelage over them by Southern Rhodesia's European minority which made London withhold the granting of independence to the federation. Gradually modern nationalist parties began to form in the three territories, and leaders to come to the fore; the young Kenneth Kaunda (born 1924) in Northern Rhodesia, Joshua Nkomo (born 1917) in Southern Rhodesia – a trade unionist like Welensky – and finally Dr Hastings K. Banda (born 1902) in Nyasaland, a man who, after decades absent in the USA, Britain, and Ghana, returned in triumph and took over the undisputed leadership of resistance to the federation. In March 1959 disturbances broke out in Northern Rhodesia and Nyasaland. As in Ghana eight years previously, a state of emergency ensued, but there was no hasty British retreat and no handing over of state power to the strongest discernible political force, which at that time in Central Africa would still have been the UFP. Instead, a British commission under Sir Patrick Devlin investigated conditions in Nyasaland. Their report, published in July 1959, for the first time threw a highly critical light on the 'partnership' policy for the public at home. Banda was released from prison on 1 April 1960. At the end of July Banda pushed through decisive constitutional reform for Nyasaland; twenty directly elected Africans beside only twelve Europeans in the Legislative Council. It was he, and not, for example, Welensky, who now stood in the position in which Nkrumah had stood in 1951 when beginning his rule of Ghana. Banda made it absolutely clear that he would demand the independence of Nyasaland (or Malawi, as he baptized it). Kenneth Kaunda, who also served a term in prison (1959–60), leaving it as the future prime minister, chose the same course for Northern Rhodesia (Zambia).

Welensky had himself asked Macmillan in 1957 for a revision of the federal constitution. He wanted federation to be retained, and he wanted independence – under his leadership. In July 1959 a royal commission under Viscount Monckton of Brenchley was convened; Britain was represented by nine people, Australia and Canada by one each, the federation by four and its territories by three each. A commonwealth commission was thus in effect here – of the old white commonwealth. Influenced by unrest in Northern Rhodesia and Nyasaland, and perhaps also by an intensification of South African apartheid policy, the Monckton Report bitterly disappointed Welensky's hopes. Although African politicians refused to co-operate with Monckton, the report placed the prospect of their ultimate goal, the collapse of the federation, within their grasp. Monckton himself recommended that it be retained for economic reasons (no one disputed success in this sphere), but nevertheless the report made it clear as the summary of its chapter on 'present attitudes' that 'the strength of African opposition in the Northern Territories is such that Federation cannot, in our view, be maintained in its present form'.[18] The individual territories were to obtain the right to secession.

The British government thus gave the green light to Banda and Kaunda. Despite the federation, competence for constitutional changes in the individual territories continued to lie with the British government and parliament. In 1962 and 1963 African majorities came about in the representative bodies of Northern Rhodesia and Nyasaland. Banda and Kaunda became chief ministers, and their countries obtained internal autonomy. But still Welensky fought back.

On 1 March 1961, Welensky met the British prime minister, the commonwealth secretary, and the colonial secretary in London; three years later, he quoted his argument as follows:

> This isn't Algeria. In the Federation we have accepted the fact
> that there will ultimately be black majorities. What I ask is some
> reason, and some sense of responsibility, in the practical applica-
> tion of this principle. But if I surrender now, it won't mean that
> the Rhodesians will accept the position. . . . You in Britain

don't seem to understand that, with us, the pace of African development has been very quick. The black man probably has progressed faster in Rhodesia, where there are white men, than anywhere else in Africa. The simple fact is that the Africans want power now, whereas I want development to go at a reasonable rate. . . .

There is growing unemployment both in Southern Rhodesia and in Nyasaland. One-fifth of the white man's income is being spent on educating African schoolchildren, but we still can't educate them fast enough. That is the heart of our problem. I don't want to fight a rearguard action. I am not negative just for the sake of being negative. Of course we could link up with South Africa; but I, for one, don't believe in South African policy.[19]

Apart from a minority in the Conservative Party (who in 1965 still wanted to make a pact with the rebels in the white minority government), this kind of talk was falling on stony ground in 1961. It had already been one year since Macmillan's celebrated speech, a phrase from which had been taken up by an editorial in *The Times*, which had spoken of the 'Wind of Change over Africa'. That had been on 3 February 1960.

Macmillan, who became prime minister after the failure of the Suez *coup de main* in 1957, had altered Britain's stance towards the conflicts between Europe and his former colonial 'hinterland'. On 8 October 1959 his party won an electoral victory. A number of younger Conservatives, prepared to undertake bolder decolonization, took their seats in the House of Commons. Determined not to give in, either in Rhodesia or in Kenya, to the demands of the white minority, and also not to pay a price for South Africa staying in the commonwealth, Macmillan set out on a trip to Africa in January 1960. On the first leg, in Ghana, he spoke already of the 'wind of change'. The world started listening in when he repeated this phrase before the South African parliament in Cape Town:

Ever since the break-up of the Roman Empire one of the constant facts of political life in Europe has been the emergence of independent nations. They have come into existence over the centuries in different shapes with different forms of government. But all have been inspired with a keen feeling of nationalism, which has grown as nations have grown.

In the twentieth century, and especially since the end of the war, the processes which gave birth to the nation-states of Europe have been repeated all over the world. We have seen the awakening of national consciousness in peoples who have for centuries lived in dependence on some other power.

Fifteen years ago this movement spread through Asia. Many countries there, of different races and civilisations, pressed their claim to an independent national life.

Today, the same thing is happening in Africa. The most striking of all the impressions I have formed since I left London a month ago is of the strength of this African national consciousness. In different places it may take different forms, but it is happening everywhere. The wind of change is blowing through the continent.

Whether we like it or not, this growth of national consciousness is a political fact. We must all accept it as a fact. Our national policies must take account of it.

Of course, you understand this as well as anyone. You are sprung from Europe, the home of nationalism. And here in Africa you have yourselves created a full nation – a new nation. Indeed, in the history of our times yours will be recorded as the first of the African nationalisms.

And this tide of national consciousness which is now rising in Africa is a fact for which you and we and the other nations of the western world are ultimately responsible. . . .

The uncommitted nations want to see before they choose. What can we show them to help them choose aright? Each of the independent members of the Commonwealth must answer that question for itself. . . .

Let me be very frank with you, my friends. What governments and parliaments in the United Kingdom have done since the war in according independence to India, Pakistan, Ceylon, Malaya, and Ghana, and what they will do for Nigeria and the other countries now nearing independence – all this, though we take full and sole responsibility for it, we do in the belief that it is the only way to establish the future of the Commonwealth and of the free world on sound foundations.

All this, of course, is also of deep and close concern to you, for nothing we do in this small world can be done in a corner or remain hidden. What we do today in West, Central, and East

Africa becomes known to everyone in the Union, whatever his language, colour, or tradition.

Let me assure you in all friendliness that we are well aware of this, and that we have acted and will act with full knowledge of the responsibility we have to you and to all our friends.[20]

South Africa took this policy of Great Britain, so openly declared, as an inducement to break with the commonwealth. At the conference of commonwealth prime ministers in May 1960, all those participating did still seek a compromise, the final communiqué remained largely silent on apartheid and South Africa's foreign minister Louw (Premier Verwoerd had been shot by a would-be assassin and had to stay at home) did at least condescend to private discussion of this 'internal matter' of his country. Nevertheless the South African government knew from now on that not one other government in the commonwealth supported it. One year later, in March 1961, Verwoerd declared the withdrawal of South Africa from the commonwealth; it is significant that it was not the 'extremist' Kwame Nkrumah who provoked the exclusion of South Africa. The initiative had come in 1960 from the Tunku Abdul Rahman of Malaya, from Julius Nyerere (although Tanganyika was not yet independent and he was consequently not present at the conference), from Sir Abubakar Tafawa Balewa of Nigeria – and from the Canadian prime minister, John George Diefenbaker. Macmillan and Macleod tried until the last to arbitrate. It is owing to their skill and to good teamwork on the part of the majority of the prime ministers that the South Africa question did not cause a rift between whites and non-whites in the commonwealth. As has already been mentioned, in the end all parties were relieved. This may be a moderate achievement in terms of diplomatic efforts, but it is better than much of the 'crisis management' which is our lot today.

The moment of truth for the Central African Federation came in 1963. The autonomous African governments in Northern Rhodesia and Nyasaland were demanding secession. London and the hardpressed federal government gave in. Southern Rhodesia had obtained a new constitution in 1961 which, if anything, shifted the status quo even more in favour of the whites. Southern Rhodesia took over the franchise split from the federation. On the A roll almost all Europeans (around 88,000) could find their place, but only 2,251 Africans; this roll was to control fifty seats. Around 11,000 Africans qualified to be on the B roll;[21] however, they held only fifteen seats in parliament. The whites could thus be sure of their dominance of Southern Rhodesia (soon to become 'Rhodesia') and could accept the dissolution of the federation on 31 December 1963. The most important part of the federal military forces – the air force – went to Rhodesia. London discharged the two northern territories into independence in 1964. It was not able to prevent the outbreak of armed struggle in the south.

Britain had not resorted for decades to the rights it reserved according to the constitutions of 1923 and 1961 in Southern Rhodesia. Never – until December 1979 – did a Rhodesian policeman receive orders from the London Colonial Office, not before 1923, when the country was governed by the private South Africa Company, and not afterwards, when the colony governed itself. In the 1960s British cabinets saw no other way than to leave the 'rebellious' white leaders of Rhodesia to the wrath of God, to outlaw them by means of UN sanctions, and otherwise to hope for a miraculous change of their hearts.

Political miracles are rare, and this one took fifteen years to happen. On 14 December 1962 the Rhodesian Front, successor to the Dominion Party, managed to out-manoeuvre their moderate adversaries. The shift to the right which the voting procedure of 1958 had still managed to conceal now came out into the open; from the A roll the front got 37,953 votes against 29,237 votes for the UFP, and this time thirty-five seats to fifteen. Winston Field became prime minister, and was replaced in April 1964 by the much tougher Ian Smith (born in Rhodesia in 1919, the son of a Scottish immigrant).

The African liberation movement boycotted these elections, thereby demonstrating how much influence it already had, particularly among those Africans who had relatively modern lifestyles; of roughly 11,000 eligible black voters, only 2,116 went to the ballot box. In so doing, the representatives of Zimbabwe – as the anti-colonial movements had begun to call Rhodesia – robbed themselves of a voice in parliament, moreover falling in 1963 into a state of discord among themselves. Their movement split; the Zimbabwe African People's Union (ZAPU) remained loyal to Joshua Nkomo, and a new Zimbabwe African National Union (ZANU) was formed, led initially by the clergyman Ndabaningi Sithole (born 1920). All efforts on the part of independent African states and the OAU to bring about a reconciliation failed. For some time ZANU and ZAPU supporters carried out bloody skirmishes among themselves in Rhodesian towns, until the police suppressed both sides. In exile, ZAPU found support from the Soviet Union and its allies, even raising a force for the 'armed freedom struggle', but suffered a severe setback in August 1967 when together with fighters from the exiled South African ANC they attempted a conventional entry across the Zambesi border towards Rhodesia.

The two foremost African leaders and rivals, Nkomo and Sithole, preferred in 1964–5 to go into Ian Smith's prisons rather than into exile. They probably hardly counted on having to stay behind bars until December 1974 and only being able to exert a diluted, indirect influence on the decisive phases of the struggle. The question is whether they could in any case have brought about a genuine united front.

First, however, it is necessary to cast a glance at the rebellious white minority (who never numbered more than 250,000), who in their estimation of the situation of course felt themselves justified by ZAPU–ZANU discord, ineffectual London policy and the powerlessness of the OAU. Who should rule Rhodesia if not they themselves, as they had been doing since 1923? White Rhodesians did not want to face the fact that they were fighting a losing battle; they did not want to foresee that they could not hold out indefinitely against guerrilla forces, if only an appreciable proportion of the 5 million blacks provided cover and passive support to the guerrillas. Obstinately, white Rhodesians once again voted for Ian Smith's party in May 1965, continuing through then until 1980. In 1965 the elections did not take place in twenty-two A roll constituencies, since the Rhodesian Front candidates stood alone and unchallenged; in the remaining twenty-seven constituencies 28,651 votes were counted for the front, and only 6,886 for twenty-four Rhodesia Party candidates (this party was the successor to the UFP) and 968 for three Independents. The front naturally obtained all the seats. From the B roll, the Rhodesia Party obtained ten seats, and five fell to Independents. All in all only 1,782 voters on the B roll voted.

The secretary of state for colonial relations in the Labour cabinet of Harold Wilson, Arthur Bottomley, drew up in September 1965 the British conditions for legal Rhodesian independence: 1. a guarantee to develop the constitution further towards majority rule (in plain English gradual transference of executive power to the Africans); 2. a guarantee against the abrogation of already granted political rights; 3. immediate improvement of the political position of the Africans; 4. a dismantling of the social colour bar; 5. proof that the entire population of Rhodesia wanted independence under these conditions – not the white minority only.

Ian Smith did not agree with this, instead declaring unilateral independence on 11 November 1965. Harold Wilson countered with the optimistic prophecy that in weeks rather than months the rebellion would be over. No intervention of British troops was ever considered in London. Instead of this it was decided to instigate economic sanctions against Rhodesia, to which the United Nations agreed.

It was with a grim kind of humour that the history of Great Britain in 1965 now stood before exactly the same formal situation as it had in 1776; a community of white colonists rebelling against the motherland. It was after 1776 that the first British Empire had crumbled in the American War of Independence. There had been begun in England the process of overseas policy stock-taking which had accompanied the rise and transformation of the second empire throughout the nineteenth and twentieth centuries. The awareness of the right of every 'nation' – however this concept may have been defined – to *self-government* – however that may have been understood – had enabled Great Britain after 1918 to build a commonwealth with its white Dominions, and after 1945 to bring about decolonization in Asia and Africa. Right at the end of this historical process, a colonists' uprising occurred again, in Rhodesia – this time only a caricature of 1776, a ghost of itself.

For almost fifteen years it looked as though London would not manage to exorcize this ghost. All initiatives towards negotiation failed in the face of Ian Smith's intransigence, regardless of whether they issued from Labour or Conservative cabinets. Sanctions did not seem to 'bite', indeed they accomplished a positive boom in Rhodesia's import substitution industry. It came as no real surprise, therefore, to discover that in the end even British Petroleum itself had been happily dodging sanctions. In January 1972, the mass of the African people in Rhodesia convincingly demonstrated their rejection of independence under white rule to a British royal commission, and therefore the fifth British condition (see above) had not been met. This demonstration of will was organized by the Methodist bishop in Rhodesia, Abel Muzorewa (born 1925), who created a new legal movement of Africans under the name of the African National Council (ANC). This, however, merely added one more to the number of rivals for the leadership of black liberation politics. The gathering of the ZAPU and the ZANU under the banner of the ANC and under the chairmanship of Muzorewa, solemnly proclaimed on 8 December 1974 by Nkomo and Sithole, who had just been released, broke up almost immediately afterwards. The Patriotic Front, which joined ZAPU and ZANU against Muzorewa in exile in the middle of 1977, was no more than a superficial alliance of convenience which made it easier for Nkomo and the new ZANU leader, Robert Mugabe (born 1924), to be recognized world-wide, and by the OAU, as authentic spokesmen for the black people.

ZANU seriously embarked at the end of 1972 on guerrilla warfare in north-east Rhodesia, supported by an alliance with FRELIMO, which had successfully undermined Portuguese authority in neighbouring Mozambique, particularly in the Tete province. In the Shona ethnic region, from which they recruited most of their cadres and soldiers, the ZANU guerrilla fighters obtained a firm foothold. Nkomo on the other hand kept back the ZAPU fighting forces, which were at least as well armed (perhaps mindful of the fiasco of 1967) in Zambia – which did not prevent the Rhodesian army and air force from striking against Zambia with reprisal actions, as they did against Mozambique.

None of the parties involved won this war. Breakthrough came somewhat surprisingly and from an unexpected quarter, after even the American diplomacy of Henry Kissinger had toiled with Rhodesia in vain, and hardly affected by the monotonous grinding of the UN mills of condemnation. In May 1979 the Conservatives in London took over the government once again, Margaret Thatcher (born 1925) – with a solid hardline reputation – becoming prime minister. She travelled at the beginning of August to the commonwealth conference in Lusaka (Zambia), and lo and behold the old club produced, like a magician conjuring a rabbit out of a hat, a solution to the Rhodesia crisis which seemed to be entirely satisfactory to Africa, the world powers, the UN, the black people of Rhodesia, and even the white stronghold of Ian Smith.

All disputing parties gathered on 10 September around the green table of time-honoured Lancaster House in London, which was imbued with the spirit of many earlier decolonization conferences. By 15 December Rhodesia's independence was home and dry; once again, and for this country actually for the very first time, a true-blue British colonial governor (Lord Soames) departed to lead peace, order, reason, and civilization to victory in darkest Africa. He managed it in eight weeks. On 14 February 1980 the whites once again voted virtually to a man for the Rhodesian Front, thereby securing for the front twenty seats in the new independence parliament. From 27 until 29 February there followed 2.7 million African voters, more than 90 per cent of those eligible, the latter consisting of all adults. The victory went to Mugabe's ZANU with 63 per cent of the votes, 57 seats, and thus an absolute majority in parliament. The runner-up was Nkomo's ZAPU, for which the Ndebele people, from whom Nkomo originates, voted *en bloc*; 24 per cent of the votes, 20 seats. Bishop Muzorewa, the hero of 1972, suffered a severe defeat; 8.3 per cent of the votes, three seats; and likewise overrun was the ZANU founder Sithole, who from 1977 had been in alliance with Ian Smith and had intrigued against Muzorewa; 2 per cent of the votes, and no seats. On 18 April 1980 came the birth of Zimbabwe – a recognized independent African state, although continuing to have a white minority living there and sharing in power.

In history and politics, of course, there are no miraculous conversions of sinners and no magic tricks. The white rebellion in Rhodesia had exhausted itself; international sanctions had 'bitten' them in the end. The brand of guerrilla warfare had done the rest in moving Smith to capitulate – he who at the beginning of 1979, very late in the day, had attempted, by using Muzorewa as a front-man prime minister, to force an internal solution in the face of London, Washington, and the rest of the world. This guerrilla war, however, was also a threat to Mozambique and Zambia, and the governments there were bound to be concerned not to suffer the fate of Lebanon, which had lost its sovereignty in 1975 in an all-out war triggered off by PLO fighters. The western powers had also been shocked by Moscow's successful intervention in Angola in 1975–6, and so may have seized the opportunity to outmanoeuvre the Warsaw Pact allies among Rhodesia's liberators – Nkomo's ZANU. The west was prepared to take the risk of a victory by Mugabe, who was also conducting a war, and who likewise favoured the language of Marxism, because Mugabe had no links with Moscow. The ZANU undoubtedly based itself on Marx – although not on Brezhnev. The opportunity offered by such a combination of forces would perhaps be available for a brief moment only and was resolutely seized by Margaret Thatcher. Mugabe submitted himself to the discipline of western parliamentary democracy, at least for a time, moreover inviting the whites (and not only any whites, but the obstinate bloc of Smith supporters) to take part in the political process in Zimbabwe. This was neither miraculous nor magical, but shrewd and therefore good politics; a conciliatory conclusion to the dissolution of the British colonial empire.

In **Kenya**, the Conservative London cabinets of the 1950s prevented the emergence of a dilemma similar to that of Rhodesia, that is, colonial responsibility combined with complete powerlessness on the actual spot. In this process, Kenya – like Malaya – had to go through a violent assault by the colonized against their rulers. The Mau Mau movement – again as in Malaya – developed along the lines of a racial conflict, its enemy being – this time unlike in Malaya – a European minority. The idea of relying on the Kenyan Europeans in the struggle against the Mau Mau and handing over political power to them must have suggested itself; all the more so since London had indeed defeated the communist Chinese partisans in Malaya by accommodating moderate Malayan nationalism, that is, an indigenous group. Things developed otherwise in Kenya, however. London realized that the white minority there was too small to take over power. The London government was fully mindful of the precedents of South Africa and Southern Rhodesia, which now distinctly alarmed them.

We have learnt that the European settlers in Kenya – around 66,000 – had been refused internal autonomy between the wars. In 1948 the settlers achieved only the granting of an 'unofficial majority' in the Legislative Council – although their eleven elected representatives remained in the minority against the twenty-nine other members (the governor and the appointed speaker, sixteen colonial officials, five elected Indians, four appointed Africans, one elected and one appointed Arab).

In 1952 Mau Mau interrupted constitutional development; in October a state of emergency was imposed. What was Mau Mau? Father Trevor Huddleston, one of the toughest white opponents of apartheid in South Africa, wrote in the Johannesburg *Star* newspaper on 12 December 1952, after a visit to Kenya:

> There are at least three features of Mau Mau technique which
> mark it off as distinct from movements elsewhere in Africa.
> First, it is in origin a tribal movement. Secondly, it is a reversion
> to primitive superstition. . . . Thirdly, it is avowedly anti-
> Christian. . . . To sum up, I would say this, Mau Mau is a

movement which in its origins and in its development, is wholly
evil. It is the worst enemy of African progress in Kenya. It has
about it all the horror of 'the powers of darkness; of spiritual
wickedness in high places'.[22]

Josiah M. Kariuki (born 1929), who was interned in a camp from
1953 to 1960 as an activist in the movement, who later spoke in the
Kenyan parliament as an advocate of the poor, and who was (therefore?) murdered on 2 March 1975, wrote differently:

> After the 1939–45 War things were changing. Our social and
> economic grievances were plainer to all and there were many
> more educated Africans who were beginning to understand that
> the social system was not immutable. Most of all was this
> happening among my own tribe, the Kikuyu. . . .
>   Normal political methods through KAU seemed to be getting
> nowhere. The young men of the tribe saw that a time of crisis
> was approaching when great suffering might be necessary to
> achieve what they believed in. It is easy enough for anyone who
> knows my people to understand that it was a spontaneous deci-
> sion that they should be bound together in unity by a simple
> oath. From what I have heard this oath began in the Kikuyu dis-
> tricts, starting in Kiambu. There was no central direction or
> control. The oath was not sophisticated or elaborate and initially
> was wholly unobjectionable. . . . Although the situation was
> dangerous, even in October 1952, it was not so dangerous that it
> could not have been put right by a few political concessions. . . .
> But the Government chose to answer it with a series of the
> harshest and most brutal measures ever taken against a native
> people in the British Empire in the twentieth century, and so the
> movement developed by action and re-action into a full-scale
> rebellion involving the soul of my people. . . .
>   I must make it clear that it did not have any special name; the
> world knows it by a title of abuse and ridicule with which it was
> described by one of its bitterest opponents.[23]

The author asserts that at an oath-swearing ceremony Kikuyu children posted as look-outs used to warn when police turned up by calling
out the meaningless phrase 'Mau Mau'. A Christian preacher seized
on this call to warn his congregation against 'heathen' oaths.

The oath itself for the beginnings of the movement is quoted as
follows in the official 1960 Corfield Report of the British government:

I will not give away the secrets of the society.

I will not help Government apprehend members of the society.

I will not sell our land to strangers.

But there were also positive clauses, such as:

I will help the society when called upon to do so with funds.

I will, if called upon to do so, render any help to members of
   the society that I am asked to do.

At the end of 1959, in the heat of the struggle, the oath is said to have
taken on the following form:

(a) To burn European crops, and to kill European-owned cattle.

(b) To steal firearms.

(c) If ordered to kill, to kill, no matter who is to be the victim,
   even one's father or brother.

(d) When killing, to cut off heads, extract the eyeballs and drink
   the liquid from them.

(e) Particularly to kill Europeans.[24]

Our African source confirms that he took two oaths at the end of
1953; first a political oath of allegiance, then the stronger oath of the
fighter, who pledges to kill and to spill his own blood. He quotes the
first oath as follows:

I speak the truth and vow before our God
And before this movement,
The movement of Unity,
The Unity which is put to the test
The Unity that is mocked with the name of 'Mau Mau',
That I shall go forward to fight for the land,
The lands of Kirinyaga that we cultivated,
The lands which were taken by the Europeans
   And if I fail to do this
   May this oath kill me,
   May this seven kill me,
   May this meat kill me.

He quotes from the second oath:

I speak the truth and vow before our God:
If I am called to go to fight the enemy
Or to kill the enemy – I shall go,
Even if the enemy be my father or mother,

199

My brother or sister,
  And if I refuse
  May this oath kill me. . . .
I speak the truth and vow before our God:
That I shall never take away the woman of another man,
That I shall never walk with prostitutes,
That I shall never steal anything belonging to another person in
  the movement,
Nor shall I hate any other member for his actions
  And if I do any of these things,
  May this oath kill me.[25]

The 'success' of the uprising was limited. According to the Corfield Report, by the end of 1956, when the British had won the struggle, Mau Mau had killed 32 Europeans, 26 Indians, and 1,819 African civilians. The military and police forces lost 63 Europeans, 3 Indians, and 101 Africans; 101 Europeans, 12 Indians, and 1,469 Africans were wounded. In contrast with these figures, 11,503 Mau Mau supporters were killed, 2,585 terrorists captured, and 26,625 others arrested; 2,714 fighters surrendered. The costs of suppressing the uprising (up to 30 June 1959) have been calculated as £55.6 million; one dead terrorist thereafter cost Britain nearly £5,000 – substantially less than in Malaya. The measures taken in order to isolate guerrilla fighters escaping into inaccessible country resembled those in both theatres of war. Sixty thousand Kikuyu were driven out of Nairobi, almost the entire nation having to be resettled in new villages. Jomo Kenyatta, who had returned to Kenya in 1946, was arrested on 22 October 1952, charged with being an influential Mau Mau leader, and sentenced on 8 April 1953 by means of a dubious trial to seven years' imprisonment.

At the same time, however, London was introducing constitutional reforms. In the middle of the state of emergency, on 13 April 1954, these came into effect; the Africans were to obtain better representation in the Legislative Council and even a minister (for 'community development') in the newly created Executive Council. The commander of the British troops, Major-General Sir George Erskine, declared openly in Nairobi that the Mau Mau problem could not be solved by military means alone. The issue was clear; it was precisely the reinforced deployment of British force and British money in Kenya, necessitated by the rebellion, which damaged the prospects for the white settlers of having their own way. One of the European parties, led by the farmer Michael Blundell (born 1907), even supported the British reforms and agreed to share political responsibility in the Council of Ministers.

In March 1957, after difficult preparations (the state of emergency was still in force), eight Africans were voted on to the Legislative Council. There were admittedly no Kikuyu among them, but the trade union leader from the Luo people, Tom M'Boya (1930–69), who won in Nairobi, proved to be a skilful representative of the aspirations of all Kenyan Africans; he took over leadership of the African MPs and later founded the Kenya African National Union (KANU). In 1960 the state of emergency was lifted. One year later an African prime minister was in office: Ronald Ngala from the coastal town of Mombasa, leader of the Kenya African Democratic Union (KADU), a party which strove to represent the interests of the minor African nations against the Kikuyu and the Luo. In the elections of 1961, it obtained only eleven seats, the KANU on the other hand nineteen; three African seats fell to Independents, ten being reserved for Europeans, eight for Indians and two for Arabs. London had thus succeeded in turning on its head the political system of 1948. The settlers had to make do with a constitutional protection for themselves as a minority which clearly bore a provisional stamp.

Since 1961 politics in Kenya has been a game for the Africans – which has not prevented whites from settling there in greater numbers than before, or from investing capital. Ngala was flexible enough not to snub the KANU, instead forming a coalition with the stronger party. As soon as Kenyatta was released in August 1961, he took over leadership of the KANU. Fresh elections in May 1963 brought seventy-five KANU and thirty-three KADU members into parliament, as well as sixteen others. Kenyatta became prime minister. After the granting of internal autonomy, which Kenya obtained on 1 June 1963, Britain needed only six months until 12 December to declare independent the colony which ten years earlier had been a stage for bloodshed and racial hatred. Kenyatta, who in his time had been apostrophized by one British politician as 'leader to darkness and death', proved in this process to be a bulwark against extremist tendencies within KANU and a great friend of the white minority, the majority of whom, in spite of the ending of their political and social privileges, in spite of the settling of Africans in the 'White Highlands', remained residents in independent Kenya.

Tanganyika had preceded its northern neighbour into independence on 3 December 1961, its decolonization proceeding in entire harmony, and thus in a manner diametrically opposed to that of Kenya. In 1955, under the leadership of the teacher (hence his honorary title *Mwalimu*) Julius K. Nyerere (born 1922), who had returned three years earlier with an MA from the University of Edinburgh, a civil servants' association transformed itself into a political party and liberation movement – the Tanganyika African National Union, TANU. No one ever seriously questioned Nyerere's leadership, and TANU never had any serious competition from another group. By 1959 the British trusteeship administration was pointing out to the Indians and Europeans who had settled in the country that they would have to forgo parity of political representation. The reasons for this general peaceableness may be sought partly in geographical and ethnic factors. In Kenya, for example, the most substantial black people, the Kikuyu, live in the centre of the country, and thus came under severe pressure during colonization. To this were added further tensions between the two largest peoples, the Kikuyu and Luo, on the one hand, and among the many smaller ethnic groups on the other. Tanganyika resembles in geographical terms a platter that is virtually empty in the middle, but densely settled at the fringes. There are numerous ethnic groups in Tanganyika, but none so strong that it could presume to claim a leading role over the whole country. In addition to these geographical considerations, the German colonial government had left the country a common African administrative language, Kiswahili, which has been in use since the end of the nineteenth century. To these factors, however, must be added an important external one concerned with international politics. Tanganyika was a trustee territory of the United Nations, a circumstance which dampened British government interest in public investment in Tanganyika to such an extent that the latter's economic development lagged markedly behind that of Kenya. Politically, London had to present regular reports on Tanganyika to the UN, where the TANU was likewise able to speak for the colonized people.

These factors alone, however, were not responsible for the degree of harmony with which Nyerere managed to lead his country into *uhuru*, independence. The personal friendship between him and the last British governor, Sir Richard Turnbull, who started his period of office in 1958, is of at least equal significance. There was thus a repetition here of what Ghana had experienced between 1951 and

1957, when Sir Charles Arden-Clarke worked side by side with Kwame Nkrumah.

Uganda's emancipation was delayed as a result of internal tensions which are reminiscent of those in Nigeria. The showcase of indirect rule, however, which blocked in both countries the way to nationalism, was in Uganda not the economically backward, Islamic-influenced north of the country, like the Fulbe emirates of northern Nigeria, but the Christian-influenced, mainly Catholic kingdom of the Baganda in the south of the country, around the capital of Kampala. In terms of economic, and hence political, significance for the country as a whole, on the other hand, the Baganda are comparable with the Kikuyu of Kenya. The Ugandan situation was further complicated, however, by a disagreement which arose between the Catholic Democratic Party, supported mainly by Baganda, and the enthusiastic supporters of their traditional monarch, the Kabaka Mutesa II (1924–69). The British deported the kabaka to England, where he stayed from 1953 to 1955, thereby in fact winning prestige as a victim of colonialism. In 1961 they tried to alleviate the dilemma by means of a federalist constitution. The kabaka became head of state, and Milton Obote (born 1926), leader of the Protestant-oriented Uganda People's Congress (UPC), became prime minister, forming a coalition with the kabaka's supporters. This political house of cards, which banished the Baganda majority into opposition, succeeded in surviving the day of independence, 9 October 1962, by a mere three and a half years.

On 10 December 1963, practically simultaneously with Kenya, the island state of **Zanzibar**, the last British possession in East Africa, followed suit, becoming independent under its Arab sultan – another relic of Indirect Rule. This experiment, however, dogged by many years of party discord, was to prove a failure even sooner than was the case of Uganda. In January 1964 a people's uprising swept the sultan from power, preparing the way for the dictatorship of Abeid Karume (1905–72) and formal union with the mainland under the new name of Tanzania. The unrest of 1964 very nearly affected the whole of East Africa. British troops were called in to put down the mutinous troops of the young states – especially those of Tanganyika. Like the Suez War of 1956, however, this episode is not relevant to a history of decolonization.

CYPRUS AND MALAYA

Two colonies of very dissimilar character went much the same way as Kenya; the road from guerrilla warfare to independence. In the case of **Cyprus** the parallel is almost perfect, since here too a former guerrilla leader – or sympathizer – became a member of the commonwealth club as an independent head of government. Archbishop Makarios (1913–77), who was deported to the Seychelles in 1956 for one year – a milder fate than the one that befell Kenyatta – won independence for his island in February 1959.

British rule in **Malaya** came to an end under different circumstances. Admittedly here too, loyal political forces made it possible to grant independence without Britain having to fear that the country would sink into enmity and extremism. The difference with Kenya and Cyprus, however, lies in the fate of the rebels; Malaya forced the communists completely out of legal politics.

The mustering and reinforcement of moderate elements within Malayan politics can be attributed to the Tunku (prince) Abdul Rahman, a son of the sultan of Alor Star, born in 1903, and trained as a lawyer. In 1951 he took over the United Malaya National Organization (UMNO), an extremely conservative association of the ruling aristocracy. He managed to unite it with the Malayan Chinese Association (MCA), thus transforming it into a party capable of action; in 1955 he also drew the Malayan Indian Congress into this alliance. In the same year, London and the tunku felt strong enough to give Malaya a new constitution, which dispensed virtually completely with a stage of internal autonomy. The alliance won fifty-one out of fifty-two of the seats in the Federal Legislative Council. Once again the communists were offered a return to legality. In the middle of November 1955 a truce was called in the partisan war, and from 28 until 30 December the tunku and the (British) chief minister of Singapore (Marshall) negotiated with the guerrilla leader Chin Peng in a village near the border with Thailand. They were not able to reach an agreement, however.

In August 1957 the Federation of Malaya obtained full independence. The constitutional commission which had prepared for this step consisted of representatives from Great Britain, Australia, India, and Pakistan – the participation of the commonwealth in the decolonization of the British Empire was even more in evidence here than it had been in the Monckton Commission. In 1963 Britain also released Singapore into independence, on the condition that it amalgamate with Malaya to form the larger Federation of Malaysia. This did happen, but the balancing act between predominantly Chinese Singapore and Malaya, with its strong Chinese minority, soon proved too difficult.

Lee Kuan Yew (born 1923), leader of the People's Action Party and prime minister of **Singapore** since 1959, where he controlled thirty-seven out of fifty parliamentary seats, proclaimed on 9 August 1965 the secession from Malaysia and the independence of his island city state.

THE WEST INDIES, THE PACIFIC, HONG KONG

We cannot conclude this history of British decolonization without recalling that in one isolated case London reassumed direct government of a colony which had already progressed on the road to independence as far as the stage of 'responsible government'. This occurred in 1953 in **British Guyana**. During the Rhodesia crisis of 1965, left-wing circles, for whose taste Harold Wilson's reactions and sanctions seemed too timid, were to recall this precedent of tough and vigorous action. They obviously overlooked the fact that Guyana had been under the authority of the London Colonial Office until the beginning of 1953. When London decided to abrogate the constitution granted only six months earlier, the governor had a tried and tested police force at his disposal. Probably the dramatic dispatching of troops and warships would not have been necessary. In 1953, however, Churchill was still prime minister – a master, if also a lover of political drama.

His adversary was the dentist Cheddi Jagan, born in 1918 of Indian descent, or rather Mrs Janet Jagan, née Rosenburg, two years younger than her husband. It is said that she had already become a communist while in her American homeland. There in 1944 she had married Jagan, who was elected to the Legislative Council of British Guyana in 1947, then founding the Progressive People's Party (PPP) in 1949 and winning eighteen out of twenty-four seats for it in April 1953. Jagan thus became the chief minister, his wife taking over party leadership. Did the two of them really want to set up, six years before the victory of Fidel Castro, a communist regime in a remote spot of the western hemisphere? The British for their part maintained that they did. In fact Jagan had difficulties overcoming Guyana's special racial problem; around 50 per cent of the 800,000 people living there were (like Jagan) of Indian origin, most of the remainder coming more or less from Africa. They prefer, as later developments showed, to be governed by one from their own ranks.

In 1957 Jagan won again in fresh elections, once again becoming chief minister, his wife party leader likewise. In 1961 the PPP won, with 42.6 per cent of vote, twenty-two seats out of thirty-five; Jagan became prime minister. The Africans, however, did not want anything to do with him.

Should a minority establish its power permanently on the strength of the British electoral procedure? The secretary of state for the colonies decided otherwise, pledging independence for 1963, but then granted Guyana a new, highly un-British electoral law: a purely proportional system. After this on 7 December 1964 the PPP did become the strongest party again (45.9 per cent), but obtained only twenty-four seats against the twenty-nine of the two rival parties. They formed a coalition, and the governor was able to invite the leader of the People's National Congress (PNC), which had polled 40.5 per cent, L. Forbes S. Burnham (1923–85), to become the new prime minister. He obtained independence promptly on 26 May 1966, and did not give up power in the country until his death.

The British had less difficulty with the decolonization of their island possessions, both in the Pacific (e.g., Fiji 1970, Papua New Guinea 1975, the Solomon Islands 1978, and the Anglo-French condominium of the New Hebrides (Vanuatu) after secessionist moves in 1980), and in the Caribbean. The larger Caribbean islands – **Jamaica**, which now has a population of some 2.5 million, and **Trinidad-Tobago**, which has more than a million inhabitants – obtained universal franchise soon after 1945, and internal autonomy a short time later. London would have liked to leave behind a West Indian Federation, and in 1958 a federal constitution was in fact drawn up. Three years later, however, Jamaica withdrew from this project, demanding and obtaining independence for itself alone on 6 August 1962. Trinidad-Tobago then followed, and over the years almost all the smaller islands; and the smallest ones as well have also become independent states within the commonwealth. Almost everywhere the queen has remained head of state; on Barbados (which became independent in 1966), Grenada (which became independent in 1974 and was in the world news for a short time in 1983), as well as St Lucia (1979), Antigua and Barbuda (1981), St Christopher and Nevis (1983). Dominica, however, declared itself an independent republic in 1978.

A tiny piece of the empire on the Central American mainland, **British Honduras**, developed little interest in independence, as it was claimed by its comparatively powerful neighbour, Guatemala. Since 1981, however, it has been a sovereign state under its new name of Belize – albeit with a British garrison.

Anyone who at this late hour of the glory of European colonial power wants to experience a genuine British colony, would do better not even to think of making a tourist visit to the island of Diego Garcia in the middle of the Indian Ocean. This once significant point within BIOT (British Indian Ocean Territory) is now chiefly a base for the US fleet, for satellite observation and probably also for missiles. Until 30 June 1997, however, the tourist can still fly to Hong Kong, where for the 5.5 million inhabitants of the city there is still a real British colonial governor, at whose suggestion the queen in London appoints all members of the Executive Council. The right of the Chinese inhabitants to self-determination, however, has made sufficient progress for them to be able to vote for twenty-four members of the Legislative Council, who none the less remain in a minority compared with the thirty-two *ex-officio* and appointed members. This thus prevents the will of the people from disturbing the circles of high diplomacy. On 19 December 1984, Great Britain and the People's Republic of China signed a joint declaration, according to which Hong Kong will fall once again under Chinese sovereignty as a 'special administrative region' on 1 July 1997. Unlike the case of the western Sahara, where Spain, the colonial power, similarly decided the fate of the country over the heads of the population, in agreement with its Moroccan neighbours, no Hong Kong liberation movement has so far called for an armed struggle.

Then, there are the **Falkland Islands**. They are claimed by Argentina on grounds rather similar to those invoked by China for claiming Hong Kong. The 'people' of the Falklands have expressed their wish to remain British. Margaret Thatcher, after having relinquished the Rhodesian whites ('rebels', indeed) to their fate, fought a war to keep the Falkland Islands a British colony in May–June 1982 – and won it. Thus the story of how the British Empire was unscrambled ends with an event to the contrary. Is it the white skin of the Falkland islanders which motivated London to act as it did? Or their loyalty? Or do we have to look to the Golden Calf of fishing rights under the New International Law of the Seas?

Chapter Nine

FRENCH DECOLONIZATION

Whereas Great Britain after 1945 went about the decolonization of its empire in a pragmatic way, doing in Nigeria what it had failed to do in India (holding heterogeneous population groups together within a federal structure) and permitting in Kenya what it had prevented in Malaya (the entry of guerrilla leaders into legitimate politics), France in the post-war period made two separate large-scale attempts at bringing its relations with the colonies into a constitutionally fixed, coherent, and progressive system. Whereas we have to feel our way intuitively into the 'club rules' of the commonwealth, the ideas of the Union Française, of a 'single indivisible republic between Dunkirk and Brazzaville', and of the Communauté, can be interpreted directly from the articles of the constitutions.

As the young Fourth Republic embarked on providing itself and its colonial empire with a new constitution, however, it had no Westminster Statute at its disposal as a model. Apart from the fact that the French were in the first place by no means disposed to learn from the British – their age-long colonial rivals – parallels were also lacking with the free and loose co-operation characteristic of relations between Great Britain and the white Dominions.

At first glance one can see that the Union Française of 1946 and the Communauté of 1958 have collapsed, whereas the British Commonwealth remained. Britain won the wars in Malaya and Kenya, whilst France lost in Vietnam and Algeria; obviously it would be fairer to compare Kenya with Cameroon, where France was likewise victorious – or at any rate saw to it that an indigenous government defeated the guerrillas after independence. Be that as it may, however, to speak of a failure of French decolonization, as is sometimes the fashion not only in Britain and the United States, would be a precipitate and unjust judgement. It cannot be denied that at the time of de Gaulle, France of all the colonial powers probably enjoyed the highest esteem in the Third World – in Asia, Africa, and Latin America. Co-operation with its former possessions was for many years excellent – apart from the case of Vietnam.

This was not only by virtue of the fact that France had always enjoyed a kind of carnival licence within the western alliance which naturally commanded respect among some non-aligned countries in Africa, Asia, or Latin America. It can also be attributed to the close cultural, and especially linguistic, ties which continued between France and almost all its former colonies. It can also be attributed to the fact that France during the Fourth and Fifth Republics was courageous enough not only to put a stop to mistakes it perceived in its colonial policy, but even to reverse them. Admittedly in the case of Vietnam and Algeria France made a U-turn only when much blood had already been spilt. It was its fixed starting-point, the constitutional harness it carried around with it wherever it went, that made it so unmanoeuvrable. The constitutional unity between France and Algeria in particular was for many of the Frenchmen who were responsible for colonial affairs – especially during the decisive and horrific years – a reality and not merely a historical showpiece, like the Indian imperial title of the British monarch.

The change in French thinking which occurred, both during decolonization itself and as a result of decolonization, is therefore all the more to be appreciated. The French are no longer the 'Cartesian' systematists they once were, but work with a full measure of pragmatism. They have become more flexible. Britain, one could argue, mastered the task of decolonization with the aid of a tried and tested technique of political thought and action. France had to pay tuition fees, but in the end also learned the lesson of decolonization.

THE CONSTITUTION OF 1946

The constitution of the Fourth Republic was treading new ground in terms of overseas matters. In no previous French constitution did the colonies figure in any appreciable way. Now the proponents of the political renewal and reinforcement being aimed for – ranging from the communists and socialists through the Catholic MRP to de Gaulle – were all in agreement that the colonized peoples, above all out of gratitude for their loyalty to the homeland, had earned a place in the institutions of the nation. In general no other goal was so in keeping with the political mood of the moment as the integration of the formerly colonized peoples into the French nation. The ideal of assimilation revived itself again, the France of 1945 drawing once again on the revolutions of 1789 and 1848.

Consequently, a number of deputies from the colonies were accepted into the First Constituent National Assembly, whereas in the Chamber of the Third Republic there had only been one member for the four coastal cities of Senegal. A preparatory committee under the chairmanship of Gaston Monnerville (born 1897) of French Guyana, who himself had African blood in his veins, even proposed the election of 120 representatives of the colonial empire. In fact de Gaulle decided that only 63 of the 522 members of the Constituent Assembly should come from overseas, and of those 63 as many as 25 represented the colonizers. This was because Paris arranged for the introduction of a two-roll electoral system for all its major colonies, essentially grouping all Europeans into the first roll and the (few) 'natives' who were eligible to vote in the second.

In party political terms the sixty-three overseas deputies[1] sought to join various factions, in particular the PCF, SFIO, and MRP ruling parties.[2] In the list of names there are some which at that time were virtually unknown, but which nowadays have a good reputation in the Third World; Félix Houphouet-Boigny, born 1905 (Ivory Coast, 2nd roll); Léopold Sedar Senghor, born 1906 (Senegal, 2nd roll); Sourou M. Apithy, born 1913 (Dahomé/Togo, 2nd roll); Gabriel d'Arboussier (1908–76) (Gabun/Congo, 1st roll), and Aimé Cesaire, born 1913 (Martinique). From Madagascar came two tough nationalists: Joseph Raseta and Joseph Ravoahangy. The members of the second electoral roll of Algeria remained insignificant, however, since from May 1945 Muslim national organizations had been banned; the victory celebrations were to degenerate into bloodshed, as will be related below. It was not until the second Constituent Assembly, which had to be elected on 2 June 1946, the constitutional project of the first having fallen through, that Ferhat Abbas and his friends were able to win eleven out of thirteen Algerian seats of the second roll, for the Union Démocratique du Manifeste Algérien (UDMA).

It was a fraught path which led the two constitutional assemblies to the text which came into effect on 27 October 1946 as the constitution of the Fourth Republic. The Union Française is codified in part VIII. Overseas members took a lively and skilful part in the discussions. For

the most part their French colleagues heard their proposals benevo-
lently, the Senegalese Senghor, by profession a *lycée* teacher of French
grammar and literature, even being entrusted with the stylistic cor-
rection of the constitution. Lively interest in the fate of colonies,
however, was rare. In general, it was harder for the native representatives to find allies in the second Constituent Assembly than it had been
in the first. At that time no member for a colony, apart from those for
Algeria and Madagascar, even called for autonomy, let alone independence. They would all gladly have done away with the two-roll
electoral law and brought about greater representation of the colonies
– and at the same time would have decentralized the republic. Assimilationist and federalist aspirations blurred into a confused mixture.
The second Constituent Assembly brought no solution in its wake;
this only happened when the socialist colonial minister, Marius
Moutet, cut through the knots with a brand new draft on 11 September 1946, putting overseas policy on the right track for some years to
come. Parliamentarians, especially overseas ones, proved disappointed. However much they criticized the text for not going far
enough, however, they did nevertheless basically applaud it. Most
importantly, a more intensive debate between colonizers and colonized had come into being. The close personal contact among them,
the continuing co-operation, chiefly of the black Africans, within the
organization of the Fourth Republic, is what characterized French
decolonization; this is the secret of its psychological success. People
came to know one another very well on the benches and in the corri-
dors of the National Assembly in the Palais Bourbon, in innumerable
committees and representative functions at the UN and in the Council
of Europe. African politicians learned in the process more about the
functioning of European politics than Nkrumah, Azikiwe, or Nyerere
did from annual commonwealth conferences, or than they could formerly have learned from their contacts with governors and commis-
sions of enquiry.

Even before the first Constituent Assembly was dissolved, it
enacted a series of colonial policy laws in order to pin down future
French assemblies at least morally, irrespective of the fate of its draft
constitution. On 26 December the currency in the colonies was
reformed, the 'franc CFA'[3] being created for Africa south of the
Sahara. On 12 March 1946 the Constituent Assembly declared
the 'old colonies' to be 'overseas *départements*'. On 11 April the
Houphouet-Boigny Act ensued – as usual named after the proposer of

the bill – concerning the abolition of forced labour in the colonies. On 30 April came the birthday of the Fonds d'investissement pour le Développement Economique et Social (FIDES), to which France was to allot around £800 million by 1958. The political crowning of this work took place on 7 May, two days after the negative result of the referendum on the draft constitution. On that day the Lamine-Guèye Act (proposed by the representative of the first electoral roll of Senegal, an African) declared all inhabitants of the colonies to be citizens of the republic, the former discrimination against 'subjects' thereby being at least symbolically done away with. If one can assert of the rest of the legislation that like the British Colonial Development and Welfare Act of 1945 it belongs under the heading of enlightened colonial policy, then the Lamine-Guèye Act can unequivocally be regarded as the prelude to decolonization.

In its final version, the constitution of the Fourth Republic also desired to give expression to decolonization; that is, the overcoming of colonization. The overseas members had proposed the following text in July 1946:

> [Article 106] France solemnly condemns the colonial system based on the annexation, conquest or dominance of overseas territories. It renounces all unilateral sovereignty over the colonized peoples. It recognizes their freedom to govern themselves [*de se gouverner eux-mêmes*] and to administer [*gérer*] their own affairs democratically. [Article 107] The French Republic forms a union with its overseas peoples: the Union Française, which is based on equality of rights and responsibilities without distinction of race or religion.[4]

In the final text, ratified by the people in their referendum, the principles of the union were shifted into the preamble and – as one can see, not without significance – modified.

> France forms a union with its overseas peoples which is based on equality of rights and duties without distinction of race or religion. The Union Française is composed of nations and peoples who unite or co-ordinate the sources of their strength and their efforts in order to develop their respective civilizations, improve their prosperity, and safeguard their security. True to its traditional mission, France intends to lead the people it has taken under its protection to freedom, to administer themselves [*de*

s'administrer eux-mêmes] and to order their own affairs in a democratic manner. Any colonial system based on arbitrary power is excluded; France guarantees to all equal access to public offices and the individual or collective exercising of the here proclaimed or confirmed rights and freedoms.[5]

That is, essentially the human and civil rights of 1789, with a few new principles added.

The 'Overseas Territories' (that is, African colonies south of the Sahara, Madagascar, and Oceania), the overseas *départements* and of course Algeria, according to the 1946 constitution, all formed, together with European France, one indivisible French Republic. The Union Française was intended to serve as a brace between the republic and its former colonies in Indochina. In Vietnam, Ho Chi Minh had just declared independence, a fact which had to be reckoned with. For this reason there were no representatives from Indochina in the Paris constituent assemblies, and similarly no Moroccans or Tunisians; France offered to the protectorates in which precolonial indigenous executive power continued, as well as to post-colonial revolutionary Vietnam, the status of 'associated states' within the union. Morocco and Tunisia, however, rejected the offer, and the Vietnam War soon prevented union with the three countries of Indochina. With the exception of its quasi-parliamentary 'assembly', which eased the path of some African politicians into politics, the Union Française was an empty shell for the duration of its existence. For years presided over by Albert Sarraut, the Assemblée de l'Union Française – seventy-five members from European France, seventy-five from overseas France, and a maximum of forty-five from the associated states – had no right either to pass or veto laws, although it did debate all draft bills relating to overseas matters. Its members thereby gained some insights into the decision-making process of the Fourth Republic.

VIETNAM

Vietnam became the touchstone of the Union Française. 'Digesting' this new, revolutionary, communist-ruled entity was its chief goal from the outset. What France hoped to achieve by this was not necessarily the elimination of the Vietmin (after all, communists also participated in government in Paris). Even de Gaulle's intentions with regard to Vietnam were left remarkably vague; in practice he pursued a policy of recolonization, without heed to the criticism of other nations. He sent Admiral Thierry d'Argenlieu to Saigon as high commissioner – a priest of a Catholic order who lived in the fantasy world of a medieval monastic knight. Before even setting foot on Vietnamese soil, d'Argenlieu proclaimed on 23 August 1945 'the will of the government of the Republic to do something new in Indochina with the freely given help of all Annamite, Cambodian and Laotian inhabitants – in the order and moderation of reason – France wishes to remain in the service of the Annamite nation, of Cambodia and Laos, and not to be served by them.'[6]

It rapidly became clear what the high commissioner meant by 'freely given help' and the 'service' being offered. Whilst at the end of September 1945 a 180,000-man strong Nationalist Chinese army was occupying Tongking and Annam as far as the 16th parallel, bringing in its retinue a number of anti-communist Vietnamese politicians, which caused problems for Ho Chi Minh, General Leclerc of France landed in Saigon on 5 October to relieve the British troops in the south. He routed the weak Vietmin units, and by February 1946 the French at least had their former Cochichine colony once again firmly in their possession. In the north, Ho kept the Chinese generals at bay with careful manoeuvring and jangling of coins, while his communist militia and the freshly recruited paramilitary units of the anti-communists fought bitterly. At last a compromise was found for the elections, which resulted on 6 February in a Vietnamese National Assembly: the Vietmin had enforced uniformist election tickets, however granting 70 out of 350 seats to the anti-communists. The people demonstrated their approval. In Hanoi Ho Chi Minh obtained 169,222 of the 172,765 votes cast, of a total of 187,880 people eligible to vote. Vo Nguyen Giap, at that time minister of the interior, managed to obtain 97 per cent of the vote for himself in his (and Ho's) home province of Nghe An; even in the imperial city of Hué 83 per cent of the vote was successfully mustered for the uniformist election ticket.

A little later France reached out towards the north. On 28 February 1946 it relinquished its concessions in Shanghai and other Chinese cities (three years after the other western powers; the formal release of China from the demeaning status of a 'semi-colony' was thus completed), in return for which Chiang Kai-shek withdrew from North Vietnam. In contrast with the case of the south, however, in the north Leclerc saw fit to make a treaty with the Vietmin.

Doggedly and unflinchingly Ho Chi Minh negotiated with Leclerc's emissaries – the former resistance fighter Jean Sainteny and General Raoul Salan – for recognition of the independence and unity of Vietnam. The Chinese card, which he attempted to play at the last minute, however, no longer had any clout. He had no alternative, therefore, but to reach an agreement with France, although it would seem he did not particularly mind doing so. A somewhat drastic saying of President Ho hails from this particular period: 'Better to smell a bit of French shit than to have to eat Chinese shit for the rest of our lives!'[7]

An uneasy compromise ensued: in the preliminary convention of 6 March 1946, France recognized 'the Republic of Vietnam as a free state with government, parliament, army and finances, forming part of the Indochinese Federation and the Union Française'.[8] The question of unity, the 'Unity of the Three Ky' (Tongking, Annam, Cochin-China) as they were then called in Vietnam, remained open. By the same token, the word 'free' did not necessarily mean sovereign or independent.

Thierry d'Argenlieu snubbed the Vietnamese immediately, on 1 June 1946, by making Cochin-China an autonomous republic, but Ho Chi Minh nevertheless persisted with his policy of co-operation. In the same month, he travelled with a Vietnamese government delegation to Europe to begin fresh negotiations in Fontainebleau – this time directly with the Paris government. On 23 June Georges Bidault, MRP leader and former president of the Resistance Council, became prime minister of the Fourth Republic, which still had no constitution, also becoming his own foreign minister. Maurice Thorez, leader of the Communist Party (PCF), remained deputy prime minister, and four ministries were headed by communists. If the communist Ho Chi Minh was hoping for support from this coalition, he was to be disappointed. Perhaps he overestimated the influence of the PCF in the government, where in fact the 'left' (the communists and socialists) were already on the retreat before the (at least relatively) 'right' force of the MRP. The PCF in any case had no overseas policy, being interested not in the colonies, but in a chance to take over power in France. A party delegation did visit Comrade Ho before the start of the conference, on 22 June, but during the negotiations themselves, which lasted from 6 July until 10 September, he received no back-up at all from the communists. Ho Chi Minh was obliged to stand alone against the representatives of the French bourgeoisie.

This in itself was no reason for the conference to fail, however. Leclerc and Sainteny were not communists, but they were still intelligent enough to recognize in Ho a legitimate spokesman for his people – at least for those of North Vietnam. Ho for his part proved ready to make compromises. At his first official meeting with Bidault on 2 July, he said:

> The infinite diversity of the French provinces is a source of astonishment to the world, but it does not prevent France from being a unified and indivisible nation. Tomorrow the Union Française, strong in the infinite diversity of free peoples, will astonish the world with its cohesion and its unity. . . . Paris has contributed no small part to allowing Vietnam and France to associate fraternally in the framework of this union. . . . We are grateful to Paris that Vietnam today is on the road of independence.[9]

Would the forces of renewal about which the France of the Resistance was so proud, prove strong or even courageous enough to catch this ball thrown into their court by Ho? In fact they did not. It is likely that they failed to recognize what role they were really playing at Fontainebleau. To reiterate: in spite of all goodwill they lacked a clear overseas policy concept. In this respect the forces of inertia – more aptly called colonial restoration – were better off, as they only needed to promote a firm grip on affairs and the protection of traditionally handed-down rights. As the last constitutional consultations and the conference of Fontainebleau were in session, the Estates General of French Colonization were also meeting in Paris from 30 July until 24 August 1946. Although representing chiefly business people and settlers from Africa, fighting with corresponding vigour for the two-roll electoral system in the overseas territories of the republic, this pressure group of colonial conservatives may nevertheless indirectly have exerted an influence on the negotiations with Ho Chi Minh.

Paris proposed the setting-up of an 'Indochinese Federation', to which Laos and Cambodia were to belong in addition to Vietnam. Both countries were still in a state of political lethargy, despite the fact that the king of Cambodia had attempted to declare independence in 1945. The monarchy of Laos was in any case itself a French creation. It is understandable, therefore, that the Vietnamese refused at Fontainebleau to ally their country with a 'federation' which could easily be manipulated by France. Instead, they called for a separate

Vietnamese army and their own diplomatic service, being prepared to lease air and naval bases to the French temporarily, whilst France on the other hand wanted to set up a unified (that is, French) supreme command. The Vietnamese (who were after all communists) reserved the right to nationalize French businesses in their country; France had after all just nationalized its own mines, electricity, gas, banks, and insurance. Bidault, however, demanded absolute protection of French private property in Vietnam.

Above all, Ho Chi Minh called for the whole of Vietnam to be a nation in its own right: 'Unity of the Three Ky'. He demanded a referendum in Cochin-China, to be organized jointly by the Vietmin and the pro-French government which was meanwhile in office in Saigon and was attempting to govern exactly the same territory which from 1956 to 1975 was to be South Vietnam. Bidault said no: communist terrorism would have to come to a stop in the south first. Bidault similarly refused to allow the word 'independence' to pass his lips. It was because of these two questions, unity and independence, that Pham Van Dong, spokesman for the Vietnamese at the last sitting on 10 September 1946, allowed the conference to break down.

Ho Chi Minh must have feared being swamped by a wave of extremism within his own party; while he was negotiating in Fontainebleau, mistrust grew in Vietnam on account of his readiness to compromise. The document waiting for signature on 10 September contained the points on which agreement had been reached: the economic and technical details of the entry of Vietnam into the Union Française. On such politically secondary issues, Ho had indeed backed down. On the key issues of unity and independence, however, on which Ho had stood firm, the document was silent. Truong Ching, general secretary of the Communist Party of Vietnam, which had integrated into the Vietmin, was already openly criticizing the president as an opportunist. Trotskyite and even expressly anti-communist politicians were singing the same tune.

Ho Chi Minh, a master of tactics even in this highly delicate situation, demonstrated national pride with one hand: his delegation left without signing the document. His other hand, however, was still outstretched to the French government; he even went so far as to stay over in Paris for several days. On 14 September he consulted again with Bidault and the colonial minister, Moutet, and shortly before midnight signed the document which had been rejected by his delegation. On 19 September Ho boarded his ship in Toulon for the journey home. This meant that his return journey would last a whole month; in the mean time he could observe the reaction of his people and his party to the move of 14 September.

The contents of the famous *modus vivendi* of 14 September 1946 are relatively unimportant. There is much talk of 'mixed committees' which were to continue discussion of all the important questions; one can read of an end to 'hostile and violent' activities in South Vietnam, of democratic freedoms and of a guarantee for French possessions and French enterprises.[10] The essential point here was to keep the thread of negotiation spinning. Alone and heavily burdened by the events of the previous months, Ho Chi Minh had thrown into the scales his authority to co-operate with a France whose plans and future were still unrevealed.

In the mean time, Vo Nguyen Giap was doing everything in his power to prepare the Vietmin fighting forces for war. Politically, however, he made his stand on the side of the president – against the extremists. On 20 October Ho Chi Minh landed at Haiphong, immediately taking the people and the government firmly in hand; a wave of purges and arrests smashed the anti-communist opposition. When parliament met on 28 October, only twenty of the seventy members of other parties were left. Ho was confirmed as president and Giap took over as minister of defence. The Vietmin were now completely masters of the house and the group around Ho masters of the Vietmin.

Co-operation with France, based on political compromise, would now have had a chance. The French military in Vietnam, however, were alarmed at the stabilization of communist power. Tension flared up among the soldiers of both sides, especially in the port of Haiphong. On 12 November 1946 the French commander posted there, Colonel Dèbes, received a telegram from his superior, General Valluy, which stated:

> We are obviously faced with a planned aggression being care-
> fully prepared by the Vietnamese army; this army no longer
> seems to obey the orders of its government. Under these circum-
> stances your worthy attempts to achieve reconciliation and
> redivision of stationing, as well as the investigation ordered by
> myself, are no longer appropriate. The moment has come to
> teach a tough lesson to those who have attacked you so treach-
> erously. You must make yourself master of Haiphong with all
> the means at your disposal. You must teach the supreme
> command of the Vietnamese army the error of its ways.[11]

Thus reads the document on the outbreak of the first Indochinese war. Dèbes ordered his artillery and warships, lying in dock, to batter down Haiphong: there were at least 6,000 dead. Giap did not 'repent', however. On 19 December his militia (not, that is, the small regular force at his disposal, which he kept back for years) attacked the French wherever they could. Forty Europeans were killed and 200 taken prisoner. The government of the Democratic Republic of Vietnam left Hanoi. Ho issued the call to battle:

> Whoever possesses a gun should arm himself with that gun.
> Whoever owns a sword should arm himself with that sword.
> Even if you have no swords, arm yourselves with pick-axes,
> spades and sticks. . . . The war of resistance will be hard, but
> our people will be victorious in selfless struggle.[12]

Initially it seemed madness to expect to defeat the French expedition corps with swords and spades. Up until March 1947, the French had 'stabilized' the military situation, that is, they had brought all important sites and communication lines under their control. Guerrilla war and terrorism continued to be waged against friends of France (in the north more energetically than in the south). Had the colonial power, however, not been putting down uprisings for decades? The French did not reckon with the all-embracing, long-term war plan of Giap, in which guerrilla warfare was only one weapon among many. In the first phase, the guerrilla fighters were to lead the struggle, so as to cut the enemy off from all connection with the population. In other words, terrorism was to be conducted in such a way that French repression would awaken an anti-colonial spirit of struggle among the whole people. In the second phase, the politico-military power of the Vietmin was then to be set up in liberated zones which were as large as possible, and a regular army established and trained at the same time. In the third phase, this army would then launch attacks from these 'base zones' against the French enclaves – especially the cities.

Giap managed both to carry out and win with his strategy. Three factors helped him: first, the military arrogance of the French generals, who expected until the very end to win the war alone, even without the dispatching of French conscripts – that is, only with volunteers, colonial troops, and the Foreign Legion; second, the proverbial 'intransigence' of Parisian policy, especially after the elections of 1951; third, and above all, the victory of Mao Tse-tung in China, which provided the Vietmin with the gift of a friendly hinterland.

When Mao's armies appeared on the border of Vietnam at the beginning of 1950, Giap evidently believed he would be able to accomplish his three-phase plan within a very short time. Immediately he took the border town of Lao Kay near the railway running from Hanoi to Yunnan. He posted five divisions (totalling just 30,000 men), armed them with American weapons which had been left behind by Chiang Kai-shek's forces when they had been disbanded, and in September 1950 overpowered the French garrison of Cao Bang, another important town in the extreme north of Tongking. Lang Son, the third key position for control of the frontier, likewise fell; Giap now believed himself sufficiently reinforced to press forward with 40,000 men to the Red River delta and throw the enemy out of Hanoi – he failed. In December 1950 Paris posted General de Lattre de Tassigny (1889–1952) to Indochina as both commander-in-chief and high commissioner – that is, also as head of the civil authorities. By 19 January 1951 he had broken Giap's offensive near Vinh Yen, 50 km north of Hanoi. Within a few weeks a series of French victories had secured the Red River delta, one of the two rice granaries of Vietnam (the other being in the south, at the Mekong delta, which was already under French control). Giap had to fall back on the first phase of his war plan, but he nevertheless fought on.

De Lattre appealed to America to step up aid. On 20 September 1951 he said on a visit to Washington:

> There is today in the world a city of enormous importance, and
> that is Hanoi, the capital of Tongking. . . . From the military
> point of view its loss would mean opening the road for the
> communist invasion to Bangkok, Singapore and many other
> roads . . . Hanoi is now for the free world of South-East Asia the
> Bastogne of December 1944 and the Berlin of 1948. . . . If
> Tongking is once lost, there will be no stopping until Suez.[13]

France was none the less left to its own resources.

De Lattre set up a network of more or less well fortified bases. This system of 'quadrillage' engaged vast numbers: more than 80,000 of the 175,000 men making up the French army in Vietnam. Above all it was unable to reawaken the trust of the population in their colonial rulers, now that it had been broken once and for all. Since the French had too few planes and almost no helicopters, the military effect of this network of outposts remained limited; it was impossible to conduct offensive mobile warfare from this network, that is, to engage in action with the fighting forces of the Vietmin, when the advantage lay on the French side. De Lattre was likewise unable to achieve a lasting successful counter-strike into the heart of Vietmin territory; his offensive against Hoa Binh on 13 November 1951, which was intended to sever the supply routes between the Chinese border and central Vietnam, ended in an embarrassing retreat. Although under the command of General Salan twelve infantry and three paratrooper battalions, reinforced by two armoured groups, had overrun Hoa Binh in the first assault, Giap countered with such strong pressure that they were compelled to evacuate their position on 25 February 1952. Even the 'pacification' of territory held by French troops proved incomplete. Throughout Vietnam the Vietmin continued to be present – be it in the form of regular administration in the 'base zones', as guerrilla and 'night-time government' in the disputed territory, or as a terrorist underground in French territory. The effect of the alliance between the French authorities and certain South Vietnamese bandit chiefs, some of whom disguised themselves under the cloak of leaders of religious sects, proved particularly disastrous. In Tongking the Catholic bishops of Phat Diem, Bui Chu, and Nam Dinh created their own power spheres, but even these did not constitute reliable bases for the French supreme command.

On 11 January 1952 General de Lattre died in a Paris clinic. Salan took over until he was relieved by General Henri Navarre (born 1898) in May 1953. The French continued to operate within a hostile or at best passive population. It was this which brought about its defeat – not Dien Bien Phu alone.

The battle of Dien Bien Phu was a well thought-out act on the part of Navarre. Giap had responded to strikes by stepping up the 'second phase', that is, by extending the communist-controlled base zones as far as possible. Ho Chi Minh had meanwhile revived the Communist Party as the Labour Party of Vietnam (Viet Nam Gang Lao Dong) in 1951, joining it with other groups to form the United National Unity Front (Lien Viet), as well as founding satellite parties for Laos and Kampuchea; the Neo Lao Hax Hat (mostly known as the 'Pathet Lao') under Prince Souphanouvong and the Khmer Issarak or 'Khmer Rouge'. Navarre expected that Giap would want to march on Laos with regular troops, and seized the chance to launch an attack on the core troops of the Vietmin, convinced that the superior weaponry of the French would be bound to defeat them. To this end, he dispatched airborne troops to Dien Bien Phu on 20 November 1953, where within a few weeks a stronghold was set up on the route to northern Laos – on the day of the enemy attack, 13 March 1954, this was occupied by twelve battalions (10,813 men), a mixture of French, North Africans, black Africans, and legionaries, ten tanks, forty-seven jeeps, forty-seven Dodge vehicles, twenty-four 10.5 cm and four 15.5 cm heavy artillery.[14]

Giap acted immediately, putting five divisions on the march to Dien Bien Phu. On 6 December 1953 he issued his order of the day:

> You must repair the roads, overcome all obstacles, overcome all difficulties. You must fight without ever despairing, you must master cold and hunger, carry heavy burdens over mountains and through valleys. You must break through to the enemy camp in order to destroy him and free our compatriots. . . . Comrades forward![15]

In addition to courage and endurance, however, the Vietmin soldiers now also had artillery. Around Dien Bien Phu American anti-aircraft guns and forty-two mountain guns supplied from China (earlier captured in Korea) had been positioned. The French had not counted on this: the enemy artillery fire upset their tactics. The French garrison in Dien Bien Phu capitulated on 7 May, and the last Isabelle field fort on 8 May 1954.

From 13 March until 5 May 449 French (including 59 officers), 624 North Africans (including one officer), 16 black Africans, 1,056 Légion Etrangère soldiers, and 603 Vietnamese fell on the French side – a total of 2,748 men. A total of almost 10,000 were taken prisoner – including 4,000 wounded. At the stronghold a total of 17 battalions were wiped out, 36 planes shot down, and 34 destroyed on the ground. According to French estimations, the attacking divisions of the Vietmin lost 7,900 dead and 15,000 wounded.

These figures need on the one hand to be compared with earlier French losses in Indochina. From 1945 until 1 April 1952 (that is, including the battles for Hoa Binh), 13,333 French fell, 5,488 men of the Foreign Legion, 5,024 North Africans, and 17,068 Indochinese.[16] On the other hand, however, one must also take into account the forces at General Navarre's disposal *before* the battle at Dien Bien Phu: 69,000 French, 30,000 North Africans, 18,000 black Africans, 20,000 legionaries and 333,000 Indochinese, including the new army of 'independent' Vietnam under Bao Dai, of whom more will be related below. The costs of the war had been rising constantly, from around

£200 million in 1948 to £600 million for 1952. Up to Dien Bien Phu a total cost of £2,000 million can be reckoned, half of which was taken up by American military aid, which poured in from 1948 onwards.[17] Seen in this context, therefore, although the outcome of the battle of Dien Bien Phu seems a genuine fiasco, and of course a thwarting of the strategic plans of General Navarre, it was by no means a military catastrophe on a scale which would have forced France to capitulate to Ho Chi Minh.

Dien Bien Phu did nevertheless make the French people aware of the political catastrophe which had been concealed behind apparently successful military operations for a considerable time. Could they have overcome the deadlock? Could they have entertained the idea of winning back the Vietnamese population? Theoretically there were even two possible solutions: either fresh negotiations with Ho Chi Minh, or the encouragement of other Vietnamese representatives to political involvement.

On 5 March 1947, appointed by the socialist Ramadier just two months before the communist ministers were thrown out of the cabinet, the high commissioner, Emile Bollaert, had sought contact with Ho Chi Minh, but had offered him unacceptable conditions for a truce: an immediate halt not only to fighting and terrorism, but also to all propaganda; a handing-over of most of the Vietmin arms; freedom of movement for French troops in the whole of Vietmin territory, and the handing-over of hostages, prisoners, and deserters.[18] Ho was bound to reject this and since then the communication lines had been down. France officially sought alternative Vietnamese representatives. It found none better than the former Emperor Bao Dai, who had retired to Hong Kong. After much haggling, a proclamation was issued on 5 June 1948 in the bay of Along (near Haiphong) in which

> France solemnly recognizes the independence of Vietnam. It is
> incumbent on the latter to implement its unity in freedom. For
> its part, Vietnam declares its membership of the Union
> Française as a state associated with France. The independence of
> Vietnam has no other boundaries than those imposed on it by
> membership of the Union Française.[19]

These were puzzling words, in which the last sentence appears to invalidate what is maintained in the first.

Politics crept along at a snail's pace throughout the war with varying success, whilst the war itself raged on at speed. It was to take almost a year for the French president, Vincent Auriol, to ratify the agreement with Bao Dai on 8 March 1949, and only now did the former emperor make his way home. It was then to take until 27 January 1950 for Bao Dai's Vietnam (now really including Cochin-China), Cambodia, and Laos to be brought into the Union Française. The 'independence' of the three associated states continued to be limited, both in their domestic and foreign policy, by all manner of clauses. Fundamentally France had set up a new type of protectorate in Indochina. Only now, on 30 January 1950, did Moscow and Peking, by way of a counter-move, accord the Democratic Republic of Vietnam under Ho Chi Minh official diplomatic recognition.

In 1952, after the fall of the French garrisons in the north of Tongking, Bao Dai was given permission to set up his own army, but this did nothing to change the situation. The action readiness of those Vietnamese troops who were on the side of the French was virtually non-existent. The whole world looked upon Bao Dai as an unhappy puppet – justifiably so. France was doing everything to show the world, including Vietnam, that it wished to create this impression; one must bear in mind that the governments of the Fourth Republic, who portrayed themselves as responsible for this vacuum in place of an Indochina policy, were under incessant pressure from right-wing and colonial pressure groups, who were accusing them of 'squandering' the overseas empire, whilst the left, including the SFIO, was having pangs of conscience about whether it could or should not after all negotiate with Ho Chi Minh. It was in this way that the climate arose in which the Vietnam War came to be regarded by the French public as '*la guerre sale*', the 'dirty war'.

Dirty war – not only at the fronts themselves, but above all behind them; not only behind the French lines, where gigantic currency profiteering was the order of the day, and where (in Hanoi) hardly a civilian took part in the parade to honour the dead of Dien Bien Phu, whilst on the same evening the nightspots were full to the brim. Behind Vietmin lines at the same time, on 4 December 1953, the tragedy of the 'land reform' decreed by the National Assembly was unfolding. Ho Chi Minh said of this: 'Land reform is a peasant revolution, which leads to class struggle in the village, a hard and complicated struggle.'[20] It is alleged that on party orders five landowners were killed in every village – a total of 100,000 – and a much greater number interned in camps.

Pierre Mendès-France, the outsider premier of the Fourth Republic, entered office on 18 June 1954 – during the Geneva Indochina Conference called by the foreign ministers of the USA, the Soviet Union, Britain, and France, in February in Berlin. The conference opened on 26 April, just as Dien Bien Phu was being condemned to its demise. Directly before this, Bidault had made an attempt to draw the two Anglo-Saxon powers into the Vietnam War. The American military were willing to give the French breathing space by means of air attacks (if necessary with atom bombs). Winston Churchill's objection on 24 April, however, meant that the undertaking failed. France was left to its own devices.

Mendès-France pressed for the expedition corps just on the point of evacuating Hanoi and the northern rice granary to be reinforced with French conscripts; all premiers before him had held back fearfully from such an 'escalation'. At the same time Mendès-France declared his desire for peace. By means of this tactic he achieved what in view of the political catastrophe and the military defeat still was achievable; the honourable withdrawal of the French from North Vietnam within 300 days (the Vietmin had only wanted to give them six months), and a restriction of communist rule to North Vietnam as far as the 17th parallel (the Vietmin had also claimed the former imperial city of Hué, and Danang). One million Vietnamese, mostly Catholics, were able to flee from the north to the south shielded by French troops, whereas only some 20,000 or 30,000 Vietmin militants took the opposite road.

The Final Declaration of the Geneva Indochina Conference, announced simultaneously with the armistice of 21 July 1954, sealed with clause 12 not only the end of French rule, but also of all French political influence in Indochina:

> All participants in the Geneva Conference pledge in their
> relations with Kampuchea, Laos and Vietnam to respect the
> sovereignty, independence, unity and territorial integrity of the
> said states and to refrain from any interference in their internal
> affairs.[21]

The USA and the Vietnam government in Saigon, headed since 26 June 1954 by the anti-French Ngo Dinh Diem and now no longer backed by Paris but by Washington, did not of course recognize this outcome of the war.

Not only Vietnam but also Laos and Kampuchea withdrew from the Union Française. Although France allowed part VIII of its constitution to remain as it was until 1958, the union thus formally remaining in existence, it no longer figured as a reality in international politics after 1954.

ALGERIA

Still under the leadership of Mendès-France, France found itself involved in another colonial war directly after Vietnam. Only a quarter of a year intervened between the end of the Geneva Conference and the night of 1 November 1954, on which Algeria began its armed struggle for independence. The Paris government was left with very little time to apply the lessons learned in Vietnam to the decolonization of its North African possessions. Here also, therefore, blood was to be shed for years – albeit in only one of the three Maghreb countries. In Morocco and Tunisia France learned the lessons of Vietnam just in time. Even in Algeria, once the fighting had been brought to an end, it succeeded in establishing firmer foundations for post-colonial co-operation than it had done in Vietnam.

As has been mentioned above, Algeria underwent an explosion of racial hatred and violence on the day of German capitulation, 8 May 1945. It is difficult to say exactly which political elements triggered off the massacre, whether it was only one side or whether it was planned at all. We do know that a police officer stepped out of the Café de France in Sétif on that day and saw a man running up to him carrying a poster with 'Long live the victory of the Allies' written on it, whereupon he shot the man outright. General carnage ensued, in which tanks and planes (the minister for the air force at that time was the communist Charles Tillon), warships and rapidly armed Italian prisoners were all engaged; some 102 Europeans died. According to official reports the Muslim population lost 1,500, according to Algerians (and the American consul) 45,000. The *Echo D'Alger*, the newspaper of the European settlers, spoke of 'the hour of the gendarmes' having struck for Algeria.

Messali, leader of the People's Party (PPA), which had only just emerged from illegality, was deported to Brazzaville, the PPA was banned once again and Ferhat Abbas likewise arrested. The authorities imprisoned a total of 4,560 Muslims; 99 death sentences and 64 life sentences were passed. Political life was not normalized again until March 1946: Abbas was freed, founding the UDMA, which represented the moderate nationalist bourgeoisie, and won the elections to the French second Constituent Assembly on the second electoral roll.

His attempts to interest the French parties in drastic reform were futile. Abbas proposed that the Paris Constituent Assembly grant to 'the Algerian Republic' a 'constitution' and internal autonomy as an associated state. Not even the communists supported him. The UDMA consequently boycotted the elections to the National Assembly in November 1946, presenting candidates only for the second chamber of the Paris parliament, the Council of the Republic (the Senate), and there it managed to win four of the seven seats allocated to the Algerian second roll. In the National Assembly, Messali attempted to bridge the gap. He had in the mean time been brought to France and enjoyed a certain limited freedom of political action. By way of a replacement for the PPA, he founded a 'movement for the victory of democratic freedoms' (Mouvement pour le Triomphe des Libertés Démocratiques – MTLD), standing as a candidate in Algiers. The administration, however, would not permit the candidature of this hated 'extremist' and also obstructed the MTLD in other constituencies. As a result they were only able to send five members to Paris, among them the subsequent leader of the FLN, Mohammed Khider.

On 20 September 1947 France proclaimed a statute for Algeria against the protests of the MTLD as well as of the UDMA, whose senators relinquished their seats. This statute left the colonial-type administration, which predominantly served the interests of the European minority, fully intact. It transformed the Délégations Financières into an 'Algerian Assembly' with 120 members, 60 of whom were to be elected from the first and 60 from the second electoral roll, thus ensuring a pro-French majority, since the first roll contained only 13 per cent Muslims, and thanks to the administration even on the second roll the electoral victory of many 'yes-men', that is, obedient tools of the authorities, could be taken for granted. In fact after the first elections of 1948 the second class of the assembly comprised only eight UDMA and nine MTLD members, as against forty-three 'independents'.

In the years that followed, the French administration of Algeria raised vote-rigging and fixing, '*truquage*' in French, to the level of a system – an almost perfect system. It is not to be wondered at, therefore, that in all by-elections to the Algerian Assembly until 1954 MTLD and UDMA support vanished into thin air, or that in the fresh election to the National Assembly in June 1951 not a single Algerian nationalist managed to get through.

Superficially, social calm and even satisfaction prevailed among the Muslims of Algeria, thanks to a solicitous administration, at the beginning of the 1950s. In reality, however, the politically aware Algerians who were willing to negotiate were being driven into illegality by this experience of contempt. Whilst the UDMA notables initially stood embittered on the sidelines, the MTLD were secretly forming a paramilitary 'Special Organization' (OS). Ahmed Ben Bella and Mohammed Boudiaf (both born in 1919), former sergeants in the French army, the Kabyle Hussein Ait Ahmed, who was five years younger, Rabah Bitat, born in 1926, and a few other young men in the OS were urging action and violence while Mohammed Khider attempted until 1951 to shield the organization by using his parliamentary immunity. He failed: the police struck in March 1950. Ben Bella escaped from prison in 1952, forming an exile group in Cairo with Ait Ahmed and Khider, whilst other members of the scattered OS at home in Algeria followed the time-honoured habit of the persecuted by fleeing to the Djebel, i.e. into the mountains. The former lance corporal Krim Belkassem (1924–70) had been organizing secret refuge in his native Kabyle region since 1947 for young men on the run from French military service and other 'problems' with the authorities. From November 1951 five courts condemned Krim to death in his absence. In 1962 he was to sign the truce of Evian as leader of the FLN delegation.

Around 1950, the political parties were still trying to build up a united front; the 'lawless ones', the 'fellagha' in the Djebel, were still a peripheral phenomenon, and the OS a safety valve for extremists. In August 1951 the MTLD and UDMA, the *ulemas* and the Algerian Communist Party met, but their 'bloc' came to no more than fine-sounding speeches. The Communist Party, whose members were still predominantly Europeans, although they had a 'Muslim' general secretary – Larbi Bouhali – supported Algerian nationalism only half-heartedly. The MTLD was inwardly corroded in 1953 by the lack of any prospect for political negotiation, their leader Messali, hero of the simple man for almost thirty years, was now (definitively) since 14 May 1952 once again under house arrest in France, and therefore guarded his authority all the more jealously. Members of the MTLD Central Committee – among them Youssef ben Khedda (born 1920) – arraigned him for having started a 'personality cult' – a topical accusation in the year of Stalin's death. As the MTLD split into Messalists and 'centrists', a handful of younger men abandoned this repugnant and hopeless enterprise, forming in March 1954 in Algiers a Revolutionary Committee for Unity and Action (Comité Révolutionnaire pour l'Unité et l'Action – CRUA) which was immediately joined by the Cairo group of émigrés. There were now nine 'conspirators': Mustafa Ben Boulaid, Murad Didouche, Larbi Ben M'hidi (who was arrested in Algiers in 1957 and found dead in his cell on 4 March), Mohammed Boudiaf, Rabah Bitat, Krim Belkassem, Mohammed Khider, Hussein Ait Ahmed, and Ben Bella.

They set the uprising for 1 November, the first areas targeted to be Krim's Kabyle region and the Aurès Mountains, which were Ben Boulaid's home. The CRUA had no more than 3,000 men with military training at their disposal, compared with the almost 50,000 French soldiers in Algeria, these being reinforced to 80,000 by February 1955. This war of liberation seemed on the face of it to have far less chance of success than the one launched by Ho and Giap, who had already been in charge of a firmly established national communist power apparatus for almost a year by the end of 1946. To begin with, therefore, French planes dropped over the Aurès some tens of thousands of leaflets, on which could be read:

> Proclamation to the Islamic population. Agitators, among whom there are foreigners, have unleashed bloody unrest in our country and have established themselves in your region in particular. They live on your possessions. They are blackmailing you and want to drag the men of your families into a criminal adventure. . . . Muslims! You will not follow them. You will immediately, before Sunday 21 November at 18.00 hours, gather your relatives and possessions in the security zones. The demarcation of these zones will be indicated by the French troops in your region and by the administrative authorities in the villages. . . . Soon a terrible calamity will fall on the heads of the rebels. Afterwards French peace will reign once again.[22]

François Mitterrand, minister of the interior in the cabinet of Mendès-France, declared on 5 November: 'Algeria is France; from Flanders to the Congo there is only one law, one nation, one parliament. The Constitution wills it so, we will it so. . . . *La seule négotiation, c'est la guerre.* [War is the only negotiation.]' On 26 January 1955 Mendès-France appointed the Gaullist assembly representative

Jacques Soustelle as the new governor-general of Algeria; Soustelle declared a month later before the Algerian Assembly: 'France will no more evacuate from Algeria than it will from Provence or Brittany. France has made her choice. She has chosen integration.'[23]

By May 1955 the rebels had formed a United Front, the Front de Libération Nationale (FLN). Messali on the other hand attempted to keep those loyal to him within the Algerian National Movement (Mouvement National Algérien – MNA). The Communist Party was silent until September 1955 and as a result fell even more in the esteem of the masses. Their loyalty was inexorably drawing them, in a process which will probably always remain hidden from history, towards the FLN, whose leaders, until then known at most to specialized police, and referred to by the French simply as bandits, were suddenly at the vanguard of fighters embodying the Algerian nation. This nation, stubbornly denied existence by official France, resorted to violence. In a war lasting more than seven years they achieved the first complete victory over a colonial power to occur in such a manner in the post-war period. Although this thesis may perhaps seem surprising one cannot assert that the first Vietnam War concluded with the complete victory of the anti-colonial side. The Vietmin conducted a war against France in order to achieve complete independence and 'Unity of the Three Ky'. The Geneva Conference brought fulfilment of the first demand, but not of the second.

France's efforts to deal with the Algerian uprising manifest a desire to take to heart the lessons of Vietnam, both in the military and in the political spheres. In military terms this meant improved 'quadrillage', in order either to prevent or reverse the emergence of FLN-dominated base zones; psychological warface aimed at isolating the FLN from the majority of the Muslim population; and most particularly the sealing-off of the eastern and western borders to block the FLN's supply lines.

The latter goal was accomplished, in spite of the fact that as a result of the dubious logic of French North Africa policy Morocco and Tunisia obtained independence in 1956 and both King Mohammed V and Habib Bourguiba simply had to support the FLN so as not to compromise themselves in the eyes of their own peoples and the entire Arab-African world. The exiled Algerian leadership thus enjoyed asylum in Morocco and Tunisia as well as in Cairo and Libya and, by no means least, in Switzerland, through whose trustworthy and discreet banks they were able to finance the running costs of the war. A total of 220,000 Algerians fled to neighbouring countries, above all Tunisia, the FLN recruiting an army (numbering at least 16,000 men) from among them, which thanks to foreign donations they were able to arm with increasingly modern weapons.[24] In March 1960 Houari Boumedienne (1925-78) took his place at the head of the general staff of this 'army across the borders'; prior to 1954 he had studied Arabic literature at El Azhar University in Cairo, having then made his way through to Oran with nine men, proving his military talent there until 1957 as commander of the Liberation Army (Armée de Libération Nationale - ALN) in wilaya number five.[25] Any later he would scarcely have managed to make it over to Tunisia, after France had secured the border with a continuous barricade zone bristling with electric wire barriers - known as the 'Morice Line' after a defence minister - which had been completed by the middle of 1957. Break-throughs in either direction by the ALN became less and less frequent. A precarious contact between the exiled leadership, the 'army across the borders' and the 'army in the six wilayas' was now only possible via the Sahara.

Although the 'ALN of the wilayas', estimated by their opponents at 15,000 men at the end of 1960, manfully held its own against the French army of occupation and the mobile units intended to engage them in combat, it was unable to secure any lasting base zones of any size. When General Salan assumed supreme command in Algeria in 1956 he saw to it that the number of French soldiers was increased from around 250,000 to 500,000. France thus had almost its entire army of conscripts posted in North Africa, having withdrawn them from NATO. Engagement in a colonial war necessitated retraining and rearmament which for the time 'spoiled' this army for any modern warfare between industrial powers. The best-known example of this was in January 1957, when Salan ordered a paratrooper general, Jacques Massu, to break up the FLN organization in the city of Algiers - without regard to the rules or moral precepts of a 'normal' war. This meant in the first instance the systematic torture of those in prison or arrested, so as to be able on the basis of their confessions to seize as many FLN underground fighters as fast as possible. Massu was the victor in this 'battle of Algiers'. On 24 September 1957 the paratroopers were even able to seize the head of the 'autonomous zone of Algiers', Yacef Saadi. The tortures became known, however, and a number of atrocity reports appeared in French books - chief among which was *La Question* of the communist journalist Henri Alleg, which was published in Paris on 26 February 1958 - soon to fill the columns of the international press. In these stories the war of French soldiers in Algeria appeared in a gruesome light, and public opinion became disturbed, both inside and outside France. Despite the fact that these were matched by similar reports of FLN atrocities, the moral victor of the battle of Algiers, in which the main weapons had been plastic explosives, electrical devices, bath tubs, etc., was in fact the FLN. On 2 July 1957 a Democratic senator from Massachusetts called in the US Senate for an 'initiative against French imperialism', moving that President Eisenhower be called on to smooth the path of Algeria to independence through NATO, and if necessary also through the United Nations: 'It is a matter today of saving France as much as free Africa.'[26] The senator was John F. Kennedy.

General Challe, who in December 1958 took over the supreme command in Algeria from Salan, destroyed one ALN base zone after another in a series of offensives lasting from February 1959 until April 1960. Only in the Kabyle region did this military success remain limited, in spite of the fact that Colonel Amirouche, the ALN commander, was killed. Everywhere else the ALN was obliged to cease organizing its men into the larger units considered necessary to introduce a 'second phase' along Giap lines; they now mostly had to fight in 'ferka' units consisting of only 35 men; even the formation of a 'katiba' (110 men), let alone a 'failek' (350 men), was managed only in exceptionally favourable circumstances.

These scattered fighters in the wilayas, however, were still not defeated. In spite of heavy losses, there were always more young men and women (which meant an internal temporary revolution in Muslim society) ready to 'take to the mountains'. At most 2,500 ALN fighters went over to the French during the war; losses in terms of those killed and taken prisoner were probably between 120,000 and 200,000. The French by contrast lost some 10,000 French soldiers and 5,000 auxiliary troops (men of the Foreign Legion, Algerian conscripts, and militiamen). According to French estimates, 2,500 Europeans and 16,000 Muslims fell victim to FLN terrorism in Algeria itself, and in the motherland 154 European and 4,172 Algerian civilians, as well as 69 soldiers and police. The material costs of the war are estimated in the same source at approximately £5,000 million.[27]

At the end of March 1960 President de Gaulle, for sound political reasons, as was to become clear a year later, relieved General Challe of his command. The offensive flagged somewhat as a result, but French troops struggled on until June 1961 to bring about their military victory. The guerrilla fighters (unlike in Vietnam) had virtually been cut off from outside supplies. In order to isolate them from their own people a gigantic resettlement programme was introduced. Some 1,625,000 Algerians were resettled in almost 2,000 villages, which of course in the eyes of the FLN were nothing but concentration camps. Here too, as in the case of the battle of Algiers, the very technical perfection with which French officers fulfilled the task in hand had the effect, on account of their lack of humanity, of bringing about a moral defeat for the French cause. However difficult practical contact between the ALN and the Algerian masses became, nothing could be done to alter the loyalty of the overwhelming majority of this people to the FLN.

The Algerians simply refused to accept the French army's presenta- tion of itself as protector, teacher, or development expert for the popu- lation in Algeria – the incessantly repeated motifs of French psycho- logical warfare. During these years French officers and men did in fact achieve an astounding amount in terms of the development of education, and indeed of other spheres also. Likewise the psychologi- cal pressure of the army did compel the Algerian Europeans in the course of the war towards a change of policy, which in 1954 would still have been regarded as a disgraceful capitulation in the face of the rabble-rousing speeches of Muslim fanatics. May 1958 witnessed the perplexing spectacle of Algerian Europeans launching a coup against Paris, thereby tossing their own privileges, in particular their two-roll electoral law, on to the funeral pyre – although admittedly there could be no question of real elections on account of the war.

From 1955 onwards the FLN, in the Djebel and in exile, evolved its own revolutionary doctrine, which mingled themes of French school teaching about 1789 with Muslim tradition, the experiences of politi- cal movements since the First World War (which applies particularly to the mistrust of the FLN for the Algerian Communist Party) and information on Mao Tse-tung and the war in Vietnam, and even with Pan-African romanticism. In August 1956 they convened a congress in the Soumman valley of the Kabyle region at which the FLN was provided by some 200 delegates with an organizational structure (headed by a five-man Co-ordination and Executive Committee – CCE) and which passed an exhaustive 'platform', that is, a preliminary programme. This document states:

In spite of its underground activity, the FLN is today the sole genuine national organization. Its influence over the entire territory of Algeria is indisputable and undisputed. The FLN has succeeded in a very short time in taking the place of all the political parties, which have existed for decades. This is no coincidence. It is the result of the concurrence of the following indispensable conditions:

1. Condemnation of dictatorship [*pouvoir personnel*] and the establishment of the principle of collective leadership, consisting of pure, honest, incorruptible, courageous people who are immune to danger, imprisonment and the fear of death.
2. The doctrine is clear. The goal to be attained is national independence. The means is revolution for the destruction of the colonial regime.
3. The unity of the people has come about in the course of the struggle against the common enemy, without sectarianism. At the beginning of the revolution the FLN declared: 'The liberation of Algeria will be the accomplishment of *all* Algerians, not of a fraction of the Algerian people.' For this reason the FLN will make room for all anti-colonial forces in its struggle, even if they are not yet under its control.
4. Unequivocal condemnation of the personality cult, open struggle against adventurers, spies, lackeys of the administration, denouncers or police. From this stems the ability of the FLN to fend off the political manoeuvring and chicanery of the French police apparatus.

This does not mean the elimination of all difficulties. Our political action was in the beginning obstructed for the following reasons:

1. numerical weakness of cadres and material and financial means;
2. the necessity for long and hard work in order to clarify policy, to expound it patiently and consistently and to overcome a serious growth crisis;
3. the strategic imperative of subordinating everything to the conduct of the armed struggle.

This weakness, at the beginning normal and inevitable, has now been put right. After a period in which the FLN responded only with words in its resistance to imperialism, it has now stepped into the real arena of political struggle. . . .

The Algerian Revolution . . . is a living reality. It has triumphed over the stupid presumption of French colonialism, which expected to destroy it in a few months. It is an organized revolution, not an anarchic revolt. It is a national struggle in order to destroy the anarchic colonial regime, not a religious war. It is a march forwards in the history of humanity, not a return to feudalism. It is a struggle for the rebirth of an Algerian state in the form of a democratic and social republic, not the restoration of a monarchy or an outmoded theocracy.[28]

The 'platform' condemned 'absent communism' as it also did 'decayed Messalism'. In fact Messali's MNA remained a bitter opponent of the FLN well into 1958; among the 300,000 Algerian workers in France, whose remittances supported 1.5 million relatives in Algeria, the MNA was initially even stronger than the FLN. Bitter infighting between the FLN and the MNA in the slums and bars of French industrial towns caused much blood to be spilled. On 29 May 1957 an FLN commando unit massacred 300 inhabitants of the Messalist village of Melouza in Algeria. It was not this terror alone, however, but the endurance of the ALN in the face of the superior power of France which in the end made the FLN the sole representative of Algerian nationalism.

In April 1956 Ferhat Abbas flew from Algiers to Cairo and joined the FLN. On 18 September 1958 he became head of the 'Provisional Government of the Algerian Republic' (GPRA), Tunis becoming its official headquarters. On 27 August 1961 he was replaced as chief minister by the younger Ben Khedda, but GPRA policy remained unchanged. It acted as the sole legitimate spokesman for the Algerian nation, took up all offers of contact – be they from Peking or Washington, Bonn or the new African states – kept its distance with appropriate revolutionary pathos from the Algerian communists, who now appeared nothing more than a hopeless clique propped up by Moscow and the French Communist Party, and waited patiently until France proved ready to negotiate with it, the GPRA alone, about the independence of Algeria.

CONTRADICTORY POLICIES OF THE FOURTH
REPUBLIC IN NORTH AFRICA

This goal was approached by the French government – or more precisely the two different regimes between 1954 and 1962 – along a fraught path. Initially the above-mentioned dubious logic of North Africa policy was in the hands of Mendès-France, who was toppled on 5 February 1955, and his successor Edgar Faure. Mendès-France's focus of interest was domestic policy; he wanted to revamp the economy and social structure of European France. Colonial problems seemed to him largely as unnecessary baggage to be discarded under the most honourable possible conditions. He had just unburdened himself of the Indochina War in Geneva, and clearly failed to realize that Algeria was embarking on a new full-blown war of liberation in 1954, judging a swift and energetic repression of the rebellion as the best means of ridding himself of the problem. He dispensed with a deeper politico-economic analysis of the North African situation and adhered instead to the gamut of legal formulas and fictions which France had churned out since 1830, these stating that Algeria was France, and Tunisia and Morocco protectorates with their own statehood. So as not to rock the boat, therefore, Mendès-France pursued in some respects the road to repression and in other respects the road to accelerated decolonization.

The governments before him, especially in 1953, had also attempted to stem the tide of imminent political unrest with classic colonial policy measures in the two outer countries of the Maghreb. In December 1951 France curtailed an experiment in co-operation with the Tunisian Neo-Destur, Habib Bourguiba being arrested on 18 January 1952. Groups of 'bandits' immediately began to form in the mountains. In Morocco in 1947 Sultan Mohammed ben Yusuf had emphasized, in a speech made on the neutral ground of Tangiers, that his country was part of the Arab world. The Independence (Istiqlal) Party, formed in 1944, was rapidly gaining ground among urban intellectuals, an alliance between it and the monarchy entrenching itself despite various manoeuvres on the part of the protectorate power. In the summer of 1953 France stirred up a revolt by privileged Berber aristocrats against the rebellious sultan. Led by the pasha of Marrakesh, Hadj Thami el Glaoui, they set out to march on Fez. The French general resident, General Guillaume, had Istiqlal supporters arrested and forced the sultan to abdicate on 20 August 1953.

Mohammed ben Yusuf was deported to Corsica and later to Madagascar. Foreign Minister Georges Bidault, although apparently inadequately informed, backed up his proconsul.

The deposed monarch nevertheless remained just as much of a symbol of the Moroccan desire for independence as the imprisoned Bourguiba was in Tunisia. Mendès-France introduced his new policy with a calculated trip to Tunisia on 31 July 1954, directly after the Geneva conference. He promised internal autonomy and the Neo-Destur returned to the government. Edgar Faure brought this policy to completion in 1955, also extending it to Morocco. On 1 June Bourguiba returned to Tunis in triumph, France again recognizing the legitimacy of Sultan Mohammed at the end of October, and the full independence of both protectorates was negotiated without any substantial problems. On 2 March 1956 Morocco disposed of French and Spanish 'protection', and Tunisia followed on 20 March.

In the mean time elections for a new National Assembly had taken place in France, the SFIO in alliance with Mendès-France achieving a narrow victory. The new premier, Guy Mollet, leader of the SFIO, who was invested on 31 January 1956, now attempted to introduce a 'liberal' policy in Algeria. In view of the protracted guerrilla war, it was difficult not to face the fact that the 'integration' of this old colony into the French motherland was now no more than a fiction. The state of emergency had even prevented in Algeria the holding of rigged elections to the National Assembly, so that Algerian seats in the Palais Bourbon in Paris were empty. What Mollet is likely to have had in the way of detailed plans is not known, for on his visit to Algiers on 6 February the Europeans greeted him with a tomato bombardment. At this he withdrew his reform plans, General Catroux, the governor-general who had been appointed by him and who was decried as a 'softie', resigning and being replaced as Algeria minister by the social-ist politician Robert Lacoste. The latter, like his predecessor Soustelle, immediately adopted the views of Algerian Europeans and the psychological warfare theories of the army. On 22 October 1956, French services hijacked a Moroccan plane intended to take Ben Bella, Boudiaf, Khider, and Ait Ahmed to Tunis, both without informing the government beforehand and in contravention of international law. The arrest of the four top FLN leaders increased the confidence of the more pugnacious in Algiers and Paris; the moderates were only just able to prevent the four of them from being condemned as criminals. The 'battle of Algiers' took its course.

It would be superfluous here to go into the *Loi Cadre* for Algeria which was being prepared by the French National Assembly in the course of drawn-out debates, and which was even enacted at the end of February 1958. This act mingled egalitarian ideals (equal voting rights for all inhabitants of Algeria) with 'communalist' clauses which could have been borrowed from the British colonial tradition, being intended to provide the Algerian Europeans with a sense of security. All of it remained on paper. In order to break up the united national front of the Algerians, Mollet and Lacoste even attempted to make use of the MNA and to transform the old Messali into a kind of Algerian Bao Dai, an undertaking which failed even more rapidly than it had in Vietnam, the prestige of the erstwhile leader of the North African Star being wrecked in the process.

In December 1957, French officers discovered a certain 'General' Bellounis in the Algerian mountains, who was said to be the leader of an MNA guerrilla army; the French allied themselves with him against the FLN, as they had previously sought alliance with Catholic bishops, sects, and pirates against the Vietmin.

Even more recalcitrantly, certain circles in France adhered to plans for a territorial division of Algeria, which was intended to preserve a home for the Europeans, to protect the strategic interests of France, and above all to keep in French hands the Sahara, out of whose barren earth crude oil and natural gas had been gushing since 26 June 1954 (near Hassi Messaoud). It had in any case become a matter of routine since the Second World War to seek to resolve disputes over countries by dividing them up. What had 'succeeded' in India and Germany, Korea, Palestine, and Vietnam, in such varied backgrounds, also seemed worth a try in Algeria. Some even dreamed of a new Israel in the centre of the Maghreb, in which the European settler population, concentrated and thereby made into a majority raring to build the place up, would show the Muslims lounging around what progress really was.

Leaving aside the question of whether the Algerian Europeans, who for generations had been accustomed to quite a different way of life, would have conducted themselves in the same manner as Jewish colonists in Palestine, these plans for a division of Algeria disappeared into oblivion, thanks to the political skill of the FLN and the superior insight of General de Gaulle.

DE GAULLE WINDS UP THE WAR

Although the founding of the Fifth Republic as such is beyond the
scope of this book, it is nevertheless necessary to take a look at those
events in Algeria around 13 May 1958 which led to the death or – as
some observers would have it – the suicide of the Fourth Republic.
The officers, especially the legendary 'colonels', who were bearers of
responsibility in terms both of psychological and military engagement, but who were nevertheless readier to seize the initiative than the
'politicized' generals, allied themselves with traditional conservatives and the newly emerged extremist leaders of Algeria's
Europeans – afraid that the new Paris premier, Pierre Pflimlin, might
'sell out' Algeria as his predecessors had 'sold out' Indochina,
Morocco, and Tunisia.

'*Algérie française*' was the battle cry of the insurgents of 13 May, and
we have no right to doubt that at least the officers seriously hoped to
build something 'new' and 'bold'. They must in 1958 have still
believed in the possibility of a genuine integration of Algerian Muslims with equal rights in the French nation, and we should not assume
that they intended to give this nation anything other than a fundamentally democratic order; after victory, therefore, there were to be full
rights of citizenship for the Muslims as well as for the Europeans!
What is astonishing and dubious, however, is the way in which
Algeria's Europeans in 1958 hailed this policy with such enthusiasm,
after having done everything in their power from the very outset of
colonial rule to keep the Muslims 'in their place', this being the place
of a politically minor people. Speculation about the honesty of this
sudden turn-about may be permissible, but is historically unimportant, since the decisive outcome of 13 May was that the Muslims turned
down the offer. Fraternization scenes at the forum of Algiers were
mere spectacles with no political effect. The FLN remained unshaken
and the war went on.

De Gaulle responded with manifest restraint to the demands of the
Algerian insurgents, his kingmakers. On only one occasion did he use
the magic formula '*Algérie française*' – at the beginning of June 1958
in Mostaganem near Oran. In his very first speech on Algerian soil, at
the Algiers forum on 4 June 1958, de Gaulle uttered darkly and
earnestly words that in retrospect may be interpreted as cynicism,
such as 'Je vous ai compris' (I have understood you) and 'Nous
verrons comment faire le reste' (We shall see what can be done).

After the truce of 1962 all was made plain: de Gaulle wanted to rid himself and France of the burden of this war as quickly as possible, to gain strength and room for manoeuvre for other tasks. Thus far de Gaulle in 1958 was not unlike Mendès-France in 1954, but three factors distinguished them: de Gaulle was planning in the first instance not internal reforms, but a new French European and NATO policy to put an end to American dominance of the western world. Secondly, de Gaulle took a good deal more time sorting out the Algerian War than Mendès-France took for Vietnam and Tunisia; at the price of several years of bloodshed, he thereby reinforced his position in French politics so well that it was not easily shaken before 1968, whereas Mendès-France had had to resign after seven months and seventeen days. Finally, de Gaulle had a much more positive relationship towards the world of the former colonies than any French head of government had had before him: decolonization meant for him a means of increasing the prestige of France in the Third World. Co-operation with the new nations of the former colonial empire and friendship with their leaders were major pieces on the chessboard of his international policy. By means of his Algeria policy, and even more his black Africa policy, de Gaulle created the sounding board for a kind of commonwealth. If not he himself, then certainly his advisers had learned in this respect directly from Great Britain. The double exile of Gaullist France from 1940 to 1944, in London and in some French colonies of Africa, made itself felt after 1958.

By the end of 1959 the hopes of the forces behind 13 May 1958 had been dashed. In October 1958 de Gaulle pledged substantial investment in development for Algeria in the 'Constantine Plan' – ostensibly intended to pacify the Europeans, but in fact a bait for the FLN, which later benefited from this investment. On 23 October de Gaulle pleaded for a 'Peace of the Brave', proposing that the guerrilla fighters trust themselves to French generosity under the 'white flag of truce'. There was of course no response to this. Although the strategy of General Challe made additional heavy strikes against the FLN in the ensuing months, on 16 September 1959 de Gaulle took a decisive step further; he offered self-determination (*autodétermination*). In March 1960 he took the opportunity of a tour of inspection of the French troops in Algeria to utter his own magic formula of '*Algérie algérienne*' – a calculated affront to '*Algérie française*'. The extremists among Algeria's Europeans had in the mean time compromised themselves with the rapid failure of the barricade coup of January 1960. This time the

FLN took de Gaulle at his word. The first negotiations took place in Melun in June 1960, breaking down at first, but now the FLN and their exile government had been recognized in principle as partners. The veterans of 13 May made a last-ditch attempt on 22 April 1961: de Gaulle had to bring his entire reputation, as well as the forces of the French left, including the communists, to bear against the coup of the four generals, Challe, Jouhaud, Zeller, and Salan, but he won. The havoc wrought by the OAS (Organisation Armée Secrète) which then began in Algeria, and which lasted until after the truce, destroyed whatever chances the European minority had had of continuing to live in an independent Algeria. One wonders how Kenya would look today if the whites there around 1960 had unleashed their own kind of 'Mau Mau' on all those of different persuasion! The OAS was none the less powerless to cause a serious obstruction to the conclusion of the drama. The second round of Franco-Algerian negotiations in Evian and Lugrin lasted from May until July of 1961, and finally from 7 to 18 March 1962 the successful third round was held – again in Evian – ending in an armistice agreement.

On 1 July the Algerians voted on their future, the final result of which reads:

eligible voters	6,562,478 (= 100 per cent)
votes exercised	6,033,622 (= 91.8 per cent)
invalid votes	23,390
valid votes	6,010,232 (= 100 per cent)
Yes (for independence in co-operation with France	5,993,754 (= 99.72 per cent)
No	16,478

The Algerian exile government led by Ben Khedda moved into Algeria, having disputed with Boumedienne and Ben Bella shortly before (the 'four martyrs' of the FLN had been free since Evian). The independence of Algeria thus began with internal unrest, which for the time being swept Ben Bella to power. The armistice agreement had essentially had the intention of persuading Algeria's Europeans to remain, an aim in which the FLN were of course also interested. The delirium of the OAS, however, caused more than 30,000 Europeans to leave the country in the first weeks of July 1962. By the time a year had passed after Evian, only a tenth of the European minority were still living in Algeria. Co-operation with France none the less continued. Both under Ben Bella and his successor Boumedienne as well as since

1978 under President Chadli, Algeria has pursued a policy which has never sought out conflict and which has always shown a willingness for friendship with France. De Gaulle's France reciprocated this stance, as also later has socialist President Mitterrand (the same man who was minister of the interior in 1954 . . .).

The cruelties and the crimes of the Algerian War are not forgotten – not in Algeria and not in France. But academic debates on how to 'master the burden of the past' seem to be a rarity in both countries. On the contrary, Algeria and France have managed to build firm foundations for the future at the eleventh hour.

BLACK AFRICA AND MADAGASCAR

In the African territories south of the Sahara and on Madagascar, the French managed to achieve a similar result without reaping violence, while the chilling example of the Algerian war undoubtedly contributed to moderation. The political barometer south of the Sahara had indicated storms more than once in the years before 1954.

On **Madagascar**, elections to the National Assembly on 10 November 1946 resulted, on the second roll, in another victory for the nationalists: in his constituency, Raseta won with only 58 per cent of the vote, but Ravoahangy won with 88 per cent, the Malagasies additionally sending the writer Jacques Rabemananjara (born in 1913) to Paris after he had obtained 67 per cent of the vote in his constituency. These three founded the Mouvement Démocratique de la Rénovation Malgache (MDRM) in February 1946. A rebellion broke out on the large island on the night of 29–30 March 1947, comparable in every way with those in Vietnam and Algeria (in the first stage). One-sixth of Madagascar became an arena for guerrilla combat, the French being forced on to the defensive for months on end. The rebels were not equipped with modern weapons, however, international support, or even encouragement, being absent. From the autumn of 1947 onwards the French struck back purposefully and brutally, engaging 15,000 troops, 'pacification' having been completed by the end of 1948: official figures totalled 1,826 killed on the side of the colonizers (including 140 French), 4,126 rebels who had fallen in combat, and 5,390 who died in the jungle. The authorities blamed the MDRM and in particular its representatives, for having organized the uprising. In fact Raseta, Ravoahangy and since his election also Rabemananjara had been advocating an autonomous Malagasy republic in Paris, using similar formulas to those of Ferhat Abbas for Algeria, or indeed those conceded by France itself to Ho Chi Minh. 'Madagascar is a free state with its own government, its own parliament, its own army and its own finances within the framework of the Union Française', as it is stated in article 2 of the draft constitution presented by the MDRM to the second Constituent Assembly on 21 March 1946 – and which never reached the stage of being debated. In the late summer of 1948 the three MPs were put on trial; Raseta and Ravoahangy were sentenced to death and Rabemananjara to life imprisonment. They were pardoned later, but a ban remained on the party. It was only shortly after independence in 1960 that the three were permitted to return home; Ravoahangy later became minister of health and Rabemananjara minister for economic affairs in the Republic of Madagascar.

In 1949 a fresh storm was brewing on the **Ivory Coast**, where once again the colonial authorities accused the leading party of an anti-French stance. This party was the African Democratic Union, the Rassemblement Démocratique Africain (RDA), which since its foundation in October 1946 had had Félix Houphouet-Boigny, the Ivory Coast representative in the National Assembly, as its president. The Africans had, at least for AOF, managed to rid themselves of the two-roll electoral law in the second Constituent Assembly, so that the sprinkling of European inhabitants of this tropical colony no longer retained their own representatives after the elections of 10 November 1946; all thirteen AOF representatives were now Africans, five of them having been elected under the auspices of the newly established RDA.

Houphouet, today president of the Ivory Coast and a living monument of conservatism among the heads of state of Africa, distinguished himself in the first Constituent Assembly by sponsoring the bill which prohibited forced labour on the request of colonial authorities in the French Empire. The RDA, under the aegis of the three-party coalition which governed France until 1947, allied with the Communist Party, thereby making itself *non grata* with the colonial authorities, who were able to give vent to their indignation as soon as the communist ministers left the Ramadier cabinet. In a debate of 1946, Houphouet had coined the sentence: 'There are no separatists on our benches', and indeed not a single representative from black Africa linked himself at that time with the desire for autonomy of the Algerians and Malagasies. Attempts by Kwame Nkrumah to make contact from London in

243

1946–7, and thus to extend implementation of the slogan of the fifth Pan-African Congress of Manchester to the leaders of the French territories, failed so completely that there has been no serious study of it to this day. It is also true, however, that the RDA was at the same time setting in motion an extremely militant anti-colonial course.

African politicians who at that time were bandying about Marxist concepts, were seeking 'emancipation' and 'individual identity' *within the French Republic*, that is, through full integration and the achievement of undifferentiated, full French citizenship for all Africans. After 1948, however, administrative chicanery of all kinds set in, and the more pronounced it became the stronger the RDA became, the Ivory Coast being particularly affected. One anti-RDA newspaper in Dakar went so far as to brand Houphouet as an 'African Stalin'. Tension reached its highest pitch at the end of January 1950 when a public prosecutor attempted to arrest Houphouet in his home village of Yamoussoukro, despite his immunity. A surprise fire attack by the police on demonstrators in Dimbokro, the district capital, cost twelve Africans their lives on 30 January.

At this moment, however, Houphouet energetically and effectively called a halt to the RDA struggle, for which there was as little prospect of success as there was for the uprising in Madagascar. He dissolved the parliamentary alliances with the communists; over the New Year of 1951 he arranged with the overseas minister then in office that in future the votes of RDA representatives would be added to those of that minister's party, which although forming part of all centrist coalitions was weak and urgently needed reinforcement. The party in question was the Union Démocratique et Socialiste de la Résistance (UDSR) and the overseas minister was François Mitterrand. This same politician, who as minister of the interior in 1954–5 so seriously misjudged the nature of the Algerian uprising, was able at the earlier date of 1950–1, by means of the tactical manoeuvre offered him by Houphouet-Boigny, to set the decolonization of black Africa on to a peaceful course. The colonial administration was now obliged, however reluctantly, to call a halt to the persecution of the RDA. At the elections to the French National Assembly in June 1951 Houphouet and two other RDA representatives were able to save their seats. By the time this legislature session had come to an end in January 1956, the RDA had regained strength to such an extent that it now, after the new elections, controlled ten out of the twenty-eight seats for West and Equatorial Africa.[29] Sekou Touré (1922–84) from Guinea and

Modibo Keita (1915–77) from Mali now took their seats in the Palais Bourbon as members of a younger RDA generation.

Only in **Cameroon** did the local RDA group, the Union des Populations de Cameroun (UPC), resolutely refuse to break with the communists. In May 1955 the UPC and the colonial authorities were thrown into bloody conflict. The party was banned, and their most prominent leaders immediately launched a guerrilla war in their home regions. This was one year after Dien Bien Phu, at a time when the FLN was just consolidating in Algeria and when the independence of Tunisia and Morocco was only a matter of months away. As a trusteeship territory, Cameroon could furthermore count on special international attention. The UPC secretary-general, Ruben Um Nyobé (1913–58), had already approached the UN Trusteeship Council with his people's desire for independence. Whatever chances for success the UPC may have estimated having when they resorted to violence came to nothing. World public opinion hardly took any notice of their guerrilla struggle, the UN gave France a free hand in Cameroon, and the UPC was able to put up little resistance to the campaigns of repression waged by the gendarmerie and certain army units. Although uncertainty, terrorism, and counter-terrorism reigned in a number of regions – chiefly in the Bamileke grassland and the port city of Douala and its hinterland, until long after independence, the UPC ceased to be a political force to be reckoned with when Um Nyobé was shot in the bush by a patrol on 13 September 1958. Exiled Cameroon politicians splintered into mutually hostile factions, and their best brain, Félix-Roland Moumié, died on 4 November 1960 – poisoned in Geneva, probably by French agents.

The Fourth Republic did nevertheless succeed in all African territories – even in Cameroon – in finding and furthering politicians who were prepared to co-operate closely with France towards harmonious and peaceful decolonization: Sekou Touré and Modibo Keita were no exception to this. These Africans strove earnestly towards the emancipation of their peoples by the path of integration within the French nation. They came up against an insuperable obstacle, however: France was really not willing to provide all the Africans colonized with full and equal rights of citizenship, and could not do so without becoming a 'colony of its colonies', as Edouard Herriot had already warned in 1946. In other respects, France went some considerable way towards meeting African demands; it improved the education system to bring it on a par with that of the motherland – if only for that small minority of youth who could obtain a place in a school. On 12 December 1952 it likewise granted African industrial and office workers social rights on the French model. This '*Code de Travail*' marked both the zenith and the final manifestation of the old assimilation policy.

It was from this modern world of industrial work, which in Africa embraced only a tiny fraction of the population, that the change came – a change of goal from that of total integration to total independence. The Franco-African trade unions left the communist, social democrat and Christian-orientated trade union associations of France in 1955–6. At this time the RDA was still closely linked with the UDSR, the group of 'Overseas Independents' around Senghor with the MRP, whilst the SFIO supported a number of local political parties in Africa. Soon, however, the parties themselves began to follow the trade union example: all constitutional debates aimed at a 'federalization' of the French Republic (how else was an emancipated Africa to find a permanent place within it?) which had been conducted since the beginning of the 1950s had run aground. Federalism would seem to be anathema to the French political temperament.

After his capitulation in the face of Algeria's Europeans in February 1956, Guy Mollet made haste to establish a new course, at least south of the Sahara. He wanted to prevent, and succeeded in preventing, what had brought disaster in Indochina and Algeria: with reforms always lagging months or even years behind the development of national liberation movements. Mollet's socialist minister for overseas affairs, Gaston Defferre, was not obliged to pluck entirely new concepts out of thin air; plans which had already been elaborated for his predecessors (predominantly MRP politicians) were to hand. It was only a question of implementing these plans in earnest and rapidly overcoming parlimentary opposition. In fact this reorientation in tropical Africa made hardly any impact at all on the colonial conservatives, whose interest between 1956 and 1959 was taken up with Algeria. The Fourth and Fifth Republics were thus able to assist at a continuous spate of births of no less than fifteen new states.

On 23 June 1956 the '*Loi Cadre* for the Overseas Territories', drafted by Defferre and rapidly pushed through the National Assembly, came into effect. It granted the African colonies semi-autonomy: parlimentary assemblies on the basis of an equal and general franchise (in AOF, for example, over 10 million people were now enrolled on unified electoral rolls, compared with 54,888 in the first and 117,700 in the second electoral class in 1945), and governments with a certain amount of parliamentary responsibility, although important French colonial administrative powers were retained. Potential states thus emerged from what had been administrative districts.

Some Africans, especially Senghor, Sekou Touré, and Modibo Keita, saw in the reform law a drawback, in that the new state institutions were based in the fifteen individual territories, some of which were indeed small, whilst no change at all took place at the macro-colonial level of AOF and AEF. In particular, France blocked all tendencies towards setting up African executive authorities in addition to the governors-general. It was quite clearly set on carrying out a 'Balkanization' of its African colonial empire. Other influential Africans nevertheless supported this policy, and indeed probably ensured that it was implemented despite French qualms; chief among these was Houphouet-Boigny, who strove earnestly for independent statehood and direct contact with France for his Ivory Coast – a relatively large and rich region capable of development, which had nevertheless always been somewhat in a state of rivalry against the AOF administrative capital of Dakar (Senegal). Houphouet-Boigny was a minister in the Mollet team and all subsequent cabinets, even in de Gaulle's first transitional cabinet in the summer of 1958. Had the Africans demanded *en bloc* the transformation of AOF and AEF into African federal states, it is likely that France would have tolerated such an experiment.

In constitutional terms, concessions were distributed equally in all territories, but in fact in those places where the Africans had the benefit of particularly energetic leaders and well-organized political parties, they were able to obtain more power for themselves than elsewhere. Backed up by his party (a branch of the RDA), Sekou Touré was able to eliminate the network of 'canton chiefs' with whose help the French district commanders had administered the colonies, replacing them with local party committees. He thereby interrupted direct contact between the French authorities and the masses long before there was any mention of independence. In Conakry Sekou Touré controlled fifty-seven out of the sixty seats after all territories held elections on 31 March 1957. Houphouet-Boigny (fifty-eight out of sixty seats) and Senghor (forty-seven out of sixty seats) similarly had the upper hand on the Ivory Coast and in Senegal respectively. In Upper Volta (today Burkina Faso), on the other hand, the RDA obtained only thirty-seven out of seventy seats. In Niger Djibo Bakary attempted to govern with forty-one representatives of his party (in fact only a random coalition) against nineteen RDA representatives.

By and large the *Loi Cadre* held its own extremely well as a transition arrangement, which is what it was intended to be, despite the hope of some French people that it marked the last stage of concessions. It was none the less difficult to make further progress in the context of the Fourth Republic, since the real political decision-making power in this regime lay with the Paris National Assembly. If African leaders wanted to continue to exert real influence on French politics as they had done up to then (which seemed to them essential for productive co-operation towards decolonization), they had to stay in the National Assembly. How could this be reconciled, however, with the fact that they wanted at the same time to extend the autonomy of their home-lands? A number of 'Young Turks', chiefly in the very loosely struc-tured party of Senghor, were already beginning to talk about the 'right to independence'. The debate which took place in Paris in 1957 and at the beginning of 1958 on the revision of part VIII of the constitution, amounted to an attempt to square the circle.

De Gaulle's return to power altered this situation at a stroke – much to the relief of the Africans. Africa knew de Gaulle from the war years – in Brazzaville he was even venerated as a sacred hero. What was above all clear from the outset, however, was that the general intended to upgrade the office of president in his new republic, and transform it into the linchpin of executive power. African leaders could thus now easily do without seats in a Parisian parliament which had effectively been deprived of power, if only they could stay close to the ear of the head of state. In terms of the political weight they carried, the Africans in the summer of 1958 were at the same time forging way ahead of their former parliamentary colleagues from the motherland; the latter having fallen into disrepute among their own people as a result of the 'suicide' of the Fourth Republic, whereas the Africans continued to be regarded as the legitimate spokesmen of their peoples. As a consequence of this, French career politicians had little success in obtaining concessions against the will of de Gaulle as the constitution of the Fifth Republic was being worked out, whereas the Africans achieved a great deal in this regard. In the Communauté, which was to take the place of the 'one and indivisible republic', they were thus to obtain full internal autonomy.

Under pressure from those who took the call of the 'Young Turks' for independence seriously, de Gaulle committed himself to a further, decisive concession, which was now finally to bring French Africa policy into line with British policy. Instead of treating the Communauté as an ideal constitutional document, and hence a static one, de Gaulle allowed a dynamic into it, the end result of which would be a harmonious transition to the very self-government which he had so roundly rejected in 1944. When the general was on his electoral campaign trip across Africa, he said in a speech in Brazzaville which drew international attention (24 August 1958):

> What proposals and what projects suggest themselves to the free and conscientious decision of all citizens? The project of the Communauté. The motherland and the overseas territories should form a community together in which each one – I repeat each one – governs itself freely and fully and in which a sphere will be jointly formed in the interests of all, embracing defence, foreign, political and economic activity, the conduct of justice and national education, as well as long-distance communication. . . . It is said: we have a right to independence. That is indeed true. Incidentally – anyone who wants independence can have it immediately. The motherland will not oppose it [lively applause]. A territory can have it immediately if it votes 'No' in the referendum on 28 September. This will mean that it wishes to continue on its way alone, at its own account and risk. In a word it votes for secession. The motherland will act accordingly. . . . More than that: if within the community any territory in the course of time, after a certain period which I will not name precisely, feels in a position to take on all the burdens and duties of independence – well, that is its own affair to be decided by its elected assembly. . . . The community will take this decision into account and arrange an agreement on the transition conditions. . . . I guarantee now that even in this case the motherland will not oppose it.[30]

Only Sekou Touré and the chief minister of Niger, Djibo Bakary, chose the 'secession' offered by de Gaulle in such grudging and warning tones, conducting a 'no' campaign for 8 September. In Niger, however, the old colonial administration was sufficiently strong to bring 78 per cent of the population to vote 'yes'. In Guinea only 4.8 per cent followed France's wishes. Guinea then declared itself independent and de Gaulle kept his word: he did not put up any opposition, but 'acted accordingly', by casting Guinea into the outer darkness of political isolation, which was intended to act as a salutary warning to the rest of French Africa. It is known that French officials moving out of Guinea even tore the sockets out of the walls of their offices.

None the less, Guinea did manage to survive under the strict leadership of Sekou Touré. His experiment, and above all the dissatisfaction prevailing in Senegal and Mali about 'Balkanization', led to a much more rapid demise of the Communauté than de Gaulle had anticipated in 1958. Was it a failure because of this? In our view it was on the contrary a success: it was elastic enough to contain the urge towards independence everywhere except in Guinea.

Cameroon and Togo, the two trustee territories of France, were not taken into the Communauté at all, being released into independence in January and April 1960 with the institutions provided them by the *loi-cadre* of 1957. Whereas the president of Togo, Sylvanus Olympio (elected against the will of France in April 1958), then pursued a policy of non-alignment between the various colonial and post-colonial zones of interest in Africa, Cameroon retained close links with France under President Ahidjo.

Senegal and Mali joined to form the Federation of Mali and, together with Madagascar, where under Philibert Tsiranana's cautious government the wounds of 1947 had finally healed, worked towards an orderly transition to independence along the lines of the second, positively intended proposal made by de Gaulle in Brazzaville in 1958. France yielded to these demands, and the Federation of Mali obtained full sovereignty on 20 June, Madagascar on 1 July 1960. De Gaulle planned a commensurate change to his constitution: a 'renewed Communauté' was to make room for independent states, but this never became reality. Houphouet-Boigny, who in 1959 was still trying to tighten rather than loosen ties with France, had no intention of being overtaken by this run towards independence. In 1960 he demanded, from one day to the next, unconditional sovereignty for the Ivory Coast. The friendly republics of Upper Volta, Niger, and Dahomey (today Benin) followed. De Gaulle agreed: the existence and prestige of Houphouet were and are a far more valuable card for the weight France carries in Africa than any constitution, however elegantly formulated. In August 1960 proclamations of independence followed one on the other in French Africa as rapidly as the guests of honour could fly from one capital to the next. The heads of these states, however, still in the 1980s consider it an honour to meet every year with de Gaulle's successor at a Franco-African summit conference, which is distinguishable from a commonwealth meeting only by the official language.

Only in one French overseas territory on the African mainland did the people's representatives decide in favour of the status quo in 1960: in Djibouti. French Somaliland, known from 1967 to 1976 as the Afar and Issa territory, remained a dependent territory for another twenty years. Only in July 1976 did Paris allow its loyal head of government, Ali Aref Bourhan, to fall, at which point 98 per cent of voters voted for independence, and on 27 June 1977 the Republic of Djibouti was declared (in which a garrison of 4,500 French soldiers continues to be stationed).

In 1987 the French tricolour, like the British Union Jack, now flies only over colonial possessions scattered in and at the edges of various oceans of the world: '*les confetti de l'Empire*', as a Paris newspaper once described them. These include French Guyana with its capital Cayenne, now no longer known for its convict island or its pepper, but as a launching-pad for Europe's space rockets. There is also Polynesia with Tahiti as a tourist attraction and with Muroroa island as a testing-ground for France's nuclear weapons.

The 'confetti' also include Martinique and Guadeloupe in the Caribbean, where the majority of the black inhabitants do not seem to want to tread the path to independence like their anglophone island neighbours, but want instead to be taken seriously by Paris as a *département* with equal rights and full integration. There is also New Caledonia in the Pacific, where there is a thoroughly active anti-colonial movement calling for independence among the Melanesian inhabitants; the Melanesians, however, in the opposite situation to that of Algeria, no longer form the majority of the population, and the French settlers as well as other immigrants would prefer to remain part of France. The cabinets of the socialist majority (1981–6) were no more able to repair this short-circuit in decolonization policy than their conservative successors have been able to since.

Finally there is the island of Mayotte near Madagascar, with just 60,000 inhabitants, part of the Comoro Archipelago, which became independent in 1974. On this one island, however, 62 per cent voted to remain part of France, although they are Muslims and of Arab-African origin, like all the half million other Comoran inhabitants. France therefore remained. The larger island of Réunion near Mauritius has in any case been French since 1638, and has the same status as a *département* of the republic as do Martinique and Guadeloupe.

Chapter Ten

THE LOSS OF THE DUTCH AND BELGIAN COLONIAL EMPIRES

The smaller West European colonial powers wasted their early opportunities after the end of the Second World War to introduce a far-reaching and long-term decolonization policy. Essentially weaker than Great Britain or France, they sought on the one hand to increase their grip on their overseas empires; on the other hand, however, they were also more vulnerable to pressure from the major powers or the United Nations when the latter advised them to withdraw. Then real evacuation followed, despite the fact that Belgium ruled over the Congo in apparent peace for many years after 1945, whilst the Dutch had been driven out of Indonesia long before – a time lag which renders comparative judgements difficult. As in earlier cases, we are interested in the scope and nature of co-operation which has been continued between colonizers and colonized since the day of independence. The Dutch were clearly far more radically ousted from decolonized Indonesia than, for example, the French were from tropical Africa or the Maghreb. The Dutch language has ceased to be used in public life, whereas French continues to be spoken in the former Belgian Congo.

There are nevertheless unmistakable similarities between the Dutch and Belgian overseas policies in their latter phases: in both cases the colony was rapidly, indeed precipitately, wrenched from the hands of the motherland as a result of pressure – some internal, but chiefly external. Whereas in the Dutch case one cannot hesitate to describe this process as a permanent defeat of the colonizers, it is still too soon to pass a similar judgement in the Belgian case.

In both cases the heaviest external pressure came from the USA, which was in the process of salving its own imperialist conscience after the end of the war. On 4 July 1946 the Philippines were granted independence or, from another point of view, the independence previously granted them by the Japanese was confirmed. Washington had as little sympathy for a restoration of **Dutch rule** in neighbouring **Indonesia** as it had for France's return to Vietnam. Whereas, however, France had been acknowledged as a major power and had to be treated with due care (if only on account of its right of veto in the UN Security Council), such considerations were not to be bestowed on the Dutch.

Great Britain, whose troops were first to set foot in Indonesia after the Japanese surrender, steered a middle course, officially supporting the Dutch claim to a reinstatement of the vested right of the colonizer, but in practice doing little to topple the new Indonesian state power which opposed this.

Sukarno had proclaimed the independence of the 'Republic of Indonesia' on 17 August 1945 in Djakarta, at the same time declaring (for the first time on 1 June 1945) the 'Five Principles' forming the basis of the new state: nationalism, internationalism, representative government, social justice, and belief in God, thereby indicating a synthesis of the ideals of western democracy, Islam, Marxism, and the traditions of indigenous village democracy. Initially, however, the Indonesian nationalists had neither time nor opportunity to devote themselves to implementing this programme of principles: Sukarno wanted to make haste in setting up a government and an effective administration before the Allies landed. He succeeded on Java and Sumatra. The proclamation of independence had of course spoken of the 'people of the archipelago', thus claiming the whole of the Dutch East Indies as the Republic of Indonesia from the outset. Sukarno formally appointed governors for all eight provinces: West Java, Central Java, East Java, Sumatra, Borneo/Kalimantan, Celebes/Sulawesi, the Moluccas, and the small Sunda Islands – but not for New Guinea. A provisional constitution was drawn up, and a 'National Committee' (Komite National Indonesia Pusat – KNIP), with 120 members of various political parties, met as a provisional parliament.

Sukarno was thus at least somewhat forearmed when the first British units landed in his capital of Batavia/Djakarta on 29 September 1945. At the beginning of October, Indonesian soldiers proved themselves for the first time during violent clashes for control of some Javanese towns – not against British troops, however, but against the Japanese troops who had been assigned by them to keep order. Dutch soldiers and authorities soon appeared, however, and were able to occupy Borneo, Celebes, and the smaller islands without resistance, immediately recruiting indigenous Moluccan troops, who had always been very loyal to them (especially the Ambonese). The towns in Java were occupied and once again placed under Dutch administration, but they remained enclaves within the republic. The governor-general, van Mook, who came to realize the strong position of Sukarno once he was on the spot, decided it would be best to compromise and negotiate with him and his government. The majority of politicians at home, however, including even the rank and file of the Labour Party, were prepared to hold talks only with 'competent', that is, docile, Indonesian partners. Catholics and Calvinists alike spoke in the Dutch parliament of the divine right of their nation to rule Indonesia, and the elections held on 17 May 1946 resulted in a victory for the conservative parties over the Labour Party.

At the beginning of November 1945, Dutch and Indonesian troops fought for control of Surabaya on Java, which was followed by a guerrilla war on Bali, whilst in south-western Celebes thousands, if not tens of thousands, of people lost their lives in the suppression of republican forces. At this point, London urged the Netherlands to start negotiations, and in the United Nations the Soviet Ukraine became the first advocate of the Indonesians. In November 1946 the British evacuated their troops, but there were to be months of toing and froing before the Dutch and Indonesians reached the stage of the preliminary Linggadjati Agreement, which was signed on 25 March 1947. Its first article reads:

> The government of the Netherlands recognizes the government
> of the Republic of Indonesia as the *de facto* existing authority over
> Java, Madura and Sumatra. Those zones occupied by Allied or
> Dutch fighting forces will gradually be included in the republican
> territory in the course of mutual co-operation.[1]

In the remainder of Indonesia, however, Holland wanted to create a different authority; for Bali, Ambo, Celebes, and the neighbouring small islands, van Mook set up a 'Greater East Indonesian State' in July 1946. To hold both states together, the Linggadjati Agreement envisaged a 'sovereign democratic state on a federal basis', to be called the 'United States of Indonesia' and to remain linked with the Netherlands in a 'union'. The Dutch had thus taken a leaf out of the book of the French, who in 1945 and 1946 were hoping for an 'Indo-chinese Federation' within the Union Française.

Both experiments were to fail under quite similar circumstances: the Dutch no more co-operated with the nationalist Sukarno than the French did (after Fontainebleau) with the communist Ho Chi Minh. On 21 July 1947 colonial troops attacked the republic on Java and overran parts of its territory. Immediately, on 30 July, India (although still not yet independent) and Australia called a meeting of the UN Security Council. On 1 August the USA managed to achieve a compromise that meant a stop to the Dutch offensive. They were formally spared the interference of an international court of arbitration, but had to put up with the 'good services' of a UN committee comprising an Australian, a Belgian, and an American representative, who were to shape the truce into lasting treaty form. Aboard the US steamer *Renville*, the committee formulated an agreement on 17 January 1948, limiting the Dutch to the 'Van Mook Line' which their soldiers had reached on 5 August 1947. Sukarno's republic survived on a reduced territory with Djogjakarta as the capital.

There was a desire to save the principles of Indonesian independence, co-operation with Holland, Indonesian federalism, and union with the Netherlands: there was much talk of testing and respecting the will of the people. Although the international committee did provisionally accept the notion of Dutch sovereignty over its former colonial empire, at the same time it offered its 'help' in future to both parties to reach 'a solution to the political conflict on Java, Madura and Sumatra'. It thus in fact appreciably limited Dutch sovereignty.

The Dutch saw to it in the first instance that it was neither the Indonesian people nor the diplomats, but guns which would keep their word. In September 1948 there was a coup in the town of Madium by Indonesian communists against the government of the republic. Although the chief minister, Hatta, managed to gain the upper hand after only two weeks, the Dutch now took the view that it was high time to eliminate Sukarno's truncated state; on 19 December 1948, therefore, they launched a surprise attack on Djogjakarta, seizing Sukarno, Hatta, and half the government – and considered the problem solved. Indeed it was now solved, but not in the way they imagined. The UN Security Council enforced an immediate cessation of the fighting and the release of the Indonesian leaders; a motion calling for a withdrawal of troops, put forward by the USSR and Chiang Kai-shek's China, was not passed, but the United States stopped its Marshall Plan payments to the Netherlands. It was this international pressure, not the guerrilla fighters on Java and Sumatra, which caused the Netherlands to give in surprisingly quickly; there were after all at the beginning of 1949 some 145,000 Dutch soldiers in Indonesia. At the round table conference which met in August at The Hague, Sukarno's republic was the chief negotiating partner. On 27 December 1949, the Netherlands handed over sovereignty of its south-east Asian empire – apart from New Guinea – to the 'United States of Indonesia'. This federal state, however, was no longer a fabric of threads woven by the Dutch, as had been planned a few years earlier. Sukarno became president, Hatta chief minister, and after a particularist uprising on the Moluccan Islands the federation became the united Republic of Indonesia on 17 August 1950.

Five and a half years later, on 13 February 1956, the union between the Netherlands and Indonesia disappeared from the vocabulary of international law, a move announced unilaterally by Sukarno after he had failed to achieve the handing-over of Dutch New Guinea after some tough negotiations. In the end, this last piece of the former Dutch East Indies empire came under his jurisdiction after all, the treaty of transferral being signed and sealed on 15 August 1962, once again under pressure from the USA (now in the Kennedy era).

When the East Indies empire of the Netherlands was already long a thing of the past in spite of all the achievements of their 'ethical policy', public opinion in Belgium was still convinced it had found the perfect answer with the very similarly conceived paternalistic government of the **Belgian Congo**, where peace and apparent contentment reigned until well into the 1950s. The Belgian colonial system continued to rest on the three time-honoured pillars of Belgian officialdom, big capital, and Catholic missions. The social emancipation of the Congolese seemed to be better provided for than that of the natives of other African countries – with the possible exception of South Africa and the two Rhodesias. There was no apparent need for political emancipation.

A. A. J. van Bilsen (born 1915), a graduate of the University of Leuven and professor of the University Institute for Overseas Affairs in Antwerp, an expert not only on the Congo, but also on South Africa, published in late 1955 in a Flemish journal, and in February 1956 in a French journal, an article with the title 'A thirty-year plan for the political emancipation of Belgian Africa'. He wrote:

257

> The period of the political emancipation of the Congo and
> Rwanda-Urundi is approaching. We have the right to expect
> from Parliament the definition and drawing up of a genuine
> colonial policy. Emancipation is coming inevitably, but it does
> not necessarily have to be catastrophic. On the contrary, it could
> become a source of mutual spiritual and material enrichment. It
> will only be painful if we allow ourselves to be surprised by it
> and to be overwhelmed by events.[2]

A time-span of thirty years! Only the socialists and some left-wing Catholics showed any interest in this plan. For the most part, Belgium, in particular representatives of colonial interests, reacted with 'shock and outrage'.[3] An opinion poll revealed that although '80 per cent were not acquainted with the actual situation' in the Congo, more than 60 per cent said that it should be defended against critics, whilst many of the remaining 40 per cent did not consider it appropriate to answer the question at all, since 'such undeserved attacks by interested parties should be treated with contempt'.[4] Were not 1,533,314 Congolese children attending school (in 1958)? That was roughly three-quarters of all school-age children in the country. For more than a million children, schooling was provided by Catholic missions. On the other hand, anti-clerical Belgians similarly saw no grounds for criticism, since the liberal colonial minister Auguste Buisseret had enthusiastically launched the establishment of a secular school system. There had after all been profits in the Congo (in 1956) from copper of almost £100 million, from cobalt of some £15 million, and from diamonds of £10 million. Between 1950 and 1957, public investment had risen from more than £17 million to nearly £57 million, and private investment from £25 million to £75 million. The real value of consumption of the 'natives' had risen from the 1950 index of 100 to 176.1 by 1957. If after seven years, therefore, so the argument ran, the Africans were nearly twice as well off, then they must be satisfied with the system. Economic crisis loomed in 1957, however, when the price of raw materials (including copper) fell, the 1956 balance of payments for the Congo dipping into the red for the first time since 1949 and the deficit growing in leaps and bounds in 1957 and 1958. The African standard of living began to fall and unemployment hit hard, particularly in the large towns. Possible rabble-rousers would nevertheless have to face the 24,000-man strong 'Force Publique', one of the largest colonial armies in the whole of

Africa and under the command of 453 Belgian officers – to name only one of the achievements of the state administration, the first pillar of the regime.

With the wisdom of hindsight we can see today that all this apparent success and fame of Belgian colonization had its darker side. Of the 1.5 million schoolchildren, for example, a mere 44,000 attended secondary schools, and only 20,000 technical schools, and at the end of 1958 a paltry 290 Africans were attending the two universities at Léopoldville (Lovanium) and Elisabethville. On the subject of the doubtless admirable achievements of Belgian entrepreneurs, especially in the Katanga mining industry, van Bilsen comments:

> The paternalism of the large enterprises and the poverty of the bush continue to dominate the Congolese economy today. The need for a substantial workforce causes the mining enterprises, in view of the sparse population and alarming birth rate statistics, to keep black workers permanently in the immediate vicinity of the mines in order to obtain a stable, acclimatized and loyal workforce. Instead of recruiting men from the interior for a period of six months . . . whole families have now been uprooted. This was an experiment undertaken with much enthusiasm, and which fundamentally altered the character of the economic conditions with which powerful mining entrepreneurs were confronted. It now became viable to invest millions over the long term in the building of decent homes, the organization of health care, maternity clinics, children's facilities and in the building of good schools for the children – those children who one day would become better qualified workers . . . . 'See how well we take care of our cattle', one of the worthiest 'paternalists' of Katanga said to me one day without the slightest hint of disparagement in his voice – a man who has sacrificed himself for the social improvement of the workers – as he led me . . . through the spick and span maternity homes and hospitals.[5]

The first to rebel in the Belgian Congo, as everywhere else in the colonies, were naturally those who were enabled as a result of modern education and their dealings with Europeans to give expression to their dissatisfaction in a manner discernible to the colonizers: that is, the '*évolués*', even if in the Congo these were only able to reach the level of a subordinate postal official (Patrice Lumumba, 1925–61), bank clerk (Antoine Gizenga, born in 1925), non-commissioned officer or journalist (Mobutu Sese Seko, born in 1930), or at best of a theology student (Joseph Kasavubu, 1910–69). In July 1956, several Catholic Congolese of this kind took up van Bilsen's plan, publishing in Léopoldville a manifesto entitled *Conscience Africaine*:

> We believe in the vocation of the Congo to become a great
> nation in the centre of the African land mass. Our national voca-
> tion: to work towards building a new, flourishing and happy
> society in the heart of Africa, on the foundations of the former
> clan society, severely shaken by development, which has been
> too rapid and which seeks a new equilibrium. We can only
> achieve this new equilibrium in a synthesis between our African
> character and temperament and the profound wealth of western
> civilization. No one can bring about this synthesis in place of the
> Congolese, or on their behalf – [but it can be done] with the
> brotherly help of westerners living in the Congo.[6]

Around this time, Kasavubu changed the cultural organization of the *évolués* of his own Bakongo people into a political party: the Alliance des Bakongo (ABAKO).

A few breaches began to appear in the invisible but effective layer of insulation which the Belgians had long ago placed around the Congo in order to prevent the 'contamination' of its Africans by alien political ideas. After 1946, everyone in Léopoldville knew that the Africans in French Brazzaville, just over the river, were no longer 'subjects' but 'citizens', and that more of them were obtaining the right to vote every year. In 1955 King Baudouin visited the colony, and to the astonishment of certain people even shook hands with some Africans. Encouraged by Pétillon, the governor-general who was in office from 1952 until 1958 and subsequently became minister in Brussels (this member of the government, however, suddenly no longer being known as colonial minister, but as 'minister for the Congo and Rwanda-Urundi'), the phrase 'Belgian-Congolese Community' came into use. Municipal elections were held in Léopoldville, Stanleyville, and Elisabethville – the first political elections in the history of the country. From now on the municipalities comprising parts of the large urban agglomerations of the Congo (similar to those around Brussels) had democratically elected African mayors; Kasavubu assumed this office in Léopoldville-Dendale.

By 1958 it was impossible to overlook the fact that things were moving rapidly in the Congo. De Gaulle was speaking of independence in Brazzaville, and even more importantly a number of Congolese were given a chance to visit Europe on the occasion of the World Exhibition in Brussels. One of the press attachés at the exhibition was Joseph Désiré Mobutu, the 28-year-old editor-in-chief of a local newspaper in Léopoldville. In December 1958, Kwame Nkrumah invited Congolese politicians to Ghana to his first 'All-African People's Conference'. Although the Belgians forbade Kasavubu to attend this 'subversive' meeting, they overlooked Patrice Lumumba, now manager of a private Léopoldville brewery. The latter had just founded the Congolese National Movement (Mouvement National Congolais – MNC) together with a few other *évolués* who did not belong to the ABAKO as they were not from the Bakongo people. Six days after Lumumba's return from Accra, on 6 January 1959, severe disturbances broke out in the Congolese capital. The Force Publique had no trouble sorting this out: forty-nine people died. It would be absurd to suggest that Lumumba had 'incited' this outburst. Whilst his account of the conference in Ghana, Nkrumah's fame, and the particular position of trust Lumumba enjoyed with this hero of Africa, may have contributed something to the flare-up, the unrest itself began with a protest march by 30,000 unemployed workers, who had other more pressing things to worry about than Lumumba's trip or party politics.

The colonial administration reacted by banning the ABAKO and arresting Kasavubu, but on 13 January 1959 the king of the Belgians officially announced a new policy. This did not of course appear out of the blue, having been in preparation since the appointment of the Christian social democrat Gaston Eyskens as prime minister on 25 June 1958. King Baudouin announced:

In pursuit of our royal intention, we have decided this day to lead the Congolese populations, without detrimental delay, albeit likewise without precipitate haste, to independence in prosperity and peace. In a civilized world, independence means a condition which unites and guarantees freedom, order and progress. It is only conceivable by means of solid, well-balanced institutions; experienced administrative cadres; well-introduced welfare, economic and financial organization in the hands of proven technical staff; the intellectual and moral education of the population, without which a democratic regime means only degeneracy, fraud and tyranny.[7]

Whilst this appraisal may sound like a mockery after the manner in which Belgium had been ruling since 1908, and which they themselves had proudly acknowledged before the world – and in spite of the fact that the announcement contained no indication of time-scale – the crucial words 'democracy' and 'independence' had none the less been uttered, which in practical terms gave the green light to the formation of more political parties in the Congo. These mushroomed throughout 1959, focusing for the most part exclusively around the interests of minor ethnic and linguistic communities, the so-called 'tribes'. Even the MNC split into two wings in July: whereas Lumumba adhered to the ideal of a united Congo, therefore advocating that Belgium leave behind a unitary state, some MNC politicians gave preference to their regional concerns, thus advocating a programme of reform with a federalist character.

The Belgian government made no attempt to stem this political flood and organize sensible transition phases to lead up to independence. On the contrary, they proceeded with considerable haste, particularly in the critical year of 1960. Colonial officials in the Congo itself probably regarded this policy as insane, but even they did little to make Brussels apply the brakes. On no account did Belgium want a repetition of the mistakes which had been made by the French in the Vietnam and Algerian wars. There were to be no perpetually late, piecemeal concessions, only to be followed by bloodshed after all. Better to grant independence at a stroke – then the Africans will soon see that they cannot manage without close co-operation with the colonizers! Such was evidently the idea behind the Congo policy of Belgium in 1959–60, both of the particularly reform-happy minister, Maurice van Hemelrijck, as well as of his successor, the more 'moderate' Auguste de Schrijver, who replaced him on 3 September 1959 under pressure from the Congo Belgians. Finding 'sensible' Africans for the new Congolese government, or for the provincial governments, was none the less essential for the success of this policy.

In Katanga, representatives of European interests unhesitatingly placed their support behind the Confédération des Associations tribales du Katanga (CONAKAT), formed at the end of 1958, and their leaders Moise Tshombé (1919–60) and Godefroid Munongo (born 1925). In the rest of the Congo, however, it was not until November 1959 that they were able to string together a large number of tribal parties to form the 'moderate' Parti National du Progrès (PNP), which was still no match for Lumumba's MNC. After a local

262

disturbance in his main power base of Stanleyville, Lumumba was imprisoned, but his party won in further local elections (December 1959) in Stanleyville, gaining 90 per cent of the vote. When a round table conference was held on 20 January 1960 in Brussels to establish how the transition to independence was to be carried out, the authorities were obliged to release Lumumba so that he could take part in it.

At that time, Tshombé and his European friends, especially during the election campaign, were preparing for the contingency of a secession of Katanga in the event of radical elements, or even elements only suspected of being radical, taking the helm in Léopoldville. Tshombé spoke of a future sovereign Katanga, adding: 'Whether a Congo Federation including a Katangese state will now prove possible or not – Katanga will seek a *Union Communautaire* with Belgium.'[8] Election results in Katanga, however, were to reveal that the CONAKAT and all political party structures in general were still on shaky foundations: only just 11 per cent of the vote was cast for the CONAKAT, 4 per cent for the rival BALUBAKAT party (a tribal-based party of the Baluba people living in the north of Katanga) and 83 per cent for isolated electoral tickets and independent candidates.

Whether it was because of this preliminary power struggle in Katanga, because of Belgian disinclination to repeat the experience of French 'Balkanization' policy, or the inability of Belgium itself to resolve its home problems by means of a federal structure, Brussels persistently blocked all attempts towards secession in Katanga right up until independence. Instead, the round table surprised the world, and not least Congolese politicians, with a straightforward 'Yes' to the most extreme demand of the Africans, that of declaring independence as early as 30 June of the same year, 1960. This decision having been taken on 27 January, a preliminary constitution had to be drawn up for the Congo in all haste, and the *Loi fondamentale* was indeed ready for proclamation on 19 May 1960. This provided for the setting-up of a federal state in which the six colonial provinces would obtain certain rights of autonomy. Ultimate power, however, lay with the central government, the executive authority being divided between the two offices of state president and prime minister. The situation was clear, therefore: if energetic, perhaps even radical 'centralists' succeeded in gaining control of both these offices, the federalist concessions contained in the constitution were condemned to oblivion – not unlike the situation in Indonesia. Parliamentary elections took place at the end of May, there being 250 electoral tickets in a total of twenty-six voting districts for the (most important) second chamber of the central parliament. House of Representatives' voting was severely splintered: despite the fact that all seats were distributed strictly according to proportional representation, in Kivu province as much as 40 per cent of the vote was rendered useless, lost on electoral lists too weak to obtain even one seat. Attendance at the polls was high by African standards, not being under 58 per cent in any constituency, and being as high as 97 per cent in parts of Léopoldville. It cannot be said, therefore, that political apathy or ignorance of the basic rules of democracy among a large majority of the population inevitably condemned the Congo to a state of chaos.

It is not surprising that a plethora of unstable factions formed in the House of Representatives. The final results showed that Lumumba controlled 41 out of 157 seats with his wing of the MNC and a few minor allies, the PNP 15, the Parti Solidaire Africain (PSA) under Gizenga, Kamitatu, and Mulele 13, the ABAKO 12, the CONAKAT 8, the federalist wing of the MNC 8, and the BALUBAKAT 7. Lumumba did not have a majority, therefore, but he did lead the strongest single faction. According to the parliamentary rules of the game, it was now incumbent upon him to form a coalition.

A good deal of horse-trading was necessary before Lumumba managed, only a matter of days before the date of independence, to muster the somewhat swelled ranks – twenty-eight ministers and ten deputy ministers – of his government team. Tshombé meanwhile kept his distance, setting himself up as provincial head of government in Katanga. The Belgians did nevertheless succeed in thwarting a concentration of African power in the central executive: the federalist Kasavubu was elected head of state.

Belgium relinquished sovereignty of the Congo as anticipated on 30 June, with Lumumba giving an impassioned, and in some places unjust, funeral oration on Belgian colonial rule. King Baudouin was offended, but a rift was once again narrowly avoided. The Belgian General Jannsens, commander of the Force Publique, however, made his view of the 'new' situation abundantly clear to his black subordinate officers, now eager for promotion, by writing on a blackboard: 'Before Independence = After Independence'. Mutinies ensued on the evening of 5 July in Thysville, spreading like wildfire over the whole country. Kasavubu and Lumumba, genuinely trying to work together, were unable to bring the situation under control. On 11 July, Tshombé declared Katanga independent. Belgian marines landing at the port of Matadi opened fire on Congolese soldiers; the government in Léopoldville severed relations with Belgium and called first on the USA and then the UN for assistance. The first international Congo crisis thus arose immediately after the decolonization of the Belgian Congo, to be followed by a number of others.

Chapter Eleven

SPAIN'S WITHDRAWAL AND PORTUGAL'S EXPULSION FROM AFRICA

Of all the European powers, the two states of the Iberian peninsula, Spain and Portugal, defended their African colonial possessions the most tenaciously. A contributory factor to this may have been that both countries were until the middle of the 1970s under quasi-fascist dictatorships, which were largely guided by a desire if possible to stop the clock of history somewhere around the 1930s period. One must also bear in mind that Spain and Portugal were the oldest colonial powers in Europe, and hence burdened to breaking-point by the traditions of their own glory. Economic historians may add to this that Spain and Portugal, because they have remained poor countries in comparison with the rest of Europe, clung all the more tenaciously to their colonies as sources of a paltry prosperity. As is generally the case, it depends on the point of view of the observer: a colonial trading association which brought little in the way of benefit, either to the Spanish or the Portuguese political economy, yielded substantial wealth for a certain group of merchants and/or bankers and/or administrative officials (rarely for industrial entrepreneurs), and was a bitterly exploitative experience for the colonized peoples in Africa.

The fact, therefore, that Franco's **Spain** managed to make the leap towards non-violent decolonization, just in time to make a favourable impression in the United Nations and among its Arab neighbours, is best explained by the quantitative lack of interesting colonial possessions. With the independence of Morocco (March 1956), Spain withdrew from its protectorate zones in the north and south of that country, with the exception of what is known as the coastal *Presidios*, that is, the towns of Ceuta and Melilla, with a total of some 130,000 inhabitants. By 1 January 1969, Madrid had also given the enclave of Ifni (south of Agadir) back to Morocco. On 10 December 1968 it transfered sovereignty to its colonies in the Gulf of Biafra in West Africa. The island of Fernando Po (subsequently renamed after the new head of state, Macias Nguema) and the mainland region of Río Muni have since joined to form the Republic of Equatorial Guinea. Only in the western Sahara did the Spanish prolong their departure, as here in April 1972 was beginning the exploitation of the rich phosphate finds of Bu-Craa, from which American and German firms also hoped to profit. At one time, Spain had 20,000 soldiers stationed in the Sahara – other estimates put the figure as high as 70,000. Three neighbouring African states had their sights set on this desert region, the population of which was estimated at about 20,000 sedentary people and 50,000 nomads: Morocco, Mauritania, and Algeria. Morocco and Mauritania finally reached an agreement to divide the Spanish Sahara between themselves, the phosphate finds falling to Morocco. Algeria was thus left empty-handed, consequently finding solace in the discovery of solidarity with the Polisario liberation front,[1] which was preparing to launch a struggle for an independent Saharan state – against Spain as long as it maintained a presence there, but chiefly against Mauritania and Morocco. Initially the Madrid government (1972–4) reacted to this by manoeuvring in the direction of 'self-determination' for the Saharan population, that is, against the Moroccan-Mauritanian claim to simple annexation. Although a decision of the International Court of Justice at The Hague in October 1975 only very partially supported Morocco's claims, Spain followed suit at this point with a change of course. After only brief negotiations, an agreement was signed in Madrid on 14 November 1975 which provided for the replacement of the Spanish administration by a Moroccan-Mauritanian one on 26 February 1976. Neither the UN Security Council nor the Organization of African Unity (OAU) proved able to influence events in view of internal African rivalries. On 4 March 1976 the Polisario front proclaimed an 'Arab Democratic Republic of the Sahara', which was immediately recognized by Algeria, Angola, Mozambique, and Guinea-Bissau, and later by half of all the OAU states, as well as by certain outposts of the Soviet camp, such as Cuba and South Yemen (although not by the USSR itself). On 14 April 1976 Morocco and Mauritania drew their boundaries across the country, but of the larger settlements only Dakhla (Villa Cisneros) was ceded to Mauritania. Polisario guerrilla war meanwhile continued, reaching the pitch in May 1976 of a surprise attack on the Mauritanian capital of Nouakchott. The Mauritanian army staged a coup and made peace with the Polisario on 5 August 1979. Morocco fought on, however, now also occupying the south of the former Spanish Sahara. The OAU suffered a serious setback in its attempts to resolve the conflict, splitting in 1980 into two factions of equal strength, one backing Morocco and the other the Polisario. In 1982 the 'Republic of the Sahara' was accepted into the OAU by a narrow majority, Morocco then becoming in 1984 so far the only African state to leave the organization.

As Spain was withdrawing discreetly from the Sahara in this manner, the demise of Portuguese rule in Africa was already history. For thirteen years **Portugal**, under the iron rule first of the dictator Antonio Oliveira Salazar (1889–1970) and then of his successor Marcello Caetano, had attempted to stem the anti-colonial tide of history by using armed force. Blood was shed in all three Portuguese colonies on the African mainland – Angola, Guinea-Bissau, and Mozambique, although the Portuguese enclave of Goa in India (taken by Affonso de Albuquerque in 1510 from the sultan of Bijapur) was taken back by India with military force, but without resistance, in December 1961. The Lisbon regime subsequently defended its African empire all the more tenaciously.

The Salazar-Caetano doctrine was simple: the overseas empire was to remain Portuguese for ever. Attempts were made to justify this on the grounds of an ostensibly centuries-old policy of assimilation, and of the 'racially blind' intermingling of the most varied ethnic and racial groups within the Lusitanian culture and nation. This was of course a fiction, as was the assertion that Portugal had had a presence in Angola for 400 years: in fact the Portuguese colonial administration had not succeeded in asserting itself in the Angolan hinterland until long after the First World War, whilst the number of people of mixed Portuguese-African blood was revealingly small in all overseas territories – some 70,000 in Angola and 30,000 in Mozambique. A genuine mingling of the white and black populations would have produced quite different demographic results.

An act of 11 June 1951 formally made all the colonies overseas provinces of the motherland, although in fact it merely enshrined Salazar's colonial legislation of 1930 within the Portuguese constitution. The former division between 'natives' (*indigenas*) and 'civilized' people or 'citizens' (*civilisados/cidadões*) was retained, the latter including Europeans, the Goanese, people of mixed race and African '*assimilados*'. The Act stipulated:

Anyone may relinquish the status of native and obtain civil rights, if he can demonstrate his ability to fulfil all five of the following conditions: 1. age of more than 18 years; 2. correct use of the Portuguese language; 3. the practice of an occupation, art or craft from which he can draw sufficient income to sustain his own person and his relatives, or other persons for whom he is responsible; or the possession of property which serves the same purpose; 4. evidence of good conduct, and the acquisition of the education and customs which are expected for full exercise of the public and private rights of Portuguese citizens; 5. no record of the applicant having avoided military service or of having deserted.[2]

In other words, the *assimilado* not only had to have obtained a rudimentary education and own some money (about £15 per month was generally recognized as an adequate sum), but also had to convince the police of his good character. In 1950 there were only 30,000 *assimilados* in Angola, and scarcely 4,300 in Mozambique, although they formed the majority of the populations of the Cape Verde Islands, São Tomé, and Principe.

From the end of the Second World War onwards, Salazar encouraged the emigration of Portuguese settlers, especially to Angola, their numbers at that time totalling some 45,000. Around 1970 there were at least 250,000, others say 300,000 in Angola, and a further 130,000 in Mozambique. In these places, therefore, new white minorities were beginning to form at a time when Africa in general was on the threshold of decolonization, the proportion of Portuguese in Angola corresponding with the white minority in Rhodesia and that in Mozambique with the Kenyan situation. We have already seen how vigorously white settlers in these two British possessions, as well as in Algeria and South Africa, held back, or even totally put a stop to, the process of decolonization. It may be said that the material contrasts between black and white were much less stark in the Portuguese territories than they were in South Africa, Rhodesia, and Kenya; in Angola many of the Portuguese were poor and even illiterate. There were white housemaids, and in Angola there were even around 7,000 white unemployed in 1960. Even in Angola, however, a white man was paid more than a black man for the same work: in the cities double, in the bush apparently five times as much.

Obviously there was no chance of the white settlers becoming uppish under Salazar: the preservation of law and order was just as much their prime civil duty as it was that of the African subjects, and the whites did indeed uphold law and order: the regime after all provided most of them with a livelihood. There was no democratic reform movement among any whites anywhere near either Angola or Mozambique which could have had an ideologically contaminating effect on Portuguese settlers (the Afrikaners of South Africa in any case had no great esteem for the Portuguese, and the feeling was mutual). The blacks within the Salazar empire, however, could not be entirely shielded from their African environment, despite the draconian police control. The ideas of decolonization were spreading from French West Africa to Guinea-Bissau, from the French and Belgian Congo to Angola, and from British East and Central Africa towards Mozambique.

This does not mean, of course, that there was no incipient indigenous movement for national liberation at all in the Portuguese colonies themselves. In Angola in particular these acted as a crystallization factor for imminent revolts. But it is no coincidence that the strongest anti-colonial group in Guinea assumed the same name as the radical anti-colonial party just being set up by young pro-communist intellectuals in neighbouring Senegal: 'African Independence Party' – in Portuguese the Partido Africano da Independéncia da Guiné a Cabo Verde (PAIGC). There is evidence to suggest that Julius Nyerere in Tanganyika advised emigrants from Mozambique to form a broad national merger movement modelled on his TANU, that the founders of FRELIMO (Frente de Libertação de Moçambique) attempted to follow this advice, and that it was Nyerere who gave the impulse for Dr Eduardo Mondlane, a sociologist living in America, to be chosen as leader of FRELIMO in 1962. As regards Angola, the MPLA (Movimento Popular de Libertação de Angola) for years thoroughly exploited the fact that its chief opponent, Holden Roberto, had spent most of his life in the Belgian Congo, recruiting his party cadres there among Angolan Bakongo emigrants, and was only able to fight the war in Angola from his external base, supported by the Congolese (Zaire) government.

In Angola, the internal rift in the African anti-colonial movement was not overcome in the course of thirteen years, and had to be fought out in a civil war after the withdrawal of the Portuguese in 1975–6. The MPLA emerged the victor of this war thanks to another outside (Cuban/Soviet) intervention. Attempts on the part of the OAU and the liberation committee it set up in 1963[3] to resolve these feuds were not only futile, but even deepened the discord, as the neighbouring states of Zaire, Congo-Brazzaville, and Zambia, who in fact set the tone of the OAU, were each supporting different Angolan groups. Until 1961 the MPLA had virtually no independent African allies: having been founded in 1956 in Luanda, predominantly by *assimilados* and intellectuals of mixed race, it contained a communist-oriented element and enjoyed close and friendly ties with the PAIGC, which was founded at the same time: Amilcar Cabral, secretary-general of the PAIGC, was working as a colonial official in Angola in 1955. The first to make his presence felt, however, as Africa pressed forwards towards independence, was Holden Roberto (born in 1925), who reformed the Union of the Peoples of North Angola, a politico-cultural interest group set up in Léopoldville in 1958 predominantly for his own Bakongo people, into the União das Populações de Angola (UPA), the chief demand of which was liberation for the whole of Angola. As a protégé originally of Guinea and Ghana, Roberto made his first international appearance at the beginning of 1960 in Tunis at the second All-African Peoples' Conference.[4] On 15 March 1961 he launched a mass rebellion against the Portuguese in the north of Angola. The terrorism of the rebels, as well as the immediately instigated massive military and police counter-terrorist measures of the colonial power, were to cost the lives of an estimated 50,000 Africans and at least 1,300 whites in the course of a few months.[5] The Portuguese scored a preliminary victory, regaining control both of the borders and of rural northern Angola. The guerrilla fighters of the UPA were pushed back to small mountainous zones in the interior, where they remained until 1974.

This uprising, although badly planned, was a disproportionately large shock for Portugal compared with the equally badly planned attempt on the part of the MPLA to capture the prison at Luanda in a surprise attack on 4 February 1961: the police had systematically begun to imprison MPLA supporters there from March 1959 onwards. The surprise attack failed. A competent MPLA leadership only re-emerged in exile, supported by foreign aid, predominantly Algerian and later Guinean.

The PAIGC experienced much the same, forming secretly in Bissau, and calling a dock workers' strike in August 1959 which was promptly quashed by the Portuguese police, Amilcar Cabral (1921/4–73) fled to Conakry, where Sekou Touré, now president of independent Guinea, gave him his backing to prepare an armed liberation struggle. None of the liberation movements of Portuguese Africa, therefore, managed without a base in exile – not even Angola's UNITA (which will be discussed below), and certainly not FRELIMO, which was founded in Dar es Salaam in September 1962.

All these movements sought political success in being able to launch 'people's struggles' as actively as possible in their country of origin, and to present themselves as the instigators of this struggle and as the authority recognized by the population in the 'liberated zones', in order to obtain recognition from the OAU as the sole legitimate representatives of their peoples. The way to the higher echelons of international legitimation at the forums of the United Nations could only be achieved through the OAU, and only through 'armed struggle' could one succeed with the OAU, which had itself stipulated this in 1963 as the appropriate political course for southern Africa. Only military might would force Portugal, the white Rhodesians, and white South Africa to introduce decolonization and transfer political power to the black African majority. Other means which had proved successful elsewhere, such as democratic elections, constitutional conferences, and various forms of negotiation were, the OAU argued, useless in the case of men such as Salazar and Ian Smith, and certainly in the case of Verwoerd and Vorster.

The models for the people's struggles in southern Africa were provided by Algeria, the Chinese civil war, and, chiefly, Vietnam. All African guerrilla commanders took the lessons of General Giap to heart, especially his three-phase theory (see p. 150). The claim of the PAIGC and FRELIMO in particular to control 'liberated zones' in Guinea and Mozambique indicated that these movements had in their own estimation reached the second phase of Giap's people's war doctrine. In reality, however, they were lacking two essential elements of the Vietnamese strategy: (1) the headquarters of the political leadership were not permanently situated in the 'liberated territory', but abroad (with the possible exception of UNITA, whose military strength remained severely limited); (2) the regular troops of the PAIGC and FRELIMO were dependent on bases in friendly neighbouring states, and were never able until the last moment to operate from the 'liberated zones' themselves. In all three of these theatres of war, the presence of liberation movements remained a presence of guerrilla units, all politico-economic activity on the part of the liberated population being subsumed within guerrilla warfare.

According to Giap's theory, on the other hand, guerrilla warfare was only to play the leading role in the first phase of a people's struggle.

These deviations from the Vietnamese model do not change the fact that the leaders of the PAIGC, of FRELIMO, and similarly of the rival Angolan parties, regarded themselves in global political terms as part of the liberation revolution, which had achieved its most spectacular victory over a European colonial army in Dien Bien Phu. The Portuguese commanders likewise strove to emulate the counterinsurgency strategies which had been employed by the French and the Americans in the war they had fought (and lost) in Vietnam. In all three African colonies, the Portuguese thus attempted to resettle as many indigenous peasants as possible in new settlements fortified by the military against both outside and inside attack. The Portuguese called these settlements *Aldeamentos*, and boasted of them to the last, as if their prime function were to acquaint the poor black peasants for the first time in their history with clean water, schoolbooks, and the hypodermic syringes of the health worker. They were above all intended to sever political contact between the guerrilla army and the people, to pluck the rebellious fish out of the water (to retain the image used by Mao Tse-tung). The Portuguese failed in this to the extent that the PAIGC and FRELIMO were in fact able to set up some liberated zones. Having achieved this much, the two movements were less concerned to control territory (they often allowed Portuguese civil and even military traffic to pass unhindered), than to commit as many people as possible to loyal work for the rebel movement, in the form of supplies, recruitment, and information services.

Emulation of the Vietnamese and Chinese models of successful peoples' struggles necessarily brought the African liberation movements into friendly contact with the communist parties now ruling in China and Vietnam. It was in this way, and not through contact with the illegal Communist Party in Portugal, that they also made firm ties with the Soviet Union. For the PAIGC and FRELIMO, and on a smaller scale for the MPLA, which was conducting only a sporadic people's struggle, the preservation of friendship with the two major communist powers was a vital necessity. Who else was to supply their soldiers with weapons and ammunition with any degree of regularity and reliability? The African states, including Algeria, were neither politically nor financially in a position to do this. There was certainly no lack of voluble declarations on the part of these states about how energetically they supported the armed struggle against Portuguese colonialism, nor of (substantially more discreet) efforts to keep the liberation movements under the control of the OAU Liberation Committee. The fact is, however, that the funds proffered by OAU states for equipping the armies of these peoples' struggles were not nearly enough. Since, moreover, no western state had any intention of taking an active part against Portugal, which was after all a NATO member, the arms suppliers and instructors of the FRELIMO, PAIGC and MPLA could only be the Soviet Union and China. Holden Roberto, however, who reformed the UPA in March and April of 1962 into the extended Frente Nacional de Libertação de Angola (FNLA), based in Kinshasa, and proclaiming a 'Revolutionary Exiled Government of Angola' (GRAE), was able to rely for the equipping of his army on his brother-in-law Mobutu, Zaire's strong man and later head of state, who diverted some American arms shipments to the FNLA. Direct CIA assistance, it seems, did not come to Roberto until 1975.[6]

The other movements were obliged to seek moral support from communist states, but it was clearly not in their interests to take sides in the Sino-Soviet dispute, which was becoming increasingly entrenched in the 1960s. The fact that FRELIMO and the PAIGC managed on the whole a successful balance between Moscow and Peking may be put down as an achievement of their diplomats. In later years, the PAIGC was chiefly interested in good contacts with the Soviet Union, since in Guinea, where they had the most military opposition from the Portuguese, they consequently had a particularly urgent need for high-level weapons. In the final phase of the war in 1973–4 the PAIGC was even using ground-to-air missiles of the SAM 7 type, which could only be supplied by Moscow. FRELIMO, on the other hand, was mainly dependent on military bases in Tanzania, where China had a much more substantial presence than the Soviet Union. The somewhat more pronounced inclination towards Peking on the part of FRELIMO[7] was counterbalanced by the fact that FRELIMO and the PAIGC together formed a solid bloc with the MPLA, maintaining a joint co-ordination centre in Algiers and constantly confirming one another as the sole genuine liberation movements of the three Portuguese colonies. The MPLA gained most from this, although its rivals the FNLA and later UNITA were not without their diplomatic successes in the African sphere. Even Pope Paul VI, wanting to make a gesture for the anti-Portuguese liberation movements in July 1970, received representatives of the PAIGC,

FRELIMO, and MPLA bloc, but never a single representative of the FNLA or UNITA.

For its part, the Soviet Union likewise concentrated its material and political aid throughout the whole duration of the war on the three above-mentioned bloc parties, in the same way supporting ZAPU in Rhodesia, the ANC in South Africa, and SWAPO in Namibia. The Peking government was less purposeful, showing an interest in UNITA at one time, as well as in the ZANU in Rhodesia and SWANU in Namibia,[8] but neglecting these contacts when they no longer seemed to be expedient in terms of Chinese foreign policy. During the Angolan civil war of 1975–6, Peking made vociferous condemnations of the MPLA and praised its opponents, although then, as earlier, doing nothing practically to build up an alternative to the bloc of liberation movements being supported by Moscow.

The military and political course of these three wars can only be outlined very briefly here. In Guinea, the PAIGC launched its guerrilla war at the beginning of 1963, after its political cadres had been working patiently among the peasants for two years. Substantial sections of the population shifted their political loyalty to the liberation movement in the course of time, enabling the PAIGC to claim half or even two-thirds of Guinea-Bissau for itself as 'liberated territory' from 1966 onwards. Only the Fulbe in the north-east of the country remained predominantly loyal to the Portuguese to the bitter end. The Portuguese initially laid a defence of their fixed bases and larger settlements, concentrating on the setting-up of *Aldeamentos* under the military governor, General Arnaldo Schultz, who was in command in Guinea from 1964 until 1968. No military or political counter-offensive was launched until later, by Schultz's successor, General António de Spínola, who spoke of Portugal now bringing the black population 'social justice and equality of all citizens in the eyes of the law', as well as 'economic and social progress'.[9] He did indeed see to the setting-up of new schools, and somewhat improved health care, also convening a 'People's Congress', in which, however, only chiefs installed by the colonial administration were permitted seats. These reforms were too little and too late to change the fortunes of the war. Although the recruitment of 17,000 black soldiers under the Portuguese flag, and offensive military tactics, made life difficult for the PAIGC, who in 1970 had only around 5,000 regular soldiers and about as many guerrilla-militiamen at their disposal, the politico-military structure of the PAIGC managed to hold off the Spínola offensive. At the end of 1970, Spínola suffered another setback with the failure of a commando mission of non-regular troops, at least tolerated, and possibly even organized, by him, to capture the Guinea capital of Conakry, and aimed chiefly against the PAIGC installations there.

On 20 January 1973, Conakry became the scene of another bloody tragedy to hit Guinea-Bissau. Renegades from the PAIGC leadership, led by the commander of the rudimentary navy (two motor-boats), murdered Amilcar Cabral and abducted his deputy Aristides Pereira. They were prevented by the Guinean military from further action, so that it is still not clear today whom their orders came from (if anyone). The party leadership regrouped under Pereira and Luiz Cabral, Amilcar's brother. As had been planned by Amilcar Cabral for months, the PAIGC proclaimed the independence of the Republic of Guinea-Bissau on 24 September 1973, allegedly on liberated territory near Madina do Boé, close to the Guinean border. They thus implicitly disclaimed state unity between Guinea-Bissau and the Cape Verde Islands, from where many of their leaders originated, including the Cabral and Pereira families. The demand for liberation of the Cape Verde Islands under the PAIGC banner, however, remained on the party agenda.

The National People's Assembly of the new state was delegated from regional councils which, as the PAIGC proudly announced to the outside world, had been directly elected by the people between August and October of 1972 in the liberated zones. In fact the voting papers had only 'Yes' or 'No' on them, the unique list of candidates having been fixed beforehand, but this practice can also be found in other countries (not only in Africa), even when there is no war. The PAIGC registered 79,680 yes votes and 2,352 no votes, of which a total of only 4,515 came from 'members of the PAIGC working outside the country'.[10] The question remains, however, why the PAIGC did not hold a vote among the 82,000 refugees who had left Guinea-Bissau for Senegal, where they were cared for in camps by the UN HCR, or among the estimated 20,000 refugees in Guinea-Conakry.

Portugal likewise held elections in Guinea-Bissau, a few months after the PAIGC, at the end of March 1973. These two elections resembled each other in one respect, that in neither case were opposition candidates permitted. The 'Legislative Assembly' of Portuguese Guinea consisted of seventeen members, of whom only five were directly elected at all, the others representing interest groups loyal to the government (six), the colonial administration (three), and chiefs installed by the Portuguese (three). The powers of the assembly in relation to Lisbon were as narrowly restricted as they would have been in a French or British colony two decades earlier. Small wonder, therefore, that people showed little interest in this reform policy. In Guinea-Bissau, only 7,824 voters enrolled, of whom 89.4 per cent then voted behind the barricades of the military bases for the candidates put up by the regime.[11] This 'election' was unable to pose a threat to the PAIGC, either in the country itself, or in the arena where they competed for international sympathy.

The Republic of Guinea-Bissau proclaimed by the PAIGC was recognized by almost all African states within a few months (even by such conservative governments as that of the Ivory Coast). At the beginning of November 1973, a vote in the UN General Assembly presented an opportunity for separating the friends of Caetano's Portugal from those of the PAIGC: sixty-five states moved a resolution protesting against the 'illegal occupation of the territory of the Republic of Guinea-Bissau by Portuguese fighting forces', among the proposers being the OAU states, the Soviet Union and its allies, and the People's Republic of China, as well as Yugoslavia, India, and Pakistan. Ninety-three delegations voted yes, thus backing the PAIGC. There were thirty abstentions, including Japan, France, and the Federal Republic of Germany. Only seven delegations openly supported Caetano's Portugal, apart from Portugal itself, these being Brazil, Greece under the colonels, South Africa, Franco's Spain, Great Britain, and the USA.

Recognizing a state which exists only in the political underground as a guerrilla force is of course a sensitive problem in international law. The PAIGC had quite intentionally decided not to form an exile government as Holden Roberto had tried to do (on the Algerian model) in Léopoldville in 1962. The PAIGC was also not in the position of being a party in a civil war, staking its claim to international recognition by constituting a government within a territory delineated by clear fronts, as, for example, the Spanish nationalists had done under Franco in 1936, or the Chinese communists in 1949 (at a point when they controlled almost the whole of the mainland). International law was tested in the case of Guinea-Bissau as to whether or not it was prepared to furnish a liberation movement which had been successful in the 'people's struggle', but still not by a long way victorious, with the rights of a sovereign government. This test only narrowly missed being taken to its conclusion in the form of an application for admission into the United Nations, because Caetano's government collapsed prior to this on 25 April 1974. Portugal's new rulers, making way for the military government, brought the African war to the speediest possible conclusion by handing over power to the liberation movements.

Before doing so, General Spínola, the temporary head of revolutionary Portugal, attempted to introduce yet another policy in some territories (especially Angola and the Cape Verde Islands), which would have given a political chance to other forces besides those of the guerrillas recognized by the OAU. In Guinea-Bissau, however, there was no question even of Spínola succeeding in this; he recognized the failure of his own earlier efforts to build an alternative to the PAIGC. After brief negotiations, Portuguese representatives (headed by the foreign minister, Mario Soares) and the PAIGC agreed 'in an atmosphere of great warmth'[12] on 26 August 1974 in Algiers on the '*de jure* recognition of the Republic of Guinea-Bissau as a sovereign state by Portugal on the date of 10 September 1974'. It was then Portugal itself which proposed the admission of Guinea-Bissau at the following General Assembly of the United Nations.

On the Cape Verde Islands, Spínola tried for an electoral decision by the people; two political parties were permitted to figure as competitors against the PAIGC. After Spínola's resignation on 30 September 1974, however, there was no further mention of them, the Portuguese military governor forming a transitional government on 30 December 1974 with the PAIGC alone. Only the PAIGC then put up candidates for parliamentary elections on 30 June 1975, obtaining, as was only to be expected, a 93 per cent turn-out. Aristides Pereira, secretary-general of the PAIGC, became head of state of the Republic of Cape Verde, which declared its independence on 5 July 1975. Even before the coup in Guinea-Bissau (14 November 1980) which ousted the Capverdians from the ruling elite of this continental African country, thereby splitting the PAIGC, there was no real effort to unite the Cape Verde Islands and Guinea into a single state. Perhaps the leaders considered it useful having two states as they kept up a balancing act between east and west. Soon, the east lost its spell as the needs of Guinea-Bissau and the 'Cape Verde Islands turned away from weapons, and towards financial aid. Both states acceded to the Lomé conventions of so many African, Caribbean, and Pacific countries with the European Community.

In Mozambique the armed struggle of the liberation movement began almost two years after that in Guinea-Bissau, FRELIMO guerrilla fighters crossing the Tanzanian border in September 1964 and infiltrating the province of Cabo Delgado. The Makonde people living on either side of the river frontier, who had always been neglected by the Portuguese authorities, gladly accepted liberation by FRELIMO, in spite of the fact that many FRELIMO leaders came from the Shangaan people living in the province of Gaza in the far south of Mozambique, around the capital of Lourenço Marques (now Maputo). Dr Mondlane was also a Shangaan, as was Samora Moises Machel (1933–86), who became president of independent Mozambique in 1974.

As fighting gradually spread to the province of Niassa, FRELIMO had to suffer a number of internal feuds. Some breakaway members tried to start up a rival movement from Zambia, but the OAU Liberation Committee never recognized them. In 1968, students at the Mozambique Institute in Dar es Salaam, a high school run by FRELIMO, and at one time headed by Mondlane's (white) American wife, rebelled against the party leadership, who had to beg for the protection of the Tanzanian police. On 3 February 1969 Mondlane was killed in Dar es Salaam opening a parcel bomb: the source of the attack has never been completely verified. In April 1969 a man influential among the Makonde, Lazaro Kavandame, at one time a member of the FRELIMO Central Committee, went over to the Portuguese. At the same time a bitter disagreement over who was to be Mondlane's successor set in among the exiled FRELIMO leadership. The vice-president Uria Simango, a Protestant clergyman who had been in office since 1962, felt threatened by Samora Machel, who had risen to the rank of military commander under Mondlane. In May 1970, Simango was dismissed and Machel confirmed as president of FRELIMO.

Around this time the Portuguese launched a huge military offensive against FRELIMO, after the arrival of General Kaúlza de Arriaga as the new commander-in-chief in March 1970. Unlike Spínola in Guinea-Bissau, he did not elaborate a politico-social programme to counter FRELIMO efforts in the 'liberated zones' of the north, being satisfied instead with rounding up as many African peasants as possible into *Aldeamentos*. He did nevertheless restore military control of the Tanzanian border by the Portuguese colonial army (70 per cent of whom in Mozambique were native Africans, the remainder being European Portuguese conscripts).

Portugal needed military protection for its largest development project in Mozambique, the building of the Cabora Bassa roller dam. This project, which had been planned for decades, was launched as soon as the Republic of South Africa had committed itself, in a treaty with Lisbon on 19 September 1969, to bear some 20 per cent of the costs and to buy a substantial proportion of the electro-energy to be produced at Cabora Bassa. In addition to Portuguese and South African firms, France, Italy, and the Federal Republic of Germany were also involved in the ZAMCO consortium formed for the building of the dam. Almost half the total value of the order (683 million DM out of the 1,553 million (or £175 million in 1970) of the first phase of building) [13] went to the German partners.

It was not until the Cabora Bassa project that West European public opinion became aware of the war in Mozambique, which had by then been going on for years. FRELIMO supporters in churches and at universities (support being much weaker in the press and in the political parties, and virtually non-existent in the unions) raised their voices in an attempt to dissuade European companies from participation in the project. Whilst a large Swedish company was forced, by the pressure of public opinion and appropriate legislation, to drop out of the consortium, both the German and other remaining partners of ZAMCO stood firm: the dam was built. Taking advantage of this sudden limelight and international interest, FRELIMO opened up a 'new front' in the province of Tete, where Cabora Bassa is situated, although FRELIMO never actually attacked the construction site, and substantial deliveries by road were only seldom troubled. Is it possible that the military protection of the Portuguese really acted as such a deterrent? Or was it that FRELIMO was so certain of victory that it calculated on being able to take over the completed project for an independent Mozambique? At all events, in the course of the discussion of Cabora Bassa in federal Germany in 1973, FRELIMO undertook a noteworthy attempt to win over the Social Democratic Party (SPD), at the time senior partner in the Bonn coalition cabinet chaired by Willy Brandt, to support the liberation cause. As has been mentioned, FRELIMO had already succeeded (like the PAIGC and other southern African movements) in securing the official sympathy of the social democratic government in Sweden. Success in Bonn would substantially have extended the political platform of FRELIMO in the western world, which would seem to be just what FRELIMO's foreign politicians were aiming for, to achieve a counterbalance for their friendly contacts within the Soviet camp and in communist China.

The SPD did not play ball, however. When a FRELIMO delegation made its visit to Bonn in August 1973, they were offered only humanitarian support, the SPD expressly refusing the requested declaration of political solidarity on the legitimacy of the struggle against Portuguese colonial rule. The FRELIMO journal subsequently published a cartoon, with Willy Brandt handing a jet-fighter to Portugal with one hand and a box of medical supplies to FRELIMO with the other.[14] FRELIMO protested – both in the cartoon and in political reality. This rejection of a liberation movement which was highly respected throughout Africa seriously damaged the prestige of the Federal Republic of Germany.

Whilst in 1972 and 1973, in spite of all Portuguese retaliation, FRELIMO soldiers were pressing forwards over the Zambesi and reached the Rhodesian border (thus enabling ZANU to embark on its guerrilla warfare in earnest in north-east Rhodesia), and whilst FRELIMO advance parties were beginning to destroy the railway and road communications between the port of Beira and Rhodesia – far to the south of their former zones of operation – the Portuguese were suffering a further defeat in the field of international psychological warfare. On 10 July 1973 *The Times* unleashed a storm of indignation against Portuguese counter-insurgency methods with a report on the massacre of Wiriyamu. The Portuguese of course also presented material on atrocities perpetrated by FRELIMO: they needed only to photograph in the hospitals the women and children who had lost arms or legs as a result of land mines, but West European public opinion was not nearly so interested in this as it had been in Wiriyamu: people began to doubt the long-term viability of Portuguese rule in Africa. In the end Europe, Portugal's ally, was spared the inconvenience of having to make up its official mind, with the coup by Lisbon officers in April 1974.

The new government of Portugal did not hesitate to any appreciable degree in handing over full political power to FRELIMO in Mozambique, as it did in Guinea-Bissau to the PAIGC. In the middle of 1974, the FRELIMO presence was still limited, even underground, to the northern half of the country; Samora Machel himself had conceded in public speeches in 1973 that FRELIMO actions in the towns of Mozambique were yet to be prepared. He had made it equally clear, however (as Mondlane had done before him), that FRELIMO would claim a political monopoly in independent Mozambique. Lisbon bowed to this claim in the very first round of negotiations, in spite of the fact that political groups had formed spontaneously in Mozambique, not only among the 130,000 whites, but also among Africans, which were not necessarily prepared to be subsumed within the FRELIMO organization marching down from the north.

On 7 September 1974 Portugal and FRELIMO signed a treaty in Lusaka, Zambia, on an immediate ceasefire and the formation of a joint transition government, to be headed by the FRELIMO leader Joaquim Chissano (born 1939) as prime minister. A short-lived revolt by white settlers in the capital led to bloody race riots, which were put down jointly by Portuguese soldiers and FRELIMO. A number of dissidents, among them Uria Samingo, who had been living in Lusaka, fell into the hands of FRELIMO and were sentenced by them. On 25 June 1975, the anniversary of the founding of FRELIMO, independence was declared and Samora Machel sworn in as president of the People's Republic of Mozambique.

Angola's transferral of sovereignty took place in a much more dramatic way, the war of the late 1960s and early 1970s having spared the country considerably more than it had the two other Portuguese colonies in Africa. Neither of the rival liberation movements proved able to put up an effective fight against Portuguese rule in the more densely populated regions of Angola. In spite of the fact that both the MPLA and UNITA claimed since 1965–6 to have 'liberated' vast areas in the east and south-east of the country, these were in fact practically uninhabited savannah regions in which the columns of guerrilla fighters were only able to move at will because the Portuguese saw no reason to stop them. The MPLA and UNITA moreover claimed to control substantial stretches of the same territories. In the north of Angola, the FNLA retained a presence in the refuges it had set up in 1961. It never claimed to have 'liberated' these zones. In the Cabinda enclave to the north of the Congo estuary, the MPLA did make some advances in 1964, but was never able to establish a lasting presence there.

The war years in Angola were characterized not only by continuing feuds between the liberation movements, but also by each organization undergoing its own internal crises and splits. A number of top functionaries of the UPA/FNLA rebelled against the personal style of leadership of Holden Roberto. In 1964, Dr Jonas Savimbi (born 1934) relinquished his post as minister of foreign affairs in the 'exiled government', founding UNITA, the National Union for the Total Liberation of Angola from Zambia – the only group which ever made a serious attempt to locate its headquarters inside Angola. Savimbi thereby gained a certain amount of respect among black Angolans, especially among his own people (the Ovimbundu), but paid for this with inadequate arms supplies to his troops, as he was unable to win over at that time any neighbouring state as a reliable base. His good relations with the People's Republic of China, where he received guerrilla training with some of his supporters, were short-lived and were in any case unable to produce results in the disruption of the Chinese Cultural Revolution. The OAU did not recognize UNITA as a liberation movement until (for a very short time) 1975.

There were a number of crises within the MPLA, even after the highly respected medical doctor and poet Agostinho Neto (1922–79) took over the presidency in December 1962 after his escape from a Portuguese prison. In 1963, the MPLA expelled their secretary-general, Viriato da Cruz. From 1972 onwards discord increased between Neto and the commander of the MPLA guerrillas on the eastern front, Daniel Chipenda, until there was an open rift, at which point Congo-Brazzaville gave its support to Neto, and Zambia to Chipenda. Attempts on the part of the OAU to mediate were as fruitless as their long years of effort to reconcile the MPLA with the FNLA. As early as October 1961 a UPA commander in North Angola had killed twenty MPLA soldiers wanting to cross his territory in order to bring supplies to a guerrilla unit up against the Portuguese. Even in later years, Roberto and the military of Zaire denied transit from Brazzaville to North Angola to the MPLA.

As long as the liberation movements and the African states impeded one another in this way, the Portuguese were able to do more in Angola than merely fight an arduous war of counter-insurgency, as they did in Guinea-Bissau and northern Mozambique. In the final years of colonial rule, Angola underwent a substantial economic upswing – albeit a colonial economic upswing. The departure of Salazar from his earlier policy of autarchy (of German-Italian persuasion) bore fruit in this respect. Foreign capital from the west flowed far more noticeably to Angola than towards Mozambique (where there was hardly any foreign investment apart from the Cabora Bassa project) – and even less to impoverished and insecure Guinea-Bissau. Angolan diamond exports increased in value by 300 per cent between 1963 and 1973, being mined mostly by *Diamang* (with British, Belgian, and French capital), although of course with the participation of the international diamond monopoly, the De Beers group. Coffee exports likewise doubled in the same period; in this case, however, African peasants also took a share of the profits. On the Kunene river in southern Angola an irrigation and power station system was constructed in partnership with South Africa. The exploitation of iron ore deposits (German, Danish, British, and French capital, with supplies to Japan among others) and of crude oils, chiefly off-shore Cabinda (mainly by the American Gulf Oil Company) was just beginning in the 1960s. In 1973 the USA (with 28.1 per cent) overtook the Portuguese homeland (with 25.3 per cent) as the no. 1 importer of Angolan goods. Portugal still occupied first place among suppliers with 29.1 per cent, followed by the Federal Republic of Germany with 13 per cent. The total imports of Angola in 1973, totalling almost 14 thousand million escudos, despite the accelerated development of the economy (including a certain amount of industrial conversion, chiefly for food production and luxury goods), was nevertheless far exceeded by its exports, which were in excess of 19 thousand million escudos.

There was, however, no corresponding political development to accompany this economic boom. It is not surprising, therefore, that the available statistics fail to provide information on where the profits from Angolan economic life accumulated. After 1973 there was still no opportunity for Angolans (black and white alike) to articulate their interests politically within the Portuguese system. The 'overseas province' of Angola did of course have the 'honourable designation' of *state* bestowed upon it by Lisbon, in an act passed on 23 June 1972, as did Mozambique.[15] All overseas provinces were now granted so-called autonomy. The newly established 'legislative assemblies' have already been described in connection with Guinea. The authoritarian constitution of Portugal, however, which was not touched by Caetano until 1974, saw to it that these new institutions were denied any authority with which to counter the directives of central government. The reform law of 1972 itself indeed spoke of the overseas provinces expressly as 'an integral part of the nation', stipulating: 'The exercise of autonomy by the overseas provinces does not affect the unity of the nation, solidarity among all parts of Portuguese territory, or the indivisible nature of its sovereignty.'

None the less, 584,000 people eligible to vote were still found to fill the electoral rolls in Angola for the elections to the Legislative Assembly at the end of March 1973. In marked contrast with its practice in former years, the administration now allowed anyone to vote who could write his name and was prepared to pay a tax of 100 escudos (at that time worth about £1); some 85.6 per cent of the enrolled voters actually voted. Unlike Guinea and Mozambique, in Angola the directly 'elected' (unopposed) representatives formed a majority in the assembly with thirty-two seats, compared with twenty-one appointed members.

No more was heard of the 'autonomous state' institutions of Angola, when Caetano was toppled from power in Lisbon on 25 April 1974. To the surprise of some observers, no one among the 250,000–300,000 white settlers[16] attempted to fill the political vacuum by seizing power in the Rhodesian style. There was no organizational base for such a step, however weakly represented the African liberation movements *in* Angola may still have been in 1974. All three naturally did their best to bridge this gap as quickly as possible. It would seem that after April 1974 the new Portuguese commanders favoured the MPLA, which in any case had the most backing among the *mestizos* and *assimilados* in the capital of Luanda. The remaining power left to the Portuguese in Angola was now increasingly limited to Luanda. In the mean time, Roberto was arming conventional troops in Zaire (now with aid from the CIA), evidently hoping to repeat the Algerian example of 1962 by seizing power at the moment of formal independence, with an army marching in from the neighbouring country at the expense of the exhausted guerrilla fighters who had managed to hold out in the interior. The white settlers of Angola had more faith in a victory of this kind for the anti-Soviet FNLA and for Savimbi's UNITA than they did in their chances of staging their own coup.

Chipenda's MPLA troops openly went over to the FNLA in 1974, while Chipenda himself took command in Namibia of a strike force armed by South Africa. Savimbi was suddenly in demand, and not only among his own people, now that the OAU could no longer avoid recognition of UNITA, thus placing it on a par with the MPLA and FNLA. Lisbon postponed the date of independence by a year, setting it for 11 November 1975. After the OAU, with the active involvement of the wise old man of Kenya, Jomo Kenyatta, had obliged the feuding movements of Angola to meet round the table of reconciliation, in a summit meeting of Neto, Roberto, and Savimbi at the beginning of January 1975 in Mombasa, Portugal concluded a transitional agreement with the three movements in Alvor. All three were thus included in the transitional government of Angola which came into existence in Luanda on 31 January 1975. This government immediately proved incapable of mutual co-operation, however, and the Portuguese administration showed itself unwilling to exert any authority in the time it had left, behaving instead rather as the British had done in Palestine in 1948, limiting themselves to an orderly retreat by their troops and leaving the country to indigenous rivals who were shooting at one another. The announcement of democratic elections withered away, never to be heard of again.

Civil war was thus the only alternative left. The three parties to the war rapidly stepped up their armament schedules, although not for guerrilla warfare, in which all three were supposed to be experienced, but for a conventional war. The victors were the MPLA of Dr Neto, by virtue of their firm comradeship with the Soviet Union. The FNLA and UNITA, however 'pro-western' their behaviour, had no such international partner, since in 1974–5 in the west there existed no common political will, let alone willingness to enter into military involvement in favour of the UNITA/FNLA coalition. South Africa sent a few soldiers across the Namibian border, but the remainder of the western world shrank back from these embarrassing allies. Whilst Secretary of State Kissinger and the US Congress were arguing it out in Washington, the West European powers maintaining a discreet silence, the Cuban back-up force of the MPLA had captured by February 1976 the whole of Angola for the People's Republic which had been declared by Dr Neto on 11 November 1975. An extraordinary summit conference of the OAU had as late as January 1976 still been split into equally strong camps for and against the MPLA.[17] On 11 February the OAU secretary-general rushed through recognition of the People's Republic of Angola with the agreement of a majority of member states, Zaire relinquishing (at least verbally) further support of the FNLA.

Decolonization of the Portuguese Empire was over, liberation achieved. Civil war, however, in Angola as in Mozambique was just about to start.

The result in historical terms of the Angolan crisis of 1975–6 is that, for the first time, the independent government of a post-colonial African state owes its authority not to election by their people, not to the pressure of their own bayonet, not to their skill in negotiating with the former colonial rulers, but to the military assistance of a superpower which had formerly been alien to Africa. This fact will continue to hold good for Angola, regardless of whether or not the MPLA will prove to be a satellite of this superpower in the long run. Other African and Asian governments which had their first taste of sitting in the saddle as the satellites of a western power have since shown themselves to be confident riders in their own right. The protracted war of liberation in the Portuguese colonies also brought with it another yield, which hopefully will prove more important for contemporary Africa. By this we mean the experience of people in the liberated zones of a politico-administrative organization which was isolated from, and consequently independent of, the constraints of the international system of our times.

Even now, very little is known of real day-to-day living conditions in the Guinea-Bissau of the PAIGC, or in FRELIMO's Mozambique before 1974. The war propaganda of the liberation movements projected to the outside world, with the help of sympathetic western journalists and academics, an idealized image of the liberated zones. According to this image there was nothing to be seen but self-sacrificing commitment, selfless working enthusiasm in the service of the noble cause, and equality and fraternity under the watchful eye of a perpetually just leadership, which was daily confirmed in its office by genuine democracy. If normal everyday human experience is anything to go by, it cannot really have been like this. The isolation of the liberated zones from the 'capitalist world market' occurred as a result of the war situation, not as a result of the free choice of political leaders, and certainly not of the choice of the populations concerned. None of this can change the fact, however, that the PAIGC and FRELIMO in the liberated zones (that is, among those people who for a full ten years transferred their loyalty from the colonial power to the revolutionaries) were obliged to a substantial degree to practise the self-reliance which many African governments in the wake of Tanzania have tried to build into their agendas, but which none of them, Tanzania included, has been able to carry out with anything approaching perfection.

The question is what ten years of real self-reliance, experienced by substantial sections of the population, organized by the core team of the present government, actually means for the future policies of the republics of Mozambique and Guinea-Bissau. Amilcar Cabral attempted to formulate an answer to this question in advance, and is rightly regarded as the foremost political theoretician among Portuguese African revolutionaries. His name evokes respect throughout

287

the whole of the Third World, his speeches and writings being studied on a par with those of Frantz Fanon, Che Guevara or even Mao Tse-tung. Amilcar Cabral not only criticized Portuguese colonial policy, but also observed at close hand the arduous attempts on the part of African states and their rulers to become truly independent after decolonization. However politely Cabral rejected direct criticism of those African states which offered him and his friends asylum and support, his reflections clearly reveal how well aware he was of the weaknesses of liberated Africa. Cabral's thoughts on the subject of how a repetition of such failures in Guinea-Bissau could perhaps be avoided are drawn from the body of Marxist theory, which views history predominantly as the history of class conflict. Even someone who does not agree with the politico-economic conclusions of Karl Marx and Marxists, however, will still find in Cabral realistic analyses, precisely directed warnings, and some practical suggestions for a better road for the decolonized peoples towards the future.

In May 1964, Cabral said during a seminar held in the Frantz Fanon Centre (Milan/Italy):

Our problem is to see who is capable of taking control of the state apparatus when the colonial power is destroyed. In Guinea the peasants cannot read or write; they have almost no relations with the colonial forces during the colonial period except for paying taxes, which is done indirectly. The working class hardly exists as a defined class, it is just an embryo. There is no *economically viable* bourgeoisie because imperialism prevented it being created. What there is is a stratum of people in the service of imperialism who have learned how to manipulate the apparatus of the state – the African petty bourgeoisie; this is the only stratum capable of controlling or even utilizing the instruments which the colonial state used against our people. So we come to the conclusion that in colonial conditions it is the petty bourgeoisie which is the inheritor of state power (though I wish we could be wrong). The moment national liberation comes and the petty bourgeoisie takes power we enter, or rather return to history, and thus the internal contradictions break out again.

When this happens . . . there will be powerful external contradictions conditioning the internal situation. . . . What attitude can the petty bourgeoisie adopt? Obviously, people on the left will call for the revolution; the right will call for the 'non-revolution', i.e. a capitalist road or something like that. The petty bourgeoisie can either ally itself with imperialism and the reactionary strata in its own country to try to preserve itself as a petty bourgeoisie or ally itself with the workers and peasants, who must themselves take power or control to make the revolution. We must be very clear exactly what we are asking the petty bourgeoisie to do. Are we asking it to commit suicide? Because if there is a revolution, then the petty bourgeoisie will have to abandon power to the workers and the peasants and cease to exist qua petty bourgeoisie. . . .

I think one thing that can be said is this: the revolutionary petty bourgeoisie is honest; i.e. in spite of all the hostile conditions, it remains identified with the fundamental interests of the popular masses. To do this it may have to commit suicide, but it will not lose; by sacrificing itself it can reincarnate itself, but in the condition of workers or peasants.[18]

Amilcar Cabral died before he was able to put the example he had himself formulated to the test. The question is whether his party comrades, or the leaders of FRELIMO in Mozambique, have withstood this test better than, for example, the petty bourgeois leaders of earlier independent governments in Ghana and Nigeria, in Guinea-Conakry and Senegal, Kenya and Zaire have come out of it. The political suicide of a group holding political power as a class, in order to be resurrected in the class conditions of workers and peasants (that means African workers without unemployment insurance, African peasants without EC subsidies) is a tall order. Even if the experience of our times should show that this demand has not been met, it is still worthy of note that the demand was once made at all.

Chapter Twelve

THE PROSPECTS IN 1988

Black Zimbabwe has emerged from white Rhodesia, Portugal's attempt to assert itself as a colonial power until the very last minute is a thing of the past. Of all the European colonial empires, only the Russian one still seems to stand unshaken; but who knows whether we can assume that Islam is really politically inert in the Soviet Central Asian republics simply because it has lain buried for decades under Marxist demands for modernization and integration? Afghanistan has become, one may argue, a Vietnam or Algeria for the USSR, even if the Muslim resistance fighters lacked the efficient central organization provided to the Vietnamese by a Communist Party. International support from a superpower is channelled to the Afghan mujaheddins, nevertheless. In fact, the commotion originating from this colonial war may be even more dangerous for the Soviet Union than the Vietnam crisis had been for the United States: college protests or large-scale refusal to go to the army are unheard of in Russia. But no state of the USA has ever been populated by Buddhists and/or communists ethnically linked to the Vietnamese. So it could be logic that motivates Mikhail Gorbachev to get out of Afghanistan faster and with still less *gloire* than Charles de Gaulle saved when he got out of Algeria.

To remain with the concerns of the west, however: the conflict in southern Africa continues. The Republic of South Africa, the last remaining white minority regime, is of course not formally a colonial power (except in Namibia), but the OAU and the United Nations accurately assess the historical connection in always having linked their appeals against Portugal and Rhodesia with those against apartheid in South Africa. South African domestic policy is a form of internal colonialism, since ruler and ruled are just as much separated by a colour bar as they were in the colonies of Britain, Belgium, and, indeed, also of France. The transformation of apartheid into another political and social system will conclude the unscrambling of Africa and the dissolution of colonialism world-wide; but the question remains: transformation into what kind of new system? No African statesman from the countries of the OAU denies white South Africans the right to live in Africa as a coherent, self-conscious, and self-reliant people. But Africa as a whole and the great majority of states represented in the UN object to their claim to keep all other South Africans in political subjugation and social discrimination.

Does democracy of a western persuasion offer a viable alternative for South Africa? 'One Man, One Vote' and majority rule as a result: that seems to be the programme on which all the exiled and internal factions of the South African liberation movement can agree for the time being. Heaven knows there are bitter quarrels among factions going back partly to the ANC/PAC split in 1959 and in what is at present their most vicious form to the break between the ANC and Chief Buthelezi's internal Inkatha organization in 1979.[1] What about the 'time being'? It is still characterized by a clear supremacy of the state apparatus of repression, including numerous black policemen, army volunteers, Bantustan forces, and vigilante groups in the black towns, over the forces of revolt.

Revolution in South Africa is not yet around the corner, that is the lesson of the youth uprisings which started in late 1984. In the long run the forces of liberation will probably win after a protracted civil war, be it of Lebanese or Ulster or Spanish (1936–9) dimensions – but how good will the prospect then be for liberal democracy? One Man, One Vote, might then be the likely outcome – as many South Africans bitterly predict – followed by another form of dictatorship. Others draw blueprints for a better South Africa on the lines of what is called 'Concordant Democracy' in academic classrooms.[2] This would mean continued existence of 'groups' not just as coherent, self-conscious, and self-reliant units, but mainly as closed political entities enjoying autonomy. The established leaders of those groups would share state power not according to numerical majority, but under a pre-arranged harmony of interests codified in a national pact. It sounds good and peaceful and stable, and there is Switzerland to support the idea in practical experience. But on the other hand, not too long ago, the prophets of Consensus Democracy were equally confident that Lebanon's political system was an asset for them.

291

General criticism of the concept remarks that internal political relations in the constituent units of such a state must by no means necessarily be democratic, that on the contrary a mosaic of oligarchies is much more likely to ensure stability, so that the whole fabric will turn out not to present harmony among truly popular interests, but just a cartel of elites. In the special case of South Africa, the constituent elements of a consensus polity would most probably not be geographical units (like Swiss cantons) or social strata (an industrial working class organized in trade unions could be an exception), but ethnic groups. What that really means is uncertain. The four 'races' established under apartheid? That would keep the whites together as one group, wielding enormous economic power under present circumstances, and traditionally inclined to patronize over others and to tell them what they really need and should want. The refusal to accept the whites as a solid bloc in liberated South Africa was the reason behind PAC protest against the Freedom Charter (the basic document of the ANC) from the late 1950s onwards. Or will the Bantustan 'tribes' form separate black units? This danger of Balkanization within the black South African nation lies behind the mistrust of ANC and UDF (the United Democratic Front created in 1983 as a legal umbrella organization of grassroot protest groups) *vis-à-vis* the Zulu-based Inkatha movement.

Some commentators expect a grand design of territorial division to be in store for South Africa, regrouping the whites (possibly with a large portion of their 'coloured' traditional servants) in the western Cape, approximately within the historical borders of the Dutch colony before 1800. This solution of the conflict seems possible only *after* a long, bloody, and inconclusive civil war which, unfortunately, becomes more likely in the course of time. It would entrust black South Africa with the running of most of the modern industrial centres, including the mines. Or would industry have to be reconstructed after thorough devastation? Some people may speculate that no conceivable government of black South Africa could avoid borrowing capital for reconstruction from, and selling the produce of industry and mines to, the western nations of the north. South Africa would still be in a stronger bargaining position than the present Angolan or Mozambican 'revolutionary' governments, but in no basically different one. Marxism-Leninism, or African socialism, or 'the suicide of the petty bourgeoisie' including its 'resurrection as workers and peasants' relegated to the realm of Sunday speeches, all would be for the best in the best possible South Africa and in the best possible universe. Is that speculation really nothing but a neo-colonialist pipe-dream?

In the mean time, the white rulers of South Africa and the politicians of the outside world are using Namibia for practice drill, practising how to manoeuvre in the labyrinthine international conflict in southern Africa.[3] It remains to be seen whether Namibia presents a re-enactment of the Rhodesian, Angolan/Mozambican or some other solution to a colonial conflict. The fact that the Republic of South Africa still administers Namibia – formerly South-West Africa – at all in 1988, is an expression of pure old-fashioned colonialism, not neo-colonialism! The UN General Assembly terminated South Africa's League of Nations mandate in 1967 because apartheid policy ran counter to the aims of the mandate. South Africa paid no heed to this resolution, and the United Nations lacked the military might to invade Namibia and establish their interim administration there. Only when in November 1977 the western veto powers in the UN Security Council – the USA, France, and Great Britain – agreed together with Canada and the Federal Republic of Germany no longer to give their backing for a South African presence in Namibia, did the Pretoria government feel compelled to make a move – apparently to allow Namibia self-determination under UN control. Free and fair elections, one man one vote, majority rule, national unity: the full spectrum of western democracy was laid out in the settlement plan conceived by the western 'Gang of Five' (as UN diplomats have jokingly called it), ratified by unanimous Security Council vote for the famous resolution no. 435 (1978) – which means it was tacitly approved by the Soviet Union, long before Gorbachev invented *perestroika* – and then accepted in principle by South Africa's new 'reformist' ruler, P. W. Botha, and by SWAPO, the Namibian liberation movement waging armed struggle against the South African Defence Force since 1966 (in earnest since the MPLA victory in Angola, 1976). Two years of intricate diplomatic horse-trading followed, South Africa raising one stumbling-block after another on the road to implementation, that is, to the entry of a UN force into Namibia charged with controlling the elections. SWAPO, on the other side, was not enthusiastic about the prospect of having to compete for ballot boxes with other political parties, forgoing thereby its recognition as 'sole and authentic representative of the Namibian people' by the UN General Assembly[4] (never repeated in any resolution of the Security Council!). But SWAPO made this concession and stuck to it during the 'Gang of Five' negotiations. Meanwhile, a new American president had to be elected; Jimmy ('Who?') Carter, whose administration had inaugurated this whole diplomatic manoeuvre in order to pull free US African policy from the apartheid connection, was defeated. Pretoria could hope that President Ronald Reagan, Carter's successor, would 'correct' the course, as indeed he did immediately after his inauguration in 1981. Obsessed by the east-west conflict, the Reagan administration invented the linkage between South Africa's military presence in Namibia, and Cuba's in Angola, calling the new operation 'constructive engagement'. In plain words, the doctrine was that forces alien to Africa should leave Africa alone, and that the Cubans were aliens while the South Africans were not.

West German diplomacy (in contrast to the French who left their chair in the 'Gang of Five' empty from 1981) was reluctant to admit the failure of its first serious involvement in African decolonization. It is history, nevertheless, that South Africa enjoys a much better opportunity, thanks to American global strategy, than Rhodesia's Ian Smith did in his time to pursue what both of them called the 'internal solution'. Namibia receives a systematic outfit of machineries for 'independent' statehood, all produced and tested by South Africa.

This development is even older than Security Council resolution 435. Beginning in 1975, South Africa assembled representatives of Namibian 'tribes' (appointed by the administration in old colonial fashion, elected at first only in the case of the privileged white tribe) in the Turnhalle building, a monument of the gymnastic endeavours of Namibia's first – German – colonizers (1884–1915) surviving in its capital, Windhoek. Out of this gathering, in due course of time, developed a system of more than a dozen political parties, every one limited by order to one ethnic group. The 'national' confederation of those parties enjoying the special attention of the South African government was called the Democratic Turnhalle Alliance (DTA). In its leadership, white and black politicians co-operated – a shame for *verkrampte* Afrikaners, but another test run in the eyes of President P. W. Botha who was planning something similar for South Africa itself. Late in 1978, while the 'Gang of Five' talks seemed well under way, South Africa staged its own 'internal' elections in Namibia, with no UN blue helmets around the ballot boxes, but plenty of South African soldiers and police. No wonder that SWAPO boycotted the test, and that the DTA won. A provisional government was established

THE PROSPECTS IN 1988

on top of the thus elected assembly. It collapsed, however, early in
1983, after minor quarrels with Pretoria over public holidays (so we
were told). After a short delay, another effort followed: no elections of
any kind were considered necessary, in 1984, to convene a multi-party
conference in Windhoek, excluding SWAPO of course, but including
some black party leaders who had previously abstained from the
Turnhalle. The number of internal political parties in Namibia now
reached and surpassed forty.[5] Is that not good proof of full democratic
freedom? The multi-party conference discussed and agreed on a fine-
sounding Bill of Rights, and a complicated constitution. It does not
follow exactly the consensus model, but seeks to guarantee minority
groups against arbitrary rule by a majority. There is no doubt that
such groups really exist in Namibia, not only in the form of the white
colonizers who are themselves divided between some two-thirds Afrikaners from South Africa, and one-third ethnic Germans. The Herero
nation, for instance, approximately as numerous as the white group,
is proud of its long history of independence and supremacy in
Namibia before 1884, and of the tragic war it waged against German
rule in 1904; at that time the nation was nearly exterminated by a
calculated German policy of genocide. Today, in an astonishing
turnabout, the Germans and the Herero of Namibia are close allies
within the DTA and the only population groups (apart from the white
Afrikaners to their right) where probably SWAPO would still find it
very difficult to secure a majority in free and fair elections.

Anyway, in 1985 a Transitional Government of National Unity
emerged in Windhoek, with blessings from Pretoria, ostensibly with a
black majority, and it called for self-government and 'self-government
now!' – as Kwame Nkrumah did in Ghana in 1951, or Houphouet-
Boigny in the Ivory Coast in 1960. Did not both these heroes of the
anti-colonial struggle have the blessing of London and Paris respectively? Has our survey not shown that every single colonial power in
Asia and Africa, from a certain point in time, was ready and more
than ready to transfer political power to independent national governments – provided they could have some influence in the choice of
leaders? Will Namibia, with rulers hand-picked in Pretoria, be more
dependent on South Africa than Cameroon, for instance, has been
dependent on France, made independent in 1960 under a president
hand-picked in Paris? There was a nationalist armed struggle going on
in Cameroon then, as there is now in Namibia. Where is the difference?

The difference is, partly, in the fact that practically nobody supported the Cameroonian guerrilla struggle in 1960, certainly no neighbouring country, while SWAPO has a military presence in Angola, under Cuban protection. More important is a difference of another kind. France is a solid nation with an overwhelming numerical majority of loyal citizens, and a democratic polity. South Africa is nothing of the sort.

At the time of writing, no good solution for the Namibian conflict is visible. SWAPO, being backed by the Cubans and Cuba being backed by the USSR, will continue to be able to wage an armed struggle, but never become strong enough to win it. The Soviet Union is highly unlikely to step up its involvement in southern Africa. The next American president may again change strategy, but he will not send his navy and army across the globe to engage white South Africa in a re-enactment of the Boer War. European governments, fairly certainly, will do exactly nothing. We must hope for some sign of wisdom and reconciliation emerging among African people, in Namibia, in exile, and in the countries of the front line, perhaps even – who knows? – in South Africa.

Happily, when winding up our survey of the dissolution of the European colonial empires, we need not look only at the imminent threat of a protracted war in southern Africa, but can pause to look at the current debate on a New International Economic Order. However fiercely this debate may have been conducted, and however much nonsense may be contained in specific drafts for restructuring the trade in raw materials, the international currency system, or the international division of labour, the fact remains that it constitutes a meeting of minds aimed at co-operation between the states of the north and the south. The north–south conflict is a serious matter. But it is not waged by means of armed struggle, and no danger exists that it ever could be. All parties concerned agree that the use of violence in this conflict would prove extremely counterproductive. The north–south stage is set for a tough bargaining dispute, modelled rather on industrial action within modern societies. Workers who go on strike usually do not smash machines any more. What Europeans are bringing into play in this meeting of north–south minds are not merely (or even mainly) remnants of their imperialist superiority complex (as they sometimes do). They are also offering (albeit to some extent falsely interpreted and clumsily presented) the experiences gained from their own bourgeois-capitalist revolutions. It is the latter which led the white nations of the north to their present position as industrial producers, polluters of the environment, and consumers of everything from crude oil to contraceptive pills, all now striven after by the nations of the south with fierce ambition – by Africans, Asians, and Latin Americans alike.

All is far from sweetness and light in north–south relations. The USA has given a third-rate burial to its 'Alliance for Progress', once so earnestly propounded by President John F. Kennedy. Neither Mexico nor Peru, however, nor even Fidel Castro's Cuba, has shut the door in the face of the giant northern neighbour. It is Washington which is shrinking back (in 1988) from Nicaragua where Sandinista power is taking root.

Some African leaders undoubtedly grin when Peking's mass media denounce the Soviet Union as a 'social imperialist' superpower. Egypt, Guinea, Mozambique and others have experiences of their own on that score. The COMECON seems to have erected a 'colour bar' against the admission of African members (a formal request by Mozambique was turned down during the early 1980s) pleading that they have got enough trouble already with the full membership of Cuba and Vietnam. The Africa of the OAU is nevertheless grateful for Soviet backing against the white regime in South Africa.

So far, sixty-six governments of the ACP (Africa-Caribbean-Pacific) group of states are not fully satisfied with the way in which the Lomé Convention is functioning, even in its third revised edition of 1984, although they show every intention of renewing this link with the European Community for another period of five years, in due time.[6] The STABEX system enshrined in the Lomé conventions which promises ACP countries financial compensation for losses of export income, cannot meet all demands in a time of shrinking economic activities.

There was a time when the EC praised STABEX as a more realistic alternative formula to the no. 1 request of the 'New International Economic Order' to stabilize commodity prices. Now the two systems are to be put into working concurrently, if we are to believe everything written down in recent treaties and conference documents. The European Common Market (to be implemented in earnest among the EC member states in 1992) has always been open to ACP raw material exports, and this is the main reason why the ACP governments agreed to the Lomé Convention in the first place, because this commodity trade established under the 'colonial pact' is the vital lifebelt for them and (some of) their people today as in the past. But the European

Common Market is still as recalcitrant to the free flow of manufactured goods from the ACP zone as it is *vis-à-vis* other regions of the Third World. Thus the African ACP governments especially fear that, under unchanged Lomé conditions, their countries will for ever remain the tail-runners of the global economy. In the EC-ACP family, further problems arise when the Europeans make 'unreasonable' noises that co-operation might be made conditional on full respect for human rights in Africa, or when they simply are not prepared to spend more money on their poor friends in the south. On the other hand, the European Development Fund (EDF) is well seen in the poorest African countries, because it has always contained a grant element approaching 100 per cent, and therefore it could never contribute to the debt crisis of the 1980s. On the whole, both sides seem to agree that the balance of the Lomé conventions nos. 1–3 is positive. This may not be an accident: in this particular model of north–south relations, partner states with long and solid colonial experience play the major role on the northern side, most notably France. The psychological basis of mutual trust, not necessarily arising from love, but from profound knowledge of each other, is one of the legacies of colonialism, and an important element for the relative success of the Lomé conventions.

We shall see if that basis remains solid only as long as the ruling elite in the former colonies belongs to a generation who sat in school under colonialism. Even the Young Turks of present-day Africa – a Thomas Sankara (1949–87) in Burkina Faso, or Yoweri Museveni (born in 1946) in Uganda – belong to such a generation. In ten years' time, things may be different.

But the most crucial question for the future of north–south relations is not the year of birth of a president in Africa, but what kind of alternative any president has to co-operation with the north (-west). We have already discarded potential co-operation with the north (-east) on a similar level.

Could post-colonial governments in Africa or Asia carry the great principle of self-reliance to the practical extreme of self-isolation? It would be unfair to answer no only on account of what the Khmer Rouge did to Kampuchea in 1975. But is the development of Burma a success story? Or Albania? The People's Republic of China, the giant of the Third World in terms of population and harnessed with not the least developed industrial structures, tried to leap forward alone, from the late 1950s until the early 1970s. Maoist propaganda of the time notwithstanding, this was unsuccessful. The course of 'modernizations' on which China has embarked since (Peking uses this term so heavily criticized in western academic circles) means co-operation with, if not imitation of, the west.

Certainly in Africa, no individual state is either large enough or economically strong enough to attempt self-isolation in earnest, and not a single statesman of Africa has ever tried it. They could, one may argue, however, have joined forces with one another, or relied on broader south–south solidarity involving Asia and/or Latin America. Brazil is energetically pushing its way upward into the top league of arms exporters world-wide: why should this country not serve as an agent for international economic growth? Equal terms do not seem to apply to these two areas of activity. Non-alignment certainly is a useful set of values to keep the large majority of former colonial territories together in a political community (Brazil, indeed, is not a member of this group of states), but still has to give proof of economic usefulness. The Group of 77, largely identical with the Non-Aligned Movement (but including the People's Republic of China) has stood well the test of seven UNCTAD meetings so far: for collective bargaining with the north, this is an experienced 'trade union' of the south. But when the question comes up how the unemployed people (in the north–south arena, this means the least developed countries and the 'marginal' strata in all Third World societies) should be accommodated in some form of burden-sharing with the workers in jobs, the Group of 77 seems to have the same internal problem as any TUC in a democratic country of the west.

Third World demands for a New International Economic Order reached a culminating point, so far, in the mid-1970s. OPEC's temporary success in raising the oil bill provided the impetus for the movement. Meanwhile, the Third World governments have, rather unanimously, lowered the tone of the debate, and indeed they have also lowered the targets. The original idea that a group of many weak nations can successfully confront the few strong ones, if only they stick together and make their voice be heard loud and clear, has given way to insights formulated politely in article 15 of the Final Act of UNCTAD VII (Geneva, 9 July–3 August 1987):

> In view of the substantial and increasing interdependence in the world economy, both among countries and across the trade, money, finance and commodity sectors, national economic policies, through their interaction with the international

economic environment, have become important factors influencing the development process. The more significant the country in terms of its economic weight, the greater is the effect of its policies on other countries. The structural characteristics of most developing countries leave them especially vulnerable to the impact of structural change and external shocks.[7]

International organizations have been in existence since 1945 in which the rule of 'One Country, One Vote' has never been applied, but in which on the contrary economic weight is the qualification for voting power. These are the World Bank and the International Monetary Fund (IMF). Consequently, IMF conditionalities are more important sources for an understanding of north–south relations at present than UN General Assembly resolutions from the 1970s publicizing the requests for a New Order. Countries like Ghana and Uganda and even Tanzania could find no way out of economic calamities other than bowing to agreements with the IMF. Many people in Africa still think that this is a shame, that it amounts to some kind of surrender of hard-won independence, that IMF terms are an expression of collective recolonization by the west. Bitterness, disappointment, and animosity between north and south are bound to fester in the near future unless there is more of an open debate on the issues, and less on the formalities. A senior African journalist, Peter Enahoro of Nigeria, gave a sarcastic comment on this trend:

> There is an unfunny story of a Nigerian soldier asked by a television interviewer what he thought of the terms set by the IMF to help ease his country out of the economic quagmire in which it has remained trapped. A changed appearance resembling the unhappy expression of a man instantly striken with bad fever clouded the soldier's countenance. 'IMF?' he hissed. 'Me I no sabby am. IMF give general too much wahallah. If I see am I go shoot am one-time. I gi' am 12 o'clock.'
>
> Which you would have gathered translates as: 'IMF? Don't know him . . . giving the president a lot of problems. If I run into him I'll shoot him without ceremony . . . between the eyes.'
>
> Believe it or not, the general level of debate concerning the present IMF's role in several African countries has not much risen above this kind of silliness, although there is some pleasure to be gained in the new conversational idiom among Freetown's taxi drivers who will blame 'the effects of IMF conditionalities'

before thievishly overcharging you. . . .

The embarrassing fact is that what the IMF is demanding of us should have been initiated voluntarily by us two decades ago.[8]

Specialists will carry the debate further. I have my own doubts if Enahoro's last remark holds water. Do IMF recipes for economic recovery really express gospel truth? When ex-colonial countries are asked to 'adapt' their economies, I do not always understand to what exactly they are supposed to adapt themselves. To those regulations which Karl Marx analysed, more than a hundred years ago, under the concept of the 'capitalist mode of production'? Are these like laws of nature (as Friedrich Engels probably believed)? I am afraid that the world would become an impossible place for human life if all nations followed the examples of present-day capitalism, colonial deformations blocking such a way of development or not: global environment will just not tolerate world-wide extension of capitalism, or industrial society, or affluent society, or whatever name we may give to a way of life which the west thought it had grasped, relying partly on economic exploitation of its colonial backyard, at a moment already history today. I am afraid some of the IMF's strategists still live in that recent past when economic growth and modernization according to the model of North America were taken for granted.

Let this question be discussed by the specialists. For the political background of north–south relations, what matters is that all parties concerned approach the problem with an open mind, with reason not excluding emotions, but controlling them, and that they always be prepared to criticize their own positions. That is the political essence of Peter Enahoro's text quoted above, and this state of mind is something that the west still has to offer to other nations. If self-criticism and rationality have been transferred to other continents by European colonialism, in the bandwagon of cruelty and exploitation – then let it be so!

Examined in the cold light of day, the market rules of the global economy, in its north–south perspective, are by no means *neo*-colonial. They are the very same rules that prevailed in the colonial period itself, or indeed in the first half of the nineteenth century when 'imperialism of free trade' was preparing the way for the conquest of colonial empires. We observe transactions between apparently free and equal partners, who in reality are totally unequal in terms of power, and therefore bound by all kinds of 'constraints'.

Post-colonial governments in Asia and Africa attempt to break free from these constraints by political action, both international and domestic. But the political development of the former colonies is not proceeding with any discernible regularity along the same lines as their socio-economic evolution, let alone the development plans most of them have failed to implement. Foreign policy orientations of nearly all former colonies have converged under the concept of 'non-alignment', but then they started to quarrel (especially at the Havana summit of the Non-Aligned States in 1979) about what this concept meant, and in the end they agreed only to disagree. On the other hand, the domestic political system of a state can still today be assessed in the old-fashioned terms of democracy, oligarchy, dictatorship (*tyrannis* is the original Greek word), and perhaps totalitarian government. The summary is rather obvious: most peoples of the ex-colonial world have submitted, more or less tacitly, to some form of dictatorship, because they were promised a short cut to progress. The promise was shown to be empty. Here and there, in Asia with considerably stronger 'people's power' behind it than so far in Africa, intellectuals and some others are now making efforts to put democracy back on the political agenda; the more careful ones call it 'participation'. Keeping in mind that peasants generally know better than bureaucrats how to grow food, we may assume that this is the right way to go. Democracy means things as simple as the freedom to express interests, to voice them collectively, to propose policy choices, and above all to exchange policies and the teams who proposed them, without killing them and thereby wasting their brains. The former colonies have no brains to waste.

Democracy further means compromise. If the north and the south are to remain united, they will have to wrestle with compromises, even dubious ones, similar to those between a trade union and an employers' association in the domestic politics of a democratic industrial state. And remain united they must on this small planet, Earth.

The process by which nations of the world have become interwoven with another, not only economically, but also in terms of social organization and political thought, is not a reversible one. It is the result and essential achievement of imperialism of the last hundred years, as well as its preliminary phases from the fifteenth century onwards. The dissolution of the colonial empires does not signify that this process is reversible. Apart from a few dreamers, no one in Asia or Africa wants to return to the state of a pre-colonial society. The common people in particular want to move forwards into a new kind of society in which they will have access to all the achievements of humanity.

It seems to us that there is only one way to look at the lessons of colonial history. The states of Europe sought with their colonial and imperial expansion to unite the globe in a way governed by their modern civilization, and indeed in the service of Europe. They succeeded. In doing so, they created not only a world economy and a world market, but also a world society. This global society, however, like the individual bourgeois societies in Europe and North America, is a kind of class society; the global society, one could say humanity itself, has been split by European colonialism into a 'class' of those who rule and a 'class' of those who are ruled. Inverted commas are necessary here, since these 'classes' cannot be defined and do not behave in the manner discerned by Marx and Engels in the nineteenth century in the case of the bourgeoisie and proletariat of Europe.

The class concept is nevertheless useful, first since it deals with the global relations of dominance and dependence, and second because it shows how rulers and ruled are part of one and the same society, not of 'two nations' which can be isolated from each other.

Moral condemnation of imperialism and neo-colonialism does not, therefore, get us very far. It is merely a way of fobbing the problem off at the level of ideas. 'Victory in people's war' at the global level would similarly not achieve a great deal, for the same reason. It is certainly possible to topple a ruling class, but a new ruling class emerges within a few years of every revolution, even in Cuba, and in global terms there is no reason to assume it would be any different after the 'victory of the village over the town' dreamed of by Lin Piao.[9]

There is no cut-and-dried solution as to how the legacy of the European colonial empires should be administered. We can only keep in mind that after the failure of UNCTAD III to V, preparations for UNCTAD VI were started, and that now in 1988 if somebody feels impatiently that the outcome of UNCTAD VII was unsatisfactory, then he will get a chance at UNCTAD VIII to revise the procedure. Perhaps, after the victory of the communists in Vietnam, FRELIMO in Mozambique, and ZANU in Rhodesia, there will be other Vietnams, as Che Guevara called for in 1967. In that case, however, there will also be further My Lais. Another such notorious war would in our eyes be a far more serious failure than a failed UNCTAD. Not to regard armed struggle as a suitable way to achieve liberation from the dependencies of international society – this is not merely a moral judgement, but also a technical evaluation.

The colonial domination by European nations and their imperialism constitutes an unhappy chapter in human history, not only because of the bloodshed it involved (a price common, unhappily, to every chapter of human history) but rather because of the conditions of poverty, and, worst of all, the immorality, with which Europe oppressed the rest of humanity during those centuries, and which we have grown accustomed to glossing over by speaking of 'underdevelopment'. The positive core of imperialism, however, was and is the unity of the globe, the drawing together of humanity into a global society. The question is whether this global society will be capable of assuming a more humane face.

Sun Yat-sen wrote in 1924:

> The road which the Great Powers are travelling today means the destruction of other states; if China, when she becomes strong, wants to crush other countries, copies the Powers' imperialism and goes their road, we will just be following in their tracks. Let us first of all decide on our policy. Only if we 'rescue the weak and lift up the fallen' will we be carrying out the divine obligation of our nation. We must aid the weaker and smaller peoples and oppose the great powers of the world . . . Then when we become strong and look back upon our own sufferings under the political and economic domination of the Powers and see weaker and smaller peoples undergoing similar treatment, we will rise and smite that imperialism. Then we will be truly 'governing the state and pacifying the world'.[10]

Can we say that these are only words, words as hollow as those of the Atlantic Charter or the United Nations Declaration of Human Rights? Or can we discern modest but real progress in this direction?

Appendix

THE COLONIAL EMPIRES
IN 1914 AND 1939

THE COLONIAL EMPIRES AT THE OUTBREAK OF WAR
IN 1914

		area in sq. km	*pop. in 1,000*
1. In British possession			
A.	Mediterranean	10	517
B.	Asia	5,199	324,114
C.	Africa	9,392	50,824
D.	America	10,407	10,082
E.	Australia and South Seas	8,267	2,508
F.	Other	18	599
	total:	33,293	388,644
2. In French possession			
A.	Asia	803	14,871
B.	Africa	9,499	30,514
C.	Other	116	807
	total:	10,418	46,192
3. In Dutch possession		2,036	38,248
4. In Russian possession		16,153	22,605
5. In Japanese possession		288	19,200
6. In German possession		2,954	13,784
7. In American possession		388	10,299
8. In Belgian possession		2,365	10,000
9. In Portuguese possession		2,244	9,146
10. In Italian possession		1,641	1,850
11. In Spanish possession		441	640

Source: Veit Valentin: *Kolonialgeschichte der Neuzeit*, Tübingen, 1915

THE COLONIAL EMPIRES AT THE OUTBREAK OF WAR
IN 1939

		area in sq. km	pop. in 1,000
1. In British possession			
A. Mediterranean		10	660
B. Asia		5,520	390,117
C. Africa		7,880	52,464
D. America		302	2,658
E. Oceania and other		65	422
	total:	13,777	446,321
2. In French possession			
A. Asia		803	25,823
B. Africa		11,043	42,031
C. Other		117	812
	total:	11,963	68,666
3. In Dutch possession		2,146	67,672
4. In Japanese possession		1,566	69,182
5. In American possession		313	16,431
6. In Belgian possession		2,391	14,720
7. In Portuguese possession		2,082	10,258
8. In Italian possession		3,513	14,084
9. In Spanish possession		334	1,000
10. In South African possession		835	365
11. In Australian possession		475	971
12. In New Zealand possession		4	76

The Dominions have not been included in British possessions; Manjukuo has been counted with Japanese, and Albania with Italian possessions. League of Nations mandates are included among the possessions of the administering powers. According to these figures, at the beginning of the Second World War almost 39,700 sq. km and almost 710 million people were under colonial rule. This represents not quite one-third (29.4 per cent) of the land surface of the world (excluding the Antarctic) – compared with more than half in 1914. The figures continue to represent one-third of humanity, however; 32.6 per cent. One should bear in mind that Soviet Russia has been left out of our calculations of the colonial empires here – not because Stalin's regime seems significantly more humane to us than the Tsarist regime, but because account simply must be taken of the different constitutional order. The stable nature of the proportion of colonized people in the global population is chiefly an expression of rapid population growth in India, Indochina, and Indonesia.

NOTES

INTRODUCTION

1 Francisco de Vitoria, *De Indis recenter inventis et de iure belli Hispanorum in Barbaros relectiones (Die Klassiker des Völkerrechts*, Vol. 2), Tübingen, 1952; see esp. I:24; III:1-4, 16, 18.

2 Frederick D. Lugard, *The Dual Mandate in British Tropical Africa*, 5th edn, London, 1965, 61.

3 Thomas Clarkson, *An Essay on the Slavery and Commerce of the Human Species*, 2nd edn, London, 1808, 146f.

4 Benjamin Disraeli, letter to Lord Derby, 30 September 1866, quoted from G. Bennett (ed.), *The Concept of Empire – Burke to Attlee 1774-1947*, London, 1953, 229.

5 V. I. Lenin, 'Imperialism, the highest stage of capitalism', ch. 6, quoted from *Ausgewählte Werke*, Vol. I, Berlin, GDR, 1961, 833.

6 Jules Ferry, 'La France et l'impérialisme colonial' (foreword to *Le Tonkin et la Mère Patrie*), quoted from R. Delavignette and C.-A. Julien, *Les constructeurs de la France d'outre-mer*, Paris, 1946, 302.

7 George Macaulay Trevelyan, *History of England*, 2nd edn, London, 1937, 674.

8 Jawaharlal Nehru, *The Discovery of India*, 4th edn, London, 1956, 324.

9 George N. Curzon, *Problems of the Far East*, London, 1894, 434f.

10 Félicien Cattier, *Etude sur la situation de l'Etat Indépendant du Congo*, 2nd edn, Brussels, 1906, 341.

11 Alfred Zimmerman, *Kolonialpolitik*, Leipzig, 1905, 6.

12 Bernhard Dernburg, *Zielpunkte des deutschen Kolonialwesens*, Berlin, 1907, 6f.

13 The speaker was d'Estournelles de Constant, who had had experience in Tunisia; quoted from Henri Brunschwig, *Mythes et réalités de l'impérialisme colonial français 1871-1914*, Paris, 1960, 144.

14 See *Towards a New Trade Policy for Development*, report by the secretary-general of UNCTAD, New York, 1964, 125 pp. (UN sales publ. 64. II. B. 4).

15 See Wolfgang Bärtschi, *Ausbeutung und Einkommensverteilung in den internationalen Wirtschaftsbeziehungen*, Berlin, 1976, 123.

16 This debate was started by Arghiri Emanuel, *L'Echange inégal*, 2nd edn, Paris, 1972. Compare Samir Amin, *L'Echange inégal et la Loi de la Valeur*, Paris, 1973.

17 David S. Landes, *The Unbound Prometheus*, Cambridge, 1969.

18 Compare Wolfgang J. Mommsen (ed.), *Der Moderne Imperialismus*, Stuttgart, 1971, and Eric J. Hobsbawm, *Industry and Empire*, London, 1968.

19 Walter Rodney, *How Europe Underdeveloped Africa*, London/Dar es Salaam, 1972.

1 THE FIRST WORLD WAR

1 Title of a booklet by Emil Zimmerman, Berlin, 1917.

2 According to an Anglo-German draft treaty of 29 August 1913, Germany was to receive almost the whole of Angola with Cabinda, and the north of Mozambique down to almost the 16th parallel, as well as the islands Sao Tomé and Principe.

3 Robert L. Hess, 'Italy and Africa – colonial ambitions in the First World War', *Journal of African History* 4 (1963), 105ff.

4 Colin Legum, *Pan-Africanism – a short political guide*, New York, 1962, 133ff.

5 Hess, op. cit., 105ff.

6 W. H. Solf, *Kolonialpolitik – mein politisches Vermächtnis*, Berlin, 1919, 81.

7 Jan Smuts, *The League of Nations – a practical suggestion*, London, 1918.

8 Hans Poeschel, *Die Kolonialfrage im Frieden von Versailles*, Berlin, 1920.

2 THE BRITISH COMMONWEALTH

1 Valentine Chirol, *India*, New Delhi, 1983, 207f.

2 At that time Edwin Montagu was secretary of state for India, and Lord Chelmsford viceroy.

3 Nehru, op. cit., 361, 368.

4 ibid., 15.

5 Translated from the German Congress Record: Liga gegen Imperialismus (ed.), *Das Flammenzeichen vom Palais Egmont*, Berlin, 1927, 57f.

6 On M. N. Roy, see pp. 144f.

7 Arthur B. Keith (ed.), *Speeches and Documents on the British Dominions 1918–1931*, London, 1961, 4.

8 ibid., 161ff.

9 ibid., 303ff.

10 The white Afrikaners are today still often referred to in Europe indiscriminately as 'Boers'. This, in my opinion, is derogatory – similar to calling black Africans 'Kaffirs'.

11 Speech given at the Municipal Congress, quoted from Bennett, op. cit., 343ff.

12 *Government Gazette*, 31 March 1936, quoted from Govan Mbeki, *South Africa – the peasants' revolt*, Harmondsworth, 1964, 27.

13 Lugard, op. cit., 58.

14 Hubert Deschamps, 'Et maintenant, Lord Lugard?' in *Africa* (London), October 1963.
15 Lugard, op. cit., 89.
16 George Padmore, *The Gold Coast Revolution*, London, 1953, 48f.
17 Ben-Gurion acknowledged parity between Jews and Arabs in 1934 in talks with the Arab notable Musa Alami, and in 1937 in correspondence with the British writer St John Philby. See Franz Ansprenger, *Juden und Araber in Einem Land*, Munich/Mainz, 1978, 72ff.

3 THE GREATER FRANCE OF THE THIRD REPUBLIC

1 J. van Vollenhoven, *Une Ame de Chef; le Gouverneur général*, Paris, 1920, 189ff.
2 Albert Sarraut, *Grandeur et Servitudes coloniales*, Paris, 1931, 121f.
3 Sarraut, op. cit., 122f.
4 The powers of the Conseil Colonial in Cochin-China and some other French colonies were similar to those of the Conseil Général in a French *département*, being very limited on account of the highly centralized French state structure.
5 Henri Bley, *France d'outre-mer; L'oeuvre colonial de la Troisième République*, Paris, 1950, 259.
6 Quoted from Henri Grimal, *La Décolonisation 1919–1963*, Paris, 1965, 101f.
7 Quoted from Charles-Henri Favrod, *Le FLN et l'Algérie*, Paris, 1962, 70.
8 *Initiation à L'Algérie*, Paris, 1957, 193. Army members appear under the heading of 'others', apart from 1891 and 1901.
9 Before the incorporation of the military districts in 1923, 2.5 million hectares of Algerian territory were divided into 296 regular municipal districts (*communes de plein exercice*), in which the citizens, that is, French settlers and naturalized Algerians, could elect the local council and mayor in exactly the same way as in European France. The 2 million Muslims of these regular municipalities had control of a quarter of the council seats before 1919, a third after that date. The remaining Algerian territory, i.e. 18 million hectares with 3.5 million inhabitants, was subdivided into seventy-eight *communes mixtes*, the administrative heads of which were appointed by the governor-general; these Muslim notables formed advisory district committees.
10 Colette and Francis Jeanson, *L'Algérie hors la Loi*, Paris, 1955, 65.
11 Charles-André Julien, 'Léon Blum et les Pays d'outre-mer'. Contribution to the symposium of the Fondation Nationale des Sciences Politiques, Paris, 1965.
12 Quoted from Favrod, op. cit., 72f.
13 Jean Mirante, *La France et les oeuvres indigènes en Algérie* (Cahiers du Centenaire no. 11), Paris, 1930, 94.
14 Favrod, op. cit., 200.
15 *Das Flammenzeichen . . .*, op. cit., 98.
16 Ferhat Abbas, *Le Jeune Algérien*, Paris, 1931, 104f.

17 Quoted from Jeanson, op. cit., 67.
18 Henri Brunschwig, *La Colonisation Française. Du pacte colonial à l'Union Française*, Paris, 1949, 265. The Caribbean colonies and the island of Réunion had conseils généraux and universal franchise from 1854 onwards.
19 *Discours prononcés par les Gouverneurs Généraux et les Gouverneurs des colonies à l'ouverture des sessions des Conseils du Gouvernement et Conseils Généraux en 1923*, Mélun, 1924.

4 THE NETHERLANDS, BELGIUM, AND PORTUGAL

1 Jan Romein, *Das Jahrhundert Asiens*, Berne, 1958, 248.
2 ibid., 252.
3 Pierre Ryckmans, *Dominer pour servir*, Brussels, 1931, 5f.
4 Schools attendance figures for 1926 were stated as 114,000.

5 FASCIST ITALY IN CLOSE PURSUIT

1 The Senussi brotherhood was founded around 1835 in Mecca. Its religious rigour is related to that of Wahabism. The brotherhood is divided into '*sauyiyas*', monastic communities which also fulfil military and political functions. Its founder, Mohammed ibn Ali es-Senussi (1787–1859), at first established the brotherhood in his native Algeria, then in Cyrenaica. His son and successor, Mohammed es-Senussi (died 1902), strengthened discipline, moved the headquarters to Kufra (1895) and was revered as Mahdi. Mohammed Idris, later King Idris I of Libya, was a grandson of the founder.
2 Quoted from Royal Institute of International Affairs (ed.), *Abyssinia and Italy*, London, 1935, 28.
3 Deyazmach and Ras are titles of the Ethiopian nobility, only roughly translatable with the terms 'count' and 'duke'.
4 According to the treaty of 29 October 1888, Britain was committed to keeping the canal open under all circumstances. But article 20 of the League of Nations Covenant states 'that this covenant is accepted as abrogating all obligations or understandings inter se which are inconsistent with the terms thereof'.

6 SUPRA-REGIONAL COLONIAL AND ANTI-COLONIAL MOVEMENTS

1 Quoted from Ernst Gerhard Jacob (ed.), *Deutsche Kolonialpolitik in Dokumenten*, Leipzig, 1938, 515ff. Schacht still stood by his speech of 1926 in 1935, but in the Third Reich emphasized the national claim to revision, his basic idea being that colonial policy would improve the German currency situation.
2 Quoted from Pierre Rondot, *Destin du Proche-Orient*, Paris, 1959, 119.
3 F. L. Schoell, 'Le deuxième congrès panafricain et la société des nations', *Genève-Afrique* (Geneva), 4 (1965), 181f.

4 W. E. B. DuBois, *The World and Africa*, New York, [2] 1965, 238f.
5 ibid., 242.
6 Schoell, op. cit., 178ff. The league's Permanent Mandates
  Commission consisted of ten members, including five representatives of
  the powers exercising mandates.
7 Geoffrey Wheeler, *Racial Problems in Soviet Muslim Asia*, London, 1960,
  12.
8 J. W. Stalin, *Werke*, Vol. 2, Berlin, 1953, 285, 319.
9 Jane Degras (ed.), *The Communist International 1919–43*, Vol. 1,
  London, 1956, 23.
10 ibid., 138.
11 *Der II. Kongress der Kommunistischen Internationale*, Wien, 1920, 152ff.
12 'Theses on the national and colonial question, adopted by the Second
   Congress', see Degras, op. cit., 139f.
13 *Das Flammenzeichen* . . . , op. cit., 223.
14 George Padmore, *Pan-Africanism or Communism?*, London, 1956, 326.

7 THE SECOND WORLD WAR AND THE COLONIES

1 Philippe Devillers, *Histoire du Viet-Nam de 1940 à 1952*, 97.
2 ibid., 110f.
3 Félix Eboué, *La Nouvelle politique indigène pour l'Afrique
  Equatoriale Française*, Paris, undated, 12.
4 *Du Manifeste à la République Algérienne,* Algiers, 1948, 21ff.
5 *La Conférence Africaine Française*, Brazzaville, 30 January–8 February
  1944, Algiers, 1944, 35.
6 ibid.
7 Wendell L. Willkie, *One World*, New York, 1943, 184f.
8 'The conferences at Malta and Yalta 1945' (Foreign Relations of the
  United States, 1945, Vol. 9), Washington, 1955, 844f.

8 THE MULTIRACIAL COMMONWEALTH

1 Nicholas Mansergh (ed.), *The Multi-Racial Commonwealth*, London,
  1955. F. H. Soward (ed.), *The Changing Commonwealth*, Toronto, 1950.
2 Bennett, op. cit., 422f.
3 Quoted from Kenneth Bradley, *Britain's Purpose in Africa*,
  London, 1959, 3.
4 Bennett, op. cit., 421.
5 The Ireland Act passed by the British parliament on 2 June 1949
  merely recognized the independence which Eire itself had proclaimed
  in the constitution of 1937.
6 This title omits reference to Christian concepts and the precedence of
  the homeland, such as are retained, for example, in the Canadian title:
  'Elizabeth the Second, by the Grace of God of the United Kingdom,
  Canada and Her other Realms and Territories Queen, Head of the
  Commonwealth, Defender of the Faith'.
7 Grimal, op. cit., 257 (translated from the French).

8 ibid., 259.
9 See Penderel Moon, *Divide and Quit*, London, 1961.
10 *Le Monde* (Paris), 7 and 8 September 1955; *Die Zeit* (Hamburg), 1 April 1966.
11 George Padmore (ed.), *History of the Pan-African Congress*, London, 1945, 55f.
12 Quoted from Padmore, *Gold Coast*, op. cit., 60. The word 'chiefs' denotes all traditional rulers from the village head to the king of the Ashanti confederation.
13 ibid., 64.
14 Kwame Nkrumah, *Ghana – The Autobiography*, Edinburgh, 1956, 96.
15 Kwame Nkrumah, *I Speak of Freedom*, London, 1961, 23.
16 *Imperial Policy: a statement of Conservative policy for the British Empire and Commonwealth*, London, 1956, 55. On p. 53 of the same booklet, the authors openly refuse to 'hand over control to a small and clamorous political group who represent little but themselves', adding: 'In "plural" societies every care must be taken to ensure that the welfare of minorities and of those whose development has advanced slowly are properly safeguarded . . . . In many Colonies, particularly in Africa, the traditional seat of authority is in the tribe, and the policy of maintaining what is best in the tribal system has much to be said in its favour.'
17 Quoted from R. Segal, *Political Africa*, London, 1961, 260.
18 *Report of the Advisory Commission on the Review of the Constitution of Rhodesia and Nyasaland* (Cmnd 1148), London, October 1960, 22.
19 Roy Welensky, *Welensky's 4000 Days*, London, 1964, 324.
20 For the full text of the speech, see appendix in Peter Calvocoressi, *South Africa and World Opinion*, London, 1961, 45–56, from which the extracts in the text are quoted.
21 These two electoral rolls were not formally linked with race until 1969. The qualifications for the A roll were (1) a yearly income of £792 or property in land to the value of £1,650; *or* (2) a yearly income of £528 or property in land to the value of £1,100 and primary school education; *or* (3) a yearly income of £330 or property in land to the value of £550 and four years of secondary education; *or* (4) appointment, by the white government, to the status of chief or headman. In 1964, 89,000 whites and 2,251 Africans were listed on this A roll.
22 Quoted from the Corfield Report: *Historical Survey of the Origins and Growth of Mau Mau* (Cmnd 1030), London, May 1960, 162.
23 J. M. Kariuki, *'Mau Mau' Detainee*, London, 1963, 48ff. KAU = Kenya African Union, founded in 1943.
24 Corfield Report, op. cit., 165ff.
25 Kariuki, op. cit., 53ff.

9 FRENCH DECOLONIZATION

1 On 12 March 1946 the first Constituent Assembly declared the so-called old colonies in the West Indies (Martinique, Guadeloupe,

French Guyana) and the island of Réunion to be overseas *départements d'Outre-Mer* (DOM). The remaining colonies (with the exception of Algeria, considered part of European France, and the North African protectorates of Morocco and Tunisia, and Indochina) were classified as *Territoires d'Outre-Mer* (TOM).

2 PCF = Parti Communiste Français; SFIO = Section Française de l'Internationale Socialiste (social democrats); MRP = Mouvement Républicain Populaire (Christian democrats).

3 CFA = Colonies Françaises d'Afrique. The fixed exchange rate for the franc of the homeland was at first 1:1.7, later 1:2.

4 François Borella, *L'Evolution politique et juridique de l'Union Française depuis 1946*, Paris, 1958, 44.

5 *Journal Officiel*, 28 October 1946.

6 Quoted from the special editions of *Univers*; 'L'Avenir de la Colonisation' (Lille), October 1945, 214.

7 Paul Mus, *Viêt-Nam – sociologie d'une guerre*, Paris, 1952, 85.

8 Devillers, op. cit., 225.

9 ibid., 290.

10 Main points of the text in ibid., 309f.

11 ibid., 336.

12 Ho Chi Minh, *Ausgewählte Reden und Aufsätze*, Berlin, GDR, 1961, 133.

13 Quoted from André Siegfried (ed.), *L'Année Politique 1951*, Paris, 1952, 236. Crucial printing errors in this source have been corrected in the translation; *'porte'* instead of *'perte'* of Hanoi, *'Le Berlin de juin 1945'* instead of '. . . 1948'.

14 For the subsequent figures on Dien Bien Phu, see also Jules Roy, *La Bataille de Dien Bien Phu*, Paris, 1963, 561ff.

15 ibid., 93.

16 Siegfried, op. cit., 236. Roy, op. cit., 465, speaks of 34,641 dead in the expedition corps by the spring of 1953, including 28,141 North Africans and legionaries, as well as 32,000 Indochinese. According to Devillers, op. cit., 472, a total of 27,562 soldiers (including the missing) fell on the French side by the end of 1951, 7,150 in 1950.

17 Roy, op. cit., 465, and Devillers, op. cit., 472. Here a total of 812.6 thousand million francs are calculated for military costs until the end of 1951, and 576.1 thousand million francs in non-military costs (building and equipment).

18 Devillers, op. cit., 389f.

19 Grimal, op. cit., 267f.

20 Ho Chi Minh, op. cit., 260ff.

21 Borella, op. cit., 381.

22 Favrod, op. cit., 128.

23 ibid., 313 and 114.

24 French estimation, according to *La Nef* (Paris), October 1962–January 1963 (special edn, 'Histoire de la guerre d'Algérie'), 15. Most of the following figures on the Algerian war are also from this source.

25 The FLN grouped Algeria into six *wilaya*: 1. Aurès; 2. the north of the Constantine *département*; 3. the Kabyle region; 4. the hinterland of

Algiers (the capital itself was an 'autonomous zone' for a time); 5. the Oran *département*; 6. the Sahara. See Favrod, op. cit., 145ff.
26 *Neuer Zürcher Zeitung*, 4 July 1957.
27 *Europe-France-Outremer* (Paris), no. 388, June 1962, 2.
28 Laroussi Khelifa, *Manuel du Militant Algérien*, tome I, Lausanne, 1962, VIII.
29 In AEF and Cameroon a two-roll electoral system was still in effect.
30 Quoted from a record distributed by French authorities.

10 THE LOSS OF THE DUTCH AND BELGIAN COLONIAL EMPIRES

1 Grimal, op. cit., 248.
2 A. A. J. van Bilsen, *Vers l'Indépendance du Congo et du Ruanda-Urundi*, Brussels, 1977 (1st edn, 1956), 165.
3 Robert Cornevin, *Histoire du Congo-Léo*, Paris, 1963, 234.
4 ibid., 235.
5 Van Bilsen, op. cit., 168f.
6 'Chronique de Politique Etrangère', special edition *La Crise Congolaise*, July to November 1960, 439.
7 *Congo 1959* (Les Dossiers du CRISP), Brussels, 1960, 101f.
8 J. Gérard-Libois, *Sécession au Katanga* (Les Etudes du CRISP), Brussels/Léopoldville, 1963, 32.

11 SPAIN'S WITHDRAWAL AND PORTUGAL'S EXPULSION FROM AFRICA

1 The abbreviation 'Polisario' stands for the People's Front for the Liberation of Saguiat el Hamra and Rio de Oro.
2 Article 56 of regulation no. 39666 of 20 May 1954. Quoted from Robert Davies, *Les Angolais*, Paris, 1965, 128.
3 Nine states originally sat on the OAU Liberation Committee. This was increased to include eleven states in 1965, seventeen in 1972; and in 1974 Guinea-Bissau became the eighteenth. Angola, Liberia, and Mozambique were added in 1976.
4 Kwame Nkrumah invited people to the first All-African Peoples' Conference in Accra in December 1958. He wanted to offer a common political forum to the governments of newly independent African states and liberation movements from those countries still ruled as colonies. The conference no longer met after its third meeting in Cairo (March 1961).
5 The whites and as many as 8,000 blacks (according to other estimates only 2,000) fell to the rebels. Figures from Michael Morris, *Armed Conflict in Southern Africa*, Cape Town, 1974, 115f.
6 See Franz-Wilhelm Heimer, *Der Entkolonisierungskonflikt in Angola*, Munich, 1979, 196ff.
7 During the war, FRELIMO preferred Chinese instructors available in Tanzania to Soviet training, which would have necessitated lengthy

stays in the USSR. In 1975–6, however, Peking became estranged
from the government of Mozambique when it made a vehement stand
against the MPLA party in the Angolan civil war.

8 On ZAPU and ZANU see 192, on ANC 194. SWAPO (South West
Africa People's Organization) and SWANU (South West Africa
National Union) are rival groups in Namibia; the OAU recognizes
only SWAPO.

9 A. J. Venter, *Portugal's War in Guinea-Bissau*, Pasadena, 1973, 191.

10 *Ein Volk in Bewegung Kann niemand aufhalten*, Berlin, 1974, 18f. This
book was published by a West German liberation support group. It
contains PAIGC documents.

11 René Pélissier, 'Afrique portugaise; les élections législatives', *Revue
Française d'Etudes Politiques Africaines* (Paris), April 1973.

12 Preamble to the Joint Declaration of the two delegations, quoted from
'Documents d'Actualité Internationale' (Paris), no. 42/1974.

13 *Cabora Bassa*, ed. in German by the Portuguese Ministry for
Information and Tourism, Lisbon/Dusseldorf, 1971, 24.

14 *Mozambique Revolution* (Dar es Salaam), no. 56, July–September 1973.

15 Act no. 5/72. Quoted from F. Ansprenger *et al.* (ed.), *Wiriyamu, eine
Dokumentation zum Krieg in Mozambique*, Munich/Mainz, 1974, 183ff.

16 As Salazar's Portugal paid lip service to assimilation, it did not collate
its population statistics according to race. The estimation that there
were some 300,000 whites in Angola after 1966 can be found in John
Marcum (*The Angolan Revolution*, Vol. 1, Cambridge, Mass./ London,
1969, 17, footnote), and in Heimer, op. cit., 3.

17 Twenty-two member states supported the MPLA, including Algeria,
Ghana, Nigeria, Tanzania, and of course Mozambique, Guinea-Bissau
and Congo-Brazzaville. Twenty-two states supported the rival groups,
including Cameroon, Ivory Coast, Egypt, Kenya, Morocco, Senegal,
Tunisia, Zambia, and of course Zaire. Two member states (Ethiopia
and Uganda) declared themselves neutral.

18 Quoted from Amilcar Cabral, *Revolution in Guinea*, London, undated
(1969), 56 ff.

12 THE PROSPECTS IN 1988

1 On ANC and PAC, see Tom Lodge, *Black Politics in South Africa since
1945*, London/New York, 1983; on Inkatha, see (an extremely critical
appraisal) Gerhard Maré and Georgina Hamilton, *An Appetite for
Power*, Johannesburg, 1987.

2 See Arend Lijphard, *Democracy in Plural Societies*, London/New Haven,
Conn., 1978; and Arend Lijphard, *Democracies*, London/New Haven,
Conn., 1984. For an application of the concept on South Africa, see
Theodor Hanf *et al.*, *South Africa – the prospect of peaceful change*, Cape
Town, 1981.

3 See André du Pisani, *SWA/Namibia: the politics of continuity and
change*, Johannesburg, 1986.

4 UN GA Res. 31/146, of 20 December 1976, passed with 107

votes against 6, and 12 abstentions. Belgium, France, the Federal Republic of Germany, Luxemburg, the UK and the USA voted against the resolution. For the context of Contact Group politics, see Franz Ansprenger, *Die SWAPO*, Mayence/Munich, 1984.

5 See Joe Pütz *et al., Political Who's Who of Namibia*, Windhoek, 1987.

6 See Christopher Stevens (ed.), *Renegotiating Lomé*, London, 1984; Robert Boardman *et al.* (eds), *Europe, Africa, and Lomé*, London/Landham, Md, 1985; John Ravenhill, *Collective Clientelism: The Lomé Conventions and North-South Relations*, Irvington, NY, 1985.

7 Final Act of UNCTAD VII (Geneva, 9 July–3 August 1987), New York, 1987, 5 (UN Doc. TD/350).

8 Peter Enahoro, 'Strong medicine', *Africa Now* (London), April 1987, 5.

9 Lin Piao, *Long Live the Victory of People's War!*, Peking, 1965 (originally published in *Renmin Ribao*, 3 September 1965; Lin Piao (1907–71) was then vice-chairman of the Central Committee of China's Communist Party, minister of defence, and vice-premier of the State Council.

10 Sun Yat-sen, *San Min Chu I (The Three Principles of the People*, translated by Frank W. Price), 'The principle of nationalism', lecture 6 (2 March 1924). Quoted from an edition from Taipei, 1981, 46f.

SUGGESTIONS FOR FURTHER READING

GENERAL QUESTIONS OF COLONIAL RULE, IMPERIALISM, AND DECOLONIZATION

Amin, S. (1973) *Le Développement Inégal*, Paris.
Apter, D. E. (1987) *Rethinking Development: modernization, dependency, and post-modern politics*, London.
Emerson, R. (1960) *From Empire to Nation*, Cambridge, Mass.
Fanon, F. (1961) *Les Damnés de la Terre*, Paris.
Fieldhouse, D. K. (1981) *Colonialism 1870-1945: an introduction*, London.
Hobson, J. A. (1902, [3]1938) *Imperialism - a study*, London.
Latham, A. J. H. (1978) *The International Economy and the Underdeveloped World, 1865-1914*, London.
Latham, A. J. H. (1981) *The Depression and the Developing World 1914-1939*, London.
Leroy-Beaulieu, P. (1874, [6]1908) *De la Colonisation chez les Peuples modernes*, Paris.
MacFarlane, S. N. (1985) *Superpower Rivalry and Third World Radicalism: the idea of national liberation*, London.
Marcussen, H. S. and Torp, J. E. (1982) *The Internationalization of Capital: the prospects of the Third World: a re-examination of dependency theory*, London.
Myrdal, G. (1970) *The Challenge of World Poverty*, New York.

GENERAL QUESTIONS OF ASIA

Kahin, G. McT. (ed.) ([2]1964) *Government and Politics of South-East Asia*, Ithaca, NY.
Panikkar, K. M. (1953) *Asia and Western Dominance*, London.

GENERAL QUESTIONS OF AFRICA

Asiwaju, A. I. (ed.) (1984) *Partitioned Africans: ethnic relations across Africa's international boundaries 1884-1984*, London.
Azikiwe, N. (1937, [2]1966) *Renascent Africa*, London.

Curtin, P. *et al.* (1978) *African History*, London.
Gann, L. H. and Duignan, P. (1967) *Burden of Empire: an appraisal of western colonialism in Africa south of the Sahara*, London/Stanford, Calif.
Gifford, P. and Louis, W. R. (eds) (1972) *France and Britain in Africa: imperial rivalry and colonial rule*, London/New Haven, Conn.
Gifford, P. and Louis, W. R. (1982) *The Transfer of Power in Africa: decolonization 1940–1960*, London/New Haven, Conn.
Hailey, W. M. Lord (1957) *An African Survey* (revised to 1956), London.
Hodgkin, T. (1956) *Nationalism in Colonial Africa*, London.
Hopkins, A. G. (1973) *An Economic History of West Africa*, London.
Iliffe, J. (1979) *A Modern History of Tanganyika*, Cambridge.
Katjavivi, P. (1987) *A History of Resistance in Namibia*, London.
Oliver, R. and Fage, J. D. (^{5}1976) *A Short History of Africa*, Harmondsworth.
Rodney, W. (1972) *How Europe Underdeveloped Africa*, London/Dar es Salaam.
Rotberg, R. I. and Mazrui, A. A. (eds) (1970) *Protest and Power in Black Africa*, London.
Sesay, A. (ed.) (1986) *Africa and Europe: from partition to interdependence or dependence?*, Beckenham.
UNESCO (1980–   ) *General History of Africa*, Vols 1 (1980), 2 (1980), 4(1984), 7(1985), Paris/London/Berkeley.

GERMAN COLONIALISM

Gann, L. H. and Duignan, P. (1977) *The Rulers of German Africa 1884–1914*, Stanford, Calif.
Gründer, H. (1985) *Geschichte der deutschen Kolonien*, Paderborn.
Iliffe, J. (1969) *Tanganyika under German Rule 1905–1912*, Cambridge.
Kum'a Ndumbe III, A. (1979) *Hitler voulait l'Afrique: les plans secrets pour une Afrique fasciste*, Paris.
Smith, W. D. (1978) *The German Colonial Empire*, Chapel Hill, NC.
Stoecker, H. (ed.) (1985) *German Imperialism in Africa*, London.
Townsend, M. E. (1930) *The Rise and Fall of Germany's Colonial Empire*, New York.

BRITISH COLONIALISM AND DECOLONIZATION (GENERAL QUESTIONS)

Bennett, G. (ed.) (1953) *The Concept of Empire – Burke to Attlee 1774–1947*, London.
Brockway, F. (1973) *The Colonial Revolution*, London.
Drummond, I. M. (1974) *Imperial Economic Policy 1917–1939*, London.
Groom, A. J. R. and Taylor, P. (eds) (1984) *The Commonwealth in the 1980s*, London.
Hobsbawm, E. J. (1968) *Industry and Empire: an economic history of Britain since 1750*, London.

Kirkman, W. P. (1966) *Unscrambling an Empire: a critique of British colonial policy 1956–1966*, London.
Mansergh, N. (^{2}1982) *The Commonwealth Experience*, 2 vols, London.
(1986) *Mission to South Africa: the Commonwealth Report*, Harmondsworth.
Perham, M. (1962) *The Colonial Reckoning*, London.
Porter, A. N. and Stockwell, A. J. (1987) *British Imperial Policy and Decolonization 1938–1964*, Vol. 1, Basingstoke.

BRITISH COLONIALISM AND DECOLONIZATION IN ASIA

Brown, J. M. (1977) *Gandhi and Civil Disobedience: the Mahatma in Indian politics 1928–1934*, Cambridge.
Cohen, Michael J. (1982) *Palestine and the Great Powers 1945–1948*, Princeton, NJ.
Gandhi, M. K. (1949) *An Autobiography: the story of my experiments with truth*, London.
Horowitz, D. and Lissak, M. (^{2}1979) *Palestine under the Mandate*, London/ Chicago.
Hungdah, Chiu *et al.* (eds) (1987) *The Future of Hong Kong: towards 1997 and beyond*, London.
Mansergh, N. *et al.* (eds) (1970) *The Transfer of Power 1942–1947*, 12 vols, London.
Nehru, J. (^{4}1956) *The Discovery of India*, London.
Philips, C. H. and Wainwright, M. D. (eds) (1970) *The Partition of India: policies and perspectives 1935–1947*, London.
Porath, Y. (1974) *The Emergence of the Palestinian-Arab National Movement 1918–1929*, London.
Short, A. (1975) *The Communist Insurrection in Malaya 1948–1960*, London.

BRITISH COLONIALISM AND DECOLONIZATION IN AFRICA AND THE CARIBBEAN

Austin, D. (1964) *Politics in Ghana 1946–1960*, London.
Best, N. (1979) *Happy Valley: the story of the English in Kenya*, London.
Brett, E. A. (1973) *Colonialism and Underdevelopment in East Africa 1919–1939*, London.
Buijtenhuijs, R. (1982) *Essays on Mau Mau*, Leiden.
Coleman, J. S. (1958) *Nigeria: background to nationalism*, Berkeley, Calif.
Davidow, J. (1984) *A Peace in Southern Africa: the Lancaster House conference on Rhodesia 1979*, Boulder, Colo.
Gann, L. H. and Duignan, P. (1978) *Rulers of British Africa 1870–1914*, London.
Kitching, G. (1980) *Class and Economic Change in Kenya: the making of an African petite bourgeoisie 1905–1970*, London/New Haven, Conn.
Leys, C. (1959) *European Politics in Southern Rhodesia*, Oxford.
Lugard, F. D. (1922,^{5}1965) *The Dual Mandate in British Tropical Africa*, London.

Macpherson, F. (1981) *Anatomy of a Conquest: the British occupation of Zambia 1884–1924*, London.

Martin, D. and Johnson, P. (1981) *The Struggle for Zimbabwe*, London/Boston, Mass.

Mosley, P. (1983) *The Settler Economies: studies in the economic history of Kenya and Southern Rhodesia 1900–1963*, Cambridge.

Nkrumah, K. (1956) *Ghana – the Autobiography*, Edinburgh.

Nwabueze, B. O. (1982) *A Constitutional History of Nigeria*, London.

Nyerere, J. K. (1966) *Freedom and Unity – Uhuru na Umoja: a selection from writings and speeches 1952–1965*, Dar es Salaam.

Okigbo, P. N. C. (1988) *National Development Planning in Nigeria 1900–1992*, London.

Padmore, G. (1936) *How Britain Rules Africa*, London.

Pearce, R. D. (1982) *The Turning Point in Africa: British colonial policy 1938–1948*, London.

Peel, J. D. Y. and Ranger, T. O. (eds) (1983) *Past and Present in Zimbabwe*, Manchester.

Sayyid, A. L. al- (1968) *Egypt and Cromer*, London.

Spencer, J. (1985) *The Kenya African Union 1944–1953,* London.

Wallace, E. (1977) *The British Caribbean: from the decline of colonialism to the end of the federation*, Toronto.

Wilson, M. and Thompson, L. (eds) (1970) *Oxford History of South Africa*, vol. 2, *1870–1967*, London.

FRENCH COLONIALISM AND DECOLONIZATION
(GENERAL QUESTIONS)

Bouvier, J., Girault, R., and Thobie, J. (1986) *L'Impérialisme à la Française 1914–1960*, Paris.

Brunschwig, H. (1949) *La Colonisation Française. Du pacte colonial à l'Union Française*, Paris.

Guérin, D. (1975) *Ci-git le colonialisme*, Paris/The Hague.

Lacouture, J. (1961) *Cinq Hommes et la France* (Ho Chi Minh, Habib Bourguiba, Ferhat Abbas, Mohammed V, Sekou Touré), Paris.

Madjarian, G. (1977) *La Question coloniale et la Politique du Parti Communiste Français 1944–1947*, Paris.

Sarraut, A. (1931) *Grandeur et Servitudes coloniales*, Paris.

FRENCH COLONIALISM AND DECOLONIZATION IN
ASIA

Devillers, P. (1952) *Histoire du Viêt-Nam de 1940 à 1952*, Paris.

Duiker, W. J. (1976) *The Rise of Nationalism in Vietnam 1900–1941*, London/Ithaca, NY.

Fall, B. B. (1966) *Viet-Nam Witness 1953–66*, London.

Giap, V. N. (1966) *Guerre du Peuple – Armée du Peuple*, Paris.

Khoury, P. S. (1986) *Syria and the French Mandate*, Princeton, NJ.

Roy, J. (1963) *La Bataille de Dien Bien Phu*, Paris.

FRENCH COLONIALISM AND DECOLONIZATION IN AFRICA

Benoist, J.-R. de (1979) *La Balkanisation de l'Afrique Occidentale Française*, Dakar.

Bourgi, R. (1980) *Le Général de Gaulle et l'Afrique Noire, 1940–1969*, Paris.

Cohen, W. B. (1971) *Rulers of Empire: the French colonial service in Africa*, Stanford, Calif.

Delavignette, R. (1946) *Service Africain*, Paris.

Favrod, Ch.-H. (1962) *Le FLN et l'Algérie*, Paris.

Johnson, W. (ed.) (1985) *Double Impact: France and Africa in the age of imperialism*, London.

Julien, Ch.-A. (1952, ²1972) *L'Afrique du Nord en Marche*, Paris.

Le Reverend, A. (1983) *Lyautey*, Paris.

Quandt, W. B. (1969) *Revolution and Political Leadership: Algeria 1954–1968*, London/Cambridge, Mass.

Salem, N. (1984) *Habib Bourguiba, Islam and the Creation of Tunisia*, London.

Schachter-Morgenthau, R. (1964) *Political Parties in French-Speaking West Africa*, Oxford.

Senghor, L. S. (1971) *Liberté II: nation et voie africaine du socialisme*, Paris.

Tronchon, J. (1986) *L'Insurrection Malgache de 1947*, Paris.

White, D. S. (1979) *Black Africa and De Gaulle, from the French Empire to Independence*, University Park, Penn.

JAPANESE COLONIALISM

Elsbree, W. H. (1953) *Japan's Role in South-East Asiatic Nationalist Movements 1940–1945*, Cambridge, Mass.

ITALIAN COLONIALISM

Baer, G. W. (1977) *Test Case: Italy, Ethiopia, and the League of Nations*, Stanford, Calif.

Del Boca, A. (1969) *The Ethiopian War 1935–1941*, London.

Khadduri, M. (1963) *Modern Libya*, Princeton.

Lewis, I. M. (²1979) *Modern History of Somalia*, London.

Pelt, A. (1970) *Libyan Independence and the United Nations: a case of planned decolonization*, New Haven, Conn.

Wright, J. (1982) *Libya: a modern history*, London.

DUTCH COLONIALISM AND DECOLONIZATION

Kahin, G. McT. (1952) *Nationalism and Revolution in Indonesia*, Ithaca, NY.

Kat Angelino, A.D.A. de (1931) *Colonial Policy*, 2 vols, The Hague.

Legge, G. D. (1964) *Indonesia*, Englewood Cliffs, NJ.

Legge, G. D. (1972) *Sukarno: a political biography*, London.

BELGIAN COLONIALISM AND DECOLONIZATION

Bilsen, A. A. J. van (1956, [2]1977) *Vers l'Indépendance du Congo et du Ruanda-Urundi*, Brussels/Kinshasa.

Gann, L. H. and Duignan, P. (1979) *The Rulers of Belgian Africa 1884–1914*, Princeton, NJ.

Kanza, T. (1972) *Conflict in the Congo: the rise and fall of Lumumba*, Harmondsworth.

Lierde, J. van (1963) *La Pensée politique de Patrice Lumumba*, Paris.

Young, C. (1965) *Politics in the Congo: the rise and fall of Lumumba*, Princeton, NJ.

SPANISH AND PORTUGUESE COLONIALISM AND DECOLONIZATION

Bender, G. J. (1978) *Angola under the Portuguese: the myth and the reality*, London.

Cabral, A. (1980) *Unity and Struggle: speeches and writings selected by the PAIGC*, London.

Chabal, P. (1983) *Amilcar Cabral: revolutionary leadership and people's war*, Cambridge.

Clarence-Smith, G. (1985) *The Third Portuguese Empire, 1825–1975: a study in economic imperialism*, Manchester.

Duffy, J. (1962) *Portugal in Africa*, Harmondsworth.

Hodges, T. (1984) *The Western Sahara: the roots of a desert war*, London.

Isaacman, A. and B. (1984) *Mozambique, from colonialism to revolution 1900–1982*, Aldershot.

Marcum, J. A. (1969, 1978) *The Angolan Revolution*, 2 vols, London/Cambridge, Mass.

Mondlane, E. (1969) *The Struggle for Mozambique*, Harmondsworth.

Rudebeck, L. (1974) *Guinea-Bissau: a study of political mobilization*, Uppsala.

Thompson, V. and Adloff, R. (1980) *The Western Saharans: background to conflict*, London.

BIBLIOGRAPHY

(compiled by Patricia Clavin)

BIBLIOGRAPHIES

Carnell, F. (ed.) (1961) *The Politics of the New States: a select and annotated bibliography with special reference to the commonwealth*, London.

Conover, H. F. (ed.) (1963) *Africa South of the Sahara: a selected, annotated list of writings*, Washington.

Duignan, P. and Gann, L. H. (1973) *A Bibliographical Guide to Colonialism in Sub-Saharan Africa* (Colonialism in Africa 1870–1960, Vol. 5), Cambridge.

Freiderich Ebert Stiftung (ed.) (1961–7) *Literatur über Entwicklungsländer*, 8 vols, Hanover.

Hazelwood, A. (ed.) (1959) *The Economics of 'Under-developed' Areas: an annotated reading list of books, articles, and official publications*, 2nd edn, London.

—— (1964) *The Economics of Development: an annotated list of books and articles published 1958–62*, London.

Maurer, D. and Schwartz, K. (1979) *Hochschulshriften zu Schwarz-Afrika 1960–1978; Deutschland-Österreich-Schweiz*, Freiburg.

Wilson, P. (ed.) (1956) *Government and Politics of India and Pakistan 1885–1955: a bibliography of works in Western languages*, Berkeley, Calif.

Winks, R. W. (ed.) (1966) *The Historiography of the British Empire/Commonwealth*, Durham, USA.

Wissenschaftl. *Ausschuss der Deutschen Afrika-Gesellschaft* (ed.) (annual volumes published for 1960–1 to 1967) *Afrika-Bibliographie, Verzeichnis der wissenschaftlichen Literatur aus Deutschland, Österreich, der Schweiz und anderen Ländern*, Bonn.

GENERAL QUESTIONS OF COLONIAL RULE, IMPERIALISM, AND DECOLONIZATION

Albertini, R. von (1966) *Dekolonisation: Die Diskussion über Verwaltung und Zukunft der Kolonie 1919–1960*, Cologne.

Behrendt, R. F. (1969) *Soziale Strategie für Entwicklungsländer*, 2nd edn, Frankfurt.

Besters, H. and Boesch, E.E. (eds) (1966) *Entwicklungspolitik – Handbuch und Lexicon*, Stuttgart/Mainz.

Betts, R. F. (1985) *Uncertain Dimensions: Western overseas empires in the twentieth century*, Oxford.

Chamberlain, M. E. (1985) *Decolonization*, Oxford.

Etherington, N. (1984) *Theories of Imperialism*, London.

Emerson, R. (1960) *From Empire to Nation*, Cambridge/Mass.

Fieldhouse, D. K. (1966) *The Colonial Empires: a comparative survey from the 18th century*, London.

Fanon, F. (1961) *Les Damnés de la terre*, Paris.

Grimal, H. (1965) *La Décolonisation 1919–1963*, Paris.

—— (1978) *Decolonization: the British, French, Dutch, and Belgian empires*, London.

Hobson, J. A. (1902) *Imperialism – a study*, London.

Holland, R. F. (1985) *European Decolonization 1918–1981*, Basingstoke.

Journal of Imperial and Commonwealth History (January 1984), special issue on 'Perspectives on imperialism and decolonization', vol. XII, London.

Kautsky, K. (1915) *Nationalstaat, imperialistischer Staat und Staatenbund*, Nuremberg.

Kemp, T. (1967) *Theories of Imperialism*, London.

Kiernan, V. G. (1969) *Lords of Human Kind: European attitudes to the outside world in the age of imperialism*, London.

—— (1983) *European Empires from Conquest to Collapse, 1815–1960*, London.

Latham, A. J. H. (1978) *The International Economy and the Underdeveloped World, 1865–1914*, London.

Lenin, V. I. (1949; lst edn, 1917) *Imperialism – the High Stage of Capitalism*, abstract (from Russian) in *Collected Works*, 45 vols, London.

Leroy-Beaulieu, P. (1908) *De la Colonisation chez les peuples modernes*, 6th edn, Paris.

Lichtheim, G. (1971) *Imperialism*, London.

Louis, R. (ed.) (1976) *Imperialism: the Robinson and Gallagher controversy*, London.

Luxemburg, R. (1969; lst end, 1913) *The Accumulation of Capital*, London.

Mack, A., Plant, D. and Doyle, U. (1979) *Imperialism, Intervention and Development*, London.

Mommsen, W. J. (1977) *Imperialismus, seine geistigen, politischen und wirtschaftlichen Grundlagen; ein Quellen-und Arbeitsbuch*, Hamburg.

—— (1980) *Theories of Imperialism*, London.

—— and Osterhammel, J. (eds) (1986) *Imperialism and After: continuities and discontinuities*, London.

Schumpter, J. A. (1953; lst edn, 1918) 'Zur Soziologie der Imperialismus', in *Aufsatze zur Sociologie*, Tübingen.

Senghaas, D. (ed.) (1979) *Kapitalistische Weltökonomie, Kontroversen über ihren Ursprung und ihre Entwicklungsdynamik*, Frankfurt.

GENERAL QUESTIONS OF ASIA

Herskovitz, M. J. and Harwitz, M. (eds) (1964) *Economic Transition in Africa*, London.

Kahin, G. McT. (ed.) (1964) *Governments and Politics of South-East Asia*, Ithaca, NY.

Panikkar, K. M. (1953) *Asia and Western Dominance*, London.

Pluvier, J. (1974) *South-East Asia from Colonialism to Independence*, Kuala Lumpur.

Romein, J. (1956) *De euw van Azie*, Leiden.

Ryan, N. J. (1967) *The Making of Modern Malaysia*, 3rd edn, Oxford.

GENERAL QUESTIONS OF AFRICA

Ajala, A. (1973) *Pan-Africanism: evolution, progress and prospects*, London.

Ansprenger, F. (1975) *Die Befreiungspolitik der Organisation für Afrikanische Einheit (DAU) 1963 bis 1975*, Munich/Mainz (Studien zum Konflikt im südlichen Afrika).

Asante, S. K. B. (1977) *Pan-African Protest: West Africa and the Italo-Ethiopian Crisis 1934–41*, London.

Azikiwe, N. (1966; lst edn, 1937) *Renascent Africa*, 2nd edn, London.

Coquery-Vidrovitch, C. and Moniot, H. (1974) *L'Afrique Noire de 1800 à nos Jours*, Paris (Nouvelle Clio 46).

Cornevin, R. (1973) *L'Afrique Noire de 1919 à nos jours*, Paris.

Crowder, M. (1968) *West Africa under Colonial Rule*, London.

Curtin, P. H. *et al.* (1978) *African History*, London.

Davidson, B. (1978) *Africa in Modern History: the search for a new society*, London.

Frage, J. D. and Oliver, R. (1976) *A Short History of Africa*, 5th edn, London.

Gann, L. H. and Duignan, P. (eds) (1969–1970) *Colonialism in Africa 1870–1960*, Vol. 1: *The History and Politics of Colonialism 1870–1914*, Vol. 2: *1914–1960*, Vol. 3 (ed. by V. Turner), *Profiles of Change: African society and colonial rule*, Cambridge.

—— (1967) *Burden of Empire; an appraisal of Western colonialism in Africa south of the Sahara*, London/Stanford, Calif.

Gibson, R. (1972) *African Liberation Movements: contemporary struggles against white minority rule*, London.

Gifford, P. and Louis, W. R. (eds) (1972) *France and Britain in Africa: imperial rivalry and colonial rule*, London/New Haven, Conn.

Hahn, L. (1960) *North Africa: nationalism to nationhood*, Washington.

Hailey, Lord (1957) *An African Survey: a study of the problems arising in Africa south of the Sahara* (revised to 1956), London.

Hargreaves, J. D. (1985) *The End of Colonial Rule in West Africa: essays in contemporary history*, London.

Hodgkin, T. H. (1956) *Nationalism in Colonial Africa*, London.

Hopkins, A. G. (1973) *An Economic History of West Africa*, London.

Iliffe, J. (1979) *A Modern History of Tanganyika*, Cambridge.

Ki-Zerbo, J. (1979) *Die Geschichte Schwarz-Afrikas*, Wuppertal.
Leibowitz, A. H. (1976) *Colonial Emancipation in the Pacific and the Caribbean*, London/New York.
Mazrui, A. A. and Rotberg, R. I. (eds) (1970) *Power and Protest in Black Africa*, London.
Pearce, R. D. (1982) *The Turning Point in Africa: British Colonial Policy 1938–1948*, London.
Robinson, R. and Gallagher, J. (1961) *Africa and the Victorians*, London.
Rodney, W. (1972) *How Europe Underdeveloped Africa*, London/Dar es Salaam.
Rotberg, R. I. (1965) *The Rise of Black Nationalism in Central Africa*, London.
—— and Mazrui, A. A. (eds) (1970) *Protest and Power in Black Africa*, London.
Turner, V. (ed.), see Gann, L. H. and Duignan, P.
Westermann, D. (1941) *Afrika als europäische Aufgabe*, Berlin.

GERMAN COLONIALISM

Bley, H. (1968) *Kolonialherrschaft und Sozialstruktur in Deutsch-Südwestafrika 1894–1914*, Hamburg.
Gann, L. H. and Duignan, P. (1977) *The Rulers of German Africa 1884–1914*, Stanford, Calif.
Hausen, K. (1970) *Deutsche Kolonialherrschaft in Afrika: Wirtschaftsinteressen und Kolonialverwaltung in Kamerun vor 1914*, Zurich.
Iliffe, J. (1969) *Tanganyika under German Rule 1905–1912*, Cambridge.
Schiefel, W. (1974) *Bernhard Dernburg 1865–1937*.
Schröder, H.-Chr (1968) *Sozialismus und Imperialismus. Die Auseinandersetzung der deutschen Sozialdemokratie mit dem Imperialismusproblem und der 'Weltpolitik' vor 1914*, Hanover.
Tetzlaff, R. (1970) *Koloniale Entwicklung und Ausbeutung. Wirtschafts- und Sozialgeschichte Deutsch-Ostafrikas 1895–1914*, Berlin.
Townsend, M. E. (1930) *The Rise and Fall of Germany's Colonial Empire*, New York.

BRITISH COLONIALISM AND DECOLONIZATION (GENERAL QUESTIONS)

Barrat-Brown, M. (1963) *After Imperialism*, London.
Beloff, M. (1969) *Imperial Sunset: Britain's Liberal Empire 1897–1921*, Vol. 1, London.
Bennett, G. (ed.) (1953) *The Concept of Empire – Burke to Attlee 1774–1947*, London.
Brockway, F. (1973) *The Colonial Revolution*, London.
Cumpston, I. M. (ed.) (1973) *The Growth of the British Commonwealth 1880–1932*, London.
Drummond, I. M. (1974) *Imperial Economic Policy 1917–1939: studies in expansion and protection*, London.

Gallagher, J. (1982) *The Decline, Revival and Fall of the British Empire*, Cambridge.

Goldsworthy, D. (1970) *Colonial Issues in British Politics, 1945–1961*, London.

Gupta, P. S. (1975) *Imperialism and the British Labour Movement*, London.

Heussler, R. (1963) *Yesterday's Rulers: the making of the British Colonial Service*, Syracuse.

Hobsbawm, E. J. (1968) *Industry and Empire: an economic history of Britain since 1750*, London.

Hyam, R. and Martin, G. (1975) *Reappraisals in British Imperial History*, London.

Kirkman, W. P. (1966) *Unscrambling an Empire: a critique of British colonial policy 1956–66*, London.

Lloyd, C. J. (1984) *The British Empire*, Oxford.

Lowe, C. J. (1967) *The Reluctant Imperialists*, 2 vols, London.

McIntyre, W. D. (1978) *The Commonwealth of Nations; origins and impact 1869–1971*, London.

Mansergh, N. (ed.) (since 1953) *Documents and Speeches on British Commonwealth Affairs 1913–1962*, London.

—— (1958) *Survey of British Commonwealth Affairs: problems of wartime co-operation and post-war change*, London.

—— (1966) *The Commonwealth Experience*, London.

Perham, M. (1962) *The Colonial Reckoning*, London.

Porter, A. (1975–6) 'Iain Macleod, decolonization in Kenya and tradition in British colonial policy', *Journal for Contemporary History*, no. 2.

—— (1986) *Victorian Shipping, Business and Imperial Policy: Donald Currie, the Castle Line and Southern Africa*, London.

Porter, B. (1968) *Critics of Empire*, London.

—— (1975) *The Lion's Share: a short history of Britain's imperialism, 1850–1970*, London.

Schlote, W. (1952) *British Overseas Trade from 1700 to the 1930s*, Oxford.

Strachey, J. (1959) *The End of Empire*, London.

BRITISH COLONIALISM AND DECOLONIZATION IN ASIA

Brown, M. J. (1977) *Gandhi and Civil Disobedience: the Mahatma in Indian politics 1928–1934*, Cambridge.

Cady, F. J. (1958) *A History of Modern Burma*, New York.

Endacott, G. B. (1973) *A History of Hong Kong*, 3rd edn, London.

Gandhi, M. K. (1940) *An Autobiography: the story of my experiments with truth*, London.

Gullick, J. M. (1969) *Malaysia*, London.

Horowitz, D. and Lissak, M. (1979) *Palestine under the Mandate*, 2nd edn, London/Chicago.

Mansergh, N. *et al.* (eds) (1970) *The Transfer of Power 1942–1947*, 12 vols, London.

Nehru, J. (1951) *The Discovery of India*, 3rd edn, London.

Pandey, B. N. (1976) *Nehru*, London.

Philips, C. H. and Wainwright, M. N. (eds) (1970) *The Partition of India: policies and perspectives 1935–1947*, London.
Porath, Y. (1974) *The Emergence of the Palestinian-Arab National Movement 1918–1929*, London.
Rothermund, D. (1966) *Die politische Willensbildung in Indien 1900–1960*, Wiesbaden.
Short, A. (1975) *The Communist Insurrection in Malaya 1948–1960*, London.
Spear, T. G. P. (ed.) (1961) *Oxford History of India*, 3rd edn, Oxford.

BRITISH COLONIALISM AND DECOLONIZATION IN AFRICA AND THE CARIBBEAN

Austin, D. (1964) *Politics in Ghana 1946–1960*, London.
Brett, E. A. (1973) *Colonialism and Underdevelopment in East Africa 1919–1939*, London.
Buijtenhuis, R. (1971) *Le Mouvement 'Mau Mau': une révolte paysanne et anti-coloniale en Afrique Noire*, The Hague/Paris.
Coleman, J. S. (1958) *Nigeria: background to nationalism*, Berkeley, Calif.
Gann, L. H. and Duignan, P. (1978) *Rulers of British Africa 1870–1914*, London.
Good, R. C. (1973) *U.D.I.: the international politics of the Rhodesian rebellion*, London.
Grant, C. H. (1976) *The Making of Modern Belize: politics, society and British colonialism in Central America*, Cambridge.
Kiewet, C. W. (1941) *A History of South Africa, social and economic*, Oxford.
Leys, C. (1959) *European Politics in Southern Rhodesia*, Oxford.
Lugard, F. D. (1965; 1st edn, 1922) *The Dual Mandate in British Tropical Africa*, 5th edn, London.
Mansfield, P. (1971) *The British in Egypt 1882–1956*, London.
Meebelo, H. S. (1971) *Reaction to Colonialism: a prelude to the politics of independence in Northern Zambia 1893–1939*, Manchester.
Munro, J. F. (1984) *Britain in Tropical Africa 1880–1960*, London.
Nyerere, J. K. (1966) *Freedom and Unity – Uhuru na Umoja; a selection of writings and speeches 1952–1965*, Dar es Salaam.
Nkrumah, K. (1956) *Ghana – the Autobiography*, Edinburgh.
Padmore, G. (1936) *How Britain Rules Africa*, London.
Ranger, T. O. (1970) *The African Voice in Southern Rhodesia 1898–1930*, London.
Robinson, R. (1981) *1920 – Africa and the Victorians*, 2nd edn, London.
Thompson, L. and Wilson, M. (eds) (1970) *Oxford History of South Africa, Vol. 2, 1870–1967*, London.
Wallace, E. (1977) *The British Caribbean: from the decline of colonialism to the end of the federation*, Toronto.

FRENCH COLONIALISM AND DECOLONIZATION (GENERAL QUESTIONS)

Andrew, C. M. (1981) *France Overseas*, London.

BIBLIOGRAPHY

Bleckmann, A. (1969) *Das französische Kolonialreich und die Gründung neuer Staaten*, Cologne.
Borella, F. (1958) *L'Evolution politique et juridique de L'Union Française depuis 1946*, Paris.
Brunschwig, H. (1949) *La Colonisation Française. Du pacte colonial à l'Union Française*, Paris.
Cohen, W. B. (1971) *Rulers of Empire: the French colonial service in Africa*, Stanford, Calif.
Delavignette, R. (1968) *Du bon usage de la décolonisation*, Paris.
Guérin, D. (1975) *Ci-git le colonialisme*, Paris/The Hague.
Lacouture, J. (1961) *Cinq Hommes et la France* (Ho Chi Minh, Habib Bourguiba, Ferhat Abbas, Mohammed V, Sekou Touré), Paris.
Sarraut, A. (1931) *Grandeur et Servitudes coloniales*, Paris.

FRENCH COLONIALISM AND DECOLONIZATION IN ASIA

Devillers, P.(1952) *Histoire du Viêt-Nam de 1940 à 1952*, Paris.
Duiker, W. J. (1976) *The Rise of Nationalism in Vietnam 1900–1941*, London/Ithaca, NY.
—— (1983) *Nation in Revolution*, London.
Fall, B. B. (1966) *Viet-Nam Witness 1953–66*, London.
—— (ed.) (1984; 1st edn, 1967) *Ho Chi Minh: On Revolution: selected writings 1920–66*, London.
Giap, V. N. (1966) *Guerre du peuple – armée du peuple*, Paris.
Honey, P. J. (1963) *Communism in North Vietnam*, Paris.
Jumper, R. (1980; 1st edn, 1962) *Vietnam: an annotated bibliography*, Salisbury, USA.
Mus, P. (1952) *Viêt-Nam – sociologie d'une guerre*, Paris.
Roy, J. (1963) *La Bataille de Dien Bien Phu*, Paris.
Rusico, R. (1985) *L'Indochine française, 1940–45*, Paris.
—— (1987) *La Décolonisation tragique: une histoire de la décolonisation française, 1945–62*, Paris.

FRENCH COLONIALISM AND DECOLONIZATION IN AFRICA

Ansprenger, F. (1961) *Politik im Schwarzen Afrika. Die moderne politischen Bewegungen im Afrika französicher Prägung*, Cologne.
Benoist, J. -R. de (1979) *La Balkanisation de l'Afrique Occidentale Française*, Dakar.
Cohen, W. B. (1971) *Rulers of Empire; the French colonial service in Africa*, Stanford, Calif.
Delavignette, R. (1946) *Service Africain*, Paris.
Elsenhans, H. (1974) *Frankreichs Algerienpolitik 1954–1962, Entkolonisierungsversuch einer kapitalistischen Metropole*, Munich.
Favrod, Ch. -H. (1962) *Le FLN et l'Algérie*, Paris.
Julien, Ch. -A. (1952, ²1972) *L'Afrique du Nord en Marche*, 2nd edn, Paris.
Le Tourneau, R. (1962) *Evolution de l'Afrique du Nord musulmane 1920–1961*, Paris.
329

Quandt, W. B. (1969) *Revolution and Political Leadership; Algeria 1954–1969*, London/Cambridge, Mass.

Schachter-Morgenthau, R. (1964) *Political Parties in French-Speaking West Africa*, Oxford.

Senghor, L. S. (1971) *Liberté II: Nation et voie africaine du socialisme*, Paris.

Smith, T. (1978) *The French Stake in Algeria 1945–62*, Ithaca, NY.

Suret-Canale, J. (1961–72) *Afrique Noire Occidentale et Centrale*, 3 vols, Paris.

Touré, S. (1959) *L'Expérience guinéenne et l'Unité africaine*, Paris.

Weinstein, B. (1972) *Eboué*, New York.

JAPANESE COLONIALISM

Bernhardt, F. (1971) *Die 'Kollaboration' asiatischer Völker mit der japanischen Besatzungsmacht im Zweitem Weltkrieg als Glied im Dekolonisationsprozess*, Hamburg.

Elsbree, W. H. (1953) *Japan's Role in South-East Asiatic Nationalist Movements 1940–1945*, Cambridge, Mass.

Jansen, M. (1975) *Japan and China: from war to peace, 1894–1972*, Chicago.

Kublin, H. (1959) 'The evolution of Japanese colonialism', *Comparative Studies in Society* and *History II*.

Lockwood, W. (1979) *The Economic Development of Japan: growth and structural change 1868–1938*, Princeton, NJ.

Mayo, M. (ed.) (1970) *The Emergence of Imperial Japan: Self-Defence or Calculated Aggression?* Lexington.

Myers, R.H. and Peatte, M.R. (eds) (1984) *The Japanese Colonial Empire, 1895–1945*, Princeton, NJ.

Nation, A. (ed.) (1973) *Korea under Japanese Colonial Rule: Studies of the Policy and Techniques of Japanese Colonialism*, Michigan.

Storry, R. (1979) *Japan and the Decline of the West, 1894–1943*, London.

ITALIAN COLONIALISM

Baer, G. W. (1967) *The Coming of the Italo-Ethiopian War*, Cambridge, Mass.

Bandin, F. (1971) *Gli Italiani in Africa: storia delle guerre coloniali 1882–1943*, Milan.

Becker, G. H. (1952) *The Disposition of the Italian Colonies, 1941–1951*, Annemasse.

Del Boca, A. (1969) *The Ethiopian War 1935–1941*, London.

Hess, R. L. (1966) *Italian Colonialism in Somalia*, Chicago.

Khadduri, M. (1963) *Modern Libya*, Princeton, NJ.

Pelt, A. (1970) *Libyan Independence and the United Nations: a case of planned decolonization*, New Haven, Conn.

Serge, C. (1974) *Fourth Shore: the Italian colonization of Libya*, Chicago.

Wright, J. (1982) *Libya: a modern history*, London.

DUTCH AND BELGIAN COLONIALISM AND DECOLONIZATION

Bilsen, A. A. J. van (1977; lst edn, 1956) *Vers l'Indépendance du Congo et du Ruanda-Urundi*, Brussels.
Congo 1959; Congo 1960 (Les Dossiers du CRISP), 4 vols, Brussels.
Dahm, P. (1966) *Sukarno's Kampf um Indonesiens Unabhängigkeit: Werdegang und Ideen eines asiatischen Nationalisten*, Frankfurt.
Gann, L. H. and Duignan, P. (1979) *The Rulers of the Belgian Africa 1884-1914*, Princeton, NJ.
Kahin, G.McT. (1952) *Nationalism and Revolution in Indonesia*, Ithaca, NY.
Kat Angelino, A. D. A. de (1931) *Colonial Policy*, 2 vols, The Hague.
Legge, G. D. (1964) *Indonesia*, Englewood Cliffs, NJ.
——(1972) *Sukarno: a political biography*, London.
Lierde, J. van (ed.) (1963) *La Pensée politique de Patrice Lumumba*, Paris.
Young, C. (1965) *Politics in the Congo: the rise and fall of Lumumba*, Harmondsworth.

SPANISH AND PORTUGUESE COLONIALISM AND DECOLONIZATION

Abshire, D. M. and Samuels, M. A. (eds) (1969) *Portuguese Africa - a Handbook*, London.
Cabral, A. (1980) *Unity and Struggle: speeches and writings selected by the PAIGC*, London.
Clarence-Smith, G. (1985) *The Third Portuguese Empire, 1825-1975: a study in economic imperialism*, Manchester.
Clausen, V. (1978) *Der Konflikt um die Westsahara*, Munich.
Davidson, B. (1975) *In the Eye of the Storm: Angola's people*, 2nd edn, London.
Duffy, J. (1962) *Portugal in Africa*, Harmondsworth.
Heimer, F. W. (1979) *Der Entkolonisierungskonflikt in Angola*, Munich.
Marcum, J. A. (1969 and 1978) *The Angolan Revolution*, 2 vols, London/Cambridge, Mass.
Middlemas, K. (1975) *Cabora Bassa, Engineering and Politics in Southern Africa*, London.
Mondlane, E. (1969) *The Struggle for Mozambique*, Harmondsworth.
Moreira, A. (1963) *Portugals Überseepolitik*, Baden-Baden.
Rudebeck, L. (1974) *Guinea-Bissau: a study of political mobilization*, Uppsala.
Thompson, V. and Adloff, R. (1980) *The Western Saharans: background to conflict*, London.

INDEX

Only persons are listed. The nationality is stated in parenthesis, whenever relevant, in the form in use in 1989.

Guevara, Ernesto 'Che' (Argentina,
    Cuba) 288, 303

Haile Selassie I (Ethiopia) 9, 119ff., 130
Haile Selassie Guksa (Ethiopia) 121
Hailey, William M., Lord (Great
    Britain) 172
Hatta, Mohammad (Indonesia) 110,
    140, 146, 257
Haya della Toree, Victor R. (Peru) 140
Herriot, Edouard (France) 81, 245
Hertzog, James B.M. (South Africa) 50,
    58, 60
Hitler, Adolf (Austria, Germany) 20,
    41, 72, 98, 126, 148, 158
Ho Chi Minh (Vietnam) 81, 83f., 139,
    148-51, 158, 214ff., 223ff., 233
Houphouet-Biogny, Félix (Ivory Coast)
    210ff., 247-50, 295
Huggins, G.M. (Lord Malvern)
    (Zimbabwe) 186
Hugo, Victor (France) 82
Hussein (Saudi Arabia) 32, 35

Ibn Saud (Saudi Arabia) 31, 35, 129
Idris I (Libya) 117
Imru (Ethiopia) 121
Irwin, Lord (Great Britain) 44
Ismail el-Azhari (Sudan) 184

Jagan, Cheddi (Guyana) 205f.
Jagan, Janet (Guyana) 205f.
Janssens, E. (Belgium) 264
Jinnah, Mohammed Ali (Pakistan) 37,
    164, 166, 171
Jonge, B.C. de (Netherlands) 109
Jouhaud (France) 241
Juin, Alphonse (France) 154
Julien, Charles-André (France) 105

Kamitatu, Cleophas (Zaire) 264
Kangethe, Joseph (Kenya) 69
Karume, Abeid (Tanzania) 203
Kasavubu, Joseph (Zaire) 260f., 264
Kassa (Ethiopia) 121
Kaúlza de Arriaga (Portugal) 279
Kaunda, Kenneth (Zambia) 187f.
Kavandame, Lazaro (Mozambique) 279
Keita, Modibo (Mali) 245, 247
Kennedy, John F. (USA) 4, 232, 257,
    297
Kenyatta, Jomo (Kenya) 69, 135, 173,
    177, 201, 204, 285

Khaled (Algeria) 96
Khider, Mohammed (Algeria) 229f.
King, Charles D.B. (Liberia) 131
King, Martin Luther (USA) 41
Kissinger, Henry (USA) 195, 286
Krim Bel Kassem (Algeria) 229

Lacoste, Robert (France) 238
Lamine-Guéye, Amadou (Senegal)
    102, 212
Las Casas, Bartholomé de (Spain) 2
Lattre de Tassigny, Jean de (France)
    220f.
Laurel, José P. (Philippines) 146f.
Laval, Pierre (France) 118
Lawrence, T.E. (Great Britain) 32, 35
Leclerc de Hautecloque (France) 214
Lee Kuan Yew (Singapore) 205
Lenin, Vladimir I. (Soviet Union) 10,
    42, 78, 128, 133, 138, 139
Leopold II (Belgium) 8, 14f., 32, 111
Lettow-Vorbeck, Paul von (Germany)
    28
Lin Piao (China) 303
Lloyd George, David (Great Britain) 51
Louw, Eric (South Africa) 191
Lugard, Frederick D., Lord (Great
    Britain) 3, 4, 64ff., 77
Lumumba, Patrice (Zaire) 259ff.
Luthuli, Albert (South Africa) 41
Lyautey (France) 87ff.
Lyttleton, O., later Lord Chandos
    (Great Britain) 182

MacArthur, Douglas (USA) 146f.
MacDonald, Ramsay (Great Britain) 47
Machel, Samora M. (Mozambique)
    279, 281
Macleod, Ian (Great Britain) 184, 191
Macmillan, Harold (Great Britain) 184,
    186, 189ff.
Macpherson, John (Great Britain) 179
Mahan, A.T. (USA) 11
Makarios III (Cyprus) 177, 204
Malugeta (Ethiopia) 121
Mandel, Georges (France) 151
Mao Tse-tung (China) 41, 84, 139, 148,
    170, 219f., 233, 273, 288
Margerie, Pierre de (France) 31
Martel, Damien de (France) 86
Marx, Karl (Germany) 42, 128, 138,
    196, 288, 303
Massu, Jacques (France) 231

INDEX